Tennessee Genealogical Records and Abstracts

Volume 1
1787–1839

Sherida K. Eddlemon

HERITAGE BOOKS
2010

HERITAGE BOOKS
AN IMPRINT OF HERITAGE BOOKS, INC.

Books, CDs, and more—Worldwide

For our listing of thousands of titles see our website
at
www.HeritageBooks.com

Published 2010 by
HERITAGE BOOKS, INC.
Publishing Division
100 Railroad Ave. #104
Westminster, Maryland 21157

Copyright © 1998 Sherida K. Eddlemon

All rights reserved. No part of this book may be reproduced or transmitted in any form or by any means, electronic or mechanical, including photocopying, recording or by any information storage and retrieval system without written permission from the author, except for the inclusion of brief quotations in a review.

International Standard Book Numbers
Paperbound: 978-0-7884-1074-1
Clothbound: 978-0-7884-8305-9

DEDICATION

John W. Eddlemon, Maury Co., TN, son of Nancy and John Eddlemon, b. 1822ca. married Louisa Rachel Jones and second, Matilda Tucker. John W. and Rachel's children were: John Frank, Nancy, James A. "Al," and Nelson Porter "Net." John W. and Matilda's children were: Harriet Macintha Minora "Kate," and Robert Enoch Lee "Grundy Bob."

John W.'s father, John Eddlemon, died as a young man leaving his wife, Nancy with two small children, John W. and Francis "Frank." His grandfather, John Eddlemon, Sr., died about the same time period. Not too much is known about the father and the grandfather. Many members of the Eddlemon family stayed in middle Tennessee and others migrated to Gibson Co., TN and the counties of Perry and Cape Girardeau, MO.

The search to link these early Eddlemon families continues.

PREFACE

In 1796 Tennessee became a state, but there is no complete census extant until 1830. Only a few of our adventurous woodsmen and pioneer settlers had ventured into the area until the turmoil of efforts to gain our independence. After the Revolutionary War was over, the other side of the mountains beckoned to settlers and our Revolutionary War veterans. Many of these veterans received military bounty land as a reward for military service by our fledgling country, the United States of America.

Virgin forests, fertile valleys, swift rivers and abundance of game awaited these new pioneers. They carved a country out of a primitive wilderness bringing families, law and order. It was not easy. Enduring the horrors of the Indian encounters, the isolation and the rigors of the time period, our pioneer ancestors prevailed. This enduring pioneer spirit is with us today as we face new challenges as the new millennium approaches.

This volume represents a collection of records from the time period before 1840. This time period is usually the most puzzling and difficult one for researchers. Records are not complete and scattered as the county boundaries changed for individuals. Pinpointing the location of an ancestor when only "Tennessee" is known for their birthplace is not easy. To close the gap left by census records, researchers must use other sources such as tax and court records to trace the footsteps of their ancestors.

Some abbreviations have been used in this volume. There are:

MD	Marriage Date
a	Acres
wp	White Pole Tax
AA	Annual Allowance
AR	Amount Received
PSD	Pension Started Date
B	Birth Date
D	Death Date

Good luck in your search for your ancestor.

TABLE OF CONTENTS

Page

BLEDSOE COUNTY
(Founded 1807 from Roane County)

Petition to the General Assembly, Feb. 25, 1809 — 1

BRADLEY COUNTY
(Founded 1836 from Indian Lands)

Tax List, 1837 — 95

BLOUNT COUNTY
(Founded 1795 from Knox County)

Marriage Records, 1795-1839 — 105

FRANKLIN COUNTY
(Founded 1807 from Bedford and Warren Counties)

Tax List, 1812 — 98

GIBSON COUNTY
(Founded 1823 from Western District)

Marriage Records, 1824-1839 — 72

GRAINGER COUNTY
(Founded 1796 from Hawkins and Knox Counties)

Insolvents Living with the Indian Boundary, 1797 — 1

HENRY COUNTY
(Founded 1821 from the Western District)

Persons Listed in the Estate Sale of Jacob Meek, 1824 — 155

JACKSON COUNTY
(Founded 1801 from Smith County)

Delinquent Tax List, 1805 — 55

LAUDERDALE COUNTY
(Founded 1835 from Dyer and Tipton Counties)

Marriage Records, 1838-1839   55

MAURY COUNTY
(Founded 1807 from Williamson County)

Purchasers of Columbia Town Lots, 1808   55

OVERTON COUNTY
(1806 from Jackson County)

Cave Spring Cumberland Presbyterian Church, 1836   94

ROANE COUNTY
(Founded 1801 from Blount and Knox Counties)

Members of the Grand Jury, December, 1804   94

ROBERTSON COUNTY
(Founded 1796 from Tennessee)

Obituary of Ewing H. Crockett   161

SEVIER COUNTY
(Founded 1794 from Jefferson County)

Tax List, 1832   156

SUMNER COUNTY
(Founded 1786 from Davidson County)

Capt. Byrn's Co. U. S. Cavalry, War of 1812   2
Tax List, 1789   71
Marks & Brands, 1787-1818   202

WASHINGTON COUNTY
(Founded 1777 from Entire State and parts of North Carolina)

Marriage Records, 1792-1839   2
Capt. Greer's Taxables, 1790   164

WILSON COUNTY
(Founded 1799 from Sumner County)

Marriages, 1806-1830   164

STATEWIDE & MISCELLANEOUS

1835 Pension Roll, Surnames A-B	56
Tennesseans on the 1885 Douglas Co., WA Territorial Census, 1885	160
Tennesseans on the Brazos Co., TX 1850 Census	161
Tennesseans on Pendleton Co., KY Delinquent Tax List, 1807	163
Tennesseans on Pendleton Co., KY Delinquent Tax List, 1808	163
Tennesseans on Pendleton co., KY Delinquent Tax List, 1809	163

Grainger County, Tennessee, List of Insolvents Living Within the Indian Boundary, 1797

James Adkins, William Allen, Thomas Anderson, John Arthur, Nathaniel Austin, Isral Baxter, John Bennet, James Bitson, Thomas Bitson, Mathew Black, Jeremiah Boling, William Bowman, John Box, John Branham, Morris Brown, James Bruton, Samuel Bruton, Julius Bunch, Charles Burdon, John Burdsong, William Burton, Archer Busham, George Callums, John Carr, Francis Chaney, Elijah Chisum, James Chisum, Thomas Clark, Stephen Claypole, Joseph Cobb, Jr., Joseph Cogdin, Andrew Cope, Barney Cope, James Cope, Mathew Cope, Alexander Cowen, Josiah Cox, Benjamin Crowley, John Cunningham, James Davis, James Davis, Jesse Dodson, Jesse Dodson ,Jr., Nimrod Dodson, William Dougherty, William Dougherty, Evan Douther, Bnjamin Drunden (?), Stephen Durham, Abrham Duvalt, William Elam, James Finley, William Finley, William Finley, Edmond Franklin, Thomas Gibbons, George Gibson, Jerry Gibson, Spencer Graham, Andrew Haines, Peter Halfacre, Nathaniel Hamit, Nathaniel Hamit, John Hamlin, Samuel Hansley, William Harding, Jonathan Harrison, John Hatfield, Joseph Hatfield, Richard Hatfield, James Henderson, Thomas Henderson, William Henderson, Thomas Hill, William Hill, David Hodgson, Robert Howard, Samuel Hughs, Theophilus Hughs, William Inglis, Jeremiah Innis, Jessee Jones, James Jonston, John Keith, Thomas Keith, Isaac Lane, Tidance Lane, Joel Lewis, Jeremiah Linch, William Livingston, Samuel Lusk, Andrew McBride, Thomas McBride, William McBride, John McDonald, William McDonald, Thomas McLellan, James Mahan, Dannel Martin, Frederick Miller, John Miller, Lewis Moore, John Morgan, John Newport, William Owen, John Payne, Elijah Peters, James Reynolds, John Reynolds, Angus Ross, George Rull, John Sears, Michael Shanley, Joseph Sharp, Jacob Shoat, James Sims, Martin Sims, Mathew Smith, James Steen, Edward Stevenson, John Stevenson, William Stevenson, Benjn Stinnet, John Stinnet, William Stinnet, Peter Sullens, Dutton Sweeton, John Sweeton, Joseph Thomas, Alexander Thompson, William Tinsley, Dennis Trammel, James Vanbiber, John Vanbiber, Peter Vanbiber, John Wallen, William Ward, John Weaver, Joseph Weaver, Samuel Weaver, Samuel Weaver, William Wier, David Womack, Jeremiah Womack, Jonathan Womack, George Yoakham,

Bledsoe County, Tennessee, Petition to the General Assembly, Feb. 25, 1809

John Anderson, Joseph Grayson, Eli Thurman, Saml. Terry, Peter Looney, James Standefer, Thomas Allred, John Portman, John Thomas, Wm. Lee, Jesse Roberts, John Smith, Benj. Grayson, John Walker. T. Coulter, Issac Stephens, Robert Lang, JameGooden, William Roberson,

John Rogers, James Roberson, Geo. Skillern, Daniel Wood, John Julien, Stephen Bishop, Michael Rawlings, George C. Cozby, John Dwiggins, Alexr Coulter, John Hutson, Timothy Hixson, Mills Robinson Archibald Beard, Jos. Hoge, Joel Hillerd, Charles Copland, J. Narramore, Ephraim Hixson, Forgason Jackson, Jesse Grayson, Wren Grayson, Stephen Chelton, Adam Lamb, John Scossy, Steven Sutton, Sr., .Richard Moon, Wm. Holland, Benj. Grayson, Sr., John Stanfill, James Hoose, Jonathan Basham

Sumner County, TN, War 1812, Captain John Byrn's Company, U. S. Cavalry Regiment of Tennessee Volunteers, Colonel John Coffee. Feb.10, 1813 - Apr. 24, 1813.

Officers: John W Bryan., Capt.; Alfred H. Douglass, 1st Lt; Noah Cotton, 2nd Lt.; Joseph Scoby, Cornet; Josiah Walton, 1st Sgt.; James Hamilton, 2nd Sgt.; Isaac Loony, 3rd Sgt.; John Cotton, 4th Sgt.; Isaac Elliot, 1st Cpl.; John Montgomery, 2nd Cpl.; Alexander Cotton, 3rd Cpl.; William Cantrell, 4th Cpl.; Allen Cotton, Trumpeter; Jacob Leavy, Saddler; Stewart Briggance, Farrier; Adam Conger, B. Smith.

Privates: Solomon Anderson, Henry Barner, John Bell, Olly Blackman, Nicholas Boyle, Richard Boyle, Charles Briggance, Nicholas Briggance, Azehiah Brown, James Byrns, John Cerly,Thomas Coffman, William Covington,Jesse Daniel, Thomas Daniel, William Daniel,John Dasset, Ingram Duff, Thomas Dugar, Jarod Dugger, Wesley Dugger, Berry Edwards, Samuel Eidson, Everlard Ellis, James Ellis, Thomas Findley, John Hunter, Benjamin Kensall, John Latimore, Nicholas Latimore, Samuel Laurence, John Lawrence, Alexander McCrory, James McKensie, Thomas Martin, Robert Moore, Isaac Morris, Robert Parks, Nofflett Perry, Simeon Perry, John Peyton, John Rice, Hardy Robertson, Samuel Rogers, Thomas Scarulock, Elijah Stallions, James Strother, Robert Strother, Archibald Thompson, John Turner, Jordan Uzzell, Thomas Wingore, Henry Winn, Peter Winn

Washington County, TN, Marriages, 1792-1839
Jonathan Tipton and ???? , (MD) Feb. 27, 1795
Joseph B. Bacon and ???? , (MD) 1815
James Acton and Zilla Bayles, (MD) Aug. 19, 1822
Alexander Adams and Lindy Brown, (MD) Oct. 14, 1826
Isaac Adams and Sarah Nelson, (MD) Nov. 25, 1831
Marten Adams and Jane Casaday, (MD) Oct. 22, 1835
John Adwell and Mary Hale, (MD) Aug. 29, 1816
J. A. Aiken and W. G. Gammon, (MD) Jun. 18, 1839
Robert Aiken and Nancy Kennedy, (MD) Sep. 4, 1822
C. Allen and C. Kiker, (MD) Oct. 27, 1839

George Allen and Esther Mitchell, (MD) Apr. 16, 1833
J. W. Allen and C. K. Maxwell, (MD) Apr. 3, 1839
James Allen and Rachel Bains, (MD) Apr. 17, 1834
Robert Allison and Elleanor Hodges, (MD) Nov. 23, 1818
Robert Allison and Margaret Williams, (MD) Mar. 27, 1833
Thomas Allman and Sarah Huffman, (MD) May 14, 1811
Daniel Allon and Allathy Hale, (MD) Mar. 27, 1788
Henry Ambrose and Rhoda Tilson, (MD) Feb. 11, 1838
Jonathan Ambrose and Mary Tinker, (MD) Apr. 28, 1829
C. Anders and I. G. Leach, (MD) Aug. 17, 1839
Reuben Anders and Rebecca Summers, (MD) Apr. 3, 1823
Alexander Anderson and Eliza Rose Deadrick, (MD) Jun. 7, 1825
John Anderson and Margaret Christian, (MD) Mar. 31, 1808
William Anderson and Hester Russell, (MD) Jan. 27, 1817
J. Andes and C. Walters, (MD) Mar. 12, 1839
John Andes and Polly Harvey, (MD) Mar. 15, 1821
Dan D. Andrew and Nancy Tyler, (MD) Mar. 14, 1821
Samuel Apperson and Milly Holland, (MD) Jan. 25, 1788
John Archer and Rebecca Smith, (MD) Dec. 4, 1827
Levi Archer and Rachel Archer, (MD) Jan. 15, 1818
James Armstrong and Nancy Horton, (MD) Jan. 24, 1837
James Arrington and Patsy Bell, (MD) Oct. 12, 1808
Thomas Arrington and Sebitha Bell, (MD) Jan. 18, 1816
John Arthurburn and Nancy Billingsley, (MD) Aug. 17, 1819
John Asten and Mary McCracken, (MD) May 31, 1832
Wilton M. Atkinson and Martha B. Macken, (MD) Feb. 26, 1817
Jesse Austin and Camilla Bean, (MD) Feb. 9, 1824
Isaac Babb and Anna English, (MD) May 5, 1821
Joshua Babb and Serrafina Smith, (MD) May 31, 1827
Philip Babb and Artemesia Hale, (MD) Dec. 4, 1821
Charles Bacon and Elizabeth Bacon, (MD) Jan. 31, 1833
Charles Bacon and Nancy Bacon, (MD) Jun. 8, 1837
Charles Bacon and Patsey Bean, (MD) Nov. 15, 1831
Charles Bacon and Anny Hale, (MD) Dec. 14, 1823
Elijah Bacon and Martha Squibb, (MD) Sep. 21, 1826
Isaac Bacon and Jane Bacon, (MD) Aug. 11, 1831
Isaac E. W. Bacon and Sarah Hunt, (MD) Aug. 21, 1819
Jacob Bacon and Elizabeth Kebler, (MD) Oct. 2, 1821
James Bacon and Marina Fawbush, (MD) Jan. 9, 1834
Jesse Bacon and Elizabeth Pritchard, (MD) Nov. 8, 1812
John Bacon and Leigh Jackson, (MD) Jun. 25, 1820
Johnny Bacon and Dorcas Jackson, (MD) Jul. 25, 1812
Jonathan Bacon and Debby Bains, (MD) Sep. 8, 1825

Joseph B. Bacon and ????, (MD). , 1815
M. Bacon and F. Hail, (MD) May 25, 1839
Thomas Bacon and Sally Barren, (MD) Dec. 15, 1825
Joseph Parker Baggatt and Mary Lansdown, (MD) Feb. 3, 1814
Stephen Bailes and Nancy Milburn, (MD) Feb. 17, 1825
William Bailes and Rachel Squibb, (MD) Aug. 12, 1813
Alner Bails and Serena Purces, (MD) Feb. 4, 1836
Caleb Bails and Margaret Iser, (MD) Apr. 18, 1831
Daniel Bails and Rebeccah Andrews, (MD) May 29, 1830
Isaac H Bails and Nancy Mulky, (MD) Oct. 20, 1836
John S. Bails and Elizabeth Nelson, (MD) Nov. 9, 1820
Joseph Bails and Mary Bails, (MD) Mar. 6, 1838
John Bains and Sarah Bains, (MD) Aug. 9, 1837
James Baird and Edy Nelson, (MD) Nov. 15, 1807
Andrew Baker and Nancy Briant, (MD) Dec. 24, 1815
Edward Baker and Lucinda Erwin, (MD) Nov. 18, 1830
Samuel Baker and Susan Mitchell, (MD) Mar. 14, 1832
William Baker and Betsy Lott, (MD) Dec. 26, 1818
Horatis Baldwin and Polly Whitakre, (MD) Feb. 22, 1809
Barton Bales and Salita Ann Bacon, (MD) Jan. 28, 1834
Andrew E. Ball and Sarah Moore, (MD) Jan. 10, 1824
Jacob Ball and Hannah Minerva Boyd, (MD) Jan. 15, 1835
Joseph Ball and Nancy Brown, (MD) Oct. 24, 1809
Samuel Ball and Mary Cole, (MD) Feb. 20, 1810
Bluford Ballinger and Sarah Sands, (MD) Oct. 13, 1836
Josiah Ballinger and Elizabeth Smith, (MD) Mar. 19, 1793
M. Banner and L. Gray, (MD) Mar. 17, 1839
Berges Barckley and Elizabeth Barckley, (MD) Jan. 29, 1818
Joseph Barger and Susannah Williams, (MD) Nov. 22, 1831
Wyland Barger and Christina Cilty, (MD) Dec. 26, 1810
John Baringer and Sabrey Embree, (MD) Sep. 30, 1834
Daniel Barkley and Jane Shields, (MD) May 20, 1823
E. M. Barkley and Polly Richard, (MD) Sep. 19, 1837
Ebenezer Barkley and Mary Taylor, (MD) Jun. 7, 1831
John Barkley and Elizabeth Charleton, (MD) Mar. 16, 1827
John Barkley and Sarah Ann McEfee, (MD) Dec. 11, 1835
William Barkley and Louisa M. Aiken, (MD) Feb. 16, 1837
Elijah Barlow and Martha Phillips, (MD) Aug. 6, 1835
John Barlow and Mary Freeman, (MD) Jun. 21, 1835
Abraham Barnes and Sarah A. Carothers, (MD) Sep. 19, 1838
Charles Barnes and Betsy Edwards, (MD) Jun. 7, 1821
Daniel Barnes and Polly Bacon, (MD) Oct. 29, 1818
E. Barnes and S. Houston, (MD) Oct. 17, 1839

George Barnes and Jemima Jackson, (MD) Mar. 24, 1818
Jacob Barnes and Ann Martin, (MD) Oct. 21, 1821
James Barnes and Margaret Grimley, (MD) Nov. 29, 1822
James A. Barnes and Deborah Carothers, (MD) Feb. 9, 1837
R. Barnes and J. R. Pain, (MD) Dec. 29, 1839
Stephen Barnes and Rhoda Brown, (MD) Aug. 13, 1831
Washington B. Barnes and Rebecca Snapp, (MD) May 24, 1832
William Barnes and Mary Blair, (MD) Jun. 26, 1809
William Barnet and Mary Edwards, (MD) Apr. 1, 1821
I. Barns and E. Cloyd, (MD) Sep. 15, 1839
Jacob Barron and Jane Murry, (MD) Oct. 20, 1831
John Barron and ???? Wright, (MD) Jan. 30, 1829
Joseph Baser and Mary Keener, (MD) Dec. 23, 1832
Christopher Bashor and Elizabeth Hymes, (MD) May 22, 1831
Henry Bashor and Elizabeth Bowman, (MD) Feb. 19, 1831
I. T. Basket and A. Hartman, (MD) Aug. 26, 1839
John Basket and Tiney Taylor, (MD) Nov. 4, 1811
Richard Basket and Lucy McNabb, (MD) Dec. 18, 1824
Richard Baskett and Rachel Hartman, (MD) Nov. 29, 1826
John Bass and Rebecca Horton, (MD) Dec. 18, 1810
Barnett Baxter and Melissa Cunningham, (MD) Dec. 7, 1828
John Baxter and Nancy Peeples, (MD) Oct. 14, 1816
Daniel P. Bayles and Lidia Flaer, (MD) Nov. 5, 1825
Elijah Bayles and John Broyles, (MD) Oct. 5, 1827
George Bayles and Nancy Goforth, (MD) Mar. 13, 1817
Hezekiah Bayles and Mary Finch, (MD) Dec. 25, 1811
John Bayles and Elizabeth Bacon, (MD) Nov. 8, 1819
Reuben Bayles and Elizabeth Moore, (MD) Jun. 27, 1808
Rheuben Bayles, Jr., and Sarah Young, (MD) Oct. 5, 1808
Samuel Bayles and Nancy Mitchel, (MD) Oct. 12, 1826
Samuel D. Bayles and Basmath Peoples, (MD) Nov. 16, 1826
Samuel G Bayles and Fernanda Brown, (MD) Aug. 7, 1821
Thomas A. Bayles and Sarah Harris, (MD) Sep. 4, 1834
William Bayles and Mary E. M. Lane Beard, (MD) Mar. 30, 1836
William Bayles and Eliza Collins, (MD) Oct. 30, 1829
William Bayles and Catherine Hare, (MD) Oct. 10, 1797
Young Bayles and Mary Phillips, (MD) Apr. 5, 1834
Jesse Bayless and Nancy Shanon, (MD) Nov. 19, 1816
Richard Bayless and Susannah Giesler, (MD) Jul. 12, 1833
John Bayley and Delilah Broyles, (MD) Feb. 2, 1828
Edmund Beagles and Manerva Medlock, (MD) Mar. 10, 1831
George Beagles and Margaret White, (MD) Jun. 2, 1834
Abner Beals and Winny Owens, (MD) Dec. 14, 1824

Isaac Beals and Anny Pitcock, (MD) Mar. 6, 1828
Joseph Beals and Mary Sherfy, (MD) Mar. 5, 1835
Levi Beals and Malinda Wyington, (MD) Dec. 17, 1812
Solomon Beals and Sally Stewart, (MD) Jun. 19, 1823
Joseph Bean and Mary Sliger, (MD) Jan. 11, 1824
Robert Bean and Patsy Crouch, (MD) Mar. 7, 1821
Robert Bean and Mary Hunter, (MD) Oct. 17, 1833
Robert Bean and Caty Sliger, (MD) Mar. 12, 1818
Charles Beane and Margaret Cloyd, (MD) Jun. 19, 1815
Robert Beard and Sarah Glasscock, (MD) Jun. 23, 1816
Samuel Beard and Catherine Bricker, (MD) Nov. 1, 1825
Thomas Beard and Jane Hall, (MD) Nov. 4, 1824
John Beaty and Ann Wood, (MD) May 7, 1788
James Beckham and Sarah Glass, (MD) Dec. 30, 1808
John Lowry Bedsalls and Mary Bacon, (MD) Oct. 27, 1827
John Bedsauls and Polly Jones, (MD) Apr. 10, 1823
George Belcher and Eliza Norton, (MD) Sep. 10, 1828
Allon Bell and Sarah Cannon, (MD) Dec. 8, 1836
Brooksey H. Bell and Elizabeth Broyles, (MD) Dec. 26, 1818
Hugh Bell and Sarah Higgins, (MD) Oct. 26, 1834
James Bell and Sarah Anders, (MD) Nov. 11, 1819
James Bell and Eliza Rogers, (MD) Apr. 5, 1837
Joseph Bell and Sarah Clark, (MD) Sep. 26, 1812
Joseph C. Bell and Nancy White, (MD) Oct. 22, 1809
Phillip Bell and Polly Ann Cannon, (MD) May 24, 1832
Samuel Bell and Nancy W. Mathes, (MD) Oct. 14, 1824
Samuel S. Bell and Lem McCray, (MD) Nov. 22, 1821
Thomas Bell and Elizabeth Ferguson, (MD) Apr. 12, 1825
Joseph Bellamy and Rebecca Taylor, (MD) Feb. 6, 1833
John Berkley and Mary Grayham, (MD) Oct. 13, 1825
David Besset and Anny Hickman, (MD) Nov. 18, 1806
Nicholas Betner and Mary E. Williams, (MD) Jul. 21, 1836
Charles Bickley and Mary Hatler, (MD) Aug. 19, 1788
Thomas Biddill and Betsy Blair, (MD) Jun. 23, 1815
James Biddle and Elizabeth Whister, (MD) Dec. 23, 1828
Samuel Biddle and Margaret Wilson, (MD) Dec. 29, 1819
Thomas Biddle and Nancy Ann Hamilton, (MD) Oct. 23, 1838
John Billingly and Polly Hale, (MD) Mar. 16, 1819
Jacob Billingsley and Rebecca Shipley, (MD) May 10, 1812
James Billingsley and Sarah Hale, (MD) May 26, 1825
Ephriam Bird and Ellianor Mauk, (MD) Sep. 30, 1829
Benjamin Birdwell and Margaret Campbell, (MD) Aug. 24, 1831
David Birdwell and Malinda Brown, (MD) Apr. 27, 1827

William Birdwell and Eliza Jobe, (MD) Aug. 30, 1832
John Bitner and Elizabeth Hatter, (MD) Nov. 3, 1790
James Black and Rachel Spring, (MD) Apr. 13, 1811
James P. Black and Mary Dyke, (MD) Sep. 26, 1837
John Black and Anne Foster, (MD) Jul. 7, 1832
Solomon Black and Elizabeth Dykes, (MD) Mar. 22, 1838
Thomas Black and Martha Clark, (MD) Sep. 13, 1831
John Blair and Margaret Blair, (MD) Dec. 17, 1794
John Blair and Hannah Carreathers, (MD) Nov. 26, 1793
John Blair and Peggy McCall, (MD) Jan. 22, 1811
John Blair and Levica Shields, (MD) Jan. 31, 1815
Robert L. Blair and Martha R. Cunningham, (MD) Nov. 1, 1838
??? Blakely and James Twedy, (MD) Oct. 12, 1792
John Blakley and Priscilla O'Neal, (MD) Jan. 5, 1802
James Bleakley and Margaret Hays, (MD) Dec. 21, 1833
Matthew Bleakley and Charity Craddick, (MD) Oct. 29, 1838
William Bleakley and Margaret Taylor, (MD) Jun. 21, 1806
Andrew Blythe and Debby Andrews, (MD) Aug. 19, 1823
Lemuel Bogard and Hannah Saylor, (MD) Jan. 24, 1833
Abraham Bogart and Elisabeth Duncan, (MD) Apr. 20, 1799
Cornelas Bogart and Elisabeth Moffet, (MD) Aug. 27, 1793
Samuel Bogart and Rachel Hammer, (MD) May 19, 1818
John Booth, Jr. and Sally Rodgers, (MD) Jan. 20, 1810
Joseph Boothe and Elizabeth Collett, (MD) Nov. 8, 1838
Abraham Boren and Sarah Robison, (MD) May 2, 1833
Absolem Boren and Hannah Litle, (MD) Oct. 5, 1793
Chana Boren and Mary Pearcefield, (MD) Sep. 21, 1796
Greenbury Boren and Mary Ruble, (MD) Oct. 11, 1807
Orry Boren and William Hart, (MD) Nov. 18, 1824
Absolom Boring and Betsy Ruble, (MD) Apr. 26, 1823
Cheney Boring and Elizabeth White Cotton, (MD) Sep. 13, 1790
Hezekiah Boring and Polly Melvin, (MD) Jul. 25, 1812
Jacob Boring and Alice Green, (MD) Feb. 11, 1819
John Tipton Boring and Elizabeth Threewit, (MD) Mar. 11, 1823
Tipton Boring and Ruth Howard, (MD) Mar. 21, 1824
Vincent Boring and Loisa Little, (MD) Mar. 13, 1826
John Bottles and Susan Patton, (MD) Jul. 8, 1822
Joseph Bottles and Ann Lineberger, (MD) Oct. 14, 1824
William Bottles and P Mary Hammonds, (MD) Oct. 11, 1820
John Bovell and Christiana Gray, (MD) Sep. 29, 1819
William Bovell and Hester M Doak, (MD) May 7, 1829
William Bovell and Minerva Tylor, (MD) Mar. 29, 1838
Francis Bowers and Elizabeth Ann Gyer, (MD) Feb. 23, 1837

Joshua Bowers and Anne Murry, (MD) Oct. 13, 1825
Lawrence Bowers and Alsey Mains, (MD) Aug. 20, 1835
Levi Bowers and Elizabeth Capps, (MD) Sep. 25, 1835
Philip Bowlin and Catherine Walters, (MD) Feb. 14, 1817
Benjamin Bowman and Ann Sliger, (MD) Apr. 8, 1838
Daniel Bowman and Alsey M Ellis, (MD) Oct. 19, 1830
David Bowman and Emiline Miller, (MD) Sep. 2, 1836
David Bowman and Sally Smith, (MD) May 11, 1815
Jacob Bowman and Sarah Campbell, (MD) Feb. 23, 1837
John Bowman and Polly Duncan, (MD) Jul. 31, 1820
John A. Bowman and Mariah Worthington, (MD) Jul. 26, 1830
John H. Bowman and Salina J. Broyles, (MD) Jul. 4, 1837
Joseph Bowman and Aley Carr, (MD) May 31, 1828
Othneal Bowman and Elizabeth Watson, (MD) Feb. 11, 1829
Samuel Bowman and Anne Crouch, (MD) Aug. 11, 1829
James Bowser and Harriet Keane, (MD) Oct. 3, 1833
James W. Bowser and Louisa M Simmons, (MD) Apr. 5, 1834
Barlley Boyd and Lercy Wood, (MD) Dec. 30, 1832
Henry Boyd and Sarah Barly, (MD) Nov. 12, 1825
Jacob Boyd and Margaret Gervin, (MD) Jun. 15, 1824
Jacob Boyd and Ruth Mallonee, (MD) May 1, 1836
James Boyd and Sarah Patterson, (MD) Jan. 24, 1828
Jeremiah Boyd and Susannah Ryker, (MD) Mar. 8, 1811
Joseph Boyd and Phebe Little, (MD) Jan. 20, 1798
Joseph Boyd and Catherine Spradling, (MD) Mar. 15, 1837
James Bradley and Levina Buck, (MD) May 30, 1825
John Bradley and Nancy Tate, (MD) Nov. 6, 1793
Charles Brannen and Maria Engle, (MD) Dec. 31, 1816
Burridge Brannon and Polly Cassady, (MD) Oct. 12, 1815
David Brannon and Sarah Mitchell, (MD) Sep. 1, 1833
Beverage Branum and Mary Ambrose, (MD) Apr. 15, 1833
William Brazelton and Martha A Gillespie, (MD) Dec. 9, 1828
James Brearly and Elizabeth Click, (MD) Oct. 29, 1825
Ira Bricker and Sally Riddle, (MD) Aug. 23, 1831
J. Bricker and E. Sisk, (MD) Nov. 18, 1839
William Bricker and Sarah Ingle, (MD) Dec. 10, 1836
William Bright and Susannah Barkley, (MD) Dec. 28, 1837
William Brit and Nancy Waller, (MD) Dec. 19, 1816
David Britt and Annah Harmon, (MD) Dec. 30, 1819
James Britt and Nancy Ford, (MD) Dec. 27, 1832
Robert Britt and Nancy Nelson, (MD) Mar. 1, 1829
William Brittan and Sally Smith, (MD) Jul. 9, 1810
Abraham Britten and Nancy Brannon, (MD) Jun. 12, 1811

Abraham Britten and Nancy Brannon, (MD) Jun. 12, 1821
John Britten and Catherine Hensley, (MD) Sep. 22, 1822
William Brizely and Sabra Britner, (MD) Jul. 20, 1826
Lewis Broiles and Elizabeth Calvert, (MD) Oct. 2, 1815
A. Brommit and Catharine Cosiah, (MD) Mar. 22, 1839
Aaron Brown and Mary Collet, (MD) Sep. 22, 1829
Abraham Brown and Sarah Franklin, (MD) May 24, 1831
Abraham Brown and Nancy Wiggins, (MD) Dec. 20, 1813
Benjamin Brown and Sarah Sevier, (MD) May 6, 1789
David Brown and Polly Campbell, (MD) Dec. 6, 1826
Elijah Brown and Betsy Glass, (MD) Dec. 23, 1815
Enoch Brown and Rebecca George, (MD) Mar. 3, 1831
Gabriel Brown and Sarah Bayless, (MD) Dec. 30, 1822
George Brown and Mary Miller, (MD) Dec. 25, 1822
George Brown and Elizabeth Sands, (MD) Mar. 25, 1830
George Brown and Elijah Wilson, (MD) Feb. 9, 1826
Hezekiah Brown and Ann Basket, (MD) Apr. 12, 1830
Jacob Brown and Susan Mitchell, (MD) Mar. 15, 1839
Jacob Brown and Sally Million, (MD) Mar. 21, 1811
Jacob Brown and Polly Salts, (MD) Jan. 23, 1816
Jacob Brown and Nancy Thompson, (MD) Oct. 3, 1805
James Brown and Rachel George, (MD) May 27, 1823
James Brown and Margaret Harvey, (MD) Oct. 20, 1839
Jeremiah Brown and Catherine Gyer, (MD) Jul. 14, 1797
Jeremiah Brown and Polly Starmer, (MD) Jul. 31, 1823
Jesse Brown and Betsy Wattenberger, (MD) Mar. 27, 1828
John Brown and Polly Barry, (MD) Aug. 27, 1827
John Brown and Nancy Clows, (MD) Dec. 26, 1822
John Brown and Rebeccah Deakins, (MD) Sep. 30, 1833
John Brown and Elizabeth Parker, (MD) Jun. 19, 1827
John W. Brown and Margaret Kincheloe, (MD) Jan. 7, 1817
Joseph Brown and Betsy Alexander, (MD) Sep. 5, 1801
Joseph Brown and Nancy Edwards, (MD) Apr. 20, 1826
Joseph Brown and Lydia Hammonds, (MD) Mar. 10, 1814
Pelig Brown and Rosamond Bean, (MD) Apr. 15, 1833
Peter Brown and Margaret H Collett, (MD) Sep. 2, 1828
Phillip Brown and Catherine Sliger, (MD) Dec. 30, 1796
Samuel Brown and Elizabeth Boyer, (MD) Jul. 8, 1824
Samuel R Brown and Nancy Balah, (MD) Sep. 28, 1819
Silas Brown and Phebe Ann Andes, (MD) Oct. 12, 1828
Solomon Brown and Mary Bayless, (MD) Mar. 30, 1797
Thomas Brown and Sarah McCray, (MD) Aug. 9, 1819
Thomas Brown and Matilda Murry, (MD) Mar. 23, 1833

Thomas Brown and Leannora Salt, (MD) Mar. 9, 1831
Valentine Brown and Catherine Edwards, (MD) Sep. 5, 1822
W. Brown and Betsy Byerly, (MD) Feb. 13, 1839
William Brown and Savannah Nelson, (MD) Oct. 8, 1816
William Brown and Catherine Sweet, (MD) Oct. 15, 1795
Zachanah Brown and Mary Haws, (MD) Jan. 24, 1834
Israel Browning and Caroline Crouch, (MD) Jul. 14, 1834
John W. Browning and Matilda Waggoner, (MD) Mar. 16, 1837
Reese Browning and Hannah Boyd, (MD) Aug. 27, 1822
Adam Broyles and Rosannah Broyles, (MD) Jun. 22, 1798
Adam Broyles and Nancy Mitchell, (MD) Apr. 13, 1838
Adam Broyles and Polly Walker, (MD) Dec. 23, 1811
Alexander Broyles and Elizabeth Mauke, (MD) Nov. 12, 1833
Cyrus Broyles and Hannah McCray, (MD) Sep. 25, 1838
E. Broyles and Nathan Kiker, (MD) Aug. 26, 1839
Ephraim Broyles and Mary Broyles, (MD) Oct. 4, 1832
Jacob Broyles and Lucinda Broyles, (MD) Dec. 13, 1827
James Broyles and Sally Shoun, (MD) Jul. 25, 1821
John Broyles and Elijah Bayles, (MD) Oct. 5, 1827
John Broyles and Lucinda Broyles, (MD) Dec. 6, 1832
Matheas Broyles and Ann Bayles, (MD) Sep. 21, 1825
Simeon Broyles and Mary Longmire, (MD) Mar. 14, 1834
William Broyles and Margaret Green, (MD) Aug. 16, 1821
Joseph Brummet and Patsy Cassady, (MD) May 12, 1814
Jonathan M Brummit and Nancy Martin, (MD) Feb. 14, 1834
Jonathan Buck and Eliza Houston, (MD) Mar. 16, 1830
Zachanah Buckingham and Mary Miller, (MD) Apr. 27, 1837
Elisha Bull and Sarah Davis, (MD) Nov. 7, 1816
Jacob Bull and Nancy Hazlett, (MD) Mar. 21, 1816
Vincent Bull and Lydia Setseller, (MD) Jul. 20, 1823
Moses Bunker and Eliza Graham, (MD) May 10, 1820
Reuben Burk and Lacy Forbes, (MD) Jul. 20, 1807
Reuben Burk and Polly Lyons, (MD) Jul. 25, 1805
William Burk and Elizabeth Thompson, (MD) Jan. 22, 1794
Arthur Burke and Mary Anderson, (MD) Feb. 25, 1788
Abraham Burket and Dorcus York, (MD) Sep. 19, 1833
Barney Burns and Mary Embree, (MD) Mar. 21, 1805
Timothy Burress and Susan Norris, (MD) Apr. 11, 1820
Elihu Burt and Mary Garret, (MD) Sep. 23, 1794
Thomas Burton and Minerva J Boyd, (MD).,
Joseph Burts and Elizabeth Young, (MD) Jan. 9, 1823
Alexander Buskill and Amanda Marshl, (MD) Feb. 6, 1836
Ira Butler and Susan Thomas, (MD) Oct. 21, 1836

Zachanah W Butler and Susan Range, (MD) Dec. 6, 1832
Michael Byerly and Patsy Thacker, (MD) May 18, 1815
Samuel Byerly and Elizabeth Williams, (MD) Feb. 25, 1820
Joseph Byler and Rebeccah Dillard, (MD) Apr. 19, 1803
Lewis Cade and Elizabeth Harmon, (MD) Nov. 29, 1832
Jonathan H. Callam and Nancy Deakins, (MD) Apr. 22, 1834
Allen Callan and Prudence Brown, (MD) Oct. 30, 1837
Alexander Campbell and Nelly Brown, (MD) Dec. 22, 1818
Alexander Campbell and Polly Strain, (MD) Oct. 18, 1810
Enos Campbell and Jane Cloyd, (MD) Jun. 22, 1826
James Campbell and Rebekah Linville, (MD) Feb. 23, 1789
James Campbell and Ann White, (MD) Oct. 30, 1828
Jeremiah Campbell and Sarah Marr, (MD) Sep. 12, 1789
John Campbell and Matilda Miller, (MD) Nov. 3, 1836
Lausen Campbell and Mary McGhee, (MD) Aug. 12, 1828
Leeroy Campbell and Ann Shields, (MD) Mar. 24, 1823
William Campbell and Sarah Recard, (MD) Nov. 18, 1828
Robert Campble and Anne Campble, (MD) Feb. 16, 1789
Ryley Cannon and Priscilla Bell, (MD) Jan. 26, 1832
Marion Carathers and Vinett Fine, (MD) Jul. 27, 1833
David Carder and Susannah Morgan, (MD) Jun. 7, 1823
Martin Carey and Anny Sherfey, (MD) Sep. 20, 1827
John Carithers and Polly Melvin, (MD) Jan. 14, 1830
William Carmichael and Patsey Blair, (MD). , 1815
Alfred Carr and Elizabeth King, (MD) Mar. 3, 1835
James M. Carr and Emiline Hartsell, (MD) Dec. 13, 1836
Jonathan Carreathers and Sarah Young, (MD) Jan. 23, 1791
Henry Carrell and Ann Strain, (MD) Jun. 20, 1815
John Carriger and Margaret Elliot, (MD) Mar. 30, 1809
John Carroll and Elizabeth Coppick, (MD) May 15, 1826
Thomas Carroll and Ann Maiden, (MD) Jan. 2, 1825
???? Carson and William Gilles, (MD) Jan. , 179
Andrew Carson and Elizabeth Hannah, (MD) Nov. 11, 1790
David Carson and Marey Burke, (MD) Apr. 26, 1794
Gannat Carson and Andrew Gammil, (MD) Mar. 5, 1793
John Carson and Hannah Carson, (MD) Dec. 26, 1811
Robert Carson and Jane Ritchey, (MD) Jul. 20, 1795
Samuel Carson and Rebekah Brandon, (MD) May 10, 1790
Samuel A. Carson and Eleanar S. McCloud, (MD) Feb. 22, 1837
William Carson and Rachel Martin, (MD) Jan. 9, 1822
William B. Carter and Eliza M. Aiken, (MD) Nov. 30, 1815
James Caruthers and Orpha Huston, (MD) Oct. 4, 1815
Abraham Casaday and Martha Wilkeson, (MD) Aug. 25, 1836

James Casaday and Rebecca Brummett, (MD) Oct. 21, 1838
Edmondson Casey and Sarah Hensley, (MD) Nov. 6, 1832
John Cash and Hannah Dosser, (MD) May 8, 1799
Martin Cash and Catharine R. Carson, (MD) May 3, 1838
William Cash and Elizabeth Mears, (MD) Mar. 28, 1833
William L. Cash and Malinda Scalp, (MD) Mar. 17, 1836
John Cass and Leney Riddle, (MD) Oct. 15, 1834
John Cassidy and Elizabeth Brummitt, (MD) Jan. 15, 1820
John E. Casson and Mary E. Harris, (MD) Dec. 1, 1824
Coderic Cazia and Christina Brown, (MD) Jun. 13, 1836
Leonard Ccollier and Charlotte Slagle, (MD) Mar. 14, 1822
Solomon Cellers and Polly Kelly, (MD) Oct. 26, 1828
Green K. Cessna and Maria L. Vance, (MD) Feb. 15, 1825
Carey Chandler and James Jackson, (MD) Mar. 6, 1838
Elkanah Chandler and Nancy Hammett, (MD) Dec. 26, 1838
Zacanah Chandler and Malinda Milburn, (MD) Sep. 9, 1838
John Chaney and Mary Fulman, (MD) Aug. 24, 1819
Ezekiel Chanler and Susannah Chanler, (MD) Mar. 16, 1812
Robert Chapman and Anna Martin, (MD) Oct. 12, 1807
Samuel Chapman and Rachael Basket, (MD) Sep. 11, 1815
William Chapman and Elizabeth Henderson, (MD) Dec. 26, 1794
Pointon Charlton and Rachel McLin, (MD) Sep. 7, 1814
Pointon Charlton and Rebeckah Miller, (MD) Apr. 12, 1819
Simpson Charlton and Sarah Collins, (MD) Dec. 11, 1821
Thomas Charlton and Jenny Glass, (MD) Dec. 5, 1805
Simpson Charton and Sussanah Page, (MD) Jul. 5, 1832
Jeremiah Chase and Hannah Hail, (MD) Oct. 6, 1831
Mark P. Chase and Eliza Campbell, (MD) Dec. 3, 1835
Walter Chase and Rebecca Elsey, (MD) Dec. 15, 1830
Walter Chase and Elizabeth Murray, (MD) Aug. 22, 1801
Jacob Cheats and Sarah Chinuth, (MD) Mar. 20, 1827
Ezra Chester and Nancy Hale, (MD) Jun. 20, 1818
Obediah Chester and Sarah Ellis, (MD) Feb. 11, 1835
Robert Chester and Martha Jones, (MD) Feb. 11, 1811
Joseph Chinnoth and Liddy Bean, (MD) Jul. 30, 1818
John A. Chinouth and Abigail Hunt, (MD) Aug. 3, 1831
Richard Chinouth and Patsy Ellis, (MD) Dec. 4, 1824
John P. Chrisley and Rebecca G. Kumray, (MD) Dec. 3, 1822
David Clark and Jemima Jester, (MD) Aug. 19, 1824
Henderson Clark and Ann West, (MD) Oct. 14, 1819
J. Clark and L. Ellis, (MD) Mar. 10, 1839
Job Clark and T. S. Nelson, (MD) Mar. 26, 1839
Joseph Clark and Polly Basket, (MD) Jun. 20, 1815

Adam Clause and Elizabeth Hutskins, (MD) Jan. 4, 1811
Martin Cleek and Merrianna Borders, (MD) Sep. 5, 1798
Michael Clem and Nancy Hunt, (MD) Sep. 19, 1822
Elijah Click and Susan Balston, (MD) Feb. 9, 1833
Martin Click and Betsy Martin, (MD) Dec. 4, 1810
Peter Click and Elizabeth Sherman, (MD) Jul. 1, 1836
Joseph Cline and Margaret Ellis, (MD) Nov. 25, 1836
Peter Cline and Rachel Leonard, (MD) Sep. 29, 1831
John Clinger and Betsy Rymill, (MD) Apr. 4, 1811
Jacob Clipper and Catharine Bowman, (MD) Dec. 23, 1817
John Clipper and Susannah Bowman, (MD) Feb. 3, 1819
Jacob Clouse and Sarah Tilson, (MD) Oct. 19, 1826
James B. Cloyd and Catherine Click, (MD) Feb. 16, 1832
John Cloyd and Rachall Boyd, (MD) May 31, 1831
John Cloyd and Mary Brown, (MD) Mar. 30, 1837
John Cloyd and Rebecca Patton, (MD) Jul. 19, 1821
R. Cloyd and Peter Northington, (MD) Oct. 24, 1839
William Cloyd and Julea Norrington, (MD) Sep. 13, 1837
William A. Cloyd and Elizabeth Cloyd, (MD) Feb. 9, 1837
Ethelred Cobb and Susanah McColm, (MD) Feb. 13, 1791
Rufus Cobb and Nancy Hail, (MD) Nov. 22, 1838
James H. Cochran and Jane Barkeley, (MD) Nov. 6, 1821
Mathias Coffman and Elizabeth Madlock, (MD) Jun. 13, 1833
James Coggburn and Jane Mercer, (MD) Feb. 13, 1828
Thomas Coldwell and Cloe Wheelock, (MD) May 27, 1826
John Cole and Catherine Layman, (MD) Aug. 9, 1814
Andrew Coleman and Mary Needy, (MD) Mar. 28, 1830
Daniel Coleman and Jane Inser, (MD) Nov. 18, 1831
James W. Collam and Elizabeth M. Campbell, (MD) Oct. 3, 1837
John Collet and Mary Britten, (MD) Jun. 3, 1829
Abraham Collett and Elizabeth Broyles, (MD) Jan. 12, 1833
John Stephens Collier and Lidia Ballenger, (MD) Jul. 26, 1836
Covington Collingsworth and Elizabeth Shipley, (MD) Apr. 16, 1816
Austin Collins and Jemima McClure, (MD) Nov. 21, 1823
Bailey Collins and Susannah McGeehan, (MD) Sep. 10, 1835
Charles Collins and Nancy Miller, (MD) Feb. 1, 1823
Henry W. Collins and Margaret Fisher, (MD) Sep. 12, 1826
J. Collins and M. Morgan, (MD) Oct. 12, 1839
James Collins and Margaret Laudermilk, (MD) Nov. 24, 1834
Jonathin Collins and Jane Bolin, (MD) Nov. 30, 1817
Thomas Collins and Elizabeth Whitson, (MD) Oct. 13, 1836
William Collins and Maria Hunter, (MD) Dec. 25, 1832
William C. Collor and Elizabeth Barnes, (MD) Jan. 12, 1827

Elijah Colson and Mary Purces, (MD) Oct. 4, 1836
Enoch Colsten and Hannah Harrison, (MD) Aug. 7, 1831
Thomas I. Colyar and Mary Bails, (MD) Feb. 15, 1835
L. Colyer and M. Spears, (MD) Feb. 10, 1839
William Combs and Nancy Conkin, (MD) Sep. 6, 1827
Judah Comby and George Irvin, (MD) Nov. 19, 1822
John Conkin and Polly Jackson, (MD) Apr. 16, 1812
David Conklin and Marey Graham, (MD) Feb. 8, 1791
James Conklin and Ruth Ronnels, (MD) Apr. 23, 1835
Josiah Conley and Mary Ann Allison, (MD) Aug. 4, 1829
Asa Cook and Margaret Hammer, (MD) Jun. 8, 1823
James Cooper and Nancy Parker, (MD) Apr. 16, 1826
Joel Cooper and Sarah Boren, (MD) Feb. 24, 1830
Joel Cooper and Elizabeth Job, (MD) Jan. 20, 1788
John Cooper and Susannah Giger, (MD) Oct. 15, 1816
H. E.. Copas and J. H. Cox, (MD) Feb. 17, 1839
Hamilton Copeland and Margaret Irwin, (MD) Jan. 13, 1827
Aron Coppeck and Olive Carrol, (MD) Jan. 12, 1827
John Coppenger and Elizabeth Rodgers, (MD) Oct. 14, 1824
Jonathan Corder and Sarah White, (MD) Jan. 15, 1826
Hiram Cornett and Sarah Winters, (MD) Jan. 30, 1834
Jacob Cosner and Peggy Delany, (MD) Jan. 28, 1811
Conrad Coughman and Ann Philip, (MD) Jul. 29, 1820
John D. Cowan and Sarah Jane Buchanan, (MD) May 29, 1834
John D. Cowan and Mary Barcroft, (MD) Mar. 15, 1838
Samuel Cowan and Jean Montgomery, (MD) Apr. 22, 1794
C Cox and Sarah Ann Billingsley, (MD) Feb. 3, 1839
Caleb Cox and Ann Carriger, (MD) Jan. 25, 1825
Charles Cox and Rebeca Elsey, (MD) Apr. 6, 1827
Charles Cox and Malinda Fitzgerald, (MD) Oct. 12, 1832
Isaac Cox and Mary Hellin, (MD) Oct. 10, 1819
Isaac Cox and Sarah Lessenbery, (MD) Mar. 28, 1818
John Cox and Ruth Gray, (MD) Aug. 20, 1817
John Cox and Priscilla Templin, (MD) Jan. 30, 1810
Joshua Cox and Nancy English, (MD) Oct. 13, 1831
Loyd A. Cox and Sarah English, (MD) Sep. 9, 1830
James Crabtree and Catherine Page, (MD) Apr. 12, 1838
John Craddick and Charlotte Mullen, (MD) Mar. 10, 1835
Hugh A. Crawford and Caroline Cox, (MD) Dec. 16, 1838
James Crawford and Elizabeth Wheeler, (MD) Nov. 4, 1815
John Crawford and Elizabeth English, (MD) Nov. 29, 1832
John H. Crawford and Susan K. Blair, (MD) Nov. 23, 1833
William Crawford and Martha Ford, (MD) Sep. 10, 1811

William Crawford and Martha Ford, (MD) Sep. 10, 1814
William Crawford and Rebecca Smith, (MD) Jan. 13, 1792
John Creamer and Margaret McNeal, (MD) Nov. 28, 1825
Samuel Criselus and Lucinda Kiker, (MD) Nov. 15, 1827
Benjamin Croggins and Margaret Starnes, (MD) Aug. 18, 1819
James Cronell and Letty Tapp, (MD) Oct. 18, 1818
John Cronwell and Mary Wheelock, (MD) Dec. 29, 1825
Elijah Crouch and Mary Ellis, (MD) Jan. 16, 1792
I. Crouch and E. Mains, (MD) Aug. 28, 1839
J. Peter Crouch and Jemima McGuise, (MD) Jul. 10, 1828
James Crouch and Susannah Bowman, (MD) May 26, 1825
John Crouch and Nancy Epperson, (MD) Nov. 2, 1818
John Crouch and Theodocia Hale, (MD) Nov. 21, 1833
John Crouch and Elizabeth Jenkins, (MD) Apr. 4, 1820
Joseph Crouch and Polly Hanley, (MD) Jul. 26, 1813
Joseph Crouch and Betsy Keyfauver, (MD) Feb. 7, 1814
Landford Crouch and Elizabeth Beam, (MD) Sep. 12, 1822
Martin Crouch and Lucinda Fitzgerald, (MD) Feb. 15, 1838
Reuben Crouch and Polly Kincheloe, (MD) Jan. 18, 1822
Thomas H. Crouch and Julia McEfee, (MD) May 26, 1835
William Crouch and Sam Hunt, (MD) May 23, 1815
Michael Crouse and Rebecca Young, (MD) Jul. 15, 1826
Thomas Crow and Sarah Ford, (MD) Mar. 2, 1834
Daniel Crown and Elizabeth Bean, (MD) Sep. 9, 1821
Solomon Crown and Susan Bowman, (MD) Aug. 24, 1820
William Cummins and Mary Nelson, (MD) Dec. 3, 1829
Alexander N. Cunningham and Margaretta Ann Eason, (MD)
    Aug. 7, 1834
John Cunningham and Mary Hampton, (MD) Jun. 16, 1832
David Davault and Marie Cox, (MD) Feb. 22, 1838
Alfred Davenport and Sarah Swingle, (MD) Sep. 4, 1834
Edward Davenport and Margaret Fawbush, (MD) Jul. 28, 1821
George Davenport and Nancy M. Fain, (MD) Sep. 14, 1837
???? Davis and Patsy Bennet, (MD) Jun. 14, 1814
Charles Davis and Martha Denton, (MD) Mar. 20, 1833
James C. Davis and Rachel Tilson, (MD) Sep. 5, 1822
Nathaniel Davis and Elizabeth Celso, (MD) Jan. 27, 1795
Rich Davis and Rebeccah Andes, (MD) Oct. 2, 1833
Samuel Davis and Sarah Letsinger, (MD) Jan. 1, 1810
Thomas Davis and Sally Moore, (MD) Oct. 11, 1817
James Davison and Mary Ellis, (MD) May 29, 1823
Jesse Davison and Phebe Fine, (MD) Sep. 3, 1833
John Davison and Rebecca Fox, (MD) Nov. 21, 1833

John Davison and Lydia Leslie, (MD) Mar. 8, 1827
Joseph Davison and Ibby Jones, (MD) Oct. 26, 1837
William Davison and Sarah Goodman, (MD) Feb. 28, 1837
Jacob Davott and Polly Hodge, (MD) Oct. 7, 1815
Thomas Day and Matilda Henley, (MD) Jan. 17, 1830
David Deaderick and Margaretta Anderson, (MD) Dec. 31, 1794
David A. Deaderick and Adelaide Eliza Jackson, (MD) Apr. 24, 1816
Joseph A. Deadrick and Emiline N. Anderson, (MD) Jan. 20, 1831
James Deakens and Anna Walker, (MD) Aug. 21, 1825
Absolom Deakins and Nancy McCray, (MD) Dec. 15, 1829
Acsean Deakins and Solomon Sherfy, (MD) Aug. 6, 1829
Charles Deakins and Rachel Nelson, (MD) Feb. 3, 1819
Henry Deakins and Rosannah Burris, (MD) Apr. 8, 1817
James Deakins and Cloe Martin, (MD) Feb. 10, 1831
John Deakins and Mary Jobb, (MD) Dec. 19, 1836
John Deakins and Jane Russell, (MD) Nov. 30, 1824
Richard Deakins and Isabella Beard, (MD) Jun. 9, 1823
Adam G. Dean and Nancy Miller, (MD) May 7, 1818
Jeremiah Dean and Susan Parks, (MD) Aug. 20, 1825
George Dearmond and Nancy Webb, (MD) May 23, 1793
Willis Debord and Catherine Lilburn, (MD) May 23, 1821
Achsah Delaney and Daniel Hufhines, (MD) Oct. 11, 1830
Daniel Delaney and Elizabeth McGhee, (MD) Dec. 6, 1821
William Delany and Elizabeth Goins, (MD) Apr. 27, 1812
Moses Delashmet and Nancy Salts, (MD) Apr. 4, 1823
Daniel Denton and Susannah White, (MD) May 5, 1812
H. Denton and I. C. Stevens, (MD) Dec. 25, 1839
William Denton and Rachel Gibson, (MD) Mar. 15, 1826
James Depew and Susannah Cox, (MD) Dec. 22, 1813
John Depew and Catherine Bacon, (MD) Feb. 8, 1816
Daniel Devault and Mary Miller, (MD) Jan. 6, 1825
John Devault and Elizabeth Kitzmiller, (MD) May 22, 1834
Peter Devault and Mary Hoss, (MD) Oct. 27, 1831
Samuel Devault and Patty Crouch, (MD) Jan. 7, 1819
Frederick Dewalt and Margarett Range, (MD) Aug. 23, 1803
William Dewoody and Hanah Alexander, (MD) Mar. 26, 1791
Alfred B. Dillingham and Delilah Caroline Stephens, (MD) Oct. 11, 1831
John Dillingham and Mary Stephens, (MD) Oct. 28, 1829
Duglas Dinkens and Sary Braden, (MD) Aug. 15, 1819
Solomon Dinkin and Susan Parker, (MD) Aug. 31, 1824
William R. Dinwiddie and Martha Blakley, (MD) Feb. 18, 1830
John N. Doak and Martha Snapp, (MD) Jun. 25, 1829
John W. Doak and Martha C. Payne, (MD) Jun. 10, 1834

Andrew J. Doherty and Mary W Phillips, (MD) Nov. 22, 1838
John Donald and Polly Kein, (MD) Oct. 24, 1816
James Dosser and Jane Shoemaker, (MD) Mar. 10, 1823
William Dosser and Malinda Rogan, (MD) Nov. 14, 1820
James Dotson and Elizabeth Overholser, (MD) Dec. 23, 1819
Peter Dotson and Margaret Stansbury, (MD) May 4, 1826
Jacob Douglas and Polly Bacon, (MD) Jun. 19, 1823
Mathew Douglas and Nancy King, (MD) May 29, 1812
John Douglass and Nancy Jobe, (MD) Nov. 18, 1838
Jonathan Douglass and Jane Young, (MD) Jul. 31, 1816
Samuel Douglass and Ann Starr, (MD) Oct. 4, 1838
Thomas Douglass and Nancy Barron, (MD) Dec. 3, 1814
Samuel Drake and Eliza Murry, (MD) Sep. 11, 1827
William Duggard and Nancy Millar, (MD) Aug. 9, 1791
John Dugger and Malvina Morris, (MD) Nov. 29, 1838
Samuel Dugles and Elizabeth Bacon, (MD) Jul. 5, 1818
Milton Dulaney and Orpha Fine, (MD) Dec. 4, 1837
Alfred Duncan and Rhody Douglas, (MD) Jan. 6, 1823
Andrew Duncan and Margaret R. Alexander, (MD) Mar. 26, 1817
Andrew Duncan and Ann Carson, (MD) Apr. 3, 1817
Ellis H. Duncan and Mary Milburn, (MD) Mar. 16, 1831
J. Duncan and A. Goins, (MD) Nov. 7, 1839
James W. Duncan and Mary A. Davault, (MD) May 24, 1838
Jesse Duncan and Sarah Dennis, (MD) Mar. 27, 1836
John Duncan and Rachel F. Duncan, (MD) Aug. 10, 1826
John Duncan and Elizabeth Hampton, (MD) Dec. 11, 1833
Joseph Duncan and Rhoda Hunt, (MD) Mar. 8, 1809
Raleigh Duncan and Mary Keer, (MD) Jul. 7, 1794
Robert Duncan and Sally Campbell, (MD) Nov. 4, 1830
Robert A. Duncan and Jane Robertson, (MD) Mar. 17, 1830
William Duncan and Elizabeth Buckingham, (MD) Apr. 22, 1830
William Duncan and Elizabeth Bayles, (MD) Sep. 21, 1827
William Duncan and Ruth Odell, (MD) Aug. 15, 1809
Thomas Dunham and Nancy Flemming, (MD) Jul. 28, 1826
Thomas Dunkin and Mary Lynch, (MD) Apr. 21, 1790
Richard Dunlap and Mary Barnet, (MD) Feb. 12, 1823
Charles Dunworth and Elizabeth Melvin, (MD) Feb. 27, 1814
William Dykes and Ginny Mare, (MD) Jan. 15, 1810
James Eagin and Hannah Whitson, (MD) Aug. 25, 1795
Felix Earnest and Rachel Embree, (MD) Jun. 2, 1831
J. W. Earnest and N. Patton, (MD) Aug. 26, 1839
Thomas Earnest and Luisa King, (MD) Apr. 9, 1833
Westley Earnest and Mary Payne, (MD) Oct. 21, 1819

John Eberly and Susannah Lineberger, (MD) Oct. 26, 1822
Johnson Edgemon and Rebecca Piercy, (MD) Oct. 26, 1823
John Edwards and Sarah Hopkins, (MD) Sep. 25, 1823
Joshua Edwards and Mary Bide, (MD) Jun. 19, 1797
Samuel E. Edwards and Elizabeth Jobe, (MD) Oct. 12, 1825
William Edwards and Eliza Brown, (MD) Jan. 12, 1829
Wilson Edwards and Ann Bradford, (MD) Nov. 15, 1837
William Egeman and Lucinda King, (MD) Jan. 5, 1820
Macajah Elherton and Rachel Farlan, (MD) Jun. 7, 1817
Clark Ellis and Nancy Lekins, (MD) Dec. 4, 1811
Daniel Ellis and Hannah Bales, (MD) Mar. 8, 1838
E. Ellis and S. M. Hunt, (MD) Dec. 31, 1839
Elijah Ellis and Jane McAdams, (MD) Mar. 23, 1823
John Ellis and Elizabeth Shipley, (MD) Dec. 28, 1830
John B. Ellis and Rebecca Trivathan, (MD) Nov. 7, 1816
L. Ellis and J. Clark, (MD) Mar. 10, 1839
William Ellis and Mary McAdam, (MD) Feb. 8, 1826
William Ellis and E. Soul, (MD) Jun. 16, 1839
William W. Ellis and Lucinda Hunt, (MD) Jan. 18, 1838
William Ellison and Sarah Williams, (MD) Nov. 25, 1824
Isaac Elsey and Ina Cone, (MD) Jun. 9, 1819
James Elsey and Sarah Hulse, (MD) Sep. 12, 1838
Elijah Embree and Mariah King, (MD) Jan. 29, 1828
Walter Emerson and Albina R. Cassen, (MD) Sep. 17, 1810
Philip Emert and Deby Lyons, (MD) Feb. 16, 1819
Thomas Emmerson and Eliza Greene, (MD) Aug. 26, 1833
Thomas Emmerson and Catherine Jacobs, (MD) Mar. 27, 1833
Peter Emmet and Rachael Caruthers, (MD) Jul. 1, 1824
John Engle and Pheta Humphreys, (MD) Nov. 25, 1822
Thomas P. Ensor and Hannah Jobe, (MD) May 8, 1818
Benjamin Epperson and Nancy Barnon, (MD) Oct. 19, 1816
Alexander Erwin and Sally Bacon, (MD) Mar. 9, 1806
Samuel Erwin and Mary Parks, (MD) Dec. 19, 1832
Samuel Erwin and Mary Tilson, (MD) Dec. 26, 1810
Samuel Erwin and Mercy Tilson, (MD) Dec. 17, 1816
William L. Erwin and Rebecca Edwards, (MD) Oct. 15, 1835
Archer Evans and Charlotte Cooper, (MD) Sep. 19, 1787
Fleming B. Evans and Margaret Atkinson, (MD) Jul. 15, 1819
John Ewing and Martha Campbell, (MD) Nov. 6, 1797
J. Fain and S. Jackson, (MD) Sep. 19, 1839
M. E. Falls and M. C. Snapp, (MD) Sep. 23, 1839
John Fannen and Polly Hinch, (MD) Apr. 29, 1812
George Farnsworth and Elizabeth Bartley, (MD) Jan. 14, 1829

Robert Faubush and Elizabeth Hinkle, (MD) May 9, 1811
David Fawbush and Sally Grills, (MD) Jul. 27, 1801
Henry Fawbush and Maria Odonnell, (MD) Nov. 8, 1838
Isaac Fawbush and Viney Summers, (MD) Nov. 23, 1834
Viney Fawbush and Ephraim Fink, (MD) Oct. 9, 1834
Dominick February and Sarah Williams, (MD) Dec. 26, 1827
William Feezle and Jerutia Pring, (MD) Nov. 12, 1822
Jacob Fellers and Hannah Brown, (MD) Nov. 21, 1805
William Felts and Peggy Lacky, (MD) Jul. 15, 1807
Elijah Fenchum and Theodocia Sargant, (MD) May 27, 1827
Thomas Ferguson and Martha Rogers, (MD) Dec. 25, 1833
John Ferjer and Teaney Slyger, (MD) Nov. 24, 1829
Charles Ferrel and Mary Odle, (MD) Nov. 21, 1823
Abraham Fine and Margaret Lusser, (MD) Jan. 4, 1815
David Fine and Viney Dulaney, (MD) Aug. 30, 1837
Vinett Fine and Marion Carathers, (MD) Jul. 27, 1833
Ephraim Fink and Viney Fawbush, (MD) Oct. 9, 1834
George Fink and Sarah Gibson, (MD) Jan. 20, 1824
George Fink and Mary Keene, (MD) Jan. 7, 1838
Levi Fisher and Elizabeth Reed, (MD) Jul. 25, 1807
Castillian Fitzimmon and Rebecca McGreer, (MD) Dec. 4, 1838
Samuel Fitzpatrick and Elizabeth Hodge, (MD) Aug. 23, 1838
James Flenn and Mary Boyd, (MD) Aug. 6, 1835
William Fletcher and Maria Robinson, (MD) Nov. 4, 1825
Isaac Floyd and Margaret Thorp, (MD) Aug. 27, 1812
Henry Fon and Sarah Isenbarger, (MD) Jul. 11, 1820
Lewis Fondwell and Ruth Ann Smith, (MD) Sep. 14, 1826
Hiram Forbush and Nancy Milburn, (MD) Jul. 12, 1824
Benjamin Ford and Polly Ford, (MD) Sep. 3, 1824
Boyer Ford and Sally Chapman, (MD) May 15, 1831
Grant Ford and Nacky Ford, (MD) Feb. 28, 1811
Horatio Ford, Jr. and Jane Careathers, (MD) Oct. 27, 1810
Isaac Ford and Caty Mowl, (MD) Dec. 4, 1817
Jonathan Ford and Jane Stone, (MD) Mar. 18, 1838
Lesley Ford and Sarah Jackson, (MD) Nov. 25, 1822
Loid Ford and Matilda Jackson, (MD) Nov. 17, 1825
Micajah Ford and Ann Briant, (MD) Apr. 14, 1812
Mordicai Ford and Nancy Hyte, (MD) Sep. 28, 1824
Thomas Ford and Margaret Chapman, (MD) Sep. 18, 1812
Thomas Ford and Elizabeth Chandley, (MD) Aug. 24, 1828
Thomas Ford and Isbel Carethers, (MD) Feb. 29, 1812
Thomas Ford and Mahala Fine, (MD) Sep. 11, 1834
Tipton Ford and Mary Ann Murry, (MD) Apr. 22, 1835

William Ford and Achsash Ford, (MD) Dec. 14, 1822
Alexander Ferguson and Mary McNutt, (MD) Apr. 21, 1796
Kenedy Foster and Rebecah Kersewn, (MD) Mar. 17, 1833
Mark Foster and Nancy Netherly, (MD) Aug. 19, 1831
I. L. Fowler and E. Mitchell, (MD) May 20, 1839
Daniel Fox and Anne Porter, (MD) Jan. 28, 1830
Solomon Fox and Eliza Whurley, (MD) Dec. 19, 1829
George Fraker and Nelly Brown, (MD) Dec. 7, 1820
Joseph Fraker and Mary Ann Simpson, (MD) Jan. 29, 1834
William Frakes and Susannah Hartman, (MD) Nov. 4, 1839
Daniel France and Martha Gervin, (MD) Apr. 14, 1829
Ephriam France and Anne Andes, (MD) Mar. 19, 1820
John France and Betsy Burris, (MD) Feb. 23, 1813
Alaxander Frazer and Charrity Bass, (MD) Sep. 30, 1794
Andrew Freeman and Nancy Jones, (MD) Sep. 4, 1821
Elbert Freeman and Margaret Smawley, (MD) Apr. 2, 1825
George Freeman and Sarah Watson, (MD) Apr. 5, 1821
Ladox Freeman and Hannah Grayham, (MD) Sep. 23, 1816
Zeadox Freman and Hannah Grayham, (MD) Sep. 23, 1810
Henry French and Catharine Watson, (MD) Dec. 29, 1817
John Peter French and Eliza Hartman, (MD) Sep. 23, 1815
Robert Fryer and Chaestain Hunter, (MD) Jul. 14, 1792
George Fulk and Sentry Leonard, (MD) Mar. 2, 1819
Alexander Fulkerson and Deborah Jackson, (MD) Nov. 1, 1815
Allen Fulkerson and Ruth Gott, (MD) Aug. 17, 1825
Isaac Fulkerson and Catherine Bacon, (MD) Feb. 12, 1825
James Fulkerson and Elizabeth Waddle, (MD) Feb. 15, 1819
James Fullen and Malinda Broyles, (MD) Oct. 21, 1818
James Fuller and Tabitha Denton, (MD) May 19, 1818
George Gabbert and Catherine Smith, (MD) Dec. 27, 1787
Honer Gaines and Josiah Parker, (MD) May 6, 1822
Daniel Galloway and Hannah Gifford, (MD) Sep. 30, 1827
John Galloway and Betsy Johnston, (MD) May 6, 1838
Thomas Galloway and Susannah Sherfey, (MD) Sep. 3, 1836
Andrew Gammil and Gannat Carson, (MD) Mar. 5, 1793
Abraham L. Gammon and Myra L. Anderson, (MD) Mar. 1, 1838
Alexander Gann and Nancy Campbell, (MD) Oct. 18, 1832
John Gann and Juda Frazier, (MD) Feb. 21, 1818
John Gann and Rebeccah Massengail, (MD) Jun. 28, 1809
John Gann and Sally Painter, (MD) Dec. 1, 1812
Reuben Gann and Eliza Clark, (MD) Jun. 2, 1814
William G. Gardner and M. G. Chester, (MD) Feb. 11, 1839
John Garin and Ruth Brummit, (MD) Apr. 5, 1822

John Garland and Camilla Bean, (MD) Mar. 10, 1827
M. H. Garland and R. I. Odwin, (MD) Oct. 15, 1839
Adam W Garner or Ganns and Sophia Giger, (MD) Jun. 25, 1829
Adam Garns and Elizabeth McAdams, (MD) Apr. 28, 1823
Robert Garvin and Martha Casady, (MD) Oct. 5, 1832
Robert Garvin and Elizabeth Denton, (MD) Oct. 22, 1837
Jacob Gates and Elizabeth Genkins, (MD) Dec. 16, 1797
John Gates and Elizabeth Cox, (MD) Jan. 24, 1833
A. Geahl and Christina Snapp, (MD) Dec. 11, 1817
C. Gibson and M. Mallone, (MD) Apr. 18, 1839
David Gibson and Mary Smith, (MD) Jul. 24, 1834
Francis Gibson and Jane Martin, (MD) Feb. 6, 1834
George W. Gibson and Mary Goin, (MD) Aug. 2, 1833
James Gibson and Mary White, (MD) Jan. 30, 1834
Jeremiah D. Gibson and Phebe Jobe, (MD) Mar. 28, 1817
John Gibson and Rhoda Barnes, (MD) May 10, 1825
John Gibson and Catherine Vaugn, (MD) May 29, 1819
Stephen Gibson and Elizabeth Ferguson, (MD) Apr. 20, 1837
Thomas Gibson and Sarah Martin, (MD) Oct. 25, 1832
John Gilles and Ann Ginkens, (MD) Sep. 13, 1794
William Gilles and ???? Carson, (MD) Jan. , 179
James H. Gillespie and Sarah Ann Young, (MD) Apr. 27, 1830
George Gilley and Nancy Sailor, (MD) Mar. 1, 1838
Abraham Gillis and Mary Sailor, (MD) Oct. 12, 1837
Laben Gillis and Nancy Mitchell, (MD) Oct. 1, 1837
Joseph B. Gilman and Sarah Gammon, (MD) Feb. 10, 1821
Jeremiah Glascock and Francis Register, (MD) Sep. 11, 1814
Larrence Glase and Hanah Humphres, (MD) Oct. 11, 1809
Robert Glenn and Noney Patton, (MD) Aug. 30, 1825
William Glover and Mary Medlock, (MD) Aug. 29, 1837
Robert Goff and Mary Ann Starns, (MD) Apr. 3, 1832
Absolom Goforth and Mary Franklin, (MD) Jun. 15, 1831
John Goforth and Nancy Chandler, (MD) Mar. 3, 1825
Ephraim Goins and Elizabeth Parker, (MD) Sep. 11, 1823
N. Goins and C. Price, (MD) Dec. 14, 1839
John Golden and Sarah Pitcock, (MD) Aug. 1, 1833
Daniel Good and Sarah Cops, (MD) Oct. 1, 1830
David Good and Mary Ann Broyles, (MD) Oct. 18, 1838
David Good and Sarah Hartsell, (MD) Jan. 5, 1811
Emanuel Good and Elizabeth Copp, (MD) Oct. 26, 1826
Emanuel Good and Nancy Rymill, (MD) Jan. 5, 1811
Jacob Good and Elizabeth Ricard, (MD) Sep. 23, 1824
John Good and Martina Hutchison, (MD) Sep. 30, 1838

John Good and Elizabeth Humphreys, (MD) May 2, 1833
Joseph Good and Ruth Irwin, (MD) Jan. 10, 1839
John Gott and Mary Evans, (MD) Feb. 13, 1793
Andrew Graham and Ruth Carson, (MD) Sep. 27, 1811
James Graham and Elizabeth Resser, (MD) Apr. 5, 1831
James Graham and Catherine Stormer, (MD) Mar. 22, 1832
John Graham and Mary Bayles, (MD) Dec. 20, 1827
James Graves and Sarah Hetherly, (MD) Nov. 18, 1789
Benjamin Gray and Matilda Lackens, (MD) Mar. 24, 1814
Daniel Gray and Isabella Mitchell, (MD) Feb. 27, 1816
Jesse Gray and Manerva Brown, (MD) Oct. 3, 1837
John Gray and Melinda Coff, (MD) Oct. 5, 1826
John H. Gray and Matilda Beard, (MD) Apr. 10, 1836
L. Gray and M. Banner, (MD) Mar. 17, 1839
David Grayham and Rachel Sands, (MD) Nov. 4, 1830
Thomas Graynn and Mary Barnes, (MD) Nov. 11, 1830
Arnold Green and Rebecca Messer, (MD) Mar. 26, 1793
James Green and Priscilla Hunter, (MD) Oct. 21, 1819
John Green and Margaret Shields, (MD) Sep. 1, 1820
Joshua Green and Sarah Fellows, (MD) Mar. 12, 1835
Joshua Green and Susannah Greenway, (MD) Dec. 19, 1810
Robert Greene and Barsha Yeager, (MD) Jun. 19, 1823
William Greenway and M. McMacken, (MD) Aug. 27, 1839
Simon Gresham and Sally Paste, (MD) Nov. 16, 1822
Richard Grier and Martha Gray, (MD) Oct. 23, 1817
W. Grimsley and A. Proffit, (MD) Jan. 20, 1839
William Grimsley and Esthe Wheelock, (MD) Sep. 30, 1813
John Grisham and Mary Shipley, (MD) Jan. 19, 1834
Christian Grove and Jane Lacky, (MD) Jan. 31, 1825
Champ Guin and Dorcas Williams, (MD) Dec. 26, 1787
J. Gwinn and William L. Humphreys, (MD) Nov. 15, 1839
William Gwinn and S. A. Hail, (MD) Aug. 8, 1839
William Gwinn and Phoebe Whisler, (MD) Nov. 9, 1837
Andrew Gwynn and Abigail Bacon, (MD) Oct. 22, 1833
Thomas Hagan and Nancy Birdwell, (MD) Sep. 15, 1801
Allison Hail and Elizabeth Kinchaloe, (MD) Nov. 27, 1836
Archibald Hail and Ann Gresham, (MD) Oct. 4, 1827
Butler Hail and Betsy Messer, (MD) Sep. 13, 1806
Chaise Hail and Clary Kinchels, (MD) Aug. 15, 1815
E. Hail and J. Sherfey, (MD) Jan. 17, 1839
F. Hail and M. Bacon, (MD) May 25, 1839
George Hail, Jr. and Ellenor Chamberlain, (MD) Sep. 19, 1797
James Hail and Jane Gray, (MD) May 12, 1816

Joshua Hail and Polly Glascock, (MD) Jan. 29, 1817
Joshua S. Hail and Ruth Hail, (MD) Jan. 31, 1816
Landon Carter Hail and Hannah Ellis, (MD) Jun. 10, 1831
Richard Hail and Ibby Hill, (MD) Jun. 23, 1827
George Haile and Nancy Shipley, (MD) Dec. 25, 1817
Christopher Haines and Deanna Job, (MD) Oct. 14, 1823
Jonathan G. Haines and Sarah Williams, (MD) Jun. 29, 1830
John Hains and Eliza Cobinger, (MD) Mar. 15, 1825
Henry Hair and Elizabeth Taylor, (MD) Jan. 26, 1819
Isaac Hair and Lavinah Susong, (MD) Jul. 22, 1822
John Hair and Aery Hail, (MD) Mar. 22, 1823
Isaac Haire and Sally Russell, (MD) Aug. 14, 1816
Chinouth Hale and Nancy Chase, (MD) Oct. 8, 1829
Enoch Hale and Pheby Haws, (MD) Apr. 19, 1820
Henry Hale and Harriet Kincheloe, (MD) Jun. 29, 1817
James Hale and Almira Bacon, (MD) Mar. 31, 1830
James Hale and Elizabeth Barkley, (MD) May 16, 1839
Jeremiah Hale and Mary Crouch, (MD) May 25, 1826
Jeremiah Hale and Nancy Hunt, (MD) Apr. 2, 1825
John Hale and Elizabeth Smith, (MD) Sep. 8, 1825
Joseph Hale and Sarah Broyles, (MD) Aug. 11, 1833
Joseph Hale and Ibby McAdams, (MD) Dec. 24, 1815
L. Hale and William H Hodges, (MD) Mar. , 1839
Mishac Hale and Jane Kennedy, (MD) Oct. 27, 1831
Nathaniel Hale and Jane Melvin, (MD) Jul. 28, 1829
Walter Hale and Nancy Smith, (MD) Nov. 10, 1816
William Hale and Elizabeth Biddle, (MD) Mar. 24, 1836
William Hale and Mary Fernsworth, (MD) Dec. 10, 1797
Alexander Hall and Susanah McColam, (MD) Jun. 14, 1793
Nathaniel Hall and Lucinda Hail, (MD) Aug. 7, 1816
Amos Haloway and Mary Hale, (MD) Feb. 12, 1833
Baultis Hamer and Sarah Carney, (MD) Mar. 16, 1791
Harvey Hamilton and Lydia Smith, (MD) Sep. 7, 1823
Isaac Hamilton and Nancy Gott, (MD) Jun. 25, 1835
Newton Hamit and Emily Hedrick, (MD) Aug. 18, 1838
Isaac Hammer and Catherine Bogart, (MD) Sep. 6, 1823
Isaac Hammer and Elizabeth Bogart, (MD) May 29, 1793
John Hammer and Martha White, (MD) Oct. 20, 1819
Thomas Hammin and Ruth Jiles, (MD) Feb. 3, 1833
Ezekiel Hammitt and Phoebe Chandler, (MD) Jun. 29, 1838
Edward Hammon and Nancy Cade, (MD) Jul. 8, 1826
David S. Hampton and Margaret Slyger, (MD) Jun. 7, 1832
Herman Hampton and Sarah Duncan, (MD) Nov. 21, 1833

John Hampton and Rosey McBroom, (MD) Jul. 10, 1836
Thomas Hampton and Joanna Renno, (MD) Dec. 17, 1824
Andrew Hannah and Jane Davis, (MD) Oct. 8, 1788
John F. Hannah and Grace Telford, (MD) May 27, 1823
Joseph Hannah and Sarah Ann Chanler, (MD) Jul. 1, 1838
Nathaniel Haris and Hannah Ford, (MD) Aug. 25, 1824
Annah Harmon and David Britt, (MD) Dec. 30, 1819
Jacob Harmon and Lucinda Gann, (MD) Feb. 19, 1824
Thomas J. Harper and Elizabeth McAlister, (MD) Nov. 16, 1837
Hugh Harris and Elizabeth Jackson, (MD) Nov. 5, 1834
I. Harris and N. Hensley, (MD) Nov. 16, 1839
James Harris and Sarah Baskett, (MD) Nov. 19, 1835
Mary E. Harris and John E. Casson, (MD) Dec. 1, 1824
Thomas I. Harris and Catherine Keplinger, (MD) Jul. 10, 1828
William A. Harris and Elizabeth Cariger, (MD) Nov. 14, 1826
Ambrose Harrison and Harriet Miller, (MD) Jul. 28, 1821
Charles Harrison and Elizabeth Kellor, (MD) Mar. 22, 1825
Jesse Harrison and Geriah Medlock, (MD) Dec. 31, 1825
John Harrison and Delilah McDaniel, (MD) Jan. 22, 1829
Peechy Harrison and Jane Clark, (MD) Dec. 24, 1824
Samuel Harrison and Elizabeth Rineheart, (MD) May 6, 1832
Elijah Harshbarger and Hannah Cox, (MD) Jan. 14, 1838
William Hart and Orry Boren, (MD) Nov. 18, 1824
Joseph Hartman and Maria Pursell, (MD) Jan. 15, 1830
William Hartman and Lucensia Register, (MD) Aug. 24, 1838
Abraham Hartsell and Rebecca Lammon, (MD) Nov. 26, 1835
Anthony Hartsell and Elizabeth Longmire, (MD) Aug. 11, 1830
Charles Hartsell and Amanda Click, (MD) Jun. 10, 1830
David Hartsell and Isabella Bayless, (MD) Aug. 2, 1831
Emiline Hartsell and James M. Carr, (MD) Dec. 13, 1836
Joshua Hartsell and Cinthea Bayles, (MD) Apr. 28, 1835
Martin L. Hartsell and Margaret Longmire, (MD) May 5, 1838
Morris Hartsell and Vilett Moore, (MD) Oct. 8, 1832
James Harvey and Armacy Clark, (MD) Mar. 23, 1820
John Harvey and Jane Elliott, (MD) May 21, 1814
John Harvey and Polly Engle, (MD) Mar. 14, 1823
Willoby Harvey and Margaret Parker, (MD) Oct. 18, 1830
John Hatcher and Eve Moris, (MD) Jan. 6, 1790
William Hatcher and Mary Boothe, (MD) Oct. 1, 1838
Elijah Hathway and Elisabeth Crouch, (MD) Sep. 2, 1801
Christian Haun and Nancy Froter, (MD) Dec. 4, 1806
James Haws and Mary Kibler, (MD) Jun. 14, 1838
James M. Haygood and Sarah Ann Case, (MD) Oct. 6, 1836

Alfred Hays and Mary J Landon, (MD) Sep. 10, 1838
Alfred Hays and Harriet Miller, (MD) Jan. 17, 1832
John Hays and Hannah Bleakley, (MD) Oct. 13, 1831
John H. Hays and Margaret Hays, (MD) Jan. 9, 1833
William Hays and Ann Overholts, (MD) Sep. 13, 1831
Charles Headrick and Margaret Salts, (MD) Dec. 12, 1838
Isaac Headrick and Elizabeth Copass, (MD) May 25, 1825
Jacob Headrick and Betsy Mygiar, (MD) Jan. 19, 1811
Jesse Headrick and Edy Faubush, (MD) Jun. 16, 1829
Sebastine Hedler and Elizabeth Kerselas, (MD) Nov. 15, 1792
Frederick S. Heiskell and Elizabeth Brown, (MD) Jul. 18, 1816
Henry M. Helvin and Nancy Shanklin, (MD) May 6, 1819
Davis Henley and Sarah H. Roberts, (MD) Dec. 10, 1830
Hennenan Henley and Flora Ann Snapp, (MD) Aug. 12, 1828
E. Henly and Thomas Waddle, (MD) Sep. 8, 1836
Eli Henry and Hannah Haunworth, (MD) Mar. 11, 1831
James Henry and Sarah Murry, (MD) Jun. 1, 1815
Robert Henry and Mary Campbell, (MD) Dec. 2, 1793
Robert Henry and Hannah Whitehead, (MD) Aug. 5, 1817
William Henry and Leander Jobb, (MD) Dec. 29, 1832
Daniel B. Herald and Elizabeth Andes, (MD) Jul. 25, 1833
Andrew L. Herrold and Ann Horton, (MD) Nov. 21, 1831
Robert Hert and Sarah Pantor, (MD) Sep. 5, 1833
John Hetherly and Nancy Wilson, (MD) Nov. 5, 1789
John Hice and Ann Cassady, (MD) Nov. 16, 1822
Anny Hickman and David Besset, (MD) Nov. 18, 1806
George Hickman and Nancy Ferguson, (MD) Mar. 26, 1829
Abraham Hicks and Elizabeth Sheppard, (MD) Jan. 6, 1828
Jater Hicks and Julia D. Nelson, (MD) Jul. 21, 1819
Jacob Hider and Elizabeth Bean, (MD) Sep. 29, 1839
Jonathan H. Hider and Martha King, (MD) Aug. 25, 1833
Joseph D. Hider and Eliza Ann Nelson, (MD) Jan. 1, 1834
Ellis Higgins and Ruth Tilson, (MD) Feb. 22, 1835
Jacob Hilbert and Esther Garber, (MD) Jun. 3, 1838
Ibby Hill and Richard Hail, (MD) Jun. 23, 1827
James Hill and Hannah Carter, (MD) Jan. 22, 1800
Noding Hill and Ruth Brown, (MD) Feb. 26, 1823
Samuel Hill and Jane Culbertson, (MD) Feb. 5, 1807
Joseph Hilton and Catharine Robinson, (MD) Oct. 9, 1827
William Himes and Mary Lemans, (MD) Dec. 22, 1836
Michael Hines and Nancy Nelson, (MD) Nov. 3, 1831
Benjamin Hinkle and Lucinda Terry, (MD) Mar. 9, 1825
George Hinkle and Ann Zetty, (MD) Sep. 27, 1821

James Hinkle and Susannah Krouse, (MD) Jan. 9, 1836
E. Hodge and Z. N. McCall, (MD) Sep. 16, 1839
Edmend Hodge and Susannah Dunkin, (MD) Apr. 13, 1811
John Hodge and Mary Acuff, (MD) Feb. 27, 1812
Robert Hodge and Elizabeth Isenbergh, (MD) Aug. 8, 1828
Anson Hodges and Harriett Gray, (MD) May 19, 1831
Howel A. Hodges and Sarah Ann Crouch, (MD) Nov. 23, 1837
James Hodges and Mary Kitzmiller, (MD) Aug. 22, 1825
Micajah Hodges and Elizabeth Gray, (MD) Jan. 30, 1818
Roland Hodges and Margaret Ellis, (MD) Aug. 17, 1823
William Hodges and Mary Ann Snyder, (MD) Jul. 31, 1823
William H. Hodges and L. Hale, (MD) Mar. , 1839
Samuel Hofman and Ruth Smith, (MD) Jun. 24, 1829
John Holleby and Phebe Brown, (MD) Jul. 3, 1815
Samuel Holmes and Rachel Miller, (MD) Apr. 5, 1823
David Holt and Isabella Templin, (MD) Jan. 3, 1826
David Honeycut and Mary White, (MD) Dec. 3, 1829
Adam Hope and Mary Carson, (MD) Apr. 24, 1824
Benjamin P. Hopkins and Ruth Tinker, (MD) Nov. 23, 1826
George Hoppers and Margaret Bain, (MD) Aug. 11, 1835
Daniel Horton and Mary Jane McCall, (MD) Sep. 7, 1838
Isaac Horton and Margaret Martin, (MD) Oct. 16, 1810
William Horton and Phebe Tylor, (MD) May 19, 1836
Calvin Hoss and Amy Deakins, (MD) Aug. 12, 1836
Elkena Hoss and Penelope Masengale, (MD) Sep. 14, 1834
Jacob Hoss and Margaret Bean, (MD) Apr. 13, 1815
John V. Hoss and Nancy Basket, (MD) Dec. 21, 1816
William Hoss and Jane Deaken, (MD) Jul. 27, 1831
Thomas House and Ann Davison, (MD) Feb. 5, 1793
Dannes Houston and Rebecca Pharez, (MD) Apr. 27, 1829
James Houston and Sarah Caruthers, (MD) Mar. 10, 1825
John Houston and Elizabeth Kelley, (MD) Oct. 16, 1824
John Houston and Mary Rose, (MD) Jul. 15, 1829
Samuel Houston and Mrs. Isabella Gray, (MD) Feb. 4, 1819
A. Howard and E. Price, (MD) Nov. 24, 1839
Elkanah H. Howard and Mary Denton, (MD) Oct. 27, 1829
John L. Howard and Margaret H. Denton, (MD) Nov. 16, 1830
Joseph Howard and Rachel Rector, (MD) Jan. 21, 1820
D. Howel and N. McIntire, (MD) Jun. 27, 1839
John Howser and Margaret Rutlet, (MD) Sep. 8, 1818
Michael Hoyle and Ann L. Mathes, (MD) Sep. 27, 1823
Jacob Huffman and Peggy Mark, (MD) Nov. 21, 1822
Daniel Hufhines and Achsah Delaney, (MD) Oct. 11, 1830

Jacob Hufhines and Anne Poore, (MD) Nov. 4, 1829
David Hufman and Rachel Buth, (MD) Jul. 20, 1821
Saml. Hufman and Rebeckah Byerly, (MD) Jan. 1, 1829
John Hulmer and Elizabeth White, (MD) Jul. 23, 1817
James P. Hulse and Ella Krane, (MD) Dec. 3, 1837
William W. Humel and S. Hartman, (MD) May 9, 1839
J. Humphreys and D. Smith, (MD) Oct. 10, 1839
L. Humphreys and J. Taylor, (MD) Aug. 9, 1838
Richard Humphreys and M. Hartman, (MD) Oct. 1, 1839
William L. Humphreys and J Gwinn, (MD) Nov. 15, 1839
Benjamin Hunt and Margaret Walker, (MD) May 27, 1827
Benson Hunt and Mary Magdalene Pope, (MD) Jun. 27, 1807
Jesse Hunt and Margaret Hale, (MD) Jul. 30, 1833
John Hunt and Sarah McBride, (MD) Oct. 27, 1831
John Hunt and Sarah Nichols, (MD) Mar. 21, 1831
John R. Hunt and Margaret Holt, (MD) Aug. 21, 1830
Joseph Hunt and Polly McAfee, (MD) Jan. 21, 1833
Peter Hunt and Lethy Bayles, (MD) Mar. 27, 1828
S. M. Hunt and E. Ellis, (MD) Dec. 31, 1839
Sam Hunt and William Crouch, (MD) May 23, 1815
Smith Hunt and Patsey Alison, (MD) Jul. 24, 1816
Smith Hunt and Jane Long, (MD) Dec. 18, 1834
Thomas Hunt and Martina Bayles, (MD) Sep. 1, 1811
Thomas W. Hunt and Mary Young, (MD) Mar. 20, 1827
Uriah Hunt and Mary Kincheloe, (MD) Sep. 3, 1832
Westley Hunt and Margaret Patton, (MD) Jul. 15, 1820
William P. Hunt and Innetta Harrison, (MD) Jan. 18, 1838
Chaestain Hunter and Robert Fryer, (MD) Jul. 14, 1792
David C. Hunter and Achsah McCray, (MD) Mar. 23, 1830
David C. Hunter and Maria Stephenson, (MD) Oct. 5, 1824
James Hunter and Jane McCord, (MD) Feb. 27, 1794
James D. Hunter and Sarah Martin, (MD) Sep. 20, 1838
Jesse B. Hunter and Malinda Catherine Rutledge, (MD) Nov. 10, 1836
John Hunter and Polly Brown, (MD) Feb. 25, 1817
Joseph Hunter and Margaret Miranda Harris, (MD) Oct. 18, 1830
Percy Hunter and Elizabeth Crouch, (MD) Jan. 8, 1838
John Hurian and Sarah Miller, (MD) Aug. 12, 1817
Alexander Hurvey and Eliza Shanklin, (MD) Dec. 13, 1829
William Huston and Jane Jenkins, (MD) Aug. 8, 1811
Moses Hutchins and Polly Carder, (MD) Sep. 10, 1810
John Hyder and Anne Worthington, (MD) Feb. 19, 1823
Moses Ingersol and Cathrine Cebler, (MD) Mar. 22, 1821
Adam Ingle and Elizabeth Sliger, (MD) Oct. 9, 1817

Allen Ingle and Eliza Bricker, (MD) Sep. 6, 1831
Henry Ingle and Amanda Graham, (MD) Aug. 21, 1826
John Ingle and Caroline McCloud, (MD) Nov. 9, 1837
Michal Ingle and Mary Slyger, (MD) Apr. 29, 1793
William Insor and Martha Lasly, (MD) Sep. 27, 1797
George Irvin and Judah Comby, (MD) Nov. 19, 1822
John Irwin and Alsey Bails, (MD) Jan. 22, 1828
Shepherd Irwin and Matilda Ann Dunham, (MD) May 13, 1813
William Irwin and Catherine Wheelock, (MD) Dec. 25, 1827
Daniel Isenbarg and Lidia Moler, (MD) Apr. 9, 1819
John Isenberg and Hannah Pitcock, (MD) Feb. 16, 1821
William Isler and Polly Spring, (MD) Jun. 19, 1811
Reuben Jacks and Hannah Irwin, (MD) Oct. 30, 1830
George Jackson and Nancy Bacon, (MD) May 12, 1813
George Jackson and Elizabeth Hale, (MD) Dec. 10, 1833
George G. Jackson and Nancy Campbell, (MD) Dec. 8, 1825
Jacob Jackson and Nancy Bacon, (MD) Nov. 1, 1821
James Jackson and Carey Chandler, (MD) Mar. 6, 1838
James W. Jackson and Margaret Odle, (MD) Jun. 21, 1831
Jemima Jackson and George Barnes, (MD) Mar. 24, 1818
Jemima Jackson and John Macanelly, (MD) Sep. 21, 1796
Laban Jackson and Nancy Elsey, (MD) Jan. 16, 1830
Peter Jackson and Ann Murray, (MD) Aug. 4, 1820
Samuel Jackson and Catharine Bacon, (MD) Feb. 15, 1816
Talbot Jackson and Jane Crow, (MD) Sep. 30, 1832
Thomas Jackson and Delilah Heartsell, (MD) Jul. 24, 1828
William Jackson and Nancy Crow, (MD) Aug. 31, 1839
Jesse I. James and Mary Anna McGuire, (MD) Jan. 12, 1829
Isaac Jaques and Peggy Grimsly, (MD) Mar. 8, 1825
Alfred Jenkins and Mary Catherine Krutzer, (MD) Feb. 1, 1838
David Jenkins and Nancy Boren, (MD) Jan. 29, 1825
George Jenkins and Polly Hodges, (MD) Jun. 2, 1827
Joseph Jenkins and Ailey Keys, (MD) Oct. 29, 1829
James L. Jennings and Mary S. Cowan, (MD) Feb. 15, 1838
Joshua Jennings and Eliza Nelson, (MD) Dec. 22, 1829
Abraham Jobb and Sarah Fain, (MD) Mar. 27, 1832
James Jobb and Nancy S Jackson, (MD) Sep. 5, 1837
James S. Jobb and Matilda Boyd, (MD) Nov. 17, 1833
Leander Jobb and William Henry, (MD) Dec. 29, 1832
William Jobb and Nancy Jones, (MD) Apr. 19, 1832
Enoch Jobe and Elizabeth Jackson, (MD) Sep. 10, 1814
John Jobe and Sarah Elsey, (MD) Nov. 4, 1828
Elan Johnson and Martha Young C. Parker, (MD) Jan. 2, 1826

James Johnson and Cristina Brown, (MD) Feb. 4, 1819
William J. Johnson and Mary Hale, (MD) Aug. 8, 1831
Henry Johnston and Mary Ann Hoss, (MD) Feb. 22, 1834
Robert Johnston and Letty Crocksell, (MD) Sep. 11, 1827
Robert Johnston and Elizabeth Suttles, (MD) May 25, 1829
Allen Jones and Nancy Carson, (MD) Sep. 18, 1828
Andrew Jones and Susannah Baker, (MD) Aug. 28, 1828
Carter Jones and Zully Ann Dryman, (MD) Oct. 20, 1830
Henry Jones and Aggey Francis, (MD) Oct. 25, 1821
Henry Jones and Rebecca Smith, (MD) Nov. 24, 1830
James Jones and Martha Hern, (MD) May 24, 1816
James Jones and Elizabeth Keebler, (MD) Jul. 14, 1831
James Jones and Hannah Maiden, (MD) Jun. 28, 1811
John Jones and Sarah Daniels, (MD) Mar. 28, 1808
John Jones and Clarissa Sevier, (MD) May 7, 1822
Katharine Jones and James Williams, (MD) Jul. 31, 1817
William Jones and Elizabeth Clouse, (MD) Oct. 22, 1811
William Jones and Nancy Koon, (MD) Mar. 28, 1812
Zachariah Jones and Rhoda Bowser, (MD) Aug. 20, 1837
William Justice and Nelly McColip, (MD) Jul. 4, 1817
J. Kagle and M. Oden, (MD) Jun. 27, 1839
John Kannon and Elizabeth Freeman, (MD) Oct. 20, 1819
Richard Kayhill and Elizabeth Anderson, (MD) Sep. 2, 1798
Eli Kean and Nancy Barren, (MD) Mar. 7, 1820
John Keath and Elizabeth Edwards, (MD) Jan. 20, 1835
Jacob Kebler and Polly Haws, (MD) Oct. 29, 1812
James Kebler and Sarah Haws, (MD) Aug. 6, 1827
Jacob Keebler and Elizabeth McClain, (MD) Oct. 12, 1830
James Keebler and Susannah Garber, (MD) Jan. 3, 1839
Jesse Keel and Mary North, (MD) Aug. 23, 1792
William Keele and Levinah Bewley, (MD) Jul. 8, 1793
Elijah Keen and Ann White, (MD) Apr. 27, 1816
Matthias Keen and Rachel Brown, (MD) Sep. 4, 1813
William Keen and Betsy Taylor, (MD) May 27, 1815
Joseph Keene and Mary Gibson, (MD) Apr. 9, 1835
Elkanah Keener and Elizabeth Lamon, (MD) Jan. 5, 1827
John Keener and Rebecca Odle, (MD) Jun. 27, 1807
Aaron Kees and Hannah Nelson, (MD) Feb. 3, 1825
Samuel Keesler and Catherine Bowman, (MD) Nov. 28, 1816
Isaac Keizer and Mary Bradley, (MD) Apr. 30, 1825
Elijah Kelby and Elizabeth Briant, (MD) Aug. 4, 1815
Fatha Kelley and Jonothan Range, (MD) Jan. 5, 1824
Henry Kellow and Eliza Snapp, (MD) Jun. 30, 1830

Daniel H. Kelly and Delila Painter, (MD) Aug. 3, 1836
Kinchen Kelly and Isabella Young, (MD) Oct. 6, 1825
David N. Kelsey and Catharine G. McCracken, (MD) Jan. 13, 1836
Robert Kelsey and Rachel Ball, (MD) Aug. 25, 1835
Samuel Kelsey and Mary McCleary, (MD) Dec. 24, 1827
William Kelsey and Evelina Astin, (MD) Jan. 19, 1827
Samuel Kenady and Lett Herrold, (MD) Sep. 23, 1792
George Kennedy and Nancy Tedlock, (MD) Oct. 4, 1827
John Kennedy and Cynthia Bakeley, (MD) Dec. 30, 1824
John C. Kennedy and Mary A Massengale, (MD) Jun. 18, 1833
Samuel Kennedy and Martha Massengale, (MD) Apr. 1, 1825
William P. Kenner and Elizabeth White, (MD) Jun. 3, 1819
Daniel Kenney and Minerva Nelson, (MD) Jul. 21, 1831
George Kennick and Catherine Parker, (MD) Oct. 17, 1837
Jacob Keplinger and Sarah E. Ruble, (MD) Sep. 24, 1828
John Keplinger and Elizabeth E. Hooker, (MD) Oct. 13, 1836
Alexander Kerl and Esther Martin, (MD) Oct. 9, 1833
Jeremiah Keys and Mary Ferguson, (MD) Jul. 6, 1826
John Keys and Rebecca Borin, (MD) Feb. 18, 1834
Young Kibler and Margaret Taylor, (MD) Jul. 11, 1833
C. Kiker and C. Allen, (MD) Oct. 27, 1839
Nathan Kiker and E. Broyles, (MD) Aug. 26, 1839
J. Kimmery and E. Morgan, (MD) Dec. 26, 1839
George Kincheloe and Amanda Brown, (MD) Feb. 9, 1837
William Kincheloe and Minerva Hale, (MD) Mar. 5, 1829
William Kincheloe and Hannah Jackson, (MD) Oct. 22, 1833
Clary Kinchels and Chaise Hail, (MD) Aug. 15, 1815
William Kindel and Caty May (MD) Jan. 28, 1811
Henry King and Eliza Young, (MD) Sep. 22, 1836
John King and Sarah White, (MD) Sep. 4, 1817
Jonas L. King and Mary Barnes, (MD) Sep. 16, 1826
Lewallen King and Susannah Crouch, (MD) Oct. 18, 1820
Thomas King and Elizabeth Rose, (MD) Apr. 19, 1825
William King and Patsy Crouch, (MD) Aug. 2, 1819
William King and Sarah Hale, (MD) Feb. 4, 1819
William F. King and Ruth Little, (MD) Feb. 15, 1812
John Kirk and Margaret Kelsely, (MD) Feb. 1, 1827
David Kitsmiller and Elizabeth Hughes, (MD) Nov. 29, 1821
Henry Kitzmiller and Elizabeth Carr, (MD) Feb. 24, 1825
John Kitzmiller and Louisa Devault, (MD) Aug. 8, 1824
E. Klouse and William Tinker, (MD) Aug. 21, 1839
John Knight and Rebecca Rhodes, (MD) Dec. 22, 1789
John Konken and Sarah Watts, (MD) Feb. 12, 1832

John Koonts and Sarah Delashmont, (MD) Jul. 18, 1819
Martin Kortz and Sarah Hunter, (MD) May 26, 1830
Allen Kyker and Malinda Bacon, (MD) Aug. 22, 1831
Jacob Kyker and Eliza Greer, (MD) Oct. 17, 1828
John Kyker and Rebecca Slyger, (MD) Jan. 2, 1831
Joseph Kyser and Jane Boothe, (MD) Mar. 31, 1802
John Lackey and Mary Rollins, (MD) Nov. 17, 1818
James Lacy and Nancy Edden, (MD) Nov. 21, 1789
Samuel Lain and Elisateh Hunt, (MD) Feb. 23, 1793
Emanuel Lamon and Kesiah Hartsell, (MD) Dec. 30, 1837
Isaac Lamon and Liddy Benley, (MD) Jun. 19, 1832
Samuel Lamon and Mary Allon, (MD) Mar. 19, 1793
Mary J. Landon and Alfred Hays, (MD) Sep. 10, 1838
Ancil Lane and Elizabeth Cash, (MD) Jan. 1, 1830
Ancil Lane and Sidney Woods, (MD) May 19, 1825
Joseph Lane and Mary L. Campbell, (MD) Aug. 17, 1813
Sammie Lane and Mary Humphries, (MD) Aug. 10, 1815
William Lashbrooks and Dorratha Cressealeas, (MD) Apr. 26, 1794
James Lather and Sarah Masannis, (MD) Dec. 14, 1822
Jacob Laudermilk and Dorcas Boren, (MD) Sep. 13, 1825
James Law and Rosanah Talford, (MD) Mar. 16, 1791
Hiram Lawrence and Sussanah Krous, (MD) Sep. 5, 1833
Davis Lawson and I A Christie, (MD) Aug. 30, 1839
John Layman and Elizabeth Coughman, (MD) Jul. 22, 1819
David Leach and Rachel Harvey, (MD) Sep. 18, 1831
John Leach and Phebe Davison, (MD) Aug. 15, 1837
John Leach and Sarah Solomon, (MD) May 3, 1792
Trenton Leach and Margaret Hufman, (MD) Feb. 5, 1830
Thomas Lee and Nancy Hail, (MD) Jun. 29, 1823
Charley Lemmon and Eve Tossen, (MD) Jun. 29, 1813
Samuel Lemmon and Lydia Boothe, (MD) May 20, 1817
Joshua Leonard and Rhoda Sweet, (MD) Sep. 28, 1826
Lawrence Leonard and Mary Guyne, (MD) Nov. 2, 1826
James Leslie and Sarah Campbell, (MD) Dec. 23, 1824
John P. Lessenberg and Elizabeth Reeves, (MD) Aug. 30, 1820
James Lewis and Lucy Holt, (MD) Jan. 18, 1819
Samuel Lewis and Elizabeth Pitcock, (MD) Aug. 5, 1821
Zaddock Lewis and Anne Marie Smith, (MD) Sep. 1, 1829
Michael P. Light and Rhoda Ellis, (MD) Sep. 11, 1828
Andrew Lilburn and Eafy Walker, (MD) Sep. 3, 1819
Asbury Lilburn and Sarah Stroud, (MD) Dec. 16, 1832
Jonah Lilburn and Mary Hertsell, (MD) Jan. 23, 1825
Thomas Linder and Ann Oliver, (MD) Dec. 4, 1824

Jacob Linebarger and Mary Barnes, (MD) Dec. 5, 1827
Daniel Linebaugh and Nancy McCollum, (MD) Dec. 6, 1819
Charles Lineberger and Ann Lopwasser, (MD) Aug. 24, 1826
Isaac Linger and Mary Yeager, (MD) Dec. 13, 1838
Richard M. Linn and Rachel Blackmoore, (MD) May 20, 1830
Charles Lisenberg and Susan Carr, (MD) Sep. 24, 1824
Lewis Lisenby and Nancy Faubush, (MD) Oct. 16, 1820
William Lisenby and Isbel Young, (MD) Mar. 2, 1817
George Little and Marey Job, (MD) Jan. 26, 1791
George Little and Barbary Kelly, (MD) Oct. 14, 1822
John Little and Ruth Boren, (MD) Dec. 11, 1824
Christian Long and Elizabeth Murr, (MD) Mar. 14, 1833
Christopher Long and Sarah Sliger, (MD) Oct. 12, 1817
Jacob Long and Mary Riddle, (MD) May 11, 1826
John Longmire and Elizabeth Range, (MD) Jan. 15, 1829
William Looney and Betsy West, (MD) Jan. 18, 1827
Dillard Love and Margaret Young, (MD) Nov. 20, 1822
Emanuel Love and Polly Sliger, (MD) Oct. 12, 1817
Robert C. Love and Elizabeth Wilkison, (MD) Jul. 10, 1837
Thomas Love and Martha Dillard, (MD) Jan. 12, 1788
Jordon Lovegrove and Elizabeth Garber, (MD) Dec. 3, 1835
William Lovelace and Rebecca Hawkins, (MD) Aug. 17, 1807
John Lowdy and Polly Wheeler, (MD) Feb. 16, 1817
William M. Lowrey and Julia Eason, (MD) Jun. 16, 1837
John Loyd and Betsy Depew, (MD) Jul. 3, 1816
John Lucas and Sussanah Hale, (MD) Sep. 1, 1790
David Ludon and Alley Bird, (MD) Jul. 19, 1819
Jesse Lunsford and Rebecca Peterson, (MD) Jan. , 1812
Nathaniel Lunsford and Eliza Waldren, (MD) Apr. 10, 1822
Henry Luntsford and Alsey Hendrixon, (MD) Dec. 4, 1820
David Luster and Sarah Garland, (MD) Oct. 12, 1808
John Lyle and Lucinda Borin, (MD) Feb. 9, 1832
Samuel Lyle and Casandra Boring, (MD) Jan. 23, 1823
James A. Lyon and Adelaide E. Deadrick, (MD) Mar. 14, 1837
Deby Lyons and Philip Emert, (MD) Feb. 16, 1819
George W. Lyons and Ruth Irwin, (MD) Nov. 26, 1835
Abraham Lysenby and Rebecca Simpson, (MD) May 22, 1817
John Macanelly and Jemima Jackson, (MD) Sep. 21, 1796
Everett Mahoney and Nancy Ann Martin, (MD) Dec. 28, 1837
John Mahoney and Mary Powel, (MD) May 3, 1831
Jonah Mahoney and Synthia Irwin, (MD) Dec. 2, 1826
Malan Mahoney and Elizabeth Rogers, (MD) Dec. 10, 1835
William Mahoney and Betsy Pardue, (MD) Jan. 5, 1815

E. Mains and I. Crouch, (MD) Aug. 28, 1839
George W Mallone and Nancy Caruthers, (MD) Dec. 27, 1832
M. Mallone and C. Gibson, (MD) Apr. 18, 1839
John Mallonee and Phoebe Wheeler, (MD) Oct. 11, 1834
Edward Malon and Margaret Castiel, (MD) Oct. 9, 1821
Joseph Mann and Elizabeth Blackburn, (MD) Apr. 20, 1831
James C. Mansfield and Rebeccah G. Chester, (MD) Feb. 7, 1821
Abel March and Anny Martin, (MD) Dec. 3, 1826
William Mares and Elizabeth Stephens, (MD) Aug. 16, 1806
Lewis A. Markwood and Sarah Isabella Deakins, (MD) Jun. 3, 1835
John Marr and Patience Tucker, (MD) Sep. 5, 1815
Alfred M. Marsh and Kuzen Lacky, (MD) Sep. 6, 1827
Henry Marsh and Scynthia Ann Kirk, (MD) Jun. 2, 1835
Joseph Marshall and Mary Hoss, (MD) Apr. 2, 1820
Richard Martain and Achah Hunt, (MD) Mar. 15, 1821
Edward L. Martan and Mariah Bartly, (MD) Oct. 1, 1818
Caleb Martin and Sally Bird, (MD) Jun. 20, 1815
Creasy Martin and John Walker, (MD) Nov. 24, 1824
Elias Martin and Ruth Nelson, (MD) Oct. 15, 1835
Henry A. Martin and Matilda Brown, (MD) Nov. 30, 1837
Isaac Martin and Polly Ellis, (MD) Dec. 25, 1818
James Martin and Margaret Long, (MD) Jan. 3, 1821
Jesse Martin and Nancy Bacon, (MD) Aug. 11, 1835
Lewis Martin and Deborah Ryester, (MD) Jan. 25, 1834
Michael H. Martin and Polly Tadlock, (MD) Jun. 17, 1813
Samuel Martin and Nancy Shields, (MD) Dec. 2, 1825
George Masingill and Hanna Jones, (MD) Nov. 15, 1813
A. G. Mason and L. Ryland, (MD) Mar. 19, 1839
John Mason and Edney Simmons, (MD) Apr. 1, 1831
John Massengail and Margaret Broyles, (MD) Feb. 7, 1809
Henry Massingale and Lavina Hoss, (MD) Mar. 21, 1827
Adam Massy and Diniah Smith, (MD) Dec. 23, 1813
Ann L. Mathes and Michael Hoyle, (MD) Sep. 27, 1823
Annie L. Mathes and David W Patten, (MD) Jan. 22, 1830
Archibald A Mathes and Christianna G. Cowan, (MD) Oct. 5, 1838
Jesse Mathes and Nancy Brown, (MD) May 29, 1825
Nancy W. Mathes and Samuel Bell, (MD) Oct. 14, 1824
William Mathes and Eleanor McLin, (MD) Feb. 28, 1827
John Matlock and Malinda Ellis, (MD) Apr. 12, 1827
Alex C. Matthes and Eliza Doak, (MD) Apr. 27, 1831
Allen H Matthews and Judith L. McConnel, (MD) Oct. 29, 1822
John Matthews and Rosannah Blackburn, (MD) Feb. 27, 1811
Ellianor Mauk and Ephriam Bird, (MD) Sep. 30, 1829

Joseph Mauk and Grace Broyles, (MD) Oct. 9, 1807
C. K. Maxwell and J. W. Allen, (MD) Apr. 3, 1839
Jane W. Maxwell and John Young, (MD) Aug. 1, 1830
Adonis May and Betsy McGinnis, (MD) May 11, 1813
Barnibas May and Margaret Ruble, (MD) Dec. 4, 1818
Caty May and William Kindel, (MD) Jan. 28, 1811
David May and Margaret Walter, (MD) Feb. 6, 1834
Thomas May and Peggy Spore, (MD) Feb. 20, 1817
Charles Mayfield and Jane Adam, (MD) Jan. 31, 1838
William Mayfield and Elizabeth Wright, (MD) Sep. 5, 1830
Samuel B. McAdams and Ann S. Duncan, (MD) Feb. 3, 1831
Thomas McAdams and Elizabeth McNeale, (MD) Nov. 6, 1828
Thomas C. McAdams and Cynthia Stephenson, (MD) Sep. 16, 1834
William McAdams and Ealenor McNeal, (MD) Dec. 23, 1830
Francis A. McAlister and John D. Murry, (MD) Apr. 22, 1838
Elkanah McBroom and Roseannah Salts, (MD) Jun. 6, 1830
Rosey McBroom and John Hampton, (MD) Jul. 10, 1836
John McCall and Elizabeth Kennedy, (MD) Mar. 28, 1829
John McCall and Polly Martin, (MD) Mar. 13, 1817
Joseph S. McCall and Malinda Cradock, (MD) Oct. 29, 1834
Mary Jane McCall and Daniel Horton, (MD) Sep. 7, 1838
Robert McCall and Jemima Wilson, (MD) Dec. 26, 1815
William McCall and Thency Shields, (MD) Aug. 23, 1806
James McCamish and Martina Bayles, (MD) Jan. 7, 1836
John McCardell and Sara Phillips, (MD) Apr. 22, 1809
Isaac McCardle and Jane Morrison, (MD) Dec. 23, 1812
James McCarroll and Sarah Forbush, (MD) Jan. 28, 1813
David G. McCarty and Elizabeth Starns, (MD) Apr. 7, 1813
Isaac B. McClellan and Margaret R. Greer, (MD) Jul. 13, 1816
John McClure and Sarah Million, (MD) Jan. 25, 1811
Robert McClure and Rebecca Mathews, (MD) Sep. 15, 1818
Robert McClure and Margaret Thompson, (MD) Jul. 28, 1808
Judith L. McConnel and Allen H Matthews, (MD) Oct. 29, 1822
David McCord and Susana Carson, (MD) May 27, 1792
John McCord and Mary Carson, (MD) Dec. 6, 1796
Jacob McCordle and Rebecca Ball, (MD) Aug. 18, 1814
Joseph McCorkel and Mary Hendry, (MD) Nov. 14, 1815
John McCorkle and Polly Cunningham, (MD) Oct. 13, 1813
Joseph McCorkle and Jean Harrison, (MD) Dec. 30, 1793
Andrew McCoy and Polly Salts, (MD) May 5, 1830
John McCoy and Hannah Lusk, (MD) Nov. 18, 1793
Henry McCracken and Katherine Hamilton, (MD). , 1816
Henry McCracken and Rebecca Wood, (MD) Oct. 25, 1832

John McCracken and Julia Nelson, (MD) Apr. 4, 1837
John McCracken and Dicey Oliver, (MD) Oct. 22, 1835
John McCracken and Hannah Tucker, (MD) Feb. 19, 1827
Joseph McCracken and Eliza Mitchell, (MD) Apr. 15, 1835
Joseph McCracken and Sarah Wood, (MD) Dec. 19, 1832
William McCracken and Jane Patton, (MD) Oct. 31, 1839
John McCraskey and Priscilla McCray, (MD) Jan. 12, 1836
Daniel McCray and Sarah Bogart, (MD) Jan. 14, 1818
Henry McCray and Marey More, (MD) Sep. 19, 1796
Lem McCray and Samuel S Bell, (MD) Nov. 22, 1821
William McCray and Maria Koontz, (MD) Jul. 1, 1807
Charles McCrea and Betsy Dickens, (MD) Mar. 25, 1788
James McCrosky and Rachael Gibson, (MD) Dec. 22, 1830
Joseph McCully and Mariam Royston, (MD) Sep. 13, 1838
John McCurrey and Sarah Embree, (MD) Aug. 9, 1824
Anguish McDonald and Polly Moore, (MD) Mar. 8, 1824
John McEwen and Eliza Stephenson, (MD) Mar. 30, 1804
Brice W. McFall and Mahala Jane Barnes, (MD) Oct. 20, 1836
Joel McFall and Deannah Tilley, (MD) Mar. 12, 1834
John McFall and Elizabeth Laudermilk, (MD) Oct. 5, 1837
John McGee and Sarah Snapp, (MD) Feb. 2, 1817
William McGee and Leoma Booyle, (MD) Sep. 26, 1793
Solomon McGhee and Lucinda Campbell, (MD) Jan. 24, 1832
Abraham McGinnis and Elizabeth Myers, (MD) Dec. 15, 1830
David McGinnis and Sarah White, (MD) Jun. 19, 1811
Jesse McGinnis and Ann Reed, (MD) Apr. 2, 1823
Joseph McGinnis and Peggy Faubush, (MD) Aug. 27, 1816
William McGinnis and Millie Conley, (MD) Mar. 10, 1808
Alexander McGinty and Elizabeth Ruble, (MD) Feb. 1, 1817
Ephriam McGloughlin and Elizabeth Barnes, (MD) Feb. 17, 1823
N. McIntire and D. Howel, (MD) Jun. 27, 1839
Gabriel McIntosh and Amy Nelson, (MD) Oct. 30, 1832
Israel McInturff and Elizabeth Webb, (MD) Oct. 29, 1828
John McInturff, Jr. and Judith Carder, (MD) Dec. 14, 1789
William McJimsey and Nancy Brown, (MD) Dec. 18, 1811
Daniel McKay and Polly Prichard, (MD) Oct. 14, 1812
Samuel McKeehan and Susannah Overhots, (MD) Aug. 25, 1824
Samuel McKeehin and Sarah Watenbarger, (MD) Aug. 9, 1835
Henry McKraken and Nancy Barclay, (MD) Jul. 25, 1811
James McLin and Jane Cunningham, (MD) May 16, 1821
Robert McLin and Ann Blair, (MD) Jun. 19, 1816
M McMacken and William Greenway, (MD) Aug. 27, 1839
Henry McMackin and Esther Stanbury, (MD) Sep. 10, 1835

John J. McMackin and Isabel C. Blair, (MD) Jun. , 1824
Thomas McMackin and Ann Blair, (MD) Aug. 27, 1823
Babtist McNabb and ??? Gray, (MD) Mar. 3, 1794
David McNabb and Peggy Whitson, (MD) Jan. 12, 1813
Manley McNabb and Polly Faubush, (MD) Oct. 9, 1819
John McNeal and Margaret Harmon, (MD) Oct. 30, 1828
John McNees and Maryane Greenway, (MD) Oct. 6, 1825
William L. McNees and Eliza Slagle, (MD) Jul. 3, 1831
Benjamin McNut and Amy Alexander, (MD) Feb. 13, 1796
Henry McPherson and Sussanah Glasscock, (MD) Aug. 20, 1808
Isaac McPherson and Elizabeth Kinnedy, (MD) Dec. 27, 1821
William McRoberts and Isabella Hunter, (MD) Jun. 18, 1828
Nathaniel McStuart and Sarah Mitchell, (MD) Aug. 21, 1827
Agness McWhorter and James Seehorn, (MD) Sep. 20, 1796
Edy Medlock and William Vaughn, (MD) Oct. 25, 1828
Geriah Medlock and Jesse Harrison, (MD) Dec. 31, 1825
Martin Medlock and Nancy Mitchell, (MD) Feb. 4, 1822
John MeGinnis and Ann Tucker, (MD) Apr. 9, 1791
John Melvin and Rachel Delaney, (MD) Dec. 6, 1821
Joseph Melvin and Sarah Delany, (MD) Jan. 16, 1818
Thomas Mercer and Henrietta Duke, (MD) Oct. 24, 1826
Thomas Messer and Elizabeth Geruin, (MD) Sep. 11, 1817
M. Milburn and Polly Harris, (MD) Oct. 13, 1839
G. W. Milhorn and Elizabeth Clepper, (MD) Dec. 29, 1836
William Millar and Susan Eastep, (MD) Oct. 11, 1833
Abraham Miller and Nancy Hale, (MD) Apr. 3, 1826
Abraham E. Miller and Elizabeth Bacon, (MD) Oct. 17, 1827
Abram Miller and Barbary Sherfy, (MD) Feb. 15, 1829
Ambrose Miller and Christian Morgan, (MD) Dec. 12, 1834
Andrew Miller and Mary Miller, (MD) Jan. 11, 1825
D. M. Miller and Rachael Wheelock, (MD) Sep. 28, 1838
Henry Miller and Jane Young, (MD) Oct. 16, 1820
Isaac Miller and Elizabeth Ann Crumparker, (MD) Nov. 5, 1828
Isaac Miller and Elizabeth Nelson, (MD) Dec. 2, 1833
Jacob Miller and Margaret Kelley, (MD) May 25, 1810
Jacob Miller and Sarah Nole, (MD) Feb. 25, 1808
James Miller and Elizabeth Devault, (MD) Mar. 24, 1827
John Miller and Elizabeth Clark, (MD) Sep. 14, 1837
John Miller and Catherine Good, (MD) May 24, 1820
John Miller and Hannah Nelson, (MD) Feb. 28, 1833
John Miller, Jr. and Mary Kelly, (MD) Jan. 28, 1819
Joseph Miller and Priscilla Hale, (MD) Jan. 4, 1821
Joshua Miller and Elizabeth Bull, (MD) Sep. 12, 1816

Peter Miller and Polly Hunt, (MD) Aug. 27, 1817
Peter R. Miller and Sarah Deakins, (MD) May 22, 1823
Samuel Miller and Artey Bean, (MD) Sep. 7, 1811
William Miller and Betsy Rebecca Arrerwood, (MD) Feb. 14, 1816
Edward Million and Ann Bayless, (MD) Sep. 29, 1825
Edward Million and Sally Mitchell, (MD) Oct. 10, 1805
Jacob Million and Mary May (MD) Jan. 2, 1810
Jeremiah Million and Tempe Salts, (MD) Jun. 24, 1827
John Million and Alliciadille Bayless, (MD) Dec. 5, 1835
Joseph Million and Elizabeth Walters, (MD) Oct. 20, 1822
Washington Million and Susan Mitchell, (MD) Aug. 6, 1836
James Miser and Ann Mitchell, (MD) Oct. 22, 1833
E. Missinger and J Kimmery, (MD) May 12, 1839
William Mitchel and Elizabeth Basket, (MD) Jul. 19, 1831
Aman Mitchell and Della Allison, (MD) Mar. 12, 1837
David Mitchell and Polly Cowpenger, (MD) Jun. 30, 1817
David Mitchell and Martha Fellers, (MD) Nov. 13, 1834
David Mitchell and Elizabeth Ingle, (MD) Oct. 25, 1832
David Mitchell and Jane McClure, (MD) May 16, 1809
Doctor William Mitchell and Elizabeth Carter, (MD) Mar. 2, 1828
James Mitchell and Elizabeth Bacon, (MD) Nov. 8, 1825
James Mitchell and Sally Starnes, (MD) Sep. 16, 1805
John Mitchell and Mary Ann Barnes, (MD) Dec. 1, 1796
John Mitchell and Elizabeth Coppinger, (MD) Dec. 24, 1818
John Mitchell and Sarah Salts, (MD) Jan. 8, 1819
Joseph Mitchell and Margaret Boyd, (MD) Jan. 16, 1822
Nelson Mitchell and Betsy Fawbush, (MD) Sep. 26, 1816
Robert Mitchell and Catherine Bails, (MD) Aug. 2, 1838
Thomas Mitchell and Polly Million, (MD) Jul. 16, 1805
Thomas Mitchell and Fanny Tucker, (MD) Apr. 11, 1799
Thomas Mitchell and Sarah White, (MD) May 8, 1828
William Mitchell and Mary Bucheighan, (MD) Sep. 16, 1824
William Mitchell and Elizabeth Bails, (MD) Jan. 5, 1837
William Mitchell and Melly Lilburn, (MD) Jun. 18, 1832
Jacob Mock and Margaret Hemp, (MD) Aug. 9, 1811
M. Monteeth and L. Page, (MD) May 17, 1839
William Moon and Mahala Scalph, (MD) Sep. 2, 1825
Abraham Moore and Polly Morgan, (MD) Sep. 20, 1815
Bayless Moore and Sarah Stroud, (MD) Dec. 16, 1832
Claibourne Moore and Sally Morgan, (MD) Apr. 17, 1823
David Moore and Mary Ball, (MD) Jul. 5, 1835
James Moore and Mary Clarke, (MD) Aug. 12, 1806
James Moore and Sarah Mitchell, (MD) Jul. 28, 1829

James Moore and Mahaley Scalf, (MD) Mar. 8, 1827
Jesse Moore and Margaret Good, (MD) Feb. 13, 1838
Jesse Moore and Elizabeth Tucker, (MD) Feb. 21, 1832
John Moore and Sarah Nelson, (MD) Mar. 13, 1821
John Moore and Margaret Tucker, (MD) May 7, 1831
John W. Moore and Nancy Northington, (MD) Jun. 5, 1836
Moses Moore and Susan Cummings, (MD) Aug. 10, 1832
Moses Moore and Elizabeth Davis, (MD) Jul. 20, 1782
Samuel Moore and Sarah Metcalf, (MD) Oct. 12, 1829
Stephen Moore and Catharine Holsinger, (MD) Feb. 9, 1836
Sterling Moore and Elizabeth Holland, (MD) Mar. 5, 1825
Christian Morgan and Ambrose Miller, (MD) Dec. 12, 1834
Cornelius Morgan and Jenny Hosier, (MD) Aug. 31, 1801
Gabriel Morgan and Mary Whitlock, (MD) Jul. 10, 1813
James Morgan and Polly Ann Riddle, (MD) Dec. 9, 1828
M. Morgan and J Collins, (MD) Oct. 12, 1839
Richard Morris and Rhoda Hodges, (MD) Jul. 1, 1830
Horatio Morrison and Ruth Ford, (MD) Feb. 18, 1826
John Morrison and Sarah Embry, (MD) Aug. 19, 1798
John Morrison and Thankful Morrison, (MD) Nov. 20, 1816
Peter C. Morrison and Luticia Kelly, (MD) Oct. 26, 1832
Thankful Morrison and John Morrison, (MD) Nov. 20, 1816
Augustine Moss and Ruth Mason, (MD) Oct. 10, 1831
Horatio Moss and Elizabeth Holts, (MD) Apr. 10, 1830
William Mowdy and N Warren, (MD) Sep. 29, 1839
William Mowdy and Nancy Warren, (MD) Sep. 29, 1826
Jonathan Mulkey, Sr. and Anna Lacy, (MD) Mar. 3, 1818
Phillip Mulkey and Ann Duncan, (MD) Jun. 2, 1831
William Mullinox and Sarah Leab, (MD) Dec. 30, 1838
Chrisey M. Mullins and Flower Mullins, (MD) Oct. 10, 1838
Flower Mullins and Chrisey M. Mullins, (MD) Oct. 10, 1838
Jesse Mullins and Betsy Tadlock, (MD) Mar. 3, 1806
George Murr and Catherine Hummond, (MD) Aug. 3, 1820
Jacob Murr and Nancy Boyd, (MD) Sep. 23, 1823
James Murr and A Ragen, (MD) Sep. 29, 1839
Jeremiah Murr and Rachel Click, (MD) Jul. 19, 1825
John Murr and Mary Brown, (MD) Dec. 22, 1798
Christopher Murray and Susan Depew, (MD) Jul. 25, 1822
Joseph Murray and Rachel Brown, (MD) Apr. 4, 1833
Morgan Murray and Sarah Ford, (MD) Jun. 9, 1812
Rowland P. Murray and Ann Gallaway, (MD) Aug. 19, 1823
Shederick Murray and Sally Hunt, (MD) Jan. 27, 1823
Shedrick Murray, Jr. and Sarah Ferguson, (MD) Aug. 2, 1827

Thomas Murray and Peggy Messer, (MD) Aug. 29, 1808
William Murray and Elizabeth Miller, (MD) Aug. 1, 1811
Duston G. Murrill and Elizabeth Emmerson, (MD) Aug. 4, 1825
Ephriam Murry and Elizabeth Snapp, (MD) Jan. 19, 1834
James Murry and Mary Hopkins, (MD) Jan. 7, 1832
John D. Murry and Francis A McAlister, (MD) Apr. 22, 1838
Phillip Murry and Mary Parker, (MD) Jan. 29, 1833
Adam Myers and Amanda Waesner, (MD) Jun. 27, 1839
Jacob L. Myers and Frances Bell, (MD) Sep. 27, 1831
Jonathan Naff and Elizabeth Massengale, (MD) Jun. 22, 1837
Jacob Naff and Amanda M. Broyles, (MD) Jun. 25, 1835
James Nasbit and Sarah Logan, (MD) Nov. 13, 1793
Henry Nash and Mary Ann Shields, (MD) Dec. 19, 1816
Thomas Nave and Louise Humphreys, (MD) Dec. 9, 1829
Charles Neal and Margaret Kennedy, (MD) Aug. 13, 1829
Ephraim Nelson and Rebecca Skiles, (MD) Nov. 29, 1831
Ephriam Nelson and Elizabeth Capp, (MD) Dec. 10, 1828
George W Nelson and Mary Harvey, (MD) Apr. 11, 1828
George W. Nelson and Martha Yeager, (MD) Sep. 17, 1835
Isaac Nelson and Martha Vauskoe, (MD) Sep. 2, 1824
James Nelson and Mary A A Atkinson, (MD) Jul. 28, 1836
James Nelson and Margaret Furgeson, (MD) Jun. 1, 1837
James Nelson and Elinor Parker, (MD) May 4, 1826
Jesse Nelson and Margaret Young, (MD) Oct. 1, 1835
John Nelson and Easter Forguson, (MD) Jul. 20, 1826
John Nelson and Lucinda Lisenby, (MD) May 10, 1824
John Nelson and Catherine Sliger, (MD) Jan. 10, 1822
John Nelson and Nancy Whitson, (MD) Jun. 11, 1837
John Nelson, Jr. and Minerva G. Sevier, (MD) Apr. 30, 1816
Joseph Nelson and Elizabeth Gilmore, (MD) Sep. 8, 1819
Levi Nelson and Betsy Ann Irwin, (MD) May 28, 1835
Moses Nelson and Hannah Gann, (MD) Mar. 19, 1817
Nathan Nelson and Elizabeth Mitchell, (MD) Oct. 8, 1828
Orville P. Nelson and Hannah Hartsell, (MD) Jan. 9, 1834
Robert Nelson and Lucy Nelson, (MD) Aug. 7, 1834
Robert Nelson and Louise Pratt, (MD) Nov. 6, 1824
Shadrack Nelson and Ibby Whitson, (MD) Mar. 23, 1826
T. A. R. Nelson and A E. Stuart, (MD) Jul. 27, 1839
T. S. Nelson and Job Clark, (MD) Mar. 26, 1839
Thomas Nelson and Delilah Mayfield, (MD) Feb. 19, 1814
Thomas Nelson and Eliza Tucker, (MD) Sep. 8, 1828
William Nelson and Sally Critzelus, (MD) Feb. 27, 1817
William Nelson and Sarah Owen, (MD) Feb. 3, 1827

William C. Nelson and Julian Slimmons, (MD) Dec. 22, 1835
James Newland and Hester Edgman, (MD) May 15, 1834
Isaac Newman and Nancy Hunt, (MD) Sep. 25, 1827
William Nicholas and Ann Overholer, (MD) Nov. 1, 1826
Henry Nichols and Patsy Watson, (MD) Dec. 28, 1820
Hagan Nine and Elizabeth Randolph, (MD) Jul. 26, 1826
Hardin Norris and Elizabeth Whitson, (MD) Jan. 27, 1827
Hugh Norris and Hannah Hartsell, (MD) Dec. 17, 1835
James Norris and Mary Brummit, (MD) Aug. 28, 1820
Peter Northington and R. Cloyd, (MD) Oct. 24, 1839
Richard Northington and Elizabeth Jenkins, (MD) Sep. 20, 1831
James Nowlan and Mary Holland, (MD) Jul. 18, 1789
Caleb Oddle and Peggy Borring, (MD) Aug. 6, 1788
Thompkin Oddle and Abigail Combs, (MD) Sep. 3, 1788
Andrew Odell and Nancy Kelsy, (MD) Aug. 15, 1826
Caleb Odell and Jane McDaniel, (MD) Dec. 1, 1788
Samuel Odell and Nancy Simpson, (MD) Jun. 22, 1830
William Odell and Margaret Sailor, (MD) Dec. 25, 1819
M. Oden and J Kagle, (MD) Jun. 27, 1839
Bartlett H. Odle and Elizabeth Quillin, (MD) Aug. 6, 1813
John Odle and Nancy Hale, (MD) Feb. 26, 1831
George Odneal and Nancy Reave, (MD) Sep. 27, 1824
E. Odum and Mary Walker, (MD) Dec. 24, 1827
Gabriel H. Odum and Sarah Bean, (MD) Jul. 27, 1837
R. I. Odwin and M. H Garland, (MD) Oct. 15, 1839
Christian Oler and Nancy Marshill, (MD) Jun. 1, 1837
Alexander Oliver and Nancy Duncome, (MD) Mar. 23, 1830
C. Oliver and E. Starns, (MD) Feb. 17, 1839
John Oliver and Elizabeth Campbell, (MD) Feb. 15, 1824
Joseph Oliver and Charlotte Hutson, (MD) Oct. 31, 1833
Lemuel Oliver and Polly Taylor, (MD) Mar. 16, 1824
Thomas Oliver and Margaret Mitchell, (MD) Apr. 16, 1829
Wesley Oliver and Elizabeth Duncan, (MD) Mar. 6, 1834
John Orindulph and Malinda Miller, (MD) Nov. 18, 1833
Sample Orr and Hester Salts, (MD) Oct. 2, 1816
Henry Osmas and Linda Price, (MD) Feb. 16, 1799
Joseph Overholser and Charley West, (MD) Aug. 2, 1838
Saul Overholt and Sarah Smith, (MD) Oct. 21, 1831
Wesley Owen and Elizabeth Winchester, (MD) Jul. 4, 1816
James Owens and Sarah Jones, (MD) Oct. 1, 1825
Jesse Owens and Nancy Jones, (MD) Aug. 26, 1828
J. H. Pain and M. Wheelor, (MD) Aug. 6, 1839
David Painter and Rebecca Car, (MD) Apr. 9, 1812

John Painter and Polly Newberry, (MD) Jun. 7, 1821
John Parker and Margarett Cashedy, (MD) Oct. 6, 1794
Josiah Parker and Hannah Easley, (MD) Jan. 28, 1837
Josiah Parker and Honer Gaines, (MD) May 6, 1822
Quillen Parker and Lucy Deen, (MD) Feb. 3, 1824
Robert Parker and Mary Andes, (MD) Mar. 17, 1831
William Parker and Mary Ensor, (MD) Oct. 13, 1815
William Parker and Cinthia Gaines, (MD) Dec. 2, 1821
William Parks and Nancy Erwin, (MD) Jun. 13, 1835
Anthony Pate and Elizabeth Lain, (MD) Dec. 25, 1818
James L. Patrick and Margaret Ralston, (MD) Feb. 11, 1830
Anthony Patten and Elizabeth Matthews, (MD) Aug. 9, 1795
David W. Patten and Annie L. Mathes, (MD) Jan. 22, 1830
William Patten and Melinda W. Jordan, (MD) Apr. 1, 1824
Adam Patterson and Margaret English, (MD) Jan. 2, 1834
Gilbert F. Patterson and Margaret Bayles, (MD) Jul. 25, 1826
James M. Patton and Elizabeth Patton, (MD) Mar. 23, 1837
John Patton and Susannah Broyles, (MD) Aug. 31, 1815
John Patton and Elizabeth Collins, (MD) Nov. 5, 1835
N. Patton and J. W. Earnest, (MD) Aug. 26, 1839
Noney Patton and Robert Glenn, (MD) Aug. 30, 1825
William Patton and Jane Hannah, (MD) Jan. 15, 1812
Eleazer Payne and Elizabeth Looney, (MD) Sep. 19, 1829
James Payne and Sarah Smith, (MD) Jan. 6, 1825
Jesse Payne, Jr. and Mary Newman, (MD) Aug. 26, 1803
Jesse Payne, Sr. and Mahaley McCoy, (MD) Oct. 1, 1825
John Payne and Rachel Parker, (MD) Aug. 6, 1794
Thomas Pearce and Susannah Myers, (MD) Mar. 5, 1822
William Penhum and Susan Baker, (MD) Jun. 25, 1827
James Penny and Polly Gann, (MD) May 27, 1807
James Penny and Mary McFarland, (MD) Jun. 4, 1794
Nathan A. Peoples and Mary May (MD) Sep. 1, 1834
John Perkins and Nancy Cooper, (MD) Jul. 23, 1832
Daniel Perkons and Betsy Beard, (MD) Mar. 22, 1815
John Peterson and Milly Carr, (MD) Apr. 28, 1821
John E. Peterson and Winny Webb, (MD) Mar. 14, 1825
James Pewit and Catharine Andes, (MD) Sep. , 1802
Baty Philips and Phebe Bayles, (MD) Feb. 11, 1818
Britton Phillips and Elizabeth Minerva Bowman, (MD) Apr. 11, 1836
Jacob Phillips and Elizabeth White, (MD) Jan. 27, 1824
Royal Phillips and Jane Bacon, (MD) Jan. 14, 1819
David B. Pickens and Rebecka A Keen, (MD) Nov. 10, 1839
Aaron Pitcock and Blanche Walden, (MD) May 5, 1827

Thomas Pitcock and Rebecca Bails, (MD) Jan. 5, 1828
Thomas Pitcock and Elizabeth Carp, (MD) May 24, 1822
Levi Pitman and Martha Copp, (MD) Aug. 23, 1832
John Pofford and Sarah Ann Thompson, (MD) May 17, 1823
George Pointer and Jane B. Temple, (MD) Jun. 15, 1824
Samuel Pointer and Hannah Johnston, (MD) May 7, 1825
Jacob Poland and Sarah Couch, (MD) Nov. 12, 1810
Robert Pore and Jane Ricker, (MD) Aug. 14, 1822
Joseph Porter and Nancy Daniels, (MD) Mar. 12, 1825
Israel Poulston and Betsy Pitcocke, (MD) Aug. 12, 1811
Jeremiah Prather and Mary Ann Snapp, (MD) Oct. 23, 1832
???? Prather and Rosanna Broyles, (MD) Nov. 24, 1823
Louise Pratt and Robert Nelson, (MD) Nov. 6, 1824
Stephen Pratt and Nancy Workman, (MD) Aug. 26, 1823
John Presnell and Jane Frances, (MD) Oct. 2, 1833
Benjamin Price and Polly Denton, (MD) Mar. 26, 1806
Dancy Price and Mary Swonger, (MD) Sep. 5, 1815
J. Price and E. Young, (MD) May 7, 1839
James Price and Esther Noland, (MD) Jan. 2, 1793
James Price and Frances Threewitts, (MD) Jan. 2, 1811
Leon Price and Polly Brown, (MD) Mar. 23, 1820
Leroy Price and Emily Young, (MD) Oct. 12, 1837
Mardicai Price and Anes Thompson, (MD) Jan. 2, 1817
Mordacai Price and Marrian Khun, (MD) Nov. 23, 1834
Thomas Price and Margaret Harrison, (MD) Jun. 22, 1812
William Primmer and Mary Elliot, (MD) Feb. 20, 1821
Nicholas Pring and Lucy Franklin, (MD) Dec. 30, 1821
George Profet and Margaret Wheelock, (MD) Oct. 28, 1828
Daniel B. Proffit and Sarah Range, (MD) Feb. 9, 1836
John Proffit and Nancy Wheelock, (MD) Oct. 27, 1835
David Pugh and Rachel Bogard, (MD) May 25, 1796
Samuel Pugh and Sarah Gray, (MD) Mar. 2, 1830
William Pugh and Mary Price, (MD) Sep. 15, 1833
John Purcell and Susan Furgeson, (MD) Oct. 18, 1838
William Purcell and Elizabeth Mulkey, (MD) Mar. 25, 1836
Richard B. Purden and Susan B. Sevier, (MD) Nov. 26, 1818
Charles Quillen and Harriet Gyre, (MD) Jun. 1, 1822
James Quimby and Elizabeth Chany, (MD) Aug. 16, 1826
William Rains and Nancy Melvin, (MD) Jan. 5, 1830
John Ralston and Margaret Starnes, (MD) May 26, 1833
Sam Randolph and Ann Bayless, (MD) Jul. 20, 1819
Isaac Range and Elizabeth Humphreys, (MD) Aug. 17, 1817
Jacob Range and Susanna Hail, (MD) Feb. 27, 1817

Jacob Range and Anne Hammer, (MD) Jun. 7, 1824
Jonothan Range and Fatha Kelley, (MD) Jan. 5, 1824
Montgomery Range and Malinda Broyles, (MD) Dec. 8, 1838
James Ranken and Mary Breser, (MD) Aug. 26, 1794
John Rankin and Jane Lowry, (MD) Jan. 1, 1816
John Rankin and Jane Weir, (MD) Nov. 20, 1806
Lewis Rankin and Mary Gray, (MD) Apr. 2, 1827
Anthony Rankins and Margaret Gray, (MD) Dec. 25, 1821
William Ray and Franky Russell, (MD) May 21, 1795
Garrett Reasoner and Margarett Rennor, (MD) Apr. 23, 1793
Nicholas Reasoner and Polly Miller, (MD) May 30, 1813
William P. Reaves and Mary Devault, (MD) Aug. 11, 1831
Enoch Rector and Polly Malinda Hall, (MD) Aug. 27, 1831
Stephen Redman and Susanna Stewart, (MD) Sep. 5, 1792
William Reece and Malinda Waldrope, (MD) Mar. 11, 1833
James Reed and Sally Hicky, (MD) Dec. 1, 1798
James Reed and Mary McCoy, (MD) Mar. 7, 1827
William Reed and Margary Miller, (MD) Oct. 10, 1834
George Reeder and James Sherrill, (MD) Nov. 2, 1818
John Reeser and Margaret Grien, (MD) Nov. 20, 1828
Samuel Reeser and Ibby Greene, (MD) Dec. 30, 1830
Isaac L. Reeves and Martha Miller, (MD) Aug. 22, 1839
Jacob Reser and Eliza Leakes, (MD) Sep. 5, 1822
John Rhea and Elizabeth Blevin, (MD) Aug. 1, 1819
George Ricard and Jemina Ellis, (MD) Dec. 12, 1817
David Rice and Jane R. Doak, (MD) Jul. 8, 1815
Isaac Richards and Peggy Snapp, (MD) Oct. 7, 1819
James Richardson and Anna Wilson, (MD) Sep. 3, 1782
John Richardson and Eliza Broyles, (MD) Jun. 4, 1833
David Richey and Elizabeth McCord, (MD) Jan. 29, 1796
Eli Richey and Nancy Duncan, (MD) Jan. 17, 1816
John Rickard and Rebecca Mash, (MD) Nov. 17, 1824
John Riddle and Lucinda Overholser, (MD) Dec. 31, 1837
Thomas Riddle and Jane Rogers, (MD) Jan. 27, 1831
John Rigesly and Maria Ellis, (MD) Dec. 26, 1826
Isaiah Riggs and Ruth Murry, (MD) Sep. 15, 1801
Jesse Riggs and Mary Ann Barron, (MD) Jul. 27, 1813
James Rigsby and Mapy Gittson, (MD) Aug. 7, 1807
Peleg Rigsby and Elizabeth Hampton, (MD) Aug. 2, 1833
William Rikert and Susannah Moler, (MD) Apr. 11, 1819
James B. Riley and Elizabeth White, (MD) Jan. 26, 1837
John Rineheart and Jane Medlock, (MD) Aug. 11, 1816
James Ritchey and Sarah Carson, (MD) Feb. 8, 1794

King Lewis Roberts and Melvina Thacker, (MD) Aug. 11, 1839
Oulen Roberts and Jain Mitchell, (MD) Nov. 17, 1819
William Roberts and Eve Ruble, (MD) Feb. 4, 1811
David Robertson and Sarah Currey, (MD) Dec. 24, 1793
Francis Robertson and Mary M. Crawford, (MD) Sep. 15, 1835
Jacob Robertson and Elizabeth Wheelock, (MD) Sep. 19, 1794
David Robinson and Nancy Jenkins, (MD) Feb. 3, 1821
John Robinson and Ann Jones, (MD) Aug. 28, 1823
Samuel Robinson and Martha Chester, (MD) Dec. 13, 1824
Daniel Robison and Polly Ritchie, (MD) Feb. 16, 1799
James Robison and Ascaia Jenkins, (MD) Apr. 11, 1827
John Robison and Jane Brown, (MD) Nov. 1, 1831
James Roddey and Elizabeth Houston, (MD) Dec. 21, 1793
Benjamin Rodgers and Artemasia Rodgers, (MD) Dec. 10, 1828
Hugh Rodgers and Nancy Thornton, (MD) Oct. 28, 178
James Rodgers and Rhoda Alexander, (MD) Mar. 20, 1793
John Rodgers and Elizabeth Asher, (MD) Jan. 17, 1788
Joseph Rodgers and Rachel Lowrance, (MD) Sep. 1, 1833
Landon Carter Rogan and Nancy French, (MD) Nov. 3, 1834
David Rogers and Martha Young, (MD) Sep. 28, 1815
Elijah Rogers and Barthena Sargent, (MD) Dec. 20, 1815
Jeramiah Rogers and Sarah Springs, (MD) Nov. 30, 1815
Reuben Rogers and Bethsheba Haile, (MD) Nov. 14, 1812
Robert Rogers and Hanna Tipton, (MD) Jul. 13, 1793
Samuel Rogers and Alsay Wine, (MD) Jun. 1, 1838
John Roland and Ann Headrick, (MD) Aug. 18, 1835
Jacob Roller and Rebecca Lartz, (MD) Oct. 9, 1816
John Rolston and Mary Shanks, (MD) Feb. 28, 1795
Frederick A. Rose and Theodocia Vance, (MD) Dec. 16, 1823
Isaiah Rose and Cassa Long, (MD) Aug. 31, 1824
Jeremiah Rose and Sarah Dotson, (MD) Feb. 4, 1837
John L. Rose and Rachel T Peoples, (MD) Dec. 6, 1834
Oliver B. Ross and Harriet Jackson, (MD) Feb. 16, 1820
Mitchell Roylston and Jane Mashburn, (MD) Feb. 9, 1837
Duke Ruble and Sarah Slaughter, (MD) Oct. 29, 1823
Henry E. Ruble and Phoebe Hunter, (MD) Jul. 31, 1825
John Ruble and Catherine Coon, (MD) May 28, 1820
John Ruble and Caty Slagle, (MD) Jan. 16, 1813
John G. Ruble and Esther Fine, (MD) Dec. 12, 1828
William Ruple and Nancy Allison, (MD) Jan. 31, 1821
Absolum W Rush and Polly Morrison, (MD) Jul. 14, 1825
Anthony Russell and Sarah Harris, (MD) Dec. 25, 1817
David Russell and Jane Stuart, (MD) Sep. 24, 1812

George Russell and Mary Fawbush, (MD) Jul. 26, 1831
James Russell and Rachel Allison, (MD) Feb. 7, 1826
James Russell and Mary W Irwin, (MD) Oct. 1, 1830
Parris Russell and Margarie Cannon, (MD) Oct. 14, 1835
Robert Russell and Elener Terry, (MD) Dec. 16, 1824
Thomas Russell and Caroline Smith, (MD) Mar. 29, 1825
Robert Rustin and Margaret McGee, (MD) Nov. 1, 1821
John Ryland and Hannah Brown, (MD) Dec. 23, 1817
John Ryland and Rebeckah Liking, (MD) Dec. 2, 1819
Sylvester Ryland and May Hays, (MD) Jan. 22, 1824
Anderson Ryley and Malinda Barger, (MD) Jan. 17, 1833
Jacob Rymal and Francis Broyles, (MD) Jul. 27, 1814
Amos Ryon and Patsy Horton, (MD) Mar. 26, 1807
Benjamin F Sackett and Evaline E. Aiken, (MD) Sep. 22, 1836
William Sailor and Rebecca Garber, (MD) Jan. 26, 1837
Daniel Salts and Rebecca McCardle, (MD) Oct. 12, 1817
John Salts and Rachel Barkley, (MD) Oct. 1, 1835
John Salts and Susan Pring, (MD) May 7, 1827
Mathew Salts and Nancy Beavers, (MD) Oct. 4, 1818
Peter Salts and Jane Bedsol, (MD) Apr. 7, 1830
Littleberry Samms and Elizabeth Burns, (MD) May 27, 1793
Barney Sanders and Mary Rigsby, (MD) Nov. 10, 1823
Abijah Sands and Polly Shields, (MD) Aug. 29, 1811
Isaac Sands and Betsy Benner, (MD) Feb. 14, 1812
Michael Sands and Elizabeth Gardner, (MD) Oct. 12, 1808
Nathaniel Sands and Sarah McCall, (MD) Aug. 1, 1832
Pleasant G. Satterfield and Hannah Smith, (MD) Oct. 4, 1835
Isaac Sawesbeer and Margaret Overholser, (MD) Dec. 24, 1833
Abraham Saylor and Abigal Melvin, (MD) Feb. 7, 1826
Berryman Scalf and Rebecca Page, (MD) Nov. 17, 1831
Lewis Scalf and Nancy Koziah, (MD) Sep. 12, 1829
Mahaley Scalf and James Moore, (MD) Mar. 8, 1827
Absolem Scott and Margaret Huffhines, (MD) Aug. 15, 1833
John Scott and Polly Clifford, (MD) Dec. 25, 1822
Wilson Scott and Mary Presser, (MD) Mar. 19, 1821
Harry Scroggs and Syntha Phillips, (MD) Mar. 14, 1833
Rufus Scroggs and Maria Miller, (MD) Dec. 2, 1828
Delitha Seaball and Frances Clark, (MD) Feb. 16, 1826
William Seahorn and Ann Williams, (MD) Feb. 25, 1823
William Seebolt and Elizabeth Baker, (MD) Mar. 4, 1828
James Seehorn and Elizabeth Good, (MD) Sep. 2, 1837
James Seehorn and Agness McWhorter, (MD) Sep. 20, 1796
Adam Sell and Margaret Miller, (MD) Jun. 19, 1822

David Sellars and Nancy Garber, (MD) Oct. 29, 1838
Solomon W. Sellars and Mary Gwynn, (MD) Oct. 14, 1833
David Sellers and Margaret Miars, (MD) Feb. 12, 1824
Samuel Serber and Eliza Andrew, (MD) Oct. 1, 1831
Stephen Shackleford and Sarah Keene, (MD) Feb. 15, 1838
Adam Shanks and Susannah Sharfey, (MD) Nov. 4, 1816
David R. Shanks and Rebekah Hair, (MD) May 1, 1821
Holden Shanks and Eliza Taylor, (MD) Jan. 17, 1830
Jacob Shanks and Mary Isenburg, (MD) Jul. 22, 1817
Michael Shanks and Hannah Cairy, (MD) Dec. 23, 1826
William Shanks and Elizabeth Roberson, (MD) Feb. 19, 1791
Elijah Shannon and Eliza Simpson, (MD) May 15, 1827
Samuel Shannon and Elizabeth White, (MD) Sep. 7, 1829
John Shaw and Mary Irwin, (MD) Aug. 11, 1788
Jacob Sheets and Sarah Chinouth, (MD) Mar. 27, 1827
Joseph Sheets and Rhody Grills, (MD) Nov. 17, 1827
George Sheffield and Mary Little, (MD) Aug. 3, 1795
Roderick Shelton and Rachel Moore, (MD) Aug. 6, 1820
Hugh Shepherd and Mary Sarten, (MD) Oct. 4, 1836
Nathan Shepherd and Ellenner Salts, (MD) Sep. 5, 1833
Jacob Sherfey and Catherine Starr, (MD) Jan. 14, 1830
Samuel Sherfey and Betsy Goodman, (MD) Mar. 3, 1813
Samuel Sherfey and Fanny Rose, (MD) Aug. 18, 1836
John Sherffey and Magdeleny Coffman, (MD) Aug. 7, 1813
Solomon Sherfy and Acsean Deakins, (MD) Aug. 6, 1829
James Sherrill and George Reeder, (MD) Nov. 2, 1818
Joseph Sherrill and Rachel Webb, (MD) Aug. 29, 1822
Archibald F Shields and Mary Hartman, (MD) May 31, 1836
Preston Shields and Lucinda Nelson, (MD) May 8, 1832
William Shields and Eliza Conway, (MD) Mar. 10, 1817
William Shields and Mary McCrackin, (MD) Mar. 9, 1837
William Shields and Polly Mathews, (MD) Dec. 27, 1825
Zachariah Shields and Nancy Sullins, (MD) Jan. 24, 1819
Adam Shipley and Catherine Brown, (MD) Dec. 27, 1824
Benjamin Shipley and Margaret Miller, (MD) Aug. 23, 1831
Elijah Shipley and Nancy Hunt, (MD) Apr. 12, 1825
Elijah H. Shipley and Margaret Bean, (MD) Feb. 25, 1834
Enoch Shipley and Elizabeth Hoss, (MD) Jul. 1, 1819
Nathan Shipley, Jr. and Hannah Miller, (MD) Dec. 30, 1826
Peter Shipley and Rebecca Sliger, (MD) May 3, 1832
Henry Short and Jane Miller, (MD) Jun. 7, 1808
Richard Silcock and Polly Aker, (MD) Oct. 9, 1816
Adam Simerly and Hannah Nowaland, (MD) Jan. 5, 1790

Elkano Simmons and Sarenay Ripley, (MD) Jul. 26, 1837
Francis W Simpson and Mary C. Blair, (MD) Sep. 4, 1834
James Simpson and Polly Hammer, (MD) Jun. 15, 1819
James Simpson and Mary Ann Murray, (MD) Apr. 6, 1826
Jeremiah Simpson and Elizabeth Lautermilt, (MD) Jul. 31, 1821
Joseph Simpson and Adalade Bayles, (MD) Dec. 4, 1838
E. Sisk and J. Bricker, (MD) Nov. 18, 1839
E. Skelton and Ruby Hale, (MD) Mar. 24, 1832
Peter Skiles and Fanny Arrenduffs, (MD) Jul. 4, 1833
Jacob Skipper and Nancy Magee, (MD) Aug. 22, 1812
Charles Slagle and Senah Meadow Wiatt, (MD) Jun. 30, 1828
Charles A. Slagle and Eliza Slagle, (MD) Dec. 22, 1831
Henry Slagle and Elizabeth Williams, (MD) Aug. 9, 1838
John Slagle and Elizabeth Delany, (MD) May 27, 1817
Peter Slagle and Misse Brumit, (MD) Oct. 30, 1824
William Slagle and Sarah Sprigo, (MD) Jul. 6, 1835
Uriah Slaton and Evelina Kurts, (MD) Jul. 27, 1838
William Slaughter and Elizabeth Miller, (MD) Oct. 31, 1834
Ferguson G. Slemmons and Nancy Roberts, (MD) Jul. 21, 1836
Adam Slieger and Catherine Brown, (MD) Dec. 4, 1797
Adam Sliger and Elizabeth Spradlin, (MD) Dec. 3, 1829
Charles Sliger and Mary Marks, (MD) Feb. 6, 1835
Henry Sliger and Catherine Keplinger, (MD) Sep. 29, 1829
John Sliger and Hester Brown, (MD) Feb. 3, 1830
Thomas Sliger and Mary Ann Kiker, (MD) Sep. 12, 1822
William Sliger and Catherine Lemon, (MD) Jan. 5, 1837
Adam Slyger and Matilda Brown, (MD) May 23, 1824
Christian Slyger and Elizabeth Brown, (MD) Jun. 29, 1830
John Slyger and Delceney Bacon, (MD) May 25, 1831
John Slyger and Mary Harmon, (MD) Oct. 16, 1792
John Slyger and Catherine Sherfey, (MD) Sep. 5, 1837
Samuel Slyger and Mary Brown, (MD) Nov. 1, 1826
Thomas Smalling and Rachel Smith, (MD) Jul. 27, 1809
Abraham Smith and Elizabeth J Stuart, (MD) Jul. 27, 1824
Brooks Smith and Rebecca Daniels, (MD) Dec. 3, 1788
D Smith and J Humphreys, (MD) Oct. 10, 1839
David Smith and Sarah Irvin, (MD) Apr. 21, 1831
Davis Smith and Latty Hombarger, (MD) Aug. 6, 1807
Elijah E. Smith and Catharine Brown, (MD) Dec. 17, 1824
George Smith and Ruth Smith, (MD) Mar. 17, 1817
Isaac Smith and Rebecca White, (MD) Jul. 20, 1839
James Smith and Elizabeth Brown, (MD) Jul. 7, 1831
James Smith and Ester McDonald, (MD) Jul. 30, 1791

John Smith and Martha Blair, (MD) Mar. 25, 1818
John Smith and Ruth Boren, (MD) Dec. 16, 1826
John Smith and Sarah Ann Fawbush, (MD) Nov. 30, 1827
John Smith and Nelly Frake, (MD) Dec. 9, 1830
John Smith and Jemima Grimes, (MD) Feb. 7, 1788
John Smith and Mary Hoss, (MD) Jan. 15, 1827
Joseph Smith and Sarah Brown, (MD) Aug. 12, 1814
Joseph Smith and Rachel M. Clark, (MD) Aug. 1, 1823
Joseph Smith and Jane McCadell, (MD) Jul. 15, 1824
Seth Smith and Elizabeth Miller, (MD) Sep. 17, 1825
Solomon Smith and Eliza Colson, (MD) Jun. 13, 1827
Solomon Smith and Eliza Colson, (MD) Jun. 13, 1829
Thomas Smith and Lauranna Archer, (MD) Dec. 18, 1834
Thomas Smith and Libby Tucker, (MD) Mar. 20, 1823
Thomas W. Smith and Rebeckah Mitchell, (MD) Jun. 10, 1805
Turner Smith and Mary Ruble, (MD) Feb. 21, 1809
William Smith and Phebe Fann, (MD) Feb. 24, 1837
William Smith and Mary Gyer, (MD) Jan. 1, 1824
William Smith and Maria McCray, (MD) Mar. 3, 1833
William W Smith and Sarah Bitner, (MD) Nov. 12, 1835
Peter Smitzer and Sally Clabaugh, (MD) Jan. 25, 1806
Abraham Snapp and Matilda Windell, (MD) Dec. 2, 1829
Jacob Snapp and Hepsabe Waddle, (MD) Jan. 6, 1829
John H. Snapp and Maria Kepple, (MD) Sep. 17, 1828
M. C. Snapp and M. E. Falls, (MD) Sep. 23, 1839
Peachy K. Snapp and Emeline Nelson, (MD) Dec. 28, 1837
William Snodgrass and Orpha Smith, (MD) Nov. 13, 1823
James L. Sparks and Margaret Greer, (MD) Oct. 18, 1836
Luisa Sparks and Henry Stephenson, (MD) Aug. 2, 1831
M. Spears and L. Colyer, (MD) Feb. 10, 1839
Tobias Speck and Hannah McCordle, (MD) Sep. 21, 1817
George Speers and Cynthia Fulkes, (MD) Dec. 30, 1824
Samuel Spurgen and Rosannah Duncan, (MD) Aug. 12, 1823
William Spurriers and Martha Ralston, (MD) May 14, 1833
John Squibb, Jr. and Sarah Kibler, (MD) Nov. 3, 1837
Payne Squibb and Dicy Hunt, (MD) Apr. 7, 1827
William B. Stackhouse and Jane McNabb, (MD) Sep. 14, 1820
Jacob Stanberry and Sarah Overholser, (MD) May 6, 1830
Edward Stanbury and Polly Ann Graham, (MD) Mar. 26, 1818
Ezekial Stanbury and Sarah Grayham, (MD) Feb. 22, 1816
Samuel Stanbury and Matilda McCollam, (MD) 1825
David Stanfield and Betsy Bailes, (MD) May 8, 1813
Robert L. Stanford and Mary Taylor, (MD) May 19, 1839

Beverly Stanton and Mary Bayly, (MD) Oct. 25, 1829
John Stanton and Margaret Piveley, (MD) May 7, 17
David Star and Betsy Combs, (MD) Jun. 20, 1816
John Star and Sarah Combs, (MD) Feb. 8, 1817
Joseph Star and Susannah Williams, (MD) Jul. 8, 1815
Frederick Starnes and Elizabeth Soltz, (MD) Mar. 14, 1810
Ira Starnes and Ann McGinty, (MD) Dec. 31, 1830
Isaac Starnes and Elizabeth Seebolt, (MD) Apr. 1, 1830
Jesse Starnes and Rosanna Brown, (MD) Feb. 19, 1807
Shepherd Starnes and Mahala Payne, (MD) Sep. 16, 1834
William Starnes and Sally Holly, (MD) Mar. 6, 1817
E. Starns and C. Oliver, (MD) Feb. 17, 1839
Ninny Steele and Rebecca Hardin, (MD) Jun. 8, 1782
Isaac Stephens and Ann Humphreys, (MD) Dec. 16, 1820
John Stephens and Jane Scott, (MD) May 12, 1824
Samuel Stephens and Eliza Jane Strain, (MD) Sep. 13, 1837
William Stephens and Elizabeth Melvin, (MD) Feb. 29, 1808
Henry Stephenson and Luisa Sparks, (MD) Aug. 2, 1831
David Stevens and Elizabeth Bacon, (MD) Jul. 21, 1831
David Stevens and Lurena Duncan, (MD) Sep. 1, 1814
I. C. Stevens and H Denton, (MD) Dec. 25, 1839
John Stevens and Margaret Duncan, (MD) Jan. 27, 1813
John Stevens and Margaret Jarrett, (MD) Feb. 20, 1828
Carder Stone and Elizabeth Stone, (MD) Nov. 18, 1838
Solomon Stone and Jone K. Hulse, (MD) Feb. 10, 1838
Daniel Stormer and Elizabeth Patterson, (MD) Oct. 9, 1828
Isaac Stormer and Catherine Reanner, (MD) Aug. 31, 1837
Alfred Stout and Eliza Harvey, (MD) Oct. 10, 1833
John Stout and Rachel Irvine, (MD) Feb. 9, 1826
Christian Stover and Margaret Wolf, (MD) Oct. 1, 1827
Robert W Strain and Nancy Biddle, (MD) Jan. 9, 1814
William B. Strain and Martha Alice Stephenson, (MD) Sep. 4, 1830
A. E. Stuart and T. A. R. Nelson, (MD) Jul. 27, 1839
Charl Stuart and Mary Blair, (MD) Mar. 12, 1792
David Stuart and Ann Allison, (MD) Jun. 25, 1792
James Stuart and Mary M. Sevier, (MD) Jul. 2, 1829
Joseph Stuart and Elizabeth Miller, (MD) Mar. 14, 1826
Richard Stuart and Serckey Sanders, (MD) Sep. 5, 1831
William Sullins and Mary Reed, (MD) Apr. 29, 1800
Malan Summer and Christina Branstutter, (MD) Jan. 15, 1836
John Summerman and Magdalean Coughfman, (MD) Aug. 8, 1818
Allen Summers and Sarah Ford, (MD) Sep. 22, 1831
Adam Surbey and Mary McLien, (MD) Oct. 10, 1822

Richard Suttles and Harriet Aleger, (MD) Feb. 6, 1827
Silvester Suttles and Margaret Jones, (MD) Jun. 26, 1836
Freelan Sutton and Lutetia Jordon, (MD) Apr. 13, 1835
Hiram Swanay and Ruth Taylor, (MD) Feb. 22, 1824
Hiram Swaney and Ruth Taylor, (MD) Feb. 21, 1825
James Swaney and Teney Oliver, (MD) Jan. 1, 1834
Watson Swatzell and Barbary Baysinger, (MD) Jun. 5, 1834
Andrew Swicegood and Sabray Owen, (MD) Sep. 29, 1839
Daniel Swords and Polly Newman, (MD) Dec. 21, 1826
Gabriel Sylvester and Maria Fletcher, (MD) May 1, 1831
John Tadlock and Polly Horton, (MD) Sep. 29, 1812
Isaac Tapp and M. Hampton, (MD) Oct. 11, 1838
Vincent Tapp and Rachel Burris, (MD) Apr. 28, 1827
John Tate and Elizabeth Parkeson, (MD) Feb. 18, 1789
Abraham Taylor and Elizabeth McCrey, (MD) Feb. 10, 1831
J. Taylor and L. Humphreys, (MD) Aug. 9, 1838
John Taylor and Rachel Hannah, (MD) Sep. 22, 1789
Robert Taylor and Anny Freeman, (MD) Sep. 15, 1827
Robert Taylor and Hannah Sands, (MD) Oct. 7, 1811
Skelton Taylor and Mary McCray, (MD) Oct. 18, 1824
Wilson Taylor and Sally Felts, (MD) Oct. 25, 1825
William Jack Tedlock and Mary Phillips, (MD) Sep. 2, 1833
Thomas Thacker and Mary Byerly, (MD) Jul. 25, 1814
John H, Thomas and Margaret Kelley, (MD) May 18, 1827
Anes Thompson and Mardicai Price, (MD) Jan. 2, 1817
Moses Thompson and Elizabeth Smith, (MD) Jan. 4, 1825
William Thresher and Elizabeth Kennedy, (MD) Aug. 12, 1807
Hellings D. Tilson and Peggy Ann Murray, (MD) Jun. 29, 1826
James Tilson and Eunis Tilson, (MD) Jun. 3, 1826
Joseph Tilson and Nancy Tompkins, (MD) Jul. 27, 1803
Joseph Tilson and Mary White, (MD) Apr. 4, 1828
Jesse Tinker and Ally Norris, (MD) Jun. 9, 1823
William Tinker and E. Klouse, (MD) Aug. 21, 1839
Abraham Tipton and Polly Boring, (MD) Feb. 7, 1814
Jacob Tipton and S. White, (MD) Jan. 30, 1839
John Tipton and Salena Headrick, (MD) Sep. 17, 1827
John Tipton and Sarah Murey, (MD) Jan. 12, 1793
Jonathan Tipton and --- ---, (MD) Feb. 27, 1795
Joshua Tipton and Rechal Hagan, (MD) Mar. 18, 1799
Thomas Tipton and Rebekah Lacy, (MD) Jul. 23, 1791
Allen Tittle and Anney Clouse, (MD) Aug. 21, 1829
John Tittle and Jain Rigsby, (MD) Nov. 25, 1807
Benjamin Tompkins and Nancy Brown, (MD) Jul. 10, 1826

Reuben Tompkins and Ceneth Lisenby, (MD) Apr. 12, 1825
Robert Treadway and Artimacy Bayles, (MD) Feb. 15, 1827
Joseph Trotter and Jane Carmichael, (MD) Sep. 9, 1793
D. H. Tucker and Mary Marten, (MD) Sep. 12, 1838
James Twedy and ???? Blakely, (MD) Oct. 12, 1792
Moses Tworkman and Jane Rector, (MD) Nov. 29, 1832
Samuel Underwood and Mary Shearer, (MD) Feb. 1, 1788
Bernard S. Vaden and Julia F. Sutton, (MD) Aug. 14, 1836
John Van and Nancy Matlock, (MD) Mar. 22, 1827
David Vance and Mary Jane McCorkle, (MD) Jun. 10, 1834
George W. Vance and Mary Malinda Morgan, (MD) Feb. 1, 1838
Hugh Vance and Rachel Blair, (MD) Aug. 18, 1829
Solmon Vance, Jr. and Elizabeth Moor, (MD) May 20, 1823
Peter Vandeventer and Mary Casner, (MD) Oct. 7, 1811
Joshua Vaughn and Edy Myers, (MD) Sep. 12, 1838
Joshua Vaughn and S Stevens, (MD) Jul. 14, 1839
Richard Vaughn and Frances Robertson, (MD) Oct. 27, 1817
Sherword Vaughn and Elizabeth Hale, (MD) Oct. 20, 1815
William Vaughn and Edy Medlock, (MD) Oct. 25, 1828
Samuel Waddell and Violet Bayles, (MD) Jan. 17, 1823
Seth Waddell and Nancy McGhee, (MD) Sep. 24, 1822
Jonathen Waddill and Hannah Greenway, (MD) Dec. 17, 1803
John Waddle and Sophia Doak, (MD) Jan. 5, 1831
John Waddle and Delila Phillips, (MD) May 10, 1832
Thomas Waddle and E. Henly, (MD) Sep. 8, 1836
Phillip Waggoner and Catherine Follon, (MD) Nov. 11, 1790
Blanche Walden and Aaron Pitcock, (MD) May 5, 1827
Andrew Walker and Sarah Brown, (MD) May 1, 1833
Isaac Walker and Sarah Huffhines, (MD) Sep. 9, 1833
John Walker and Creasy Martin, (MD) Nov. 24, 1824
Joseph Walker and Jane Chandler, (MD) Aug. 25, 1825
William Walker and Mary Brown, (MD) Dec. 18, 1834
Armstee Wall and Harriet Ross, (MD) Sep. 21, 1835
Jesse C. Wallace and Mahala Bleakley, (MD) Jul. 24, 1832
John Wallace and Elizabeth Messer, (MD) Jul. 21, 1818
Pleasant Wallace and Anne Gann, (MD) Mar. 7, 1811
Jesse Waller and Elizabeth White, (MD) Sep. 17, 1835
C. Walters and J. Andes, (MD) Mar. 12, 1839
John Walters and Margaret Kyker, (MD) Sep. 16, 1822
Peter Walters and Mary Ann Cressaleus, (MD) Oct. 20, 1833
William Walters and Nancy Cummings, (MD) Jul. 26, 1838
William Walters and Nancy Kiplinger, (MD) Dec. 19, 1829
Edmund Waren and Jenny Baker, (MD) Apr. 14, 1809

John H. Warren and Margaret Good, (MD) Sep. 30, 1828
N. Warren and William Mowdy, (MD) Sep. 29, 1839
Frederick Watenbarger and Emeline Charliton, (MD) Feb. 1, 1838
Jacob Watenbarger and Susan Barger, (MD) May 18, 1834
Jacob Watenburger and Hannah Citty, (MD) Aug. 11, 1815
Spencer H Watkins and Mary McCoy, (MD) Aug. 23, 1832
Peter Watleberger and Margaret Slyger, (MD) Mar. 9, 1819
John Watson and Christianna Headerick, (MD) Nov. 26, 1793
Mulkey Watson and Elizabeth Templin, (MD) Dec. 31, 1832
Thomas Watson and Harriet Job, (MD) Feb. 6, 1826
Thomas Watson and Marian Royston, (MD) Oct. 2, 1823
George Wattenberger and Nancy Collet, (MD) Jul. 28, 1833
Michael Wattenberger and Nancy Whistler, (MD) Sep. 9, 1824
William Wattinberger and Elizabeth Kennedy, (MD) Jan. 21, 1821
Daniel Weatherford and Nancy Briant, (MD) Mar. 3, 1827
Daniel Weatherford and Nancy Briant, (MD) Mar. 3, 1828
John Webb and Nancy Clouse, (MD) Nov. 22, 1816
Winny Webb and John E. Peterson, (MD) Mar. 14, 1825
Hugh Weir and Sally Duncan, (MD) Apr. 6, 1813
John Wesleck and Rebecca Shawley, (MD) Nov. 13, 1834
Charley West and Joseph Overholser, (MD) Aug. 2, 1838
Edward West and Elizabeth Humphreys, (MD) Dec. 25, 1793
John West and Rachel Overholster, (MD) Feb. 6, 1834
Joseph West and Eliza Roberts, (MD) Feb. 13, 1833
Robert J West and Leah Crouch, (MD) Jul. 11, 1832
Edward Weston and Elizabeth Humphres, (MD) Dec. 28, 17
Daniel Wetheford and Catherine Leaman, (MD) Aug. 24, 1820
John William Wheat and Mary Williams, (MD) Sep. 14, 1791
Elija Wheeler and Nancy Keys, (MD) Oct. 8, 1835
James Wheeler and Emeline Jobb, (MD) Sep. 14, 1837
William Wheeler, Jr. and Elizabeth Little, (MD) Nov. 4, 1813
Enoch Wheelock and Lucy Irwin, (MD) Apr. 14, 1818
M. Wheelor and J. H. Pain, (MD) Aug. 6, 1839
N. Wheelor and I. Whitlock, (MD) Aug. 13, 1839
Merriwether Whilock and Sophia Burgner, (MD) Jan. 25, 1838
Elias Whisler and Anna Jane Gann, (MD) Dec. 28, 1837
Abner White and B. J Waggoner, (MD) Oct. 5, 1838
George White and Sally Nelson, (MD) Oct. 10, 1815
Jacob White and Nancy Carbury, (MD) Feb. 2, 1814
James White and Peggy Bayles, (MD) Feb. 24, 1820
James White and Anne Humphries, (MD) Jan. 11, 1830
James White and Margaret Yeager, (MD) Oct. 30, 1838
John White and Sarah Beard, (MD) Jan. 4, 1835

John White and Kesiah Smith, (MD) Oct. 20, 1830
John M. White and Rachael Taylor, (MD) Jun. 17, 1837
Lewis White and Ruth Carson, (MD) Sep. 25, 1799
Thomas White and Jane Young, (MD) Mar. 8, 1820
William White and Jane Mitchell, (MD) Jun. 26, 1817
William White and Nancy White, (MD) May 6, 1839
John Whitlock and Marcia Mullinaux, (MD) Oct. 31, 1812
Abraham Whitson and Margaret Norris, (MD) Jan. 1, 1831
Charles Whitson and Sarah Davis, (MD) Mar. 11, 1833
Charles Whitson and Nancy Dunkin, (MD) Aug. 15, 1816
Enoch Whitson and Elizabeth White, (MD) Mar. 26, 1828
James Whitson and Jemima Ramsey, (MD) Aug. 22, 1822
James Whitson and Mary Toney, (MD) Aug. 31, 1832
Thomas Whitson and Susannah Willett, (MD) Jan. 2, 1816
William Whitson and Sarah Eliza McGempsy, (MD) Jan. 11, 1832
Peter Wian and May Eva Overholt, (MD) Oct. 21, 1824
Lawrence B. Wiles and Jane Wheelock, (MD) Dec. 23, 1834
James W. Wiley and Eliza Gillespie, (MD) May 19, 1823
Nathan Wilkinson and Rebeckah Wear, (MD) Aug. 30, 1792
Dulaney Willard and Caroline Clak, (MD) May 11, 1837
James Willcox and Sarah Doan, (MD) Dec. 2, 1797
G. W. Willett and Eliza Crookshanks, (MD) Aug. 7, 1834
Charlton Williams and Darcus McGhee, (MD) Aug. 5, 1838
David Williams and Hannah Murry, (MD) Nov. 13, 1834
Francis Williams and Matilda Stephens, (MD) Mar. 31, 1836
James Williams and Katharine Jones, (MD) Jul. 31, 1817
James Williams and Mary Tilson, (MD) Nov. 30, 1823
John Williams and Susannah Sehorn, (MD) Jan. 2, 1821
John L. Williams and Elizabeth Price, (MD) Sep. 11, 1820
Joseph Williams and Nancy Collier, (MD) Feb. 16, 1812
Norris Williams and Margaret Needham, (MD) Sep. 2, 1828
Notty Williams and Ruth Collins, (MD) Feb. 5, 1789
Owen Williams and Elizabeth Slagle, (MD) Sep. 28, 1828
Samuel Williams and Rebeca Morison, (MD) Jun. 27, 1825
William Williams and Sally Wilhite, (MD) Jul. 15, 1816
Joseph Willit and Susan Stout, (MD) Mar. 10, 1825
John Wills and Carline Boren, (MD) Mar. 30, 1823
Garland Willson and Mary Cook, (MD) Jun. 3, 1795
John Willson and Sarah Winberg, (MD) Feb. 15, 1791
Joseph Willson and Sarah Cutbert, (MD) Aug. 27, 1794
Robert Willson and Jane Martin, (MD) Nov. 25, 1780
Solomon W. Willson and Mary Glaze, (MD) Oct. 5, 1833
Thomas J. Willson and Eliza Embree, (MD) Sep. 30, 1833

Alex W. Wilson and Ann L. Patton, (MD) Nov. 22, 1833
David Wilson and Anne Glaze, (MD) Dec. 12, 1829
Elijah Wilson and George Brown, (MD) Feb. 9, 1826
George Wilson and Elizabeth Messemore, (MD) Feb. 25, 1830
Hiram Wilson and Mary Smith, (MD) Jul. 8, 1828
Levi Wilson and Margaret Alexander, (MD) May 28, 1838
James Winders and Jean Forbush, (MD) Feb. 28, 1798
Henry Winkle and Susannah Wilson, (MD) Jun. 30, 1831
Abraham Winkler and Elizabeth Stormer, (MD) Mar. 25, 1822
Christian Winkler and Hannah Smilser, (MD) Aug. 24, 1803
Solomon Wittenbarger and Polly Humphreys, (MD) May 6, 1824
Henry Wolf and Nancy Kincheloe, (MD) Apr. 10, 1824
John Wolf and Anny McKihen, (MD) Oct. 25, 1818
James Wood and Mary Fulkerson, (MD) Aug. 11, 1836
Lercy Wood and Barlley Boyd, (MD) Dec. 30, 1832
Calvin Woodruff and Elizabeth Million, (MD) Jul. 2, 1836
Jeremiah Woodruff and Mary Ann Click, (MD) May 5, 1831
William Woodruff and Elizabeth Nelson, (MD) Feb. 21, 1831
Jesse Woods and Margaret McCracken, (MD) Dec. 28, 1831
Joseph Woods and Catherine Grayham, (MD) Jul. 21, 1817
Sidney Woods and Ancil Lane, (MD) May 19, 1825
Gilbert Woolsey and Hannah Tucker, (MD) Oct. 4, 1832
Benjamin Worham and Rebeccah Johnston, (MD) Jun. 11, 1809
Andrew M. Workman and Nancy Rector, (MD) Dec. 20, 1838
John Worley and Sarah Range, (MD) Nov. 3, 1819
John Wortman and Elizabeth Thompson, (MD) Sep. 7, 1807
Hosea Wrenshey and Mary McAdams, (MD) Dec. 22, 1822
Daniel Wright and Phebe Porter, (MD) Feb. 26, 1808
Samuel Wright and Sarah Price, (MD) Nov. 11, 1818
Thomas I. Wyatt and Seranah Cashedy, (MD) Jul. 26, 1834
John J. Wyett and Matilda Toppin, (MD) Jan. 11, 1831
Harris Wylie and Arty Taylor, (MD) Oct. 4, 1790
Barsha Yeager and Robert Greene, (MD) Jun. 19, 1823
Cornellia F. Yeager and Salina Hoss, (MD) Dec. 24, 1834
Samuel Yearly and Delilah Hartsil, (MD) Feb. 16, 1811
E. Young and J. Price, (MD) May 7, 1839
Henry Young and Deborah Hammer, (MD) Sep. 17, 1829
Henry Young and Catherine Miller, (MD) May 6, 1825
Hugh P. Young and Esther Beard, (MD) Jun. 27, 1823
John Young and Jane W Maxwell, (MD) Aug. 1, 1830
Robert Young and Cassy Ann Hendry, (MD) Jul. 30, 1835
William H. Young and Emilin Jikes Tipton, (MD) Oct. 30, 1826
Daniel Zimmerman and Catharine Miller, (MD) Aug. 25, 1824

Jacob Zimmerman and Sarah Bowman, (MD) Mar. 21, 1825

Jackson County, TN, Delinquent Tax List, 1805, As of the March Term, 1806
    William Christmas (223a, Occuppied by B. Blackburn); Oliver Smith (640a); Robert Fenner (640a); Archibald Lytle (640a); William Walton (640a); Hugh martin (5,000a); Leonard Southfield (3,840a); Benjamin William (1,800a); John B. Gobson (2,160a).

Maury County, TN, Purchasers of Town Lots in Columbia, September, 1808.
    Christopher Stump, Thomas Deaderick, Perry Lohea, Kinchen Massengale, John S. Williamson, John M. Goodloe, Abner Pillow, John Davison, Peter Bass, John Carothers, Gilbert G. Washington, Robert Weakley, Norton Guin, William McGee, John Lyon, Allen Yates, David Shannon, Robert Sawyers, John Keenan, Wm. Breadshaw, Joseph Hodge, Wm. Berryhill, Nicholas T. Perkins, James Welch, John Palmore, Peter Cheatham, Wm. Lentz, John Rains, Jr.; Joel Oldham, John Spencer, Newton cannon, Henry Anderson, James Bruce, James Gullet, L. B. Estes, George Calum, Isaac Roberts, Joseph Rhodes, Isaac Crow, C. B. Neilson, N. Cannon, Samuel M'Clusky, John White, Wm. Thompson, James Dobbins, Osburn P. Nicholson, Lucy White, John White, Thomas H. Hooland, A. M. Gilbert, James M. Lewis, John Williams. John Williams (saddler); Richard Garrett, Zachariah Drake, Lawrence Thompson, David Hughes, John Bell, John Linzey, Wm. Frierson, Wm. Daniel, Samuel Taylor, O. P. Nicholson, Wm. W. Thompson, John Williams, Richard Hanks, John Russell, Joseph B. Porter, Robert B. M'Lean, E. E. Davidson, Joseph Brown, David Orton, Richard Orton, Dennis Wright, Jabez Nowlin, James Welch, John Spencer, Wm. Badger, David Shannon, Isaac Adair, Thomas H. harden, Benjamin F. Spencer, Faulkner Cox, Joseph Lemaster, Micajah Davis, Samel Cowson, Nicholas Cobler, Hezekiah Almon, Richard Anderson, John Webb, Hugh Shaw, Edmund Harrison, George Coburn.

Lauderdale County, TN, Marriages 1838-1839
Thomas Arnold and Malinda J. Walker, (MD) Mar. 3, 1838
Joseph Balderson and Martha Payne, (MD) Sep. 13, 1838
W. Boydstun and Mary Lusk, (MD) Aug. 30, 1838
David A. Bradford and Margaret Burk, (MD) Feb. 12, 1839
Matthew Brandon and Jane Miskelly, (MD) Aug. 1, 1838
A. J. Burton and Mary Ann Wardlaw, (MD) Mar. 7, 1839
Benjamin M. Flippin and Eliza Jane Caldwell, (MD) Jul. 22, 1838
William J. Fudge and Susan Humphreys, (MD) Aug. 25, 1839
Thomas J. Hill and Mary R. Kennelly, (MD) Jul. 21, 1839

John W. Holloman and Nancy McClelland, (MD) Dec. 28, 1838
Alexander Howard and Francis A. Lee, (MD) Nov. 30, 1838
William Hulene and Margarett Prescott, (MD) Mar. 29, 1838
Abraham Humble and Jane Addams, (MD) Dec. 13, 1838
Edmonson John and Milly Stephens, (MD) Oct. 16, 1839
Martin H. Johnson and Penelope Morris, (MD) Nov. 28, 1839
William A. Johnson and Mary Walpole, (MD) Aug. 31, 1839
John Langley and Ann Deason, (MD) Nov. 28, 1839
Roland Ledbetter and Manah S. Bowman, (MD) Dec. 3, 1839
Leroy T. Lockard and Nancy Wood, (MD) Sep. 13, 1839
George Millsaps and Elizabeth Vickery, (MD) May 29, 1839
Thomas Milsap and Elizabeth Alread, (MD) Mar. 31, 1839
James Jose Osteen and Malinda Bowman, (MD) Mar. 5, 1838
A. J. Smith and Nancy M. Kirby, (MD) Oct. 18, 1838
Viney Smith and A. J. Fullen, (MD) May 17, 1838
Marsall Starnes and Sarah Golding, (MD) Dec. 5, 1838
Wiert F. Still and Millisy W. Stone, (MD) Aug. 5, 1839
Gordan W. Stone and Elizabeth C. Thompson, (MD) Jun. 19, 1839
Salen A. Thompson and M. E. Stone, (MD) Apr. 11, 1839
John B. Walpole and Elizabeth Roberson, (MD) Jul. 31, 1839
John J. Willis and Miza Simpson, (MD) Jul. 8, 1839

Tennessee Pension Roll of 1835, Surnames A-B
John Abbott: (CO) Grainger. (RK) Sgt. (SRV) North Carolina Cont'l Line (AA) $96.00, (AR) $236.80. (PSD) Jan. 9, 1826. (A) 70, (D) May 10, 1828
David Abernathy : (CO) Giles, (RK) Private, (SRV) North Carolina Line, $33.33, (AR) $69.99, (PSD) Sept. 25, 1833, (A) 75
John A. Acillis alias John A. Honey (CO) Claiborne, (RK) Private, (SVC) W. White's Regiment, (AA) $96.00, (AR) $1,344.00, (PSD) Apr. 30, 1821, (A) 74
Jacob Acor : (CO) Washington, (RK) Private, (SRV) Connecticut Contl., (AA) $96.00, (AR) $1,448.00 (PSD) May 19, 1819, (A) 74, (D) Jun. 18, 1833
Cronamus Acre : (CO) Roane, (RK) Private, (SRV) Maryland Contl., (AA) Line $96.00, (AR) $1,517.33, (PSD) Oct. 8, 1819, (A) 37, (CMTS) Listed on TN 1830 census as Cronamus Acred.
James Acree : (CO) Knox, (RK) Private, (SVC) Virginia Contl., (AA) $96.00, (AR) $773.06, (PSD) May 15, 1826, (A) 78
John Acree : (CO) Sullivan, (RK) Private, (SVC) Virginia Militia $40.00, (AR) $120.00, (PSD) Jan. 11, 1834, (A) 74
John Adams : (CO) Montgomery, (RK) Private, (SVC) Virginia Line $66.66, (AR) $199.98, (PSD) Sep. 19, 1833, (A) 75

Micajah Adams : (CO) Sullivan, (RK) Private, (SVC) Virginia Militia $43.32 , (AR) $129.99 , (PSD) Feb. 18, 1833 , (A) 75
John Adcock : (CO) Davidson, (RK) Private, (SVC) Virginia Contl., (AA) Line $96.00 , (AR) $1,374.73 , (PSD) Apr. 2, 1822 , (A) 79
Thomas Adcock : (CO) Morgan, (RK) Private, (SRV) North Carolina Line, $60.00 , (AR) $180.00 , (PSD) Sep. 26,1833, (A) 73
James Aiken : (CO) Roane, (RK) Private, (SVC) Virginia Line $73.33, (AR) $219.99, (PSD) Feb. 20, 1833, (A) 74
George Ailesworth : (CO) White, (RK) Private, (SVC) Virginia Contl., (AA) Line $96.00 , (AR) $504.00 , (PSD) Feb. 12, 1829, (A) 76
Early Albertson : (CO) Overton, (RK) Private, (SVC) North Carolina Militia, (AA) $21.22 , (AR) $63.66 , (PSD) Jul. 10, 1833 , (A) 78
Dan Alexander : (CO) Hardiman, (RK) Private, (SVC) North Carolina Militia, (AA) $40.00 , (AR) $120.00 , (PSD) Jun. 18, 1834 , (A) 76
Dan Alexander : (CO) Marion, (RK) Private, (SVC) North Carolina Line, (AA) $60.00 , (AR) $180.00 , (PSD) Oct. 18,1833 , (A) 70
Elijah Alexander : (CO) Maury, (RK) Private, (SVC) North Carolina Line, (AA) $20.00 , (AR) $60.00 , (PSD) May 3, 1833 , (A) 74
Matthew Alexander : (CO) Henry, (RK) Private, (SVC) South Carolina Line, (AA) $66.66 , (AR) $199.98, (PSD) Sep. 11, 1831, (A) 77
William Alexander : (CO) Maury, (RK) Private, (SVC) North Carolina Volunteers, (AA) $96.00, (AR) $572.53 , (PSD) Feb. 11, 1825, (D) Aug. 4, 1830
William Alexander: (CO) Knox, (RK) Private, (SVC) Virginia Line, (AA) $31.98 , (AR) $95.94, (PSD) Feb. 25, 1833, (A) 83
William Alexander : (CO) Maury, (RK) Private, (SRV) North Carolina Line, $60.00, (AR) $150.00, (PSD) Mar. 9, 1833, (A) 74
John Alford : (CO) Davidson, (RK) Private, (SVC) Virginia Line, (AA) $23.33, (AR) $69.99, (PSD) Mar. 16, 1833, (A) 74
Samuel Allay : (CO) Sumner, (RK) Private, (SVC) Virginia Line, (AA) $30.00, (AR) $90.00, (PSD) Dec. 19, 1832, (A) 87
Charles Allen: (CO) Williamson, (RK) Private, (SRV) North Carolina Line, (AA) $36.66, (AR) $109.98, (PSD) Jul. 19, 1833, (A) 76
John Allen: (CO) Davidson, (RK) Private, (SVC) Virginia Contl. Line, (AA) $96.00, (AR) $1,033.06, (PSD) Aug. 9, 1819, (A) 80, (CMTS) Transferred from Madison Co., AL on Mar. 4, 1825, (D) Aug. 10, 1829
John Allen : (CO) Madison, (RK) Private, (SVC) Virginia Contl. Line, (AA) $96.00, (AR) $1,033.06, (PSD) Aug. 9, 1819, (A) 75,

(CMTS) Transferred from Alabama on Mar. 4, 1825, (D) Aug. 10, 1824
Moses Allen : (CO) Wilson, (RK) Sergeant. (SVC) Virginia Line, (AA) $120.00, (AR) $360.00, (PSD) November 2,1832, (A) 80
Richard Allen: (CO) Roane, (RK) Private, (SVC) Virginia Line, (AA) $73.33, (AR) $219.99, (PSD) Feb. 15, 1833, (A) 75, (CMTS) Listed on TN 1830 census p. 30.
William Allen: (CO) Sumner, (RK) Sergeant, (SVC) Tennessee Militia, (AA) $48.00, (AR) $288.00, (PSD) Apr. 23, 1828
James Alley : (CO) Roane, (RK) Private, (SVC) Virginia Line, (AA) $50.00, (AR) $150.00, (PSD) Dec. 7, 1833, (A) 81
John Allgood: (CO) Monroe, (RK) Private, (SVC) Virginia Line, (AA) $80.00, (AR) $240.00, (PSD) Feb. 15, 1833, (A) 74
John Allison: (CO) White, (RK) Private, (SVC) North Carolina Line, (AA) $46.66, (AR) $116.65, (PSD) Aug. 14, 1833, (A) 71
Thomas Allmond: (CO) Stewart, (RK) Private, (SVC) Lee's Legion, (AA) $100.00, (AR) $830.00, (PSD) Dec. 11, 1828
Alexander Anderson: (CO) Stewart, (RK) Private, (SVC) Virginia Militia, (AA) $23.33, (AR) $69.99, (PSD) May 3, 1833, (A) 73
George Anderson: (CO) Henderson, (RK) Private, (SVC) North Carolina Line, (AA) $46.6, (AR) $140.01, (PSD) Jun. 6, 1834, (A) 73
James Anderson: (CO) Bedford, (RK) Private, (SVC) Virginia Militia, (AA) $30.00, (AR) $90.00, (PSD) Feb. 28, 1833, (A) 69
James Anderson: (CO) Jefferson, (RK) Private, (SVC) North Carolina Militia, (AA) $20.00, (AR) $60.00, (PSD) Aug. 17, 1833, (A) 74, (T1836JF) Dist No. 14 James Anderson (84a); James Anderson (111a)
John Anderson: (CO) Davidson, (RK) Private, (SVC) Virginia Line, (AA) $50.00, (AR) $150.00, (PSD) Nov. 12, 1832, (A) 76
Peter Anderson: (CO) Hawkins, (RK) Private, (SVC) Virginia Militia, (AA) $30.00, (AR) $90.00, (PSD) Jun. 1, 1833, (A) 79
Robert Anderson: (CO) Jackson, (RK) Private, (SVC) Pennsylvania Line, (AA) $80.00, (AR) $240.00, (PSD) Jan. 24, 1833, (A) 73
Athelston Andrews : (CO) Henderson, (RK) Private, (SVC) Mass. Line, (AA) $40.00, (AR) $120.00, (PSD) Mar. 13, 1833, (A) 73
John Andrews: (CO) Henderson, (RK) Sergeant, (SVC) 8th Infantry, (AA) $72.00, (AR) $950.60, (PSD) Dec. 1, 1820
Lewis Armstrong: (CO) Anderson, (RK) Private, (SVC) Virginia Line, (AA) $36.66, (AR) $109.98, (PSD) Jun. 26, 1833, (A) 72
James Armstrong: (CO) Maury, (RK) Private, (SVC) South Carolina Militia, (AA) $80.00, (AR) $240.00, (PSD) Jul. 26, 1833, (A) 70
John Armstrong: (CO) Smith, (RK) Private, (SVC) North Carolina Contl.

70
John Armstrong: (CO) Smith, (RK) Private, (SVC) North Carolina Contl. Line, (AA) $96.00, (AR) $788.00, (PSD) Jan. 25, 1826, (A) 81
Thomas Armstrong: (CO) Lincoln, (RK) Private, (SVC) North Carolina Line, (AA) $28.21, (AR) $70.52, (PSD) Jul. 26,1833, (A) 78
Benjamin Arnold: (CO) Warren, (RK) Private, (SVC) South Carolina Militia, (AA) $31.66, (AR) $94.98, (PSD) Nov. 25, 1833, (A) 71
Francis Arnold: (CO) White, (RK) Private, (SVC) Virginia Contl. Line, (AA) $96.00, (PSD) Jun. 1, 1819, (CMTS) Pension dropped May 1, 1820
James Ashlock (CO) Sumner, (RK) Private, (SVC) Virginia Contl. Line, (AA) $96.00, (AR) $120.26, (PSD) Sep. 5, 1820, (A) 62 (D) Apr. 4, 1821
Jesse Ashlock: (CO) Overton, (RK) Private, (SVC) North Carolina Militia, (AA) $40.00, (AR) $120.00, (PSD) Jun. 5, 1833, (A) 79
George Askins: (CO) Rutherford, (RK) Private, (SVC) South Carolina Contl. Line, (AA) $96.00, (AR) $1,076.26, (PSD) Jun. 2, 1820, (A) 80
Thomas Aslin or Thomas Asselin : (CO) Lincoln, (RK) Private, (SVC) Virginia Contl. Line, (AA) $96.00, (AR) $128.43, (PSD) Jan. 12, 1828, (A) 77
John Aspley : (CO) Sumner, (RK) Sergeant Major (SVC) North Carolina Contl., (AA) Line $96.00, (AR) $577.06, (PSD) Mar. 22, 1828, (A) 78
Thomas Asselin or Thomas Aslin : (CO) Lincoln,, West (RK) Private, (SVC) Virginia Contl. Line, (AA) $96.00, (AR) $128.43, (PSD) Jan. 12, 1828, (A) 77
Thomas Atchley : (CO) Sevier, (RK) Private, New Jersey Line, (AA) $28.22, (AR) $84.66, (PSD) Aug. 2, 1833, (A) 79
Lewis Atkins: (CO) Henry, (RK) Private, (SVC) North Carolina Line, (AA) $56.66, (AR) $141.65, (PSD) Sep. 11, 1833, (A) 77
John Atkinson: (CO) Williamson, (RK) Private, (SVC) Pennsylvania Militia, (AA) $20.00, (AR) $60.00 (PSD) Jun. 23, 1834, (A) 89
Robert Ausburne: (CO) Williamson, (RK) Private, (SVC) North Carolina Line, (AA) $48.33, (AR) $144.99, (PSD) Aug. 2, 183, (A) 80
John Austin: (CO) Sumner, (RK) Private, (SVC) Virginia Contl. Line, (AA) $96.00, (AR) $1,510.93, (PSD) Jun. 2, 1819, (A) 80, (D) Jun. 19, 1833
George Avery : (CO) Wilson, (RK) Sergeant, (SVC) Virginia Line, (AA) $120.00, (AR) $360.00, (PSD) Nov. 2, 1832, (A) 80

(AA) $80.00, (AR) $200.00, (PSD) Mar. 13, 1831, (A) 80, (D) Sep. 22, 1833

Seth Babb, Sr.: (CO) Greene, (RK) Private, (SVC) Virginia Line, (AA) $20.00, (AR) $60.00, (PSD) Feb. 20, 1833, (A) 74

William Bacchus: (CO) Wilson, (RK) Private, (SVC) North Carolina Line, (AA) $46.66, (AR) $139.98, (PSD) May 7, 1833, (A) 78

James Baggel: (CO) Montgomery, (RK) Private, (SVC) South Carolina Contl., (AA) Line $96.00, (AR) $618.66, (PSD) Sep. 17, 1819, 78, (CMTS) Dropped May 1, 1820, Restored Jan. 22, 1829

John Bailey: (CO) ?, (RK) Private, (SVC) 1st Regiment Rifle, (AA) $48.00, (AR) $240.00, (PSD) Apr. 19, 1820, (A) Jul. 4, 1814, (Heirs) Tabitha Bailey, Mary Bailey, Thompson B. Bailey, Hiram Bailey, Elizabeth Bailey

Henry B. Baker: (CO) Sevier, (RK) Private, (SVC) South Carolina Contl. Line, (AA) $96.00, (AR) $453.33, (PSD) Mar. 31, 1819, (A) 77, (D) Apr. 16, 1823

John Baker: (CO) Davidson, (RK) Private, Georgia Contl. Line, (AA) $96.00, (AR) $652.00, (PSD) Jul. 21, 1819, (A) 78, (D) Jan. 28, 1825

Peter Baker: (CO) White, (RK) Private, Dragoons, (SVC) North Carolina Line, (AA) $93.33, (AR) $180.16, (PSD) Feb. 13, 1833, (A) 78, (D) Feb. 7, 1833

Samuel Baker: (CO) Giles, (RK) Private, (SVC) North Carolina Contl., (AA) Line $96.00, (AR) $212.80, (PSD) Dec. 16, 1831, (A) 80

Squire Baker: (CO) Stewart, (RK) Private, Mass. Contl. Line (AA) $96.00, (AR) $89.60, (PSD) Aug. 31, 1819, (A) 81, (CMTS) Dropped May 1, 1820

Amos Balch: (CO) Bedford District (RK) Private, Sergeant, (SVC) North Carolina Militia, (AA) $32.77, (AR) $81.93, (PSD) Jul. 3, 1833, (A) 75

Alexander Ballard : (CO) Hawkins, (RK) Private, (SVC) New Jersey Line, (AA) $31.33, (AR) $93.99, (PSD) Apr. 21, 1834, (A) 82

Joseph Ballew : (CO) Shelby, (RK) Private, (SRV) North Carolina Line, (AA) $50.00, (AR) $150.00, (PSD) Jul. 20, 1833, (A) 77

Epperson Bandy: (CO) Wilson, (RK) Private, (SVC) Tennesse Militia, (AA) $48.00, (AR) $410.93, (PSD) Oct. 31, 1825

Thomas Bandy: (CO) Sumner, (RK) Private, (SVC) Virginia Militia, (AR) $60.00, (PSD) Jan. 18, 1834, (A) 86

Edward Banks or Edward Brus: (CO) Washington, (RK) Private, (SVC) Virginia Contl., (AA) Line $96.00, (AR) $65.06, (PSD) Februaury 5, 1810, (A) 83

John Barclay : (CO) Rutherford, (RK) Private, (SVC) North Carolina Line, (AA) $25.00, (PSD) Jun. 26, 1833, (A) 72

James Barfield : (CO) Carroll, (RK) Private, (SVC) Tennessee Militia, (AA) $48.00, (AR) $184.00, (PSD) Feb. 8, 1828
George Barker: (CO) Maury, (RK) Private, (SVC) North Carolina Line, (AA) $20.00, (AR) $60.00, (PSD) Jan. 15, 1834, (A) 75
James Barkley: (CO) Warren, (RK) Private, (SVC) North Carolina Militia, (AA) $23.33, (AR) $69.99, (PSD) Oct. 15, 1833, (A) 73
Henson Barlow: (CO) Jefferson, (RK) Private, (SRV) 7th Regiment Infantry, (AA) $96.00, (AR) $642.40, (PSD) Apr. 12, 1822, (T1836JF) Not listed
Jonathan Barnard (CO) Claiborne, (RK) Private, (SVC) Mass. Contl. Line, (AA) $96.00, (AR) $1,479.46, (PSD) Feb. 9, 1819, (A) 75
James Barnes: (CO) Smith, (RK) Private, (SVC) Virginia Contl. Line, (AA) $96.00, (AR) $175.46, (PSD) Jul. 3, 1823, (A) 77, (D) Apr. 1825
James Barnes: (CO) Davidson, (RK) Private, (SVC) North Carolina Line, (AA) $50.00, (AR) $150.00, (PSD) Nov. 12, 1832, (A) 74
John Barnes: (CO) Sumner, (RK) Private, (SVC) North Carolina Militia, (AA) $70.00, (AR) $210.00, (PSD) Mar. 13, 1833, (A) 74
William Barnes: (CO) Sullivan, (RK) Private, (SVC) Pennsylvania Line, (AA) $33.33, (AR) $99.99, (PSD) Feb. 18, 1833, (A) 82
Michael Barnet: (CO) Jefferson, (RK) Private, (SVC) Virginia Line (AA) $80.00, (AR) $240.00, (PSD) Dec. 31, 1833, (A) 72, (T1836JF) Dist. No.1, Michael Barnet (320a)
Carter Barnett: (CO) Roane, (RK) Private, (SVC) North Carolina Line, (AA) $20.00, (AR) $60.00, (PSD) Nov. 19, 1833, (A) 71
Lance James Barnett: (CO) Franklin, (RK) Private, (SVC) South Carolina Contl. Line (AA) $96.00, (PSD) Jun. 3, 1819, (A) 82, (CMTS) Dropped May 1, 1820
William Barnett : (CO) McMinn, (RK) Private, (SRV) North Carolina Line, (AA) $43.33, (AR) $129.99, (PSD) Feb. 5, 1834, (A) 73
James Barr : (CO) Sumner, (RK) Private, (SVC) Tennessee Rangers, (AA) $48.00, (AR) $936.00, (PSD) Jul. 16, 1818
William Barron : (CO) Washington, (RK) Private, (SVC) North Carolina Line, (AA) $28.33, (AR) $84.99, (PSD) Feb. 20, 1833, (A) 79
John Bartlett : (CO) Davidson, (RK) Private, (SVC) Virginia Contl. Line, (AA) $96.00, (AR) $1,210.93, (PSD) May 23, 1822, (A) 70, (CMTS)Transferred from Jefferson, Ky Mar. 4, 1825
Peter Bashaw : (CO) Davidson, (RK) Private, (SVC) Virginia Militia, (AA) $33.33, (AR) $99.99, (PSD) Aug. 2, 1833, (A) 71
James Bass: (CO) Bedford, (RK) Private, (SVC) Virginia Militia, (AA) $60.00, (AR) $120.00, (PSD) May 22, 1833, (A) 74
James Bassford : (CO) Madison, (RK) Private, (SVC) 39th Regiment.

U. S. Infantry, (AA) $96.00, (AR) 342.13, (PSD) Aug. 25, 1817
David Baswell: (CO) Williamson, (RK) Private, (SVC) Virginia Line, (AA) $25.00, (AR) $62.50, (PSD) May 29, 1833, (A) 74
Isaac Bates: (CO) Shelby, (RK) Private, (SVC) Col. Armstrong's Regiment, (AA) $67.20, (AR) $907.20, (PSD) Dec. 1, 1820, (CMTS) Transferred from North Carolina
James Bates : (CO) Sullivan, (RK) Private, (SVC) North Carolina Militia, (AA) $20.00, (AR) $60.00, (PSD) Aug. 16, 1833, (A) 73
Andrew Bay: (CO) Wilson, (RK) Sergeant, (SVC) North Carolina Line, (AA) $120.00, (AR) $300.00, (PSD) Apr. 20, 1833, (A) 78
Elijah Baylis : (CO) Sumner, (RK) Private, (SVC) Virginia Line, (AA) $20.00, (AR) $60.00, (PSD) Mar. 27, 1833, (A) 74
John Bayliss: (CO) Knox, (RK) Private, (SVC) Virginia Contl., (AA) $96.00, (AR) $773.06, (PSD) Jun. 12, 1819, (A) 84, (D) Aug. 6, 1824
Robert Beard: (CO) Washington, (RK) Private, (SVC) Virginia Line, (AA) $23.33, (AR) $56.51, (PSD) Jan. 25, 1833, (A) 71, (D) Aug. 6, 1833
Samuel Beard: (CO) Henderson, (RK) Private, (SVC) Virginia Line (AA) $20.00, (AR) $60.00, (PSD) Jun. 6, 1834, (A) 80
William Beard : (CO) Sumner, (RK) Private, (SVC) Pennsylvania Line (AA) $40.00, (AR) $120.00, (PSD) May 17, 1833, (A) 72
John Bearden : (CO) Bedford, (RK) Private, (SVC) South Carolina Line, (AA) $63.38, (AR) $148.33, (PSD) May 17, 1833, (A) 79
Andrew Beaty: (CO) Fentress, (RK) Private, (SVC) North Carolina Line, (AA) $30.00, (AR) $90.00, (PSD) May 29, 1834, (A) 74
Walter Beaty : (CO) Hawkins, (RK) Private, (SVC) Virginia Contl. Line, (AA) $96.00, (AR) $1,490.13, (PSD) Jan. 21, 1819, (A) 82
James Beatty : (CO) Rutherford, (RK) Private, (SVC) North Carolina Line, (AA) $40.00, (AR) $100.00, (PSD) Jul. 26, 1833, (A) 79
John Beavert : (CO) Rutherford, (RK) Private, (SRV) North Carolina Line, (AA) $20.00, (AR) $60.00, (PSD) Jul. 20, 1833, (A) 73
Jacob Beeler : (CO) Sullivan, (RK) Private, (SVC) Virginia Line , (AA) $80.00, (AR) $240.00, (PSD) Dec. 19, 1832, (A) 72
Bartlet Belcher: (CO) Hawkins, (RK) Private, (SVC) Virginia Line, (AA) $33.33, (AR) $99.99, (PSD) Jul. 39, 1833, (A) 69
John Bell : (CO) Madison, Lieutenant, (SVC) Russell's Company Spies, (AA) $120.00, (AR) $195.00, (PSD) Jan. 9, 1816
Thomas Bell : (CO) Montgomery, (RK) Private, (SVC) North Carolina Line, (AA) $20.00, (AR) $60.00, (PSD) Dembember 7, 1833, (A) 73
Thomas Bell : (CO) Washington, (RK) Private, (SVC) Virginia Line,

(AA) $20.00, (AR) $60.00, (PSD) Dec. 14, 1833, (A) 78
William Bell : (CO) Sumner, (RK) Private, (SVC) North Carolina Line, (AA) $23.33, (AR) $69.99, (PSD) Nov. 28, 1832, (A) 75
Daniel Bender : (CO) Sumner, (RK) Private, (SVC) North Carolina Line, (AA)$20.00, (AR) $60.00, (PSD) Jan. 18, 1834, (A) 84
Levin Benson : (CO) Lincoln, (RK) Private, (SVC) Delaware Line, (AA) $80.00, (AR) $240.00, (PSD) May 22, 1833, (A) 83
Spencer Benson: (CO) Rhea, (RK) Private, (SVC) Delaware Line, (AA) $20.77, (AR) $62.31, (PSD) Nov. 19, 1833, (A) 78
Jeremiah Bentley : (CO) Giles, (RK) Private, (SVC) Virginia Contl. Line, (AA) $96.00, (AR) $1,464.00, (PSD) Sep. 18, 1819, (A) 75
David Benton: (CO) Warren, (RK) Private, (SVC) North Carolina Contl. Line, (AA) $96.00, (AR) $153.33, (PSD) Apr. 16, 1819, (A) 77, (CMTS) Dropped May 1, 1820
Enock Berry: (CO) Warren, (RK) Private, (SVC) North Carolina Line, (AA) $23.10, (AR) $69.30, (PSD) Oct. 15, 1833, (A) 73
John Berry : (CO) Monroe, (RK) Private, (SVC) Pennsylvania Militia, (AA) $30.00, (AR) $85.33, (PSD) Dec. 18, 1820, (CMTS) Transferred from Pennsylvania
Sandford Berry: (CO) Franklin, (RK) Private, (SVC) South Carolina Line, $40.00, (AR) $100.00, (PSD) Sep. 27, 1833, (A) 71
Alexander Berryhill: (CO) Franklin, (RK) Private, (SVC) North Carolina Line, (AA) $33.33, (AR) $99.99, (PSD) May 3, 1833, (A) 71
John J. Bethel: (CO) Jefferson, (RK) Private, (SVC) Virginia Line, (AA) $45.60, (AR) $135.00, (PSD) Oct. 18, 1833, (A) 78
Thomas Bibee: (CO) Cocke, (RK) Private, (SVC) Virginia Line, (AA) $56.66, (PSD) Mar. 31, 1834, (A) 100
Jacob Biffle : (CO) Maury, (RK) Private, (SVC) South Carolina Line, (AA) $30.00, (AR) $75.00, (PSD) Jul. 26, 1833, (A) 71
Robert Bigger : (CO) Montgomery, (RK) Private, (SVC) North Carolina Line, (AA) $20.00, (AR) $60.00, (PSD) Mar. 2, 1833, (A) 73
Andrew Bigham : (CO) McMinn, (RK) Private, (SRV) North Carolina Line, (A) $73.33, (AR) $219.99, (PSD) Oct. 11, 1833, (A) 75
William Bigham : (CO) Bedford, (RK) Private, (SVC) North Carolina Militia, (AA) $63.33, (AR) $189.99, (PSD) Oct. 17, 1844, (A) 77
Ezekiel Billington : (CO) Bedford, (RK) Private, (SVC) New Jersey Line, (AR) $159.99, (PSD) Dec. 3, 1832, (A) 75
Benjamin Bingham: (CO) Blount, (RK) Private, (SVC) Virginia Militia, (AA) $35.00, (AR) $87.50, (PSD) May 13, 1833, (A) 78
James Blackburn : (CO) Anderson, (RK) Private, (SVC) Virginia Contl. (AA) $96.00, (AR) $180.26, (PSD) Jan. 13, 1819, (A) 74, (CMTS) Dropped May 1, 1820

George Blackmore : (CO) Lincoln, (RK) Private, Drummer, (SVC) South Carolina Line, (AA) $46.22, (AR) $138.66, (PSD) Nov. 19, 1833, (A) 72

George D. Blackmore : (CO) Lincoln, (RK) Private, (SRV) Maryland Line (AA) $80.00, (AR) $240.00, (PSD) Feb. 6, 1833, (A) 74

David Blackwell : (CO) Roane, (RK) Private, (SVC) Virginia Militia, (AA) $34.41, (AR) $103.23, (PSD) May 29, 1833, (A) 75

John Blair : (CO) Washington, (RK) Lieutenant, (AA) $96.00, (AR) $484.17, (PSD) Apr. 8, 1811

Samuel Blair : (CO) McMinn, (RK) Private, (SRV) North Carolina Line, (AA) $40.00, (AR) $120.00, (PSD) May 23, 1834, (A) 76

Thomas Blair: : (CO) Maury, (RK) Private, (SVC) South Carolina Line, (AA) $43.33, (AR) $129.99, (PSD) Jul.18, 1833, (A) 70

Charles Blalack : (CO) Wilson, (RK) Private, (SRV) North Carolina Line, (A) $60.00, (AR) $180.00, (PSD) Sep. 11, 1833, (A) 72

Daniel Blalack : (CO) Fayette, (RK) Private, (SRV) North Carolina Line, (AA) $40.00, (AR) $120.00, (PSD) Mar. 14, 1834, (A) 83

John Blalock : (CO) Carter, Lieutenant (SVC) Virginia Line, (AA) $160.00, (AR) $480.00, (PSD) Aug. 16, 1833, (A) 72

Thomas Blanton : (CO) Rutherford, (RK) Private, (SVC) Virginia Contl. Line, (AA) $96.00, (AR) $1,202.66, (PSD) Feb. 20, 1822, (A) 73

Jacob Bledsoe: (CO) Carroll, (RK) Private, Lieutenant, (SRV) North Carolina Line, (AA) $33.33, (AR) $99.99, (PSD) Mar. 14, 1834, (A) 72

Jacob Bletcher : (CO) Bedford, (RK) Private, (SRV) North Carolina Line, (AA) $96.00, (PSD) Jun. 7, 1828, (A) 74, (CMTS) Transferred from Orange Co., NC Sep. 4, 1832

Daniel Blevens : (CO) Morgan, (RK) Private, (SVC) North Carolina Militia, (AA) $40.00, (AR) $120.00, (PSD) Jun. 25, 1834, (A) 81

Henry Blivin: (CO) Hawkins, (RK) Private, (SRV) North Carolina Line, (AA) $80.00, (AR) $240.00, (PSD) Jun. 13, 1833, (A) 75

Edward Blurton: (CO) Wilson, (RK) Private, (SVC) North Carolina Contl. Line, (AA) $96.00, (AR) $731.20, (PSD) May 12, 1826, (A) 76

John Boisseau: (CO) Simpson, (RK) Private, (SVC) Virginia Line, (AA) $40.00, (AR) $120.00, (PSD) Feb. 4, 1834, (A) 69

James Bole: (CO) Rutherford, (RK) Private, (SVC) Pennsylvania Line, (AA) $53.33, (AR) $159.99, (PSD) Sep. 11, 1833, (A) 85

John Bolen : (CO) Sullivan, (RK) Private, (SVC) Virginia Line, (AA) $23.66, (AR) $70.98, (PSD) Mar. 1, 1833, (A) 74

Reuben Boin: (CO) Hawkins, (RK) Private, (SVC) Virginia Line, (AA)

$80.00, (AR) $240.00, (PSD) May 2, 1833, (A) 78
Edmund Boling: (CO) Green, (RK) Private, (SVC) Virginia Contl., (AA) $96.00, (AR) $489.33, (PSD) Mar. 19, 1829, (A) 74
Henry Bonar : (CO) Davidson, (RK) Private, (SVC) Pennsylvania Line, (AA) $20.00, (AR) $60.00, (PSD) Jun. 8, 1833, (A) 79
William Bond: (CO) Warren, (RK) Private, (SRV) North Carolina Line, (AA) $30.00, (AR) $90.00, (PSD) Sep. 27, 1833
Wright Bond : (CO) Hawkins, (RK) Private, (SVC) Virginia Line, (AA) $40.00, (AR) $120.00, (PSD) Jul. 30, 1833, (A) 79
John Bonner : (CO) Wilson, (RK) Private, New Jersey Militia, (AA) $30.00, (AR) $90.00, (PSD) May 13, 1833, (A) 70
Wm. Bonner : (CO) Henry, (RK) Private, Infantry and Cavalry (SVC) North Carolina Militia, (AA) $71.66, (AR) $214.98, (PSD) May 13, 1833, (A) 78
George Booth: (CO) Rutherford, (RK) Private, (SVC) Virginia Line, (AA) $80.00, (AR) $240.00, (PSD) Mar. 21, 1833, (A) 76
Christopher Boston: (CO) Claiborne, (RK) Private, (SVC) North Carolina Contl. Line, (AA) $96.00, (AR) $833.86, (PSD) Jul. 13, 1825, (A) 74
Miles Bottom : (CO) Warren, (RK) Private, Infantry And Cavalry (SVC) Virginia Militia, (AA) $48.33, (AR) $144.99, (PSD) Feb. 19, 1834, (A) 82
Leonard Bowars : (CO) Carter, (RK) Private, (SRV) Maryland Line, (AA) $80.00, (AR) $240.00, (PSD) Aug. 16, 1833, (A) 74
Elias Bowden : (CO) Henry, (RK) Private, (SVC) Virginia Line, (AA) $20.00, (AR) $50.00, (PSD) Aug. 14, 1833, (A) 72
William Bowden : (CO) Maury, (RK) Private, Infantry and Cavalry, (SVC) South Carolina Line $26.21, (AR) $78.63, (PSD) Aug. 14, 1833, (A) 92
James Bowers : (CO) Montgomery, (RK) Private, (SVC) New Jersey Militia, (AA) $60.00, (AR) $150.00, (PSD) Oct. 16, 1833, (A) 77
Daniel Bowman : (CO) Rutherford, (RK) Private, (SVC) Virginia Line, (AA) $20.00, (AR) $60.00, (PSD) May 26, 1833, (A) 75
John Bowman: (CO) Roan, (RK) Private, (SVC) Virginia Contl. Line, (AA) $96.00, (AR) $1,041.60, (PSD) May 29, 1823, (A) 81
Sparling Bowman: (CO) Green, (RK) Private, (SRV) Maryland Line, (AA) $40.00, (AR) $120.00, (PSD) Jan. 10, 1833, (A) 82
William Bowman: (CO) Knox, (RK) Private, (SVC) Virginia Militia, (AA) $30.00, (AR) $60.00, (PSD) Sep. 19, 1833, (A) 76
Edward Box: (CO) Perry, (RK) Private, (SVC) South Carolina Militia, (AA) $80.00, (AR) $240.00, (PSD) Jan. 2, 1834, (A) 78
Samuel Box: (CO) Jefferson, (RK) Private, (SVC) South Carolina Militia,

(AA) $72.44, (AR) $217.32, (PSD) Aug. 16, 1833, (A) 89,
Jacob Boy: (CO) Sullivan, (RK) Private, (SVC) Virginia Militia, (AA) $60.00, (AR) $132.66, (PSD) Jun. 1, 1833, (A) 83, (D) May 20, 1833
John Boyd: (CO) Blount, (RK) Private, (SVC) Pennsylvania Contl. Line, (AA) $96.00, (AR) $1,520.53, (PSD) Nov. 2, 1818, (A) 82
William Boyd: (CO) Roane, (RK) Private, (SRV) North Carolina Line, (AA) $60.00, (AR) $180.00, (PSD) Feb. 15, 1833, (A) 73
Wm. Boydston: (CO) Cooke, (RK) Private, (SVC) Virginia Militia, (AA) $46.66, (AR) $116.65, (PSD) Jun. 13, 1833, (A) 81
Michael Boyers: (CO) Claiborne, (RK) Private, (SVC) Pennsylvania Militia, (AA) $33.33, (AR) $99.99, (PSD) Jun. 17, 1834, (A) 78
William Bradford : (CO) Sumner, (RK) Private, (SVC) Virginia Contl. Line, (AA) $96.00, (AR) $340.80, (PSD) Mar. 6, 1828, (A) 74
John Bradley : (CO) Rutherford, (RK) Private, (SVC) Virginia Militia, (AA) $80.00, (AR) $200.00, (PSD) Mar. 13, 1833, (A) 75
Richard Bradley : (CO) Sumner, (RK) Private, Sergeant, (SVC) North Carolina Contl. Line, (AA) $96.00, (AR) $516.18, (PSD) Jun. 24, 1822, (D) Aug. 20, 1827
Wm. Bragg: (CO) Cocke, (RK) Private, (SVC) Virginia Militia, (AA) $20.00, (AR) $60.00, (PSD) Oct. 18, 1833, (A) 69
Charles Brandon : (CO) Bedford, (RK) Private, (SVC) South Carolina Line, (AA) $33.33, (AR) $99.99, (PSD) Nov. 2, 1832, (A) 85
Josiah Brandon : (CO) Lincoln, (RK) Private, (SRV) North Carolina Line, (AA) $80.00, (AR) $240.00, (PSD) Aug. 9, 1833, (A) 74
Thomas Brannon: (CO) Bledsoe, (RK) Private, (SVC) North Carolina Contl. Line, (AA) $96.00, (AR) $918.93, (PSD) Jun. 7, 1819, (A) 100, (D) Mar. 22, 1828
Morris Brashears : (CO) Roane, (RK) Private, (SRV) Maryland Line, (AA) $80.00, (AR) $240.00, (PSD) Jun. 15, 1833, (A) 78
Charles Bratcher: (CO) Campbell, (RK) Private, (SVC) Virginia Line, (AA) $21.11, (AR) $51.42, (PSD) Oct. 18, 1833, (A) 72, (D) Aug. 11, 1833
William Bratcher : (CO) Maury, (RK) Private, (SVC) South Carolina Contl. Line, (AA) $96.00, (AR) $632.53, (PSD) Aug. 5, 1819, (A) 94
William Brawley : (CO) Maury, (RK) Private, (SRV) North Carolina Line, (AA) $20.00, (AR) $50.00, (PSD) Sep. 26, 1833, (A) 71
William Brechen, Sr. : (CO) Bedford, (SRV) North Carolina Line, (AA) $27.21, (AR) $81.63, (PSD) May 17, 1833, (A) 79
Charles Breden : (CO) Wilson, (RK) Private, Sergeant, (SRV) North Carolina Line, (AA)$29.55, (AR) $88.65 (PSD) Aug. 2, 1833, (A) 81

John Breden (CO) Claiborne, (RK) Private, (SVC) Virginia Line, (AA) $32.33, (AR) $96.99, (PSD) Sep. 27, 1833, (A) 74

Peter Breakkill : (CO) Monroe, (RK) Private, (SVC) Virginia Line, (AA) $36.66, (AR) $109.98, (PSD) Sep. 28, 1833, (A) 74

John Brent : (CO) Smith, (RK) Private, (SVC) Virginia Contl. Line, (AA) $96.00, (AR) $1,437.86, (PSD) May 6, 1819, (A) 81, (D) Jul. 20, 1833

Benjamin Brevard: (CO) Humphries, (RK) Private, (SRV) North Carolina Line, (AA) $20.00 , (AR) $60.00, (PSD) Nov. 29, 1833, (A) 72

William Brewer: (CO) Blount, (RK) Private, (SRV) North Carolina Line, (AA) $30.00, (AR) $90.00, (PSD) Nov. 12, 1832, (A) 82

Benjamin Bridwell : (CO) Sullivan, (RK) Private, (SRV) North Carolina Line, (AA) $20.00, (AR) $60.00, (PSD) Feb. 20, 1833, (A) 69

John Briggs: (CO) Green, (RK) Private, (SVC) Pennsylvania Line, (AA) $80.00, (AR) $160.00, (PSD) Feb. 22, 1833, (A) 82

James Bright : (CO) Sullivan, (RK) Private, (SRV) Maryland Contl. Line, (AA) $96.00, (AR) $1,155.46, (PSD) Dec. 24, 1822, (A) 82

William Brimer: (CO) Sevier, (RK) Private, (SVC) North Carolina Militia, (AA) $46.66, (AR) $139.98, (PSD) Feb. 11, 1833, (A) 75

Obed Britt: (CO) Perry, (RK) Private, Sergeant, (SVC) Virginia Militia, (AA) $99.33, (AR) $297.99, (PSD) Oct. 16, 1833, (A) 75 Philip

Brittain : (CO) Bedford, (RK) Private, (SVC) North Carolina Contl. Line, (AA) $96.00, (AR) $165.33, (PSD) Apr. 16, 1819, (A) 74, (CMTS Dropped May 1, 1820

Joseph Britton : (CO) Hawkins, Lieutenant (SVC) Virginia Contl. Line, (AA) $240.00, (AR) $1,844.67, (PSD) Feb. 5, 1819, (A) 65, (CMTS) Dropped May 1, 1820; Restored Dec. 13, 1824

Joseph Britton : (CO) Hawkins, Lieutenant Gist's (SRV) Maryland Regiment, (AA) $320.00, (AR) $2,830.00, (PSD) Sep. 3, 1828

Leroy Brizendine : (CO) Sumner, (RK) Private, (SVC) Virginia Line (AA) $50.00, (AR) $125.00, (PSD) Apr. 16, 1833, (A) 73

John Broadway: (CO) Wayne, (RK) Private, (SVC) South Carolina Contl. Line, (AA) $96.00, (AR) $464.00, (PSD) Jun. 4, 1829, (A) 74

John Brochus: (CO) Grainger, (RK) Private, (SVC) Virginia Contl. Line, (AA) $96.00, (AR) $561.60, (PSD) Jan. 12, 1819, (A) 77, (D) Apr. 14, 1824

Dudley Brook : (CO) Robertson, (RK) Private, (SVC) Virginia Line, (AA)$23.33, (AR) $69.99, (PSD) Jul. 18, 1833, (A) 72

David Brooks (CO) Claiborne, (RK) Private, (SVC) Virginia Line (AA) $80.00, (AR) $240.00, (PSD) Sep. 20, 1833, (A) 75

John Brooks: (CO) Fayette, (RK) Private, (SRV) Maryland Line, (AA)

$23.33, (AR) $69.99, (PSD) Dec. 7, 1833, (A) 82
Joseph Brooks: (CO) Overton, (RK) Corporal, (SVC) 2nd Regiment U. S. Rifles, (AA) $60.00, (AR) $97.50, (PSD) Nov. 10, 1815
Littleton Brooks : (CO) Hawkins, (RK) Private, (SVC) Virginia Line , (AA) $80.00, (AR) $240.00, (PSD) Feb. 20, 1833, (A) 76
Wm. Brotherton : (CO) Green, (RK) Private, (SRV) North Carolina Line, (AA) $80.00, (AR) $240.00, (PSD) Feb. 20, 1833, (A) 75
Arthur Brown : (CO) Carroll, (RK) Private, (SVC) North Carolina Contl. Line, (AA) $96.00, (AR) $1,507.20, (PSD) May 28, 1819, (CMTS) Transferred from Caldwell County, KY Mar. 4, 1826
Benjamin Brown : (CO) McMinn, (RK) Private, (SRV) North Carolina Line, (AA) $61.66, (AR) $184.98, (PSD) May 3, 1833, (A) 76
Benjamin Brown : (CO) White, (RK) Private, (SRV) North Carolina Line, (AA) $20.00, (AR) $60.00, (PSD) Jul. 18, 1833, (A) 83
David E. Brown : (CO) Davidson, (RK) Private, (SVC) North Carolina Contl. Line $96.00, (AR) $408.53, (PSD) Jun. 7, 1819, (A) 84, (CMTS) Suspended May 1, 1820; Continued May 17, 1826
George Brown : (CO) Washington, (RK) Private, (SRV) North Carolina Line, (AA) $25.00, (AR) $75.00, (PSD) Dec. 19, 1832, (A) 79
Hiram Brown : (CO) Sullivan, (RK) Private, (SVC) 1st Regiment Rifle, (AA) $48.00, (AR) $240.00, (PSD) Mar. 5, 1818, (Heirs) Polly Ann Brown,
Aaron Brown : (CO) Monroe, (RK) Private, (SVC) Virginia Line, (AA) $80.00, (AR) $240.00, (PSD) Jan. 14, 1834, (A) 78
Isaiah Brown : (CO) Roane, (RK) Private, (SRV) North Carolina Line, (AA) $20.00, (AR) $40.00, (PSD) Apr. 6, 1833, (A) 74, (D) Apr. 29, 1833
Isham Brown : (CO) Giles, (RK) Private, (SVC) Virginia Contl. Line, (AA) $96.00, (PSD) Dec. 16, 1819, (A) 85, (CMTS) Dropped May 1, 1820
Jacob Brown : (CO) Washington, (RK) Private, (SRV) North Carolina Line, (AA) $38.33, (AR) $95.83, (PSD) Feb. 12, 1833, (A) 82
James Brown : (CO) Smith, (RK) Private, (SVC) Virginia Contl. Line, (AA) $96.00, (AR) $1,222.93, (PSD) Mar. 24, 1821, (A) 80, (D) Jun. 21, 1832
James Brown : (CO) Davidson, (RK) Private (SVC) Virginia Line, (AA) $28.96, (AR) $86.88, (PSD) Nov. 12, 1832, (A) 82
Joseph Brown : (CO) Knox, (RK) Private, (SVC) Pennsylvania Militia, (AA) $33.33, (PSD) Jul. 25, 1834, (A) 75
Morgan Brown : (CO) Davidson, (RK) Lieutenant, (SVC) South Carolina

Line, (AA) $320.00, (AR) $960.00, (PSD) Nov. 6, 1832, (A) 77
Moses Brown : (CO) Davidson, (RK) Private, (SVC) South Carolina Line, (AA) $50.00, (AR) $150.00, (PSD) Nov. 12, 1832, (A) 82
Richard Brown : (CO) Giles, (RK) Private, (SVC) South Carolina Line, (AA) $73.33, (PSD) Jan. 9, 1834, (A) 78
Robert Brown : (CO) Warren, (RK) Private, (SRV) North Carolina Line, (AA) $80.00, (AR) $240.00, (PSD) Jan. 9, 1834, (A) 76
Stephen Brown: (CO) Bledsoe, (RK) Private, (SVC) Virginia Militia, (AA) $31.11, (AR) $93.33, (PSD) May 24, 1833, (A) 78
Thomas Brown: (CO) Grainger, (RK) Private, (SVC) Virginia Line, (AA) $100.00, (AR) $30.00, (PSD) Jun. 22, 1833, (A) 71
Thomas Brown : (CO) Giles, (RK) Private, (SRV) North Carolina Line, (AA) $46.66, (AR) $139.98, (PSD) Jan. 17, 1834, (A) 81
William Brown : (CO) Bedford, (RK) Private, (SVC) New Jersey Militia, (AA) $30.00, (AR) $90.00, (PSD) May 13, 1833, (A) 82
Daniel Broyles : (CO) McMinn, (RK) Private, (SVC) Virginia Line, (AA) $23.33, (AR) $69.99, (PSD) Oct. 18, 1833, (A) 73
Michael Broyles : (CO) Washington, (RK) Private, (SVC) Virginia Line, (AA) $20.00, (AR) $60.00, (PSD) Dec. 14, 1833, (A) 94
George Bruce : (CO) Rutherford, (RK) Private, (SVC) North Carolina Contl. Line, (AA) $96.00, (AR) $1,202.66, (PSD) Feb. 20, 1822, (A) 73
John Bruce : (CO) Rutherford, (RK) Private, (SVC) Regiment Mounted Men, (AA) $72.00, (AR) $170.00, (PSD) Oct. 22, 1819
William Bruce : (CO) Sumner, (RK) Private, (SVC) Virginia Line, (AA) $20.00, (AR) $60.00, (PSD) Aug. 2, 1833, (A) 72
Thomas Brummet : (CO) Anderson, (RK) Private, (SVC) Virginia Contl. Line, (AA) $96.00, (AR) $1,476.80, (PSD) Jan. 15, 1819, (A) 79
Jacob Bruner : (CO) Green, (RK) Private, (SRV) Maryland Line, (AA) $40.00, (AR) $120.00, (PSD) Feb. 20, 1833, (A) 71
Edward Brus or Edward Banks (RK) Private, (SVC) Virginia Contl. Line, (AA) $96.00, (AR) $65.06, (PSD) Feb. 5, 1819, (A) 83
Michael Bryan : (CO) Rutherford, Bombard. (SVC) Virginia Contl. Line, (AA) $96.00, (AR) $462.93, (PSD) Nov. 10, 1821, (A) 71
James Bryant: (CO) Grainger, (RK) Private, (SVC) Virginia Line, (AA) $80.00, (AR) $240.00, (PSD) Dec. 15, 1832, (A) 85
Jesse Bryant, (CO) Cocke, (RK) Private, (SVC) Virginia Contl. Line, (AA) $96.00, (AR) $89.60, (PSD) Oct. 6, 1818, (CMTS) Suspended May 1, 1820
William Bryant : (CO) Davidson, (RK) Private, (SVC) Virginia Contl. Line, (AA) $96.00, (AR) $1,524.80, (PSD) Dec. 9, 1818, (A) 99

Samuel Bryson : (CO) Wilson, (RK) Private, (SRV) North Carolina Line, (AA) $30.00, (AR) $90.00, (PSD) Sep. 27, 1833, (A) 80

James Buckley: (CO) Weakley, (RK) Private, Sergeant, (SVC) Virginia Line, (AA) $26.66, (AR) $79.98, (PSD) Jul. 18, 1833, (A) 72

John Bullard : (CO) Rutherford, (RK) Private, (SVC) Virginia Line (AA) $33.33, (AR) $99.99, (PSD) Jul. 18, 1833, (A) 77

Philip T. Burford : (CO) Fayette, (RK) Private, (SRV) North Carolina Line, (AA) $73.33, (AR) $219.99, (PSD) Oct. 1, 1833, (A) 72

Joseph Burk Cocke County (RK) Private, (SVC) North Carolina Militia, (AA) $20.00, (AR) $60.00, (PSD) Jan. 18, 1834, (A) 72

Robert Burk : (CO) Roane, (RK) Private, (SRV) North Carolina Line, (AA) $41.66, (AR) $124.98, (PSD) Feb. 1, 1834, (A) 70

Elisha Burke : (CO) Marion, (RK) Private, (SVC) North Carolina Contl. Line, (AA) $96.00, (AR) $795.20, (PSD) May 9, 1826, (AA) 71

Isham Burke: (CO) McNairy, (RK) Private, Georgia Line $75.00, (AR) $225.00, (PSD) Jan. 8, 1834, (A) 73

Samuel Burkes: (CO) Rutherford,t (RK) Private, (SRV) North Carolina Line, (AA) $44.44, (AR) $111.10, (PSD) Jul. 26, 1833, (A) 69

Frederick Burkett: (CO) Green, (RK) Private, (SVC) Virginia Line, (AA) $30.00, (PSD) Jan. 11, 1834, (A) 82

Frederick Burkett: (CO) Hawkins, (RK) Private, (SVC) Virginia Militia, (AA) $30.00, (PSD) Jul. 25, 1834, (A) 83

John Burns: (CO) Hardiman, (RK) Private, (SVC) Tennessee Militia, (AA) $48.00, (AR) $642.93, (PSD) May 12, 1821

John Burns : (CO) Bedford, (RK) Private, (SRV) North Carolina Line, (AA) $25.66, (AR) $64.15, (PSD) Mar. 27, 1833, (A) 81

Laird Burns : (CO) Roane, (RK) Private, (SVC) South Carolina Line, (AA) $66.66, (AR) $199.98, (PSD) Jul. 18, 1833, (A) 78

William Burnitt: (CO) Rutherford, (RK) Private, (SVC) Virginia Line, (AA) $30.00, (AR) $90.00, (PSD) Feb. 12, 1833, (A) 75

Jacob Burris: (CO) Smith, (RK) Private, (SVC) Virginia Line, (AA) $80.00, (AR) $131.50, (PSD) Nov. 23, 1833, (A) 77, (D) Oct. 1, 1832

Henry Burton: (CO) Humphreys, (RK) Private, (SVC) North Carolina Contl. Line, (AA) $96.00, (AR) $1,148.00, (PSD) Sep. 5, 1822, (A) 75

Isham Busby: (CO) Smith, (RK) Private, SVC) Infantry and Cavalry, (SRV) North Carolina Line, (AA) $38.33, (AR) $95.83, (PSD) Apr. 26, 1833, (A) 75

Enoch Bush: (CO) Roane, (RK) Private, (SVC) Virginia Line, (AA) $40.00, (AR) $120.00, (PSD) Mar. 31, 1834, (A) 86

George Bushong: (CO) Sullivan, (RK) Private, (SVC) Tennessee Militia,

(AA) $72.00, (AR) $669.00, (PSD) Mar. 4, 1818
Matthew Bussell (CO) Claiborne, (RK) Private, (SVC) Virginia Line, (AA) $75.00, (AR) $215.00, (PSD) May 14, 1834
William Bussell : (CO) Hawkins, (RK) Private, (SRV) North Carolina Line, (AA) $20.00, (AR) $60.00, (PSD) Nov. 19, 1833, (A) 75
Benjamin Butler: (CO) Henderson, (RK) Private, (SVC) Virginia Line, (AA) $23.33, (PSD) Jun. 6, 1834, (A) 69
James Butler Rhea County (RK) Private, (SRV) North Carolina Line, (AA) $80.00, (AR) $240.00, (PSD) Jan. 6, 1834, (A) 85
Thomas Butler : (CO) Morgan, (RK) Private, (SVC) North Carolina Militia, (AA) $20.00, (AR) $60.00, (PSD) May 6, 1834, (A) 70
William Butler: (CO) Jackson, (RK) Private, (SVC) Tennessee Militia, (AA) $48.00, (AR) $363.20, (PSD) Sep. 12, 1826
William Butler : (CO) Anderson, (RK) Private, (SRV) North Carolina Line, (AA) $23.33, (AR) $69.99, (PSD) May 6, 1834, (A) 96
Zachariah Butler: (CO) Maury, (RK) Private, (SVC) Virginia Line, (AA) $23.33, (AR) $69.99, (PSD) Sep. 11, 1833, (A) 70
Zachariah Butler : (CO) Sullivan, (RK) Private, (SRV) Maryland Militia, (AA) $20.00, (AR) $60.00, (PSD) Jun. 1, 1833, (A) 80
Michael Byerly : (CO) Washington, (RK) Private, (SVC) Virginia Line, (AA) $23.33, (AR) $69.99, (PSD) Feb. 12, 1833, (A) 77
William Byers : (CO) Williamson, (RK) Private, (RK) Sergeant, (SVC) South Carolina Line, (AA) $24.48, (AR) $73.44, (PSD) Jan. 18, 1834, (A) 87
Thomas Byant: (CO) Green, (RK) Private, (SVC) Virginia Line, (AA) $80.00, (AR) $240.00, (PSD) Feb. 18, 1833, (A) 75
Charles Byles : (CO) Henry, (RK) Private, (SRV) North Carolina Line, (AA) $26.66, (AR) $79.98, (PSD) Aug. 2, 1833, (A) 85
John Bynum: (CO) Rutherford, (RK) Private, Sergeant, (SVC) Georgia Line, (AA) $51.66, (AR) $154.98, (PSD) Jul. 20, 1833, (A) 77

Sumner County, Tennessee, Tax List, 1789
Danl. Smith. Robert Bell, Joshua Campbell, Robert Erspy, James Hannah, William Bowan, Thomas Thompson, Isaac Walton, Simeon Kuykendall, Edward Williams, Cornelius Glasgow, Kasper Mansker, John Cravins, Alexander Montgomery, Elijha Agilfry, William LaMar. William Frazier, Joseph Thompson, James Hambleton, Henry Rule, James Frazier, Richard Carr, Francis Hakins, Thomas Conyer, David Beard, Thomas Jones, William Walton, Laurence Thompson, William Montgomery, Edward Hogan, Isaac Towel, Ephriam Payton, John Hambleton, Lewis Crane, John Norris, Ezekiel Douglass, Peter Looney heirs, Elmore Douglass, Isaac Lindsey, Charles Carter, James McKeen, Mathew H?? son,

Zachariah Green, David Brigham, Thomas Egnew, John Brigham, William McNeeley, William Snoddy, Joseph McKelwrath, William Baldwin, Richard Hogan, Thomas Hendricks, Mathew Kuykendall, Peter Kuykendall, James Shepperd, Hugh Crafferd, Edward Duglass, Thomas Martin, Rueben Duglass, James Duglass, Henry Houdeshell, James McKeen Jr., Peter Looney, John Hardin, Zachariah Cross, Thomas Kilgore, Charles Harrington, William Hacker, Jesse Sumner, Philip Trammel, Thomas Hampten, John Sutton, James Yates, John Kuykendall, David Milburn, John Hacker, Ezekiel Norris, Richard Cavit, David Hughes, George Martin, William Starr, John Hughes, Robert Campbell, Peter Hughes, William Maxwell, Michael Cavit, Joseph Kuykendall, Ramsey, David Crady , William Halls heirs, John Morgan, Henry Gambul, Armsthad Morgan, Robert Desha, Thomas Simpson, John Doke Hannah, Michall Shaour, Thomas Billeu, Alexander Neeley, Jordon Gipson, Jacob Zeigler, Robert Steel, Hugh Rogan, Thomas Peal, Charles Morgan, David Wilson, John Wilson, James Wilson, Thomas Patton, Joseph Dickson, Joseph Maxey, John Morrison, James Lynn, Thomas Ramsey, John Hicks, Gallant Lemana, John Dunihoo, Isaac Bledsoe, George Winchester, James Harrison, George D. Blackemore, David Shelby, William Bowman, Anthony H. Bledsoe, Obediah Terrell, Jesse Hughes, Anthony Rho, Benjamin Morgan, George Ridley, George Weals

Gibson County, TN Marriages, 1824-1839
James A. Harwood and Salley Tincle, (MD) Dec. 8, 1824
Gilbert Cribbs and Nancy Martin, (MD) Dec. 22, 1824
Johnston Cribbs and Sary Bane, (MD) Sep. 7, 1824
Elijah Davis and Jane Alexander, (MD) Nov. 29, 1824
Colbert Mathews and Jane Lovewell, (MD) Feb. 2, 1824
Elzey Rutledge and Judith Terrell, (MD) Apr. 6, 1824
Leonard Worley and Aney Harley, (MD) Mar. 2, 1824
Vinson R. Allen and Patsey Hurley, (MD) Dec. 22, 1825
Joseph Curtice and Manie Mayo, (MD) Jun. 30, 1825
William Jones and Sarah Young, (MD) Dec. 29, 1825
John Smith and Elizabeth G. Pullen, (MD) Jan. 31, 1826
Tibetha C. Harper and Sarah J. Blakemore, (MD) Jul. 6, 1826
Solomon C. Harpole and Sarah J. Blakemore, (MD) Jul. 6, 1826
Felix Parker and Mary O. Gibson, (MD) Jun. 22, 1826
Leroy H. Bell and Elizabeth Spencer, (MD) Jun. 27, 1826
Wm. G. Moore and Sally Hickey, (MD) Feb. 2, 1826
James V. Walker and Mary Bradford, (MD) Nov. 22, 1826
Edmund V. Tucker and Abegail McClay, (MD) Dec. 4, 1826
William Boling and Elizabeth Moss, (MD) Sep. 23, 1826

John Cole and Francis Mobley, (MD) Dec. 1, 1826
James Connell and Rebecka Roach, (MD) Jul. 25, 1826
William Cribbs and Jane Harbour, (MD) Jun. 16, 1826
Barnett Ferguson and Lucinda Woods, (MD) Sep. 21, 1826
John McIntosh and Susana Boreing, (MD) Nov. 11, 1826
Abraham Patton and Elizabeth Woods, (MD) Nov. 6, 1826
Stephen Roach and Elizabeth Bane, (MD) Feb. 27, 1826
Robert Sellers and Rebecca Fletcher, (MD) Nov. 6, 1826
Edmond Woods and Rebecka Crockett, (MD) Nov. 22, 1826
William Young and Leir Smith, (MD) Nov. 11, 1826
Ephraim Blair and Polly C. Miller, (MD) Apr. 12, 1827
Moses A. House and Sally M. Craig, (MD) Feb. 5, 1827
Salmon Sedwick and Fanny P. Fly, (MD) Jan. 22, 1827
Nathan Barksdale and Sarah S. Davis, (MD) Jul. 25, 1827
Samuel Zericor and Nancy S. Blakemore, (MD) Jan. 4, 1827
Green B. Chambers and Sally Thedford, (MD) Oct. 24, 1827
Thos. M. Witherspoon and Lucinda Owens, (MD) Nov. 2, 1827
James P. Stewart and Docia McLeary, (MD) Oct. 4, 1827
Daniel W. Crafton and Sarah Moss, (MD) Jul. 19, 1827
Thomas Boling and Sarah Hopkins, (MD) Nov. 21, 1827
Singleton Cock and Peggy Dickson, (MD) Jul. 11, 1827
Alexander Cooper and Rebecca Brown, (MD) Sep. 24, 1827
Zebulm Dill and Polly Fox, (MD) Jun. 14, 1827
Benjamin Edwards and Elizabeth Smith, (MD) Oct. 6, 1827
William England and Polly Walker, (MD) Feb. 28, 1827
Mosses Fite and Elizabeth Lytaker, (MD) Aug. 27, 1827
David Gordon and Sarah Usher, (MD) Mar. 21, 1827
Jacob Harbour and Peggy Childress, (MD) May 8, 1827
James Kennedy and Katharine Jones, (MD) Mar. 5, 1827
Jesse Maxwell and Martha Claiborne, (MD) Jul. 24, 1827
Abraham McLemore and Sally Erwin, (MD) May 4, 1827
Nathan McMullen and Malinda Richardson, (MD) May 7, 1827
Ruben Pearce and Elizabeth Mobly, (MD) May 13, 1827
Francis Perry and Elizabeth Pollard, (MD) Dec. 3, 1827
Thomas Runolds and Matilda Conwell, (MD) Feb. 24, 1827
James Taylor and Deborah Parker, (MD) Nov. 15, 1827
Samuel Webb and Polly Smith, (MD) Aug. 28, 1827
Allen White and Nancy Cribbs, (MD) Dec. 19, 1827
Henry Brown and Sarah A. Mitchel, (MD) May 14, 1828
Henderson Conlee and Mary A. Tyson, (MD) Mar. 7, 1828
Wm. C. Love and Susanah C. Williams, (MD) Jun. 1, 1828
Ephraim Blair and Polly C. Miller, (MD) Apr. 12, 1828
Wm. N. Dillard and Eliza G. Hogg, (MD) May 13, 1828

John N. Jack and Eliza G. Hogg, (MD) May 13, 1828
James Castles and Harriet H. Welch, (MD) Sep. 2, 1828
Saml D. Spate and Rebecca J. Mathews, (MD) Oct. 13, 1828
Daniel Tinkle and Amanda Katharine Williams, (MD) Oct. 11, 1828
Nicholas L. Lankford and Margaret W. Craig, (MD) Sep. 21, 1828
Thos. C. D. Howell and Lirzah Scott, (MD) Dec. 1, 1828
Absolum A. White and Piercy Bradberry, (MD) Jan. 5, 1828
Wm.W. B. Langley and Nancy Roberts, (MD) May 12, 1828
James G. Hall and Sally Hickey, (MD) Feb. 2, 1828
Andrew J. Ross and Polly Kennedy, (MD) Sep. 28, 1828
Wm. G. Stephens and Dolly Cocke, (MD) Nov. 18, 1828
Augustus W. King and Polly Harrisson, (MD) Sep. 17, 1828
Benj. W. Perry and Elizabeth Lattie, (MD) Nov. 15, 1828
Samuel Baker and Anne Forrester, (MD) May 25, 1828
Elijah Billingsley and Emeline Northcott, (MD) Feb. 21, 1828
Elijah Billingsley and Rebecca Pipkins, (MD) Feb. 25, 1828
Wilson Brown and Polly Glasscock, (MD) Nov. 18, 1828
John Charlton and Susan Adones, (MD) Mar. 12, 1828
Henry Colyear and Lidia Dixon, (MD) Jan. 5, 1828
John Cribbs and Nancy Harbor, (MD) Jan. 18, 1828
Hiram Davis and Sally Lowery, (MD) Jun. 5, 1828
John Duncan and Leah Brummet, (MD) Oct. 2, 1828
Benjamin Edwards and Elizabeth Smith, (MD) Oct. 6, 1828
John Edwards and Mary Bayne, (MD) Jun. 25, 1828
Joseph England and Martha Walker, (MD) Jan. 21, 1828
Alen Fox and Jane Hall, (MD) Apr. 11, 1828
Robert Franklin and Elizabeth Page, (MD) Aug. 19, 1828
Benjamin Fuel and Rachel McMahon, (MD) Nov. 20, 1828
William Fulghum and Elizabeth Seat, (MD) Mar. 13, 1828
Thomas Geylard and Polly Seratt, (MD) Aug. 1, 1828
Jesse Grady and Sally Elder, (MD) Jun. 13, 1828
James Lammons and Milly Dial, (MD) Apr. 2, 1828
Obadiah Lewis and Malinda Malone, (MD) Oct. 23, 1828
Jessee Maxwell and Martha Claiborne, (MD) Jun. 24, 1828
Jerry McGee and Betsey Baley, (MD) Dec. 31, 1828
Donald McIver and Matilda McClary, (MD) Mar. 14, 1828
Joel Miller and Sally Baley, (MD) Mar. 26, 1828
John Mixon and Mary Mason, (MD) Jun. 3, 1828
Harrison Phillips and Emily McKendrick, (MD) Mar. 4, 1828
Stephen Pollard and Ann Stephens, (MD) Feb. 24, 1828
John Roach and Nancy Morgan, (MD) Jan. 15, 1828
Elijah Robbins and Milly Moody, (MD) Feb. 18, 1828
John Sellers and Julian Fonville, (MD) Jun. 12, 1828

Richard Sharrod and Milly Hains, (MD) Mar. 4, 1828
Nathaniel Sherrod and Hanah Hanes, (MD) Apr. 5, 1828
William Thedford and Harriet Littlefield, (MD) Oct. 18, 1828
David Thomas and Malinda Murphy, (MD) Feb. 25, 1828
Samuel Webb and Polly Smith, (MD) Aug. 25, 1828
Thomas Williams and Sabry Davidsson, (MD) Oct. 18, 1828
Jonathan Woodard and Elizabeth James, (MD) Oct. 30, 1828
Wineford Avery and Miss F. L. W McEwen, (MD) Aug. 7, 1829
Herbert A. Ragasdale and Francis H. King, (MD) Jun. 27, 1829
Denis Thedford and Hester H. Gray, (MD) Aug. 4, 1829
Ebenezar Dunlap and Mary L. Harbour, (MD) Apr. 20, 1829
Francis A. Bledsoe and Sally Holmes, (MD) Dec. 8, 1829
Hugh A. Fullerton and Frances Dyer, (MD) Mar. 7, 1829
Munroe B. Elder and Rachel Reed, (MD) Feb. 24, 1829
Isral C. Moore and Elizabeth Bain, (MD) Feb. 5, 1829
Wm. C. Robertson and Susan Weatherspoon, (MD) Nov. 2, 1829
Wm. E. Wade and Sally Little, (MD) Mar. 9, 1829
Thos. J. Baysinger and Wineford Avery, (MD) Aug. 7, 1829
James L. Totten and Sally Staton, (MD) Oct. 13, 1829
James N. Higgins and Martha Pruitt, (MD) Dec. 22, 1829
Wm. N. Jones and Jane Patterson, (MD) Feb. 20, 1829
Wm. N. Mitchell and Ellenor Bledsoe, (MD) Nov. 10, 1829
Philemon Y. Bowers and Margaret McDougle, (MD) Jul. 2, 1829
Thomas Baker and Levina Smith, (MD) Dec. 22, 1829
Alen Betts and Sally Parker, (MD) Dec. 15, 1829
Zacheriah Biggs and Sally Dunagan, (MD) Jul. 10, 1829
Elisha Billingsly and Martha Fite, (MD) Dec. 14, 1829
George Blackwell and Fanny Elder, (MD) Jan. 3, 1829
James Boals and Desdimony Moss, (MD) Nov. 4, 1829
John Britingham and Sally Ormes, (MD) Dec. 29, 1829
Edmund Britt and Betsey Sammons, (MD) May 20, 1829
Hiram Dawson and Nancy Johnston, (MD) Aug. 29, 1829
David Dickey and Anna Nelson, (MD) Mar. 23, 1829
William Elder and Eliza Harper, (MD) Mar. 4, 1829
William Ferguson and Maryan Cole, (MD) Aug. 26, 1829
Boldin Finch and Lively Pitchford, (MD) May 23, 1829
Joseph Fletcher and Rebecka Forrester, (MD) Sep. 8, 1829
John Ford and Vilet Hall, (MD) Sep. 28, 1829
Mark Forest and Rebecca Pollard, (MD) Jan. 24, 1829
John Gambell and Rebecka Hopkins, (MD) Jul. 21, 1829
William Hall and Lidia Hall, (MD) Jan. 5, 1829
Pennell Kell and Elizabeth Scallarn, (MD) Dec. 23, 1829
Drury Martin and Elizabeth Dunnegan, (MD) Nov. 4, 1829

William McBride and Sarah Thomas, (MD) Sep. 23, 1829
Joseph McClure and Elizabeth McBride, (MD) Jun. 2, 1829
James Morris and Rebecca Ford, (MD) Jan. 1, 1829
Alfred Neding and Telitha Hodges, (MD) Jun. 15, 1829
Lewis Needham and Matty Oglesby, (MD) Jun. 6, 1829
Elisha Oglesby and Polly Morgan, (MD) Dec. 8, 1829
John Pruitt and Rossan Champain, (MD) Aug. 8, 1829
William Thedford and Elizabeth Crockett, (MD) Nov. 3, 1829
Joshua Wilburn and Jane Bryant, (MD) Feb. 19, 1829
Arthur Williams and Mary McBride, (MD) Dec. 21, 1829
William Crafton and Hester Ann Dial, (MD) Mar. 27, 1830
Andrew J. Hodges and Nancy M. Fisher, (MD) Nov. 16, 1830
Valcian C. G. Wright and Caroline Harrisson, (MD) Jun. 24, 1830
Lions C. Scott and Mrs. Brassfield, (MD) Feb. 4, 1830
James G. Hall and Fanny Bradford, (MD) Apr. 7, 1830
John H. Terry and Adeline Northcut, (MD) Feb. 27, 1830
Wellington H. Bledsoe and Matilda Bruff, (MD) Jan. 6, 1830
J. J. Fielder and Jane Hicks, (MD) Feb. 17, 1830
Wm. J. Davidson and Jane Hicks, (MD) Feb. 17, 1830
Andrew P. Foster and Darthul Lewis, (MD) Apr. 8, 1830
Robert P. Edmundston and Wine Bane, (MD) Jan. 5, 1830
Turner R. Gibbs and Mary Rains, (MD) Jun. 23, 1830
John W. Hutson and Elizabeth Sellars, (MD) Mar. 2, 1830
James Baker and Polly Mitts, (MD) Jan. 8, 1830
Green Boland and Jane McMillin, (MD) Apr. 2, 1830
Robert Boles and Nancy Lamons, (MD) Mar. 3, 1830
Elijah Boyt and Susan Crane, (MD) Apr. 25, 1830
John Briant and Matilda Jackson, (MD) Jan. 12, 1830
John Childras and Eland McMillin, (MD) May 20, 1830
William Crockett and Clorence Boytt, (MD) Mar. 18, 1830
Wm. Cribbs and Elizabeth York, (MD) Oct. 1, 1830
Edward Curtis and Lucinda Mahon, (MD) Jan. 25, 1830
John Dunagan and Sally Davidson, (MD) Nov. 11, 1830
Salesbury Fasthing and Martha Haley, (MD) Dec. 14, 1830
Thomas Fletcher and Sarah Lewis, (MD) Nov. 27, 1830
Wm. Cromes and Sally Montgomery, (MD) Jun. 23, 1830
Wile Flowers and Margaret Crockett, (MD) Mar. 22, 1830
William Forester and Mary Runaldo, (MD) Dec. 31, 1830
Paton Fox and Catharine Murphey, (MD) Mar. 5, 1830
Joseph Hamilton and Margarett McClary, (MD) Aug. 3, 1830
Joseph Hamilton and Margarett McClary, (MD) Aug. 3, 1830
Samuel Henry and Roda Ross, (MD) Apr. 12, 1830
Henry Hunter and Anna Stacup, (MD) Nov. 7, 1830

Abraham King and Elizabeth Bloys, (MD) Apr. 17, 1830
Edwin Mathis and Patsey Sparkman, (MD) Dec. 13, 1830
David McBride and Angeline Cross, (MD) Sep. 11, 1830
Luny McDaniel and Nancy Adcock, (MD) Mar. 6, 1830
Abraham McKirby and Sally McDaniel, (MD) Jan. 11, 1830
James Morris and Rebecca Ford, (MD) Jan. 15, 1830
David Patton and Elizabeth Cook, (MD) Jul. 28, 1830
Stephen Rains and Clary Daugherty, (MD) May 15, 1830
William Ridgeway and Sarey Glason, (MD) Apr. 3, 1830
John Scallorn and Lovina Jackson, (MD) Dec. 20, 1830
Samuel Sewell and Wynne Anders, (MD) Oct. 25, 1830
James Smith and Elizabeth Reed, (MD) Jan. 26, 1830
Henderson Trusty and Julian Mitchell, (MD) Jan. 16, 1830
Milichi Watts and Matilda Totten, (MD) Nov. 13, 1830
Joshua Wilburn and Jane Bryant, (MD) Feb. 19, 1830
William Wilson and Nancy Howard, (MD) Jun. 30, 1830
Wm. Fletcher and Nancy Fisher, (MD) Jul. 14, 1830
Charles Parish and Francis O. L. McCullock, (MD) Aug. 29, 1831
Joshua Monan and Mary Ann Harris, (MD) Jul. 6, 1831
George Patton and Rhoda Ann McWhorter, (MD) Feb. 26, 1831
John Russell and Hester Ann Mitts, (MD) Jul. 16, 1831
Zachariah Smith and Mary Ann White, (MD) Sep. 5, 1831
F. G. Goodman and Sarah B. Rust, (MD) Oct. 18, 1831
John S. Fullerton and Mary C. Gentry, (MD) Dec. 14, 1831
Sherod S. Paul and Mary C. Gentry, (MD) Dec. 14, 1831
Robert Seat and Martha E. Gilchrist, (MD) Jul. 7, 1831
William Sham and Luize E. Lyon, (MD) Feb. 19, 1831
John Fly and Mary F. Lile, (MD) Nov. 29, 1831
Thomas G. Jones and Levina I Dickson, (MD) Oct. 3, 1831
Edwin Fonville and Ann Jane Bush, (MD) Dec. 12, 1831
Wm. P. Gillum and Ann Row Hall, (MD) Sep. 22, 1831
Caswell Miller and Mary V. Stoddard, (MD) Nov. 11, 1831
Robt A. H. McCorkle and Nancy Putnam, (MD) Dec. 22, 1831
James P. H. Grundy and Elizabeth Kirsey, (MD) Feb. 14, 1831
James P. H. Grundy and Elizabeth Kirsey, (MD) Feb. 14, 1831
John W. H. Mays and Louiza Webb, (MD) Dec. 8, 1831
Philip R. K. Claiborne and Louisana Hess, (MD) Oct. 31, 1831
Robt A. Rankin and Martha Bell, (MD) Apr. 1, 1831
James A. Richardson and Elizabeth Murphy, (MD) Dec. 12, 1831
Cooper B. Jones and Malinda Glasscock, (MD) Sep. 24, 1831
Elgin C. White and Mariah Stanley, (MD) Sep. 5, 1831
D. G. Boyett and Anna Stalcup, (MD) Nov. 7, 1831
Jas. H. Sheron and Unity Campbell, (MD) Jul. 2, 1831

Wm. E. Tinkle and Eliza Avery, (MD) Mar. 25, 1831
Thomas J. Walton and Rebecka McWhorter, (MD) Feb. 23, 1831
Lindsey K. Tinkle and Sarah Willson, (MD) Nov. 29, 1831
Thos. L. Boswell and Rebeckha Taylor, (MD) Feb. 19, 1831
Jno. M. Carroll and Winey Harrisson, (MD) Sep. 1, 1831
George O. Richmon and Sarah Patterson, (MD) Mar. 7, 1831
Wm. Goodman, Jr. and Jane Coop, (MD) Jun. 30, 1831
P P. Patterson and Emaline Russ, (MD) Dec. 13, 1831
Daniel R. Hendrick and Rachel Frazer, (MD) Dec. 23, 1831
Edmond W. Rains and Margarett Fulerton, (MD) Jan. 8, 1831
Ruben W. Biggs and Martha Hector, (MD) Jun. 25, 1831
George W. Dickey and Merica Hawkins, (MD) Jul. 16, 1831
Thomas W. King and Mary Terrell, (MD) May 9, 1831
James Babb and Elizabeth Craig, (MD) Mar. 6, 1831
Andrew Blair and Nancy Sellars, (MD) Oct. 8, 1831
Robert Boles and Nancy Leamons, (MD) Mar. 5, 1831
Elijah Boyt and Susan Crane, (MD) Apr. 25, 1831
Frederick Bryant and Martha Jones, (MD) Jul. 27, 1831
Addison Corrington and Judia Whitley, (MD) Jul. 10, 1831
Alexander Cox and Elizabeth Fox, (MD) Aug. 31, 1831
Dr. Cribbs and Nancy Harbour, (MD) Aug. 11, 1831
James Curtis and Penelope Griffee, (MD) Dec. 27, 1831
Sampson Curtis and Charlotte Grayor, (MD) Jul. 4, 1831
Daniel Delph and Margarett Bratton, (MD) Nov. 10, 1831
William Erwin and Narcissa Wilborn, (MD) Oct. 15, 1831
Allen Ferguson and Mcula Cole, (MD) Nov. 14, 1831
Reuben Fletcher and Elizabeth Baysinger, (MD) Sep. 21, 1831
William Fletcher and Margaret Griffee, (MD) Apr. 28, 1831
Dillard Forester and Malinda Cantrell, (MD) May 28, 1831
William Freeman and Mary Muirhead, (MD) Jan. 20, 1831
William Goodman and Ann Hardister, (MD) Jul. 27, 1831
Hendleton Ingram and Charlotte Dowell, (MD) Dec. 10, 1831
John Jackson and Lucenda Elder, (MD) Nov. 21, 1831
John Kinley and Lucinda Harbour, (MD) Mar. 17, 1831
Robert Landran and Lucresa Wilson, (MD) Apr. 28, 1831
William Leonard and Sary Dickey, (MD) Feb. 5, 1831
Giles Marchbanks and Mary Lewis, (MD) Oct. 11, 1831
Haden McCormack and Polly Smith, (MD) Feb. 16, 1831
Josiah Moore and Lucy Smith, (MD) Jun. 10, 1831
Enoch Muirheid and Martha Simons, (MD) Apr. 21, 1831
Lewis Needham and Matty Oglesby, (MD) Jun. 6, 1831
John Nobles and Sally Diggins, (MD) Oct. 14, 1831
Terry Odell and Sally Davis, (MD) Oct. 25, 1831

Isaac Parker and Susan Moore, (MD) Dec. 15, 1831
Joseph Parker and Nancy Nobles, (MD) Feb. 24, 1831
Watson Pridy and Sally Cook, (MD) Jul. 5, 1831
Samuel Reed and Elizabeth Parks, (MD) Aug. 6, 1831
Joseph Robins and Nancy Rody, (MD) Jan. 9, 1831
Overall Sanderson and Eliza Lyon, (MD) Apr. 7, 1831
Louis See and Deborah Parker, (MD) Dec. 13, 1831
Samuel Shane and Rebecka Umstead, (MD) Dec. 5, 1831
Daniel Stephison and Martha Shane, (MD) Nov. 7, 1831
Joseph Suratt and Malissa Baker, (MD) Aug. 16, 1831
Thomas Taylor and Juliana Gilchrist, (MD) Sep. 19, 1831
Reuben Tyson and Exaline Boyt, (MD) Jul. 30, 1831
Littleton Ward and Elizabeth Mitchell, (MD) Sep. 7, 1831
Edwin Warrin and Elizabeth Hendrick, (MD) May 8, 1831
Young Kirksey and Mary E. C. Asher, (MD) Aug. 27, 1832
James Scott and Vilett B. Roddy, (MD) Dec. 8, 1832
John D. Wright and Elizabeth C. Davis, (MD) Feb. 9, 1832
H. W. Wright and Nancy C. Williams, (MD) Aug. 25, 1832
James Hicks and Susanah C. Sanford, (MD) Aug. 15, 1832
David B. Dixon and Harriett H. Carroll, (MD) Aug. 4, 1832
William Smith and Harriat Jane Bledsoe, (MD) Apr. 25, 1832
Peleg Bailey and Eliza N. Bailey, (MD) Sep. 13, 1832
Ira Spight and Mary R. Dickson, (MD) Jan. 31, 1832
Stewart Flinter and Charity T. Thompson, (MD) May 31, 1832
Andrew A. Carr and Elizabeth Massey, (MD) Dec. 25, 1832
N. B. Jones and Elizabeth Welch, (MD) Oct. 8, 1832
David B. Mason and Lorindo Roach, (MD) Sep. 26, 1832
Thomas C. Jordian and Jane Baily, (MD) Apr. 10, 1832
Wm. A. Lemmons and Elizabeth Massey, (MD) Dec. 25, 1832
Wm. A. Estes and Harriett Joslin, (MD) Sep. 27, 1832
Eliza E. Walker and Nancy Smith, (MD) Sep. 3, 1832
James E. Vickers and Jane Smith, (MD) Nov. 23, 1832
V. H. Bell and Drucilla Culp, (MD) Jul. 10, 1832
Wilson L. Davidson and Elizabeth Richardson, (MD) Oct. 11, 1832
James P. Alexander and Julian Butler, (MD) Nov. 17, 1832
William Baxter and Sarah Berry, (MD) Jan. 7, 1832
James Bell and Michel Bell, (MD) May 8, 1832
William Blann and Zaby McKnight, (MD) Jan. 10, 1832
Johnathan Dausson and Alee Kelly, (MD) Nov. 14, 1832
Henry Dowland and Matilda Williams, (MD) Jan. 16, 1832
John Flowers and Margaret Gregory, (MD) Sep. 1, 1832
Spivy Fuller and Letha Dickson, (MD) Mar. 12, 1832
Thos. Gaskins and Delila Rains, (MD) Nov. 16, 1832

Thomas Hail and Elizabeth Luster, (MD) Dec. 25, 1832
Blaney Harper and Elizaeth Griffy, (MD) Sep. 3, 1832
Blaney Harper and Winneford Toller, (MD) Jan. 7, 1832
John Holmes and Elizabeth Singleton, (MD) Sep. 3, 1832
Calvin Jackson and Sarah Bhass, (MD) Oct. 22, 1832
Abraham Kirksey and Elizabeth Boon, (MD) Jun. 28, 1832
Wiliam Leeton and Elizabeth Cole, (MD) Dec. 18, 1832
Eli McMullin and Harriett Davidsson, (MD) Dec. 22, 1832
John Oakes and Winney Fowler, (MD) Feb. 10, 1832
Joseph Pecks and Honey Thedford, (MD) Dec. 25, 1832
Isaac Pollard and Maniza Legate, (MD) Nov. 24, 1832
Charles Porter and Cary Baley, (MD) Feb. 11, 1832
James Rackley and Rila McDermitt, (MD) Nov. 24, 1832
James Rackly and Elizabeth Cole, (MD) May 5, 1832
Samuel Rankin and Mercilla Goodman, (MD) Sep. 18, 1832
Joseph Robbins and Nancy Rodey, (MD) Jan. 9, 1832
Magilba Rogers and Nancy Staton, (MD) Dec. 8, 1832
Wm. Carradine and Emely Hall, (MD) Jan. 21, 1832
Robert Sellars and Margarett Miller, (MD) May 10, 1832
Mark Selph and Millia Holder, (MD) Nov. 20, 1832
Erwin Smith and Susannah Oglesby, (MD) May 19, 1832
James Tipton and Rachael Puckett, (MD) Sep. 20, 1832
Winneford Toller and Blaney Harper, (MD) Jan. 7, 1832
Gideon Tucker and Cely Johnson, (MD) Jul. 28, 1832
Hinton Willis and Ann Holder, (MD) Nov. 15, 1832
Jefferson Wilson and Mary Mayfield, (MD) Dec. 22, 1832
John Wood and Ana Bradley, (MD) Sep. 21, 1832
Wm. Sammons and Hinna Nobles, (MD) Apr. 10, 1832
Ely Evans and Mary A. Joslin, (MD) Jul. 17, 1833
Russell Conlee and Mary Ann King, (MD) Aug. 15, 1833
Absolem Knox and Sarah Ann Higgins, (MD) Apr. 13, 1833
Daniel H. Barns and Margaret C. Patterson, (MD) Mar. 10, 1833
William Bowen and Easter D. Craig, (MD) Feb. 4, 1833
Johnson Williams and Elizabeth D. Robb, (MD) Aug. 27, 1833
Wm. K. Love and Sarah Eliza Dyer, (MD) Jun. 19, 1833
James Porter and Sarah J. Craddock, (MD) Oct. 14, 1833
Allen L. Wood and Eliza Jans Freeman, (MD) Oct. 5, 1833
Hearvy Bledsoe and Mary L. Bledsoe, (MD) Mar. 18, 1833
John Hutchins and Caroline M. James, (MD) Apr. 7, 1833
John Hutchins and Caroline M. James, (MD) May 7, 1833
Solomon Human and Nancy P. Porter, (MD) Dec. 17, 1833
Wilie Umstead and Mary P. Campbell, (MD) Oct. 3, 1833
Steve Johnston and Gabriel S. Tyler, (MD) Mar. 18, 1833

Jesse Mydyett and Adaline T. Mitchell, (MD) Oct. 24, 1833
Benjamin Roach and Polly T. Bradberry, (MD) Sep. 11, 1833
H. L. M. Barton and Martha Fletcher, (MD) Sep. 7, 1833
John B. Hays and Judia Bates, (MD) May 11, 1833
John B. Stuart and Elizabeth Watson, (MD) Dec. 28, 1833
Wm. B. Moore and Nancy Fowler, (MD) Sep. 16, 1833
Wm. C. McClour and Aly Jones, (MD) Mar. 7, 1833
Jno. L. Flippin and Elizabeth Shane, (MD) Feb. 14, 1833
Allen L. Woods and Elizabeth Parker, (MD) May 24, 1833
Wm. H. Rains and Tempy Chronister, (MD) Jan. 18, 1833
Samuel S. Rust and Steve Johnston, (MD) Mar. 18, 1833
Milton T. Tarvin and Nancy Boyls, (MD) Dec. 9, 1833
Epperson W. Harper and Mary Mastisa, (MD) Aug. 31, 1833
Joshua Bell and Louisa Bledsoe, (MD) Oct. 19, 1833
Alexander Black and Narcissa Bell, (MD) Sep. 25, 1833
James Bodkins and Elizabeth Speres, (MD) Apr. 23, 1833
Thomas Bowers and Obediance Baley, (MD) Mar. 13, 1833
John Crockett and Mary Patterson, (MD) Oct. 15, 1833
Robert Edmonson and Mary Clark, (MD) Jan. 5, 1833
William Ervin and Narcissa Wilbourne, (MD) Dec. 16, 1833
Pleasant Fisher and Sarah Etheredge, (MD) Nov. 15, 1833
Thomas Gaskins and Delila Rains, (MD) Nov. 16, 1833
Edward Haley and Jans Hardister, (MD) Sep. 17, 1833
Henry Hardester and Jane Stone, (MD) Nov. 25, 1833
Edward Haley and Jans Hardister, (MD) Sep. 17, 1833
Henry Hardester and Jane Stone, (MD) Nov. 25, 1833
Jobe Hicks and Elizabeth McAlelly, (MD) Dec. 14, 1833
Pleasant Hill and Martha Reynolds, (MD) Jun. 1, 1833
Herrod Holt and Sarah Gilland, (MD) Dec. 28, 1833
Preston Holt and Honey Thetford, (MD) Aug. 23, 1833
Isham Johnson and Mary Ferguson, (MD) Feb. 6, 1833
Joseph Kelley and Lavina Thompson, (MD) Jun. 13, 1833
Alen King and Malinda Bratton, (MD) Mar. 4, 1833
Benjamin May and Delitha Becton, (MD) Oct. 28, 1833
Richard McAllelly and Nancy McKeown, (MD) Apr. 10, 1833
Middleton McCortney and Charity Flinter, (MD) Oct. 18, 1833
Nathan Parker and Huldy Durley, (MD) Jul. 18, 1833
Acy Rains and Rebecca McMahan, (MD) Jan. 15, 1833
Willoughby Self and Mary Self, (MD) Apr. 2, 1833
Harmon Simpson and Margarett Trayner, (MD) Jan. 8, 1833
Owen Smith and Louana Sphere, (MD) Sep. 7, 1833
Aaron Stanley and Mary Lacey, (MD) Sep. 11, 1833
Coburn Stone and Rachael Etheredge, (MD) Oct. 5, 1833

Thomas Trainer and Elizabeth Ward, (MD) Jan. 3, 1833
Joseph Williams and Ann Jordan, (MD) Mar. 22, 1833
Ruffin Yates and Nancy Crockett, (MD) Mar. 12, 1833
Charles Yearbory and Susannah Stellar, (MD) Apr. 15, 1833
Wm. P. S. Fielder and Elvira L. Roundtree, (MD) Nov. 18, 1834
Green Jacobs and Mary Ann H. Wallingsford, (MD) Oct. 21, 1834
Hugh S. Stone and Mary J. H. Rolls, (MD) Dec. 13, 1834
James G. Carter and Angeline J. L. Seat, (MD) Sep. 29, 1834
John W. Bratton and Eliza A. Hunt, (MD) Apr. 9, 1834
James A. W. Hess and Mary Ann Petis, (MD) Feb. 17, 1834
R. T. S. Avery and Virlinda C. Beazly, (MD) Jul. 22, 1834
William Elder and Sarah F. Ramsey, (MD) Jul. 23, 1834
Wm. G. Bledsoe and Jane G. Hall, (MD) Nov. 27, 1834
Daniel B. Crider and Lean G. Dibrill, (MD) Sep. 4, 1834
John D. Hannah and Elizabeth G. Fields, (MD) May 14, 1834
Thomas B. Blair and Sarah H. Medeoris, (MD) Nov. 15, 1834
Silas M. McKnight and Charlott H. Alsabrooks, (MD) Oct. 16, 1834
Johnson Isbell and Elizabeth H. Sloan, (MD) Dec. 24, 1834
Samuel McLary and Jane Isabella McKnight, (MD) Nov. 18, 1834
Wm. S. Dougherty and Matilda J. Fielding, (MD) May 17, 1834
John H. Elder and America J. Thomas, (MD) Aug. 30, 1834
Hugh M. Bigham and Bitha Lavina Northcutt, (MD) Jun. 14, 1834
James B. Blakemore and Martha T. Fly, (MD) Oct. 18, 1834
James T. Hains and Matilda W. Gant, (MD) Jul. 8, 1834
John B. Hubbard and Mary Fly, (MD) May 21, 1834
Robert B. Davidson and Mahaly Billingsly, (MD) Feb. 13, 1834
Alex C. Ridgway and Nancy Taner, (MD) Jun. 19, 1834
Boyd F. Bryant and Elizabeth Thetford, (MD) Feb. 8, 1834
Albert G. Love and Nancy Baldridge, (MD) Dec. 9, 1834
John H. Elder and Louisa Mirack, (MD) Apr. 2, 1834
Ransom H. Byrne and Mary Richardson, (MD) Jan. 30, 1834
Alexander H. Vaughn and Rutha Walker, (MD) Apr. 1, 1834
Wm. F. McKnight and Elizabeth Thetford, (MD) Feb. 8, 1834
Fair M. Little and Pripy Jackson, (MD) May 5, 1834
John W. Crockett and Mary Ward, (MD) Jul. 3, 1834
George W. Durley and Martha Carrahan, (MD) Nov. 22, 1834
Bryant Andrews and Dorcas Jackson, (MD) Feb. 4, 1834
Josiah Baker and Mary Forester, (MD) Dec. 2, 1834
Ephraim Burrow and Elizabeth Bobbett, (MD) Apr. 2, 1834
James Carroll and Mary Singleton, (MD) Jan. 25, 1834
Wm. Banister and Elizabeth Conell, (MD) Dec. 18, 1834
John Cummings and Rachell Kenady, (MD) Mar. 15, 1834
William Dowell and Malinda Lowry, (MD) Dec. 30, 1834

William Downey and Martha Colyer, (MD) Feb. 24, 1834
Henry Fletcher and Mary Wilkins, (MD) Jul. 17, 1834
Alex Foren and Sarah Stiller, (MD) Jul. 5, 1834
Watson Forest and Sarah Crafton, (MD) Nov. , 1834
Kinchin Freeman and Rutha Murchean, (MD) Jun. 11, 1834
Stephen Fuqua and Caroline Gentry, (MD) Feb. 4, 1834
Mark Gosey and Nancy Diggins, (MD) Dec. 28, 1834
Stanley Griffin and Polly Clements, (MD) Apr. 28, 1834
Stanley Griffin and Polly Clements, (MD) Apr. 28, 1834
Richard Heath and Elizabeth Cole, (MD) Dec. 20, 1834
John Huckabee and Susan Boyd, (MD) Mar. 3, 1834
Joshua Little and Jane Jackson, (MD) Sep. 15, 1834
Finas Lytaker and Elizabeth Stanley, (MD) Mar. 3, 1834
Micajah Mackleroy and Elvira Myrick, (MD) Oct. 7, 1834
Jackson Mathis and Mary Crockett, (MD) Oct. 15, 1834
Alexander McDougald and Elanor Wade, (MD) Aug. 8, 1834
Radford McFarland and Mahaly Lowry, (MD) Feb. 3, 1834
Elvira Myrick and Micajah Mackleroy, (MD) Oct. 7, 1834
Wesley Myrick and Dorcas Myrick, (MD) Oct. 7, 1834
Hearvy Nettles and Nancy Welch, (MD) Sep. 9, 1834
Robert Pope and Elizabeth Smith, (MD) May 16, 1834
Melvin Ross and Rebecca Smith, (MD) Aug. 23, 1834
Absolom Smith and Mahaly Conlee, (MD) Dec. 22, 1834
Barnett Smith and Mary Bell, (MD) Dec. 20, 1834
Thomas Spight and Catharine Evans, (MD) Jun. 5, 1834
Walter Thetford and Barbary Holt, (MD) Oct. 4, 1834
James Trosper and Rachael Glasscock, (MD) Jul. 12, 1834
Adam Trout and Francis Gilliland, (MD) Nov. 23, 1834
Gideon Tucker and Ann Bradberry, (MD) Jun. 11, 1834
Saunders Utley and Nancy Robertson, (MD) Jan. 14, 1834
Enoch Walker and Elizabeth Walker, (MD) Dec. 23, 1834
David Watson and Catharine Stiller, (MD) Jul. 5, 1834
Seth Williams and Mary Dunwoody, (MD) Feb. 15, 1834
Thomas Word and Rosonna Crider, (MD) Sep. 25, 1834
Edwind York and Caroline Spears, (MD) Dec. 5, 1834
Wm. Connell and Polly Sandford, (MD) Oct. 16, 1834
Jessee J. McCloud and Martha A. McMinn, (MD) Feb. 17, 1835
James Forester and Mary A. McKinney, (MD) Aug. 5, 1835
John Morgan and Susana A. Bysinger, (MD) Apr. 23, 1835
John D. Little and Ann E. Higgins, (MD) Aug. 15, 1835
Hugh D. Neilson and Amanda G. Gilchrist, (MD) Jun. 9, 1835
Banks M. Burrow and Rebecca G. Richardson, (MD) Oct. 3, 1835
Jeremiah Cherry and Sarah G. Bunting, (MD) Nov. 6, 1835

James B. Carnahan and Anna H. Newhouse, (MD) Dec. 22, 1835
William Hobbs and Sally H. Knight, (MD) Feb. 2, 1835
Nelson I. Hess and Rebecca J. Mays, (MD) Feb. 12, 1835
Humphrey Donaldson and Judith J. Davidson, (MD) Nov. 5, 1835
John D. Hannah and Julia L. Davidson, (MD) Mar. 15, 1835
John W. Moore and Martha M. Crafton, (MD) Aug. 25, 1835
Daniel McDougald and Susan N. Morton, (MD) Aug. 13, 1835
John D. Shaw and Rebecca W. Pettus, (MD) Sep. 9, 1835
John Steuart and Elizabeth W. Taliaferro, (MD) Jun. 16, 1835
John B. McLary and Nancy Lattie, (MD) Jul. 29, 1835
Sterling B. Hogg and Mira Jourden, (MD) Dec. 21, 1835
Sterling B. Haley and Martha Fowler, (MD) Jan. 15, 1835
John B. Crafton and Mary Bowers, (MD) Aug. 25, 1835
John B. Hogg and Sarah Stewart, (MD) Jun. 15, 1835
John D. Scott and Zella Mainor, (MD) Sep. 20, 1835
John D. Robbins and Sarah Dial, (MD) Jun. 24, 1835
Wm. B. Howard and Sarah Nobles, (MD) Jan. 10, 1835
Joseph E. Matthews and Nancy Aiken, (MD) Nov. 16, 1835
P. E. Holmes and Caroline Howard, (MD) May 27, 1835
Wm. D. Chamberling and Nancy McCaslin, (MD) May 15, 1835
Charles H. Ross and Mary Yates, (MD) Feb. 28, 1835
Wm. H. Bridges and Sarah Beckham, (MD) Dec. 12, 1835
Benjamin M. Adair and Nancy Boyles, (MD) Dec. 9, 1835
Luke M. Edwards and Kisiah Sellars, (MD) Jun. 29, 1835
Samuel P. Rust and Nancy Clemons, (MD) Jan. 26, 1835
Gabriel S. Tyler and Nancy Rooker, (MD) Nov. 12, 1835
Wm. S. Runaldo and Anna Beaver, (MD) May 2, 1835
George W. Mitchell and Sarah Lynch, (MD) Aug. 4, 1835
George W. Bledsoe and Elizabeth Flowers, (MD) Sep. 29, 1835
John W. Flowers and Sobina Yates, (MD) Oct. 29, 1835
Benjamin W. Murphy and Clarissa Young, (MD) Dec. 16, 1835
Nathan Barron and Elizabeth Sherron, (MD) Dec. 17, 1835
Andrew Blair and Nancy Sellars, (MD) Oct. 8, 1835
Steel Bodkin and Nancy Meurhead, (MD) Sep. 16, 1835
Nathan Carry and Ann Carry, (MD) Nov. 26, 1835
Francis Edney and Nancy Bowling, (MD) Apr. 23, 1835
Thomas Edwards and Mary Robertson, (MD) Nov. 26, 1835
Richard Ellington and Ruthy Watson, (MD) Dec. 19, 1835
Phebe Fite and Lewis Levy, (MD) Jul. 15, 1835
Thomas Fletcher and Elizabeth Miller, (MD) Nov. 17, 1835
Thomas Fletcher and Lucratis Whitley, (MD) Mar. 19, 1835
Hillorry Flowers and Nancy Thetford, (MD) Apr. 4, 1835
Samuel Glidwell and Nancy Dill, (MD) Feb. 6, 1835

Jerome Griffin and Caroline Thomas, (MD) Aug. 22, 1835
John Heathcock and Harriet Donel, (MD) Jan. 14, 1835
William Hendrick and Rachael Coope, (MD) Nov. 7, 1835
Edward Jeffreys and Penelope Simmons, (MD) Apr. 8, 1835
Henry Kenneday and Susannah Mainor, (MD) Aug. 12, 1835
Lewis Levy and Phebe Fite, (MD) Jul. 15, 1835
Samuel Malone and Elizabeth Philips, (MD) Dec. 12, 1835
William Maxley and Sarah Watson, (MD) Jul. 13, 1835
Green McCaslin and Mary Holmes, (MD) Nov. 6, 1835
Unica McGehee and Archells Thompson, (MD) Aug. 6, 1835
Jeremiah McWhorter and Martha Boon, (MD) Oct. 1, 1835
Cincematus Roach and Lethia Bruff, (MD) Aug. 25, 1835
Thos. Ross and Rachael Smith, (MD) Sep. 12, 1835
Archells Thompson and Unica McGehee, (MD) Aug. 6, 1835
Owen Tombs and Lucenda Glasscock, (MD) Feb. 28, 1835
Jesse Turner and Elizabeth Alford, (MD) Jun. 15, 1835
Wilban Webb and Nancy Crockett, (MD) Jun. 11, 1835
James Welch and Francis Fields, (MD) Sep. 29, 1835
Reuben Whichard and Lucrecca Nobls, (MD) Dec. 13, 1835
Jeremiah Wright and Francis Jeffers, (MD) Oct. 2, 1835
Ben Littlefield and Miss B. M. McGarrity, (MD) Jun. 11, 1836
James J. Bradberry and Miss M. A. E. Mitchell, (MD) Jul. 2, 1836
Thomas W. Goff and Julia A. Fields, (MD) Jan. 30, 1836
John Smith and Mary A. Martin, (MD) Dec. 1, 1836
Jno. Baysinger and Mary Ann Morgan, (MD) Nov. 10, 1836
William Counts and Elizabeth Ann Davidson, (MD) Jul. 12, 1836
William Mathis and Martha Ann Harber, (MD) Sep. 16, 1836
Thomas Smith and Mary Ann Ross, (MD) Mar. 2, 1836
Henry Gately and Martha B. Wallingsford, (MD) Mar. 7, 1836
Phillips Holcomb and Sarah B. Harlean, (MD) Oct. 27, 1836
F. E. Becton and Elizabeth E. Mosely, (MD) Sep. 26, 1836
Samuel B. Mixon and Nancy F. Allison, (MD) May 12, 1836
Crawford Prewitt and Margrat G. Griffin, (MD) Oct. 25, 1836
John R. King and Sarah H. Gibson, (MD) Jun. 22, 1836
Aaron Word and Precilla H. Freeman, (MD) Apr. 15, 1836
Thomas H. McAvery and Violet L. Carr, (MD) Sep. 11, 1836
Joseph J. Etheridge and Louisiana L. Jones, (MD) Apr. 21, 1836
James T. Hunt and Mary L. McClary, (MD) Jul. 8, 1836
Robert F. Finley and Dillia P. Woodson, (MD) Dec. 15, 1836
David Todd and Amey P. Mayfield, (MD) Aug. 19, 1836
John Robertson and Mary R. Mayfield, (MD) Feb. 5, 1836
Daniel M. Wallice and Sarah S. White, (MD) Jun. 18, 1836
Henry Flowers and Mary T. Halliburton, (MD) Sep. 20, 1836

John W. Webb and Martha W. Ragan, (MD) Dec. 21, 1836
F. L. W McEwen and Nancy Harley, (MD) Dec. 1, 1836
Abner C. Roach and Hester Crockett, (MD) Jan. 7, 1836
Hugh D. Neilson and Narcissa Gailard, (MD) Jan. 30, 1836
Wm. D. McDermet and Polly Lane, (MD) Sep. 5, 1836
Henry H. Hunter and Susan Walker, (MD) Dec. 26, 1836
Richard H. Berge and Louisa Kevit, (MD) Jul. 26, 1836
Ezra I. Arnold and Mary Hignight, (MD) Feb. 29, 1836
Asberry M. Webb and Catherine Jones, (MD) Jul. 28, 1836
Harvey M. Latta and Sarah Barnes, (MD) Jan. 19, 1836
John M. Saunders and Nancy Handcock, (MD) May 26, 1836
Wm. J. Spencer and Abigal Davis, (MD) Oct. 15, 1836
Harrod P. Welch and Elizabeth Thompson, (MD) Sep. 29, 1836
Thomas R. Harrisson and Francs Sloan, (MD) Jan. 5, 1836
Thomas S. Stone and Martha Laughter, (MD) Jun. 16, 1836
Abraham S. Dial and Malissa Waldrip, (MD) Jan. 18, 1836
James T. Hains and Polly Babb, (MD) Oct. 13, 1836
Charles W. Williams and Clarissa Young, (MD) Dec. 16, 1836
Wm. T. Blakemore and Sarah Glasscock, (MD) Nov. 22, 1836
James Arnold and Mary Thedford, (MD) Apr. 6, 1836
Benjamin Bean and Eliza Bass, (MD) Nov. 21, 1836
Thos. Bell and Elizabeth Goodman, (MD) Dec. 17, 1836
Martin Briant and Dicy Smith, (MD) Jan. 28, 1836
Thompson Bruff and Sarah Smith, (MD) Mar. 12, 1836
James Carter and Jane Hart, (MD) Jul. 6, 1836
Noah Curtis and Mary Bran, (MD) Sep. 28, 1836
Eli Dickason and Margaret Basinger, (MD) Feb. 4, 1836
John Dill and Eda Smith, (MD) Jul. 5, 1836
Wesley Ely and Elizabeth Anderson, (MD) Nov. 1, 1836
Briant Flowers and Susan Strauther, (MD) Aug. 4, 1836
Jacob Flowers and Margaret Thedford, (MD) May 21, 1836
William Foren and Arreana Griffin, (MD) May 9, 1836
Richard Freeman and Margaret Nevils, (MD) May 6, 1836
Arthur Fuller and Levina Moore, (MD) Dec. 5, 1836
Leathen Fuller and Thos McKneely, (MD) Nov. 21, 1836
William Gentry and Lavina Scallion, (MD) Jan. 9, 1836
Rigdon Grady and Nancy Gleason, (MD) Aug. 1, 1836
Johnathan Henry and July Strother, (MD) Apr. 15, 1836
Solomon Hines and Malinda White, (MD) Jul. 23, 1836
Dickson Jackson and Tibatha Rasberry, (MD) Nov. 5, 1836
John Laymon and Elizabeth Stuart, (MD) Nov. 24, 1836
David Little and Sarah McGarett, (MD) Jan. 28, 1836
James McDummet and Charity Webb, (MD) Mar. 16, 1836

Thos. McKneely and Leathen Fuller, (MD) Nov. 21, 1836
James Montgomery and Mahaly McKezick, (MD) Dec. 17, 1836
William Nedry and Nancy Boyt, (MD) Aug. 23, 1836
Joseph Pate and Nancy Glasscock, (MD) Jun. 22, 1836
Burrell Patterson and Pricilla Boun, (MD) Jul. 9, 1836
John Phaling and Izabellar Alexander, (MD) Sep. 20, 1836
Washington Scallion and Margarett Toten, (MD) Oct. 12, 1836
Stephen Snowden and Nancy Fletcher, (MD) Jan. 25, 1836
Elijah Spencer and Hannah Jackson, (MD) Feb. 27, 1836
Thomas Staton and Lavina Spellings, (MD) Jan. 21, 1836
Jerry Traynor and Harriet Forran, (MD) Apr. 23, 1836
Henry Welch and Caroline Smith, (MD) Feb. 15, 1836
Isack Word and Rachael Freeman, (MD) Dec. 5, 1836
Macca Write and Martha Bone, (MD) Jul. 23, 1836
S. Shaw and Miss M. A. Clay, (MD) Apr. 28, 1837
John J. McKnight and Miss H. H. Hopkins, (MD) Feb. 22, 1837
John Ashlin and Margaret L. B. McDowell, (MD) Jul. 25, 1837
Jas. M. Lassiter and Eliza A. H. Burton, (MD) Oct. 30, 1837
John Campbell and Aley A. H. Welch, (MD) Aug. 24, 1837
Allen Griffin and Miss E. J. Care, (MD) Oct. 31, 1837
Wm. B. Convill and Lucy A. . Baber, (MD) Nov. 2, 1837
John A. Haley and Tabitha A. Legat, (MD) Oct. 10, 1837
John B. Wallingford and Eliza A. Harpoll, (MD) Oct. 7, 1837
Robert H. Goodlow and Mary A. Hail, (MD) Dec. 23, 1837
James H. McDowell and Frances A. White, (MD) May 29, 1837
Zachariah Biggs and Martha A. Penney, (MD) Nov. 23, 1837
O Conlee and Juley A. Richardson, (MD) May 29, 1837
Nathanial Dickson and Martha A. Kirksey, (MD) Aug. 24, 1837
William Jackson and Polly A. Lacy, (MD) Jan. 6, 1837
Obed Nicholasson and Elizabeth A. Donaldson, (MD) Jan. 26, 1837
Bryant Ringgold and Mary A. Nobles, (MD) Dec. 28, 1837
Austin A. King and Martha Ann Bledsoe, (MD) Jul. 31, 1837
Bird B. Stone and Martha Ann Hickman, (MD) Oct. 6, 1837
James H. Dyson and Martha Ann Bean, (MD) Feb. 15, 1837
Scarlet M. Glasscock and Martha Ann Walker, (MD) Aug. 22, 1837
James Hays and Mary Ann Finey, (MD) Apr. 13, 1837
Wm. W. Gooden and Rebecca C. Humphris, (MD) Mar. 8, 1837
Winiford Fly and Minor C. Cole, (MD) Sep. 15, 1837
Benjamin H. Hubbard and Ann D. Moore, (MD) Jul. 22, 1837
John W. James and Lucenda D. McWherter, (MD) Dec. 6, 1837
Simpson Shaw and Elizabeth D. Jones, (MD) May 30, 1837
Wm. B. Moore and Susana E. Mathis, (MD) Jul. 26, 1837
John D. Cabler and Nancy E. McKnight, (MD) Feb. 6, 1837

Thomas M. Watson and Martha E. Thomas, (MD) Dec. 14, 1837
Wm. Bowman and Eliza G. Crisp, (MD) Dec. 21, 1837
John A. Taliaferro and Elizabeth H. Reed, (MD) Mar. 13, 1837
Hudson W. Moss and Cary H. Massee, (MD) Jun. 22, 1837
Jas. W. Glasgow and Mary Jane Fisher, (MD) Oct. 25, 1837
Henry Shearer and Pennlope June Berry, (MD) Jan. 16, 1837
John H. Herod and F K. Peary, (MD) Feb. 22, 1837
John A. Haley and Evelina L. Clay, (MD) Oct. 9, 1837
Richard J. Smith and Ellendor L. Thomas, (MD) Feb. 21, 1837
Charlete Jones and Thos L. Boswell, (MD) Oct. 6, 1837
John D. Whitson and Ann M. Hawkins, (MD) Jul. 17, 1837
John Stewart and Roseana M. Bates, (MD) Aug. 23, 1837
John Kimbro and Sarah P. Bellew, (MD) Aug. 12, 1837
Milton H. Johnson and Hudson W. Moss, (MD) Jun. 22, 1837
Mathew A. Glass and Nancy Arnold, (MD) Jul. 29, 1837
Thos. B. Murphrey and Margaret Edwards, (MD) May 26, 1837
Thomas B. Lourence and Sarah Farris, (MD) Jan. 5, 1837
Moses B. Hawkins and Mahaly Allen, (MD) Jan. 2, 1837
James C. Williams and Susan Ellen, (MD) Dec. 6, 1837
Samuel C. Leggatte and Elizabeth Serratt, (MD) Jun. 17, 1837
Abner D. Thomas and Julia Donaldson, (MD) Oct. 30, 1837
John D. Davidson and Martha Pound, (MD) Feb. 6, 1837
Wm. C. Jack and Winiford Fly, (MD) Sep. 15, 1837
Wm. C. Page and Elizabeth McMahon, (MD) Jan. 6, 1837
Stephen J. Roach and Centha Vickers, (MD) Aug. 24, 1837
Robert J. Gilchrist and Leer Smith, (MD) Sep. 14, 1837
F. K. Peary and Charlete Jones, (MD) Oct. 6, 1837
Josiah L. Thedford and Nancy Barton, (MD) Oct. 18, 1837
James M. Brewer and Mary McClure, (MD) Jun. 5, 1837
James M. Walker and Liddy Gilliland, (MD) Aug. 9, 1837
John M. White and Ruth Jones, (MD) Jun. 24, 1837
James M. Woods and Mahetable Ballintine, (MD) Jan. 9, 1837
James M. Balleu and Carroline Bryant, (MD) Nov. 6, 1837
Julius M. Hall and Margarett Tyson, (MD) Dec. 5, 1837
James P. Reed and Elizabeth Vaughn, (MD) Jul. 12, 1837
Luke P. Seay and Jane Cross, (MD) Sep. 7, 1837
James W. Carten and Jane Harts, (MD) Jul. 6, 1837
Gideon W. Mainard and Dovey Smith, (MD) Aug. 21, 1837
John W. Pope and Haskey Dennis, (MD) Apr. 30, 1837
Daniel W. Word and Lucinda Hawkins, (MD) May 16, 1837
Joseph Y. Diskill and Elizabeth Williamson, (MD) Sep. 28, 1837
Joseph Bellue and Mary McCleur, (MD) May 29, 1837
Samuel Blackley and Mulinda Treumen, (MD) Jan. 28, 1837

Major Bledsoe and Centha Shaw, (MD) Dec. 22, 1837
Zachariah Bowen and Hanah Holaway, (MD) Sep. 21, 1837
Mark Bullington and Nancy Browning, (MD) Sep. 26, 1837
Thos. Canady and Elizabeth Canadey, (MD) Apr. 6, 1837
Julus Clarke and Jane Calhoun, (MD) Dec. 30, 1837
John Connell and Mary Bates, (MD) May 29, 1837
Freeman Cross and Nancy Patterson, (MD) Jun. 19, 1837
James Cunningham and Catharine Robertson, (MD) Nov. 29, 1837
Elisha Easterwood and Nancy Sellers, (MD) Dec. 27, 1837
Edward Fox and Mary Morris, (MD) May 2, 1837
James Gibson and Elizabeth Battle, (MD) Nov. 22, 1837
Lucy Hall and Abron Kenaday, (MD) Aug. 28, 1837
Christopher Hite and Mary Care, (MD) Feb. 21, 1837
Carroll Holt and Mary Connell, (MD) May 13, 1837
Robert Jackson and Catherine Tincle, (MD) Jan. 14, 1837
John Keith and Polly Robertson, (MD) Nov. 11, 1837
Abron Kenaday and Lucy Hall, (MD) Aug. 28, 1837
Andrew Littlefield and Elizabeth Bellew, (MD) Aug. 17, 1837
Berry Patterson and Lucenda Gibson, (MD) Jun. 13, 1837
Andrew Porter and Polly Howell, (MD) Jan. 2, 1837
Elijah Quick and Sarah Moss, (MD) Jun. 17, 1837
James Runolds and Nancy Jenkins, (MD) Nov. 2, 1837
Everett Smith and Margrett Newell, (MD) Sep. 17, 1837
Wm. Thedford and Polly Williams, (MD) Oct. 13, 1837
Mulinda Treumen and Samuel Blackley, (MD) Jan. 28, 1837
Isah Webb and Mary Moore, (MD) Jun. 21, 1837
John P. Steller and Miss L. B. Williams, (MD) Sep. 13, 1838
John C. Bates and Nancy A. Burkhart, (MD) Aug. 1, 1838
David L. Haley and Sarah A. Bryant, (MD) Feb. 3, 1838
H. T. Burnam and Elizabeth A. Horskins, (MD) Aug. 20, 1838
John J. Fielder and Caron Ann Turpin, (MD) Sep. 1, 1838
William Dozer and Edney Ann Simmons, (MD) Jul. 3, 1838
Eli Howard and Centha Ann Melton, (MD) Dec. 14, 1838
Henry Lowary and Julia Ann Dowell, (MD) Mar. 5, 1838
Franklin Wood and Mary Ann McKee, (MD) Oct. 10, 1838
Minor C. Cole and Mary C. Page, (MD) Apr. 21, 1838
Nicholas W. Cabler and Tibetha C. Harper, (MD) Aug. 22, 1838
Joseph D. Rentfro and Jamima E. Durley, (MD) Nov. 14, 1838
Peter S. Reeves and Meriah E. Landin, (MD) May 5, 1838
Pressilla Harper and F E. Becton, (MD) Feb. 17, 1838
Henson Howard and Eliza E. Walker, (MD) Jul. 30, 1838
H. B. Hoover and Eliza H. Rigsby, (MD) May 26, 1838
Preston Holland and Sarah H. Cole, (MD) Oct. 1, 1838

Wm. A. Bridgemon and J. J. Fielder, (MD) Sep. 1, 1838
Wm. M. Irwin and Rebecca J. Alsabrooks, (MD) Dec. 18, 1838
Purcell C. Vaughn and Eliza J. Montgomery, (MD) Nov. 28, 1838
Smith H. Gee and Louisa J. Akins, (MD) Nov. 29, 1838
Samuel Hodge and Margaret J. Allison, (MD) Dec. 18, 1838
Merris Horn and Thos. J. Baysinger, (MD) Sep. 8, 1838
John S. Mayfield and Rachal L. Thomas, (MD) Jul. 24, 1838
Woodson Rountree and Rosannah L. Biard, (MD) Jun. 18, 1838
Mulindy Cole and Julius M. Hall, (MD) Mar. 28, 1838
Roenna McCalvy and Thos M. Witherspoon, (MD) Jan. 23, 1838
John D. Davidson and Lucy R. Smith, (MD) Jun. 18, 1838
John Keath and Hannah R. Hollan, (MD) Jan. 29, 1838
John D. Stone and A. S. Davidson, (MD) May 5, 1838
David D. Blair and Willie S. Harvy, (MD) Oct. 1, 1838
Henry Head and Elizabeth S. Beazley, (MD) Jan. 13, 1838
Benjamin Boon and Unicy T. Hunt, (MD) May 16, 1838
Abner C. Beacham and Nicholas W. Cabler, (MD) Aug. 22, 1838
John F. Rogers and Sophia W. Woods, (MD) Jan. 15, 1838
James A. McKnight and Everlina Rony, (MD) Sep. 12, 1838
Richard B. Hutcherson and Mary Hendricks, (MD) Dec. 24, 1838
Nicholas C. Stone and Catharine Smith, (MD) Jul. 3, 1838
Wm. A. Fonville and Juliana Craige, (MD) Dec. 24, 1838
Jesse D. Partee and Sarah Lite, (MD) Oct. 30, 1838
Hugh D. Hays and Sarah Atkenson, (MD) Jul. 6, 1838
Wm. C. Northcutt and Elizabeth McMahon, (MD) Jan. 6, 1838
Walter E. Daniel and Margrett Odle, (MD) May 21, 1838
Meriah E. Landin and Louisa Genest, (MD) Feb. 20, 1838
Wm. C. Webb and Martha Chafero, (MD) Feb. 22, 1838
David F. Matthews and Charinda Crews, (MD) Aug. 17, 1838
E. H. Crocker and Martha Glascock, (MD) Nov. 12, 1838
James H. Martin and Centhy Bledsoe, (MD) Apr. 1, 1838
John H. Reed and Preston Holland, (MD) Oct. 1, 1838
Hiram H. Banks and Emely Webb, (MD) Dec. 7, 1838
Wm. D. Bethell and Pressilla Harper, (MD) Feb. 17, 1838
Wm. D. Fly and Henson Howard, (MD) Jul. 30, 1838
Samuel J. Crider and Dorraty Bobbitt, (MD) Aug. 30, 1838
David L. Haley and Susan Bobbett, (MD) Sep. 15, 1838
Benjamin L. Rodgers and Polly Adair, (MD) Aug. 8, 1838
Frances M. Crocker and Nancy Smith, (MD) Jan. 1, 1838
George M. Fisher and Jane Trosper, (MD) Sep. 15, 1838
Jas. M. Halford and Mulindy Cole, (MD) Mar. 28, 1838
Jno. M. Northern and Rutha Canaday, (MD) Jul. 3, 1838
J. M. White and Roenna McCalvy, (MD) Jan. 23, 1838

Wm. J. Ferguson and Merris Horn, (MD) Sep. 8, 1838
Alexander R. McFall and Mary Billingsley, (MD) Jan. 18, 1838
Mack R. Cook and Martha Howell, (MD) Jun. 20, 1838
Wm. P. Wilson and Sibly Johnston, (MD) Feb. 17, 1838
Wm. R. Sawyers and America Barnes, (MD) Aug. , 1838
Wm. S. Williams and Mary Miller, (MD) Jun. 19, 1838
John W. Davidson and Frances Montgomery, (MD) Oct. 18, 1838
Garland Adams and Elizabeth Cook, (MD) Aug. 11, 1838
Isaack Alexander and Sarah Word, (MD) Sep. 11, 1838
Merradett Alvin and Mary Bradford, (MD) Oct. 1, 1838
Arther Barns and Frances Shern, (MD) Dec. 18, 1838
Aaron Branch and Catherine Harrison, (MD) Dec. 5, 1838
Simeon Butram and Elizabeth Fletcher, (MD) Feb. 5, 1838
Jesse Carray and Elizabeth Keathly, (MD) Apr. 16, 1838
John Crews and Sarrah Edmundston, (MD) Aug. 14, 1838
Humphrey Curtis and Elizabeth Grice, (MD) Dec. 26, 1838
Peletha Curtis and Marcus Holeman, (MD) Mar. 30, 1838
Joshua Donaldson and Emela Jackson, (MD) Dec. 19, 1838
James Doxey and Ellenander Etherage, (MD) Jan. 11, 1838
Nany Dozer and Wiley Taylor, (MD) Jul. 7, 1838
Jackson Dunning and Nancy Williams, (MD) Jan. 11, 1838
John Edmundson and Mulindy Trosper, (MD) Aug. 25, 1838
John Flowers and Parzada Borrin, (MD) May 24, 1838
Jackson Fox and Dilly Morris, (MD) Oct. 27, 1838
William Gibson and Sarah Edmundson, (MD) Oct. 20, 1838
Thomas Hamack and Margratt Warren, (MD) Apr. 26, 1838
Numan Haynes and Susanah Jones, (MD) Oct. 10, 1838
Marcus Holeman and Peletha Curtis, (MD) Mar. 30, 1838
Edmund Holland and Hawkins Hall, (MD) Sep. 17, 1838
Samuel Houghs and Nancy Gleason, (MD) Aug. 19, 1838
Eli Jackson and Margarett James, (MD) Feb. 22, 1838
Willis Joslin and Mary Dorset, (MD) Nov. 8, 1838
Henry Long and Martha Pate, (MD) Sep. 8, 1838
Duncan Massey and Mary Olsabrooks, (MD) May 12, 1838
James McClary and Emley James, (MD) Feb. 3, 1838
William McFarland and Lucinda Jacobs, (MD) Sep. 18, 1838
William Murphy and Rebecca Adams, (MD) May 9, 1838
Henry Patison and Lavina Oneal, (MD) Feb. 24, 1838
Solomon Pinion and Anny Brunson, (MD) Jul. 21, 1838
William Price and Maria Hess, (MD) Dec. 31, 1838
Wm. Pritchett and Lucinda Traynor, (MD) Jun. 7, 1838
Bennet Ragan and Susan Yancy, (MD) Apr. 17, 1838
Nathan Ray and Emaline Bledsoe, (MD) Feb. 6, 1838

Wm. Reason and Levina Tatom, (MD) Jul. 7, 1838
Richard Robertson and Sarah Griffin, (MD) Nov. 24, 1838
John Ronalds and Patsey Smith, (MD) Mar. 17, 1838
William Sain and Frances Lathain, (MD) Jul. 10, 1838
James Scott and Mary Landers, (MD) Jun. 14, 1838
James Sexton and Tennessee Mathews, (MD) Sep. 4, 1838
Aaron Sherron and Elizabeth Hailey, (MD) Dec. 3, 1838
Arther Smith and Martha Warrin, (MD) May 7, 1838
Wm. Smith and Elizaeth Gilliland, (MD) May 8, 1838
Wiley Taylor and Nany Dozer, (MD) Jul. 7, 1838
Ephram Thompson and Elizabeth Brown, (MD) Dec. 4, 1838
Jeremiah Webb and Peggy Stafford, (MD) Oct. 31, 1838
Wm. T. Huckby and Rebecca A. Page, (MD) Jul. 22, 1839
Samuel Aslin and Mary A. Barham, (MD) Dec. 19, 1839
Orvill Conlee and July A. Richardson, (MD) May 29, 1839
Green Williams and Nancy A. Philips, (MD) Jan. 1, 1839
S. C. Harpoll and Martha Ann Williams, (MD) Oct. 16, 1839
A. S. Davidson and Mary Ann Nuckles, (MD) Dec. 14, 1839
Jackson Brown and Lyda Ann Bunnell, (MD) May 20, 1839
William Harron and Sarah C. Hubbard, (MD) Jul. 24, 1839
William Warran and Elizabeth C. Keathley, (MD) May 11, 1839
Benjamin F. Spellings and Hulda E. Mayfield, (MD) Jan. 12, 1839
Robert W. Barton and Harratt E. Davidson, (MD) Dec. 5, 1839
Edmond W. Goodrich and Susan E. Harcey, (MD) Sep. 3, 1839
Jessee Flowers and Dibby E. Robertson, (MD) Nov. 19, 1839
George Himbrough and Rebecka E. Crockett, (MD) Feb. 25, 1839
Needham Holland and Ann E. Donaldson, (MD) Dec. 7, 1839
Michal McNutty and Angaline E. Davis, (MD) Dec. 23, 1839
Mira Jordan and Albert G. Love, (MD) Jun. 24, 1839
Walter M. Thedford and Martha H. Morton, (MD) Oct. 28, 1839
Hugh Y. Bone and Martha Jane Robb, (MD) Apr. 25, 1839
Gilbert Boon and Nancy L. Hatchett, (MD) Mar. 29, 1839
George P. Muyrhead and Hannah M. Britenham, (MD) Jul. 30, 1839
Caleb Howell and Ann M. Hobbs, (MD) Jun. 24, 1839
Allen Reed and Frances M. Crider, (MD) Aug. 8, 1839
Robert R. Sloan and Nancy R. Robertson, (MD) Jan. 29, 1839
Andrew A. Patterson and Cintha W. Bridges, (MD) Jan. 23, 1839
John B. Lowry and Catharine Rucker, (MD) May 30, 1839
Moses B. Wallingsford and Elizabeth Haguewood, (MD) Jul. 23, 1839
Jonathan B. Dryden and Berlinda Turner, (MD) Mar. 28, 1839
Philip B. Carter and America Hayns, (MD) Dec. 27, 1839
John C. Porter and Sarah Ing, (MD) Sep. 15, 1839
Alex C. Ridgway and Elizabeth Serratt, (MD) Jun. 17, 1839

Wilson D. Hunt and Sarah Carroll, (MD) Jun. 10, 1839
Jacob F. Penn and Emeline Merritt, (MD) Sep. 18, 1839
John G. Warren and Mira Jordan, (MD) Jun. 24, 1839
Wm. D. Scott and Rebecca Richardson, (MD) Sep. 26, 1839
Cary H. Massee and Patience White, (MD) Aug. 11, 1839
Thomas J. Hines and Martha Morphus, (MD) Jan. 23, 1839
Wm. H. Clemmont and Fanny Carter, (MD) Jan. 23, 1839
Wm. H. Ivy and Elizabeth Bledsoe, (MD) Aug. 20, 1839
Parson M. Sherman and Emeline Wilkins, (MD) Aug. 2, 1839
Jerramiah P. Woodard and Delila Short, (MD) Jan. 7, 1839
Wm. L. Goodman and Polly Adair, (MD) Aug. 8, 1839
T R. Turner and Nancy Borran, (MD) Nov. 30, 1839
James R. Witherspoon and Sarah Fields, (MD) Mar. 29, 1839
John W. Avery and Margaret Hicks, (MD) Jan. 8, 1839
George W. Crockett and Elizabeth Wilks, (MD) Apr. 15, 1839
E. W. Hale and Martha Jordian, (MD) Oct. 23, 1839
E. W. Hale and Martha Jordian, (MD) Oct. 23, 1839
George W. Terrill and Ann Bell, (MD) Sep. 5, 1839
Ezechal Armstrong and Margarett Armfield, (MD) Apr. 19, 1839
Wm. Bailey and Hollan Patrick, (MD) Jun. 3, 1839
Franklin Barrott and Sarah Massee, (MD) Oct. 3, 1839
Harvy Belew and Rachal Holcomb, (MD) Aug. 14, 1839
Madison Conlee and Sarah Rigsly, (MD) Dec. 9, 1839
Samuel Craige and Carroline Alvis, (MD) Feb. 16, 1839
Henry Duffy and Margaret Latty, (MD) Oct. 22, 1839
Robert Edmundson and Nancy Edmundson, (MD) Jan. 11, 1839
Charles Forrester and Kizza Sellers, (MD) Oct. 23, 1839
Hardy Fowler and Sarah Dockings, (MD) Mar. 15, 1839
Alvadas Hill and Mary Bowlen, (MD) Aug. 13, 1839
Rachal Holcomb and Harvy Belew, (MD) Aug. 14, 1839
Isah Holland and Eliza Flowers, (MD) Aug. 27, 1839
Elleson Howard and Jane Hawkins, (MD) Dec. 25, 1839
Tucker Hutchens and Sarah Stan, (MD) Dec. 12, 1839
Thos. Johnston and Martha Pope, (MD) Apr. 9, 1839
Wm. Jones and Manurva Roberts, (MD) Aug. 13, 1839
John Knox and Ellen Bell, (MD) Dec. 4, 1839
John McLeod and Ann McDougold, (MD) Aug. 20, 1839
Samuel O'Neal and Mary Greggory, (MD) Nov. 4, 1839
William Patterson and Mary Sexton, (MD) Mar. 13, 1839
Rubin Price and Susan Volentine, (MD) Apr. 15, 1839
John Rackley and Elizabeth Guess, (MD) Jan. 3, 1839
Milton Ray and Pheby Furgarson, (MD) Jun. 26, 1839
John Richardson and Sarah Mathews, (MD) Nov. 21, 1839

Peter Sexton and Martha Woods, (MD) Sep. 12, 1839
Joseph Sharp and Jurasha Taylor, (MD) Mar. 6, 1839
John Smith and Sarah Bartlett, (MD) Mar. 20, 1839
Alfred Stewart and Joan Goff, (MD) Oct. 7, 1839
James Thompson and Letha Campbell, (MD) Mar. 22, 1839
Eli Tilghman and Nancy Crain, (MD) Jul. 20, 1839
Robert Warrin and Sina Keathley, (MD) Sep. 11, 1839
John Wolard and Peney Pope, (MD) Oct. 30, 1839
Ruffin Yates and Harriett Word, (MD) Feb. 27, 1839

Roane County, TN, Members of the Grand Jury, December, 1804.

Jared Hotchkiss, foreman; John Hicky, Jesse Blackwell, Hugh Johnston, Joseph Looney, Cumberland Rector, James Hallaher, William Lampkin, Robert Burk, George Moore, Bazzell Davis, John Hellman, Henry Miller, Benjamin Grayson.

Cave Spring Cumberland Presbyterian Church, Cave Spring, Overton County, Tennessee

October 22, 1836, p. 2

Jobe Carlock, Abraham Hayter, John M'Donnald, Susannah L. M. Lansdon (d. Feb. 4, 1841), Judeth Lansden, Elizabeth Car- lock, B. L. Carlock, Polly Hayter, Sarah Copeland, Andrew T. Hayter, Eliza Hayter (Carlock), Wm. T. Hayter, Robt. L. Fer- ril, Polly McDonnold, Thomas C. McDonnold, John J. Hayter, Thomas Hayter, Eleanor Ferril, Charlotte Ferril, Sally Hunt, Nelson F. Harward, Eliza Ann Harward, Alfred Tate, Margaret Hunt, Wm. McDonnold, Susannah McDonnold, Mary Ann Harward, Anna Hites, Alsey Jackson, Lucinda Elder, John Smith, Thos. K. McDonnold, Catharine Hayter, Catharine Smith, Tabitha Lee, Merril Ledbetter, Sarah McDonnold (Hayter), Polley Ledbetter (Quales), Lucinda M'Ky (sic)(Lemmins), Wm. M. Martin, Campbell Hayter, Nancy Martin, Robert Coleman, Donna Taylor, Mgaries (?) Johnston, Polly Stewart, Job Carlock, Jr., Evan Campbell, Quintin Elder, Samuel Tate, Dawson Jackson, Silas Lemans, Benjamin McDonnold, Sussannah Smith, Catherine Worley, Saomi Worley, Rebeckah Worley, Elizabeth J. Carlock, Florah M'Millan, Mary Martin, Margaret McMillon, Nancy C. Bates, Jane McMillon, James S. Lansdon, Fanney Ledbetter, Libuton D. Hayter, Harriet J. McDonnold, Carline Means, F. J. Robbins, Sarah McDonnold (woman of colour), James Johnson, Carline Martin (woman of colour), Margaret Ledbetter, B. H. Ledbetter, Nancy Ledbetter (Jones), Rollings H. Johnson.

Bradley County, Tennessee, Tax List, 1839, (Note: All persons were taxed 1 white pole. If the tax is different, it is indicated after the name in parentheses.)

District No. 1

Amos Atchley, Seth Atchley, John Atchley, Thomas Bets, James Bruton, Nathan Brimlet, Samuel Brooks, Hiram Branden, William Braden, John Brown, Thomas Barns, Benjamin Chester, Thomas Clark, John carter, Yowell Coffy, Kinsy Claborn, James Claborn, Jeremiah Dearin, John Davis, Thomas Davis, David Funderbulk, Araba Fitzjarell, Garrett Forester, James Gibson, Jeremiah Foster, David Gibson, James Gibson, Joseph Gibson, Jesse Grissam, James Grissam, Thomas Gearin, Isaac Gearin, Harmon Gady, James Grigsby, Malin Gilbreth, Andrus Hooper, William Howard, Dickson Hudson, John Hicks, Leroy Hicks, Anderson Hiden, James Haris, Steph. Harris, James Hill, Edward Jonston, Weldin Keling, William Keling, Edward Kinging, Joel Kirkpatric, Thomas Lain, Anderson Lane, Simeon Legg, Isaac Legg, Sion Level, Daniel Lewis, George Loson, John Lawson, James Lawson, Robert Mohon (1s), John McBride, William McBride, Singleton McKeel, William McMinn, Humphrey McCamish, James McRunnals, John McFearson, Washington Nichols, Bengeman O'Kelly, Francis D. O'Kelly, Bengeman O'Kelly (sic), Hesachiah H. Posey, William Poter, James Prechet, John Rogers, Sr. (6s), William W. Rogers, Henry Roach, Ephiam Ragan, George Real, Silas Suttel (1s), Joseph Stewart, John Seebolt, John S??dly, Frances Striply, Edward Sharp (2s 1wp), John Turner, Adam H. Tiner (1s 1wp), Dan?? D. Taylor, Ha?er Turner, Enoch Thomas, Isaac Taylor, James Taylor, Josiah Vernon, John Vernon, James Wilhight, William Wilhight, Caleb Wilhight, Michel Wilson, R. K. Walker, Wm. S. Wicker.

District No. 2

Thomas Akens, Loranzey Alexander, Bengeman Abbott, Hiram Bedwell, Elijah Bollanger, John Benton, James Brott, Jesse brown, Allan Blair, John Borden, Armrous Bradley, Richard Burch (?), William Barrow, William Brown, Isaac Brazelton, Elisha Borden, William T. Bradley, R. R. Barksdel, Robert Cates, John Carter, James Causey, Samuel Crage, John Collins, Jesse Collins, Isaac Day (s 1wp), Josiah Davenport, John Earnest, Thomas Elaeradge (4s), Thomas Fulton (2s 1wp), James R. Finley, Lewis Fous, John Ford, Robert Darmer, William F. Glaves, William Grant (2s 1wp), John W. Goodner, Sr., Thomas Gather, Harrison Gather, John W. Goodner (1s 1wp), Sr., Lahue Glenn, A. P. Grimmett, Jefferson Hoobs, Jefferson Hodges, Jackson Hodges, Reason Humbert, Wiatt Hambelton, R. C. Humphries, Nathaniel W. Hays, Sims Harris, Mikel Howel, John Jonston (1s 1wp), Z. P. Jones (1s 1wp), Bengeman Jimeson, Samuel K. King, Franses Kincannon, Samuel Lane, Curtis Lain, Thomas Lane, W. T. McCoy (2s 1wp), ???ea??ed McCrackin, Bengeman McCarty, William

McCarty, Thomas McCarty, Richard McFall, Richard G. McFall, John Mills, John Mount, John Morten, John McMinn, L. B. Miller, Samuel McSpadon, Joseph McSpaden (1s 1wp), Henry Norman, John Onley, George Orr, James Ogel, Jackson Parks, Bengeman Parkens, James M. Parker, Josiah Price, James C. Price, David Pridey, Samuel Parkes (3s), Sampson Prowel (2s), John Rains, William Roper, T. Andrew Rogers, John Robertson, Joel Scott, Alexander Russel, Andrew Stephens, George W. Sally, Lewis T. Templeton. Araham Slover, Jeptha Sivels, George Shelton, Ezekel Sprigs (5s 1wp), Stephen Scott (5s), Alpherd (sic) Taylor, William Vernon, Conaway Mount, Harden Woodey, Robet Woodet, William Wooden Robert Woodey, Sr. (1s), Samuel West, William Woodey, John W. Waker, Harvy Woods, A. C. Wilson, James Webb. John Wilson, Ephraim Whitaberry, Jesse Wimpy.

District No. 3

Robert J. Allan, John Allan, Samuel L. Akens, William Blare, Caleb Bedwell, John Buster, James Bates, Jesse Billingsley, Ezekel Bates, Joseph Billingsley, George Cates, John Cates, Samuel Cates, Joseph Cowan, John D. Chaton, William Cowen (1s 1 wp), John H. Cowen, George W. Casel, Richard Collen, Andrew J. Cate, Charles Dodd, William Davis, Andrew Defoor, Isaac Edwards, Thomas Eperson, Harvey Frey, Newel Frey, George Fulks, John Fulks, Thomas Gipson, Sampson Hurst, Jabes Huderson, James Hawkins, A. B. Howlet, George Haynes, John H. Hips, David Jenkins, Linsay James, William D. Kelley, William Kerr, Sr. (1s), William Kerr, Jr. (1s 1wp), Daniel Kenner, Isaac Killingsworth, Isaac Long, John F. Larreson, John Lambert, Joseph Mee (3s), Isaac Mee, Isaac Marten, George E. Mountcastel, James May Stephen McCaselin, Joseph McMillion, William McMillion (2s 1wp), Jesse McClane, William May (2s), Asa May George Murrel (3s 1wp), David Ogle, David Peoples, John W. Price, Jacob Ruth, Uriah Shipley, William H. Shane, Andrew Seflett, John Simmons, Isham Simmons, Wesley Simmons, Archabal Taylor, Bengeman F. Taylor, George Yoakin, Ira Webb, Isaac Worrell, Robert White, Allen Burk.

District No. 4

John Allan, William Allan, John Allan (sic), Stephen Blanckingship, William Back (1s 1wp), William Ballard, Jeremiah Brannam, Mark Black, Mark Black (sic), Elbert E. Chooper (sic), Meagh Clack, David Clark, William Clark, Absolam Carson, Isaac Crumwill, John Crumwell, Joseph Chookson, John Chilertt, Robert Carr, John Carr, Samuel Dunn, Ruban Dodson, Simeon Dickson, Alpherd Dickson, John Dunn, Walter Edwards, Hans H. Fisher, Elias Fite, Hiram Gremitt Gilbert Gaston, John Gaston, James Grigsby, Thomas Gowen, William Galahan, E. A. Gowing, Michel Hamby, James Hesse, John Hesse, Joel Y. Harvey, John Hodges, Robert Howel, James Johnston, Aaron Jarret, Joel Longley, David Lay, Hugh

Lusk, James Mayfield, James Maclester, Eliajh Maus, James Motise, David Melter, Isaac Mandinssall, William McColiser, Thomas Moody, Wesley McColester, John Murrey, John S. Nelson, Isaac Potts, George Richardson, Mager (sic) Russell, Alexander Seahorn, Mathew Safford, Nathan Safford, Eum (sic) Steovell, John Shook, Alexamder Turmin, Silas Wann, Robert T. Weatherley, William Weatherley, John Yoakim.

District No. 5

Thomas Adams, Isaac Adams, Elijah Adams, James Butcher, George Baker (1s 1wp), James Brown, William Biggs, John Carson (1s 1wp), Davis Curmuss, Joseph Chookson, Isaac Couch, John Catron, Even Camil, Joseph Dail, Anthony Dale, David Dale, Samuel Deugin, Hinton Daugherty, Evens Dunahoo, Robert Deuggen, Hugh Deugin, James Evens, John Evens, John E. Evens, Henry Erby, William Fogg, Isaac Fitsgeral, Eligah Gillinwatters, Almon Guinn, Elisha Green, Joseph Green, William Howell, William Higens, William Henry, James Helemes, Robert Hood, Valantine Harveson, Tinsley Jones, Thomas Jones, Levi J. Jones, William Jones, Sr., William Jones, Jr., Rubn, Kinester, Joshua Kilpatrick, David L. Knox, Jeramiah Lilard, Nelson Lawson, Noah Lilard, Stephen Lawson, Beard Lane, Hiram Linder, Abraham Liliard, Samuel Merrett, Mathew McNabb, Jesse McCalester, JohnOnele, Robert Orr, John patterson, Nathaniel Peake, Robert Pharris, William Pharris, Ephriam pringe, Thomas L. Ray, John Ru, James Rogers, Jarges Rogers (1s 1wp), David Ragen, John Randolph, William Randolph, William S. Ray Solomon Summary, Bengeman Sanford, Cutbreth Shelton, Thomas Swafford, Samuel H. Summens, Elisha Williams, John Williams, Isaac Williams.

District No. 6

Levi Brotherton, James Booker, James cathey, Flemuel Childers, William Childers, James A. Fletcher, William Grogen, Welsey Gassaway, Abraham W. Hagler, Jr., Benjemon Muray, David McNear (4s), Shearwood Orsburn (1s 1wp), James Pettet (10s), John Ross, Michal Reed, Archabel Sackran, Thomas Skelton, James Satterfield, Isaac Smith, John Towns (4s 1wp), Roling Tanckersley, Jesse Vonn, George Wilson, David Westfield (5s 1wp), John Wear, James W. Wilson.

District No. 7

Charles Adkins, Edward Auston, John P. Angsley, Henry Akins, J. R. Bates, Burrey Buckner, E. P. Burnett, John Bean, S. Blackwells, Wm. B. Brumfield, John Bredon, Allan Blevens, Andrew Carr, George Colvelle, Erbey Colyer, James Campbell, Plesant Casey, William Chapion, Ellison Dearman, John A. Dearman, William Davis, James Ellidge, Robert Elison, A. B. Foster, T. B. Foster, Parrish Garner, Asa F. Gerrel, Amos Hambright, Charles F. Hardwick, Bengemon Hackson, Hugh Hannah, Joseph Henry, James Harlin, John Hughs, John Hardwick, Thomas Hannah, William Hammones, William Hunbert, Zachariah Harewood,

Beldin Herrel, William Jones, John Igor, Joseph Igor, Robert Johnston, George Kincannon, Mathew Kincanon, Thomas Kerbey, Daniel Lain, George Long, James Lay, Joseph Lusk, J. G. Lea, Alpherd McNabb, Daniel McJunklin, George McGhee, James McNutt, James Mitchell, Samuel McGaugho, John McJunkin, James Officer, John T. Price, Edmon Ramsey, James Riddel, John Reel, Abraham Smedley, George Smith, George Sewel, A. K. Smedley, James Slanton, N. G. Spring, Samuel Smith, Thomas D. Smedley, William Sampels, Jackson Sewel, A. J. Sewel, John Smith, Henderson Taylor, John D. Traynor, Paterson Thomas, Robert Thornhill, S. M. Taylot, Levi Truhutts, Casey Willliams, David White, George Weslvency, Robert Williams, Shadrik Williams, William White.

District No. 8

Thomas Atchley, John Ahart, Henry Arehart, Michel Arehart, Lea P. Allan, Samuel Aley, Joshua Atchley, Levi Bookout, Lewis Bibel, William Burwick, John Burk, Henry bennett, Bartley S. Benson, William M. Bennett, Ralph R. Barksdel, Nathanuel Barksdel, William Buster, David Boon, Thomas Benton, James Chooper, Edward Childers, Maxwell Chambers, Henry Childers, John Cox, Alexander A. Clingan, John Claboo, Charles Callon, Wiett Coffel, George W. Cox, Bengemon Cox, Phillip Cox, James Collan, James D. Davis, Thomas Duckett, John Davis, Willaim Dotson, Samuel Ervin, James Ervin, Joseph H. Ervin, Bengemen Ervin, Anderson Fitsgeral, Bird Farmear, Euel Gross, Ire Gotherd, Thomas Gorge, Samul. George, William Gent, Edward George, James Henry, Samuel Howard (s 1wp), Isaac Hufaker, Logen Howerd, William Hockins, Robert Hackens, Elias Hutcherson, Allison Hawerd, Bryant Havens, George Harvey, John B. Ingram, Elim Johnston, Joseph Johnston (1s 1wp), John W. Johnston Nathen Jones, John Kincannon, Martin Langston, Thomas McNutt, James Luderdeal, Andrew Lowry, John Long, James Maron, William Mahonn, Plesant Manesse, Jesse Mayfield (6s 1wp), Clabourn Maness, Larkin Maness, March McGhee, Joseph McNutt, William Moor, Dickson Price, Alexander Perry (1s 1wp), Johnathen Price, James Pate, Amos Potts, William Riddel, Hiram Reece, Euil Rives, James Smith, Jesse Swesesher, John Silcuerk, Henry Swisher, James H. Smith, Jesse Smith, William J. Thompson, William Thournburgh, Churchwell B. Tucker, William Treplett, (1s 1wp), Henry Trotter, William Williams (2s 1wp), Wood Williams, King Williams, Willis White (1s 1wp), Frederic Williams, Elijah Wiett, William Woods, A. G. M. McCulley, Phillip Coffitt, Isaac Coffitt.

Franklin County, Tennessee Tax List 1812

John Adkerson, Jesse Bean, Robert Bean, George Bean, Joab Bean, John Bean, William Bean, Jr., John H. Bean, Joel Bean, Jesse Bean, Jr.,

John Bell, Edmond Bean, David Bell, Robert Bell, William Brown, Nathaniel Brown, Samuel Berry, John Barnett, Zachariah Brown, John Briscoe, Richard Benge, Peter Bellieu, Ralph Crabb, Thomas Crabb, Francis Crabb, David Carson, Carter Collins, William Cowan, George Counts, John Carnaham, William Caperton, Thomas Cridley, Thomas Collins, Richard Callaway, Charles Duncan, James Dougan, John Dougan, Thomas Dougan, Sharp Dougan, Robert Dougan, Ephraim Drake, James Drake, George Dickey, John Dickey, Ephraim Dickey, Ephraim Dickey, Jr., Thomas Duglass, William Duncan, Wallace Estill, James Estill, Daniel Eans, Charles Frazier, Moses Ginn, Jesse Ginn, George Gifford, Daniel Givans, Solomon George, Samuel Henderson, William Hinshaw, James Holloway, William Hudspeth, William Hudspeth, William Heslip, Thomas Heslip, Samuel Handley, James Estill, John Handly, James M. Hall, Thomas Hall, Christopher Hawk, Robert Hudspeth, James Harris, Archabald Hatchett, John Holder, Nathaniel Hall, Robert Hall, Thomas Hall, Samuel A. Harris, John Ireland, William Kincaid, Samuel Leord, David Larkins, John Larkins, Field Moore, James Moore, Jesse McAnally, William McCloud, David McCord, Richard Miller, William Moore, Federick Mayberry, Bartly Marshal, Ezekiel Owens, John Owens, James Patton, William Quisenbury, Nathan Robert, James Richey, Hugh Robertson, Isaac Robertson, Jacob Rich, Thomas Rich, Barton Rice, Gabriel Rice, Daniel Robertson, Abel Sparks, Benjamin Sparks, John Sparks, Soloman Sparks, Reubin Sanders, Humphry Scoggins, Nathan Spencer Michael Spencer, George Stovall, John Staples, Samuel Smith, Elisha Stovall, Alexander Simon, Charles Simons, William Simmons, Simon Trent, ??? Trent, ???? Taylor, Jacob Vanzant, Jacob Vanzant, Jr., John Woods, James Woods, Peter Woods, John Woods, Jr., Charles Woods, Andrew Woods, Archabald Woods, William Woods, William Wright, Henry Willis, Lewis Beck, Richard White, Robert Box, Nimrod Mitchell, Samuel Webber, Charles McDaniel, John Wilson, William McDaniel, John Jones, Jesse Goodwin, Nathaniel Russell, Dutton Sweeton, Thomas L. Duncan, James Downing, Francis Smtih, Stephen Hun, Thomas L. Page, James Lett, Amon Aryes, William Proctor, Daniel Cook, Jacob Tarwater, Benjamin Roberts, Samuel Yeager, Reubin Jorden, George Tubb, Philip Jones, Jeremiah Street, Jeremiah Beck, James Smith, John Deloach, Boykin Deloach, John Arra Smith, John W. Salmon, King Patterson, James Holly, John Smith, Thomas Smith, John Beasley, Thomas Dowly, Mathew Dowly, Charles Rowlin, Daniel Havern, John Goodwin, Peter Wileman, John Graham, James Wooten, John Phips, John Dobs, Henry Painter, John Painter, John Jorden, Thomas Harison, Abraham Hargess, Harrison Sartain, James Sanders, Solomon Sanders, William Forsyth, Henry Gotcher, Joshua Gotcher, William Cook, Burril Cook, Archabald Gesel, Robert Jones, Lemuel Johnson, Silas Johnson, John

Burris, Mater Sheckel, James Bonner, James Nazworthy, Jacob Box, William Trussell, William Tubb, Daniel Hill, John Sweeton, Stephen Fulyers?, Elizha Ivey, Gabriel Jones, John Brumsent, John Winn, Antony Burris, Obediah Bean, John Burrows, Moses Sweeton, Burrel Bagget, John Robins, James Brooks, Nathan Price, Silas Tucker, James Sertain, Jacob Beck, Henry Beck, Frederick Beck, Lewis Watson & Co., Lewis Watson, Lewis Powell, John C. Smith, William Morgan, John Box, John Morris, William Burgiss, John Armstrong, Jacob Dean, David Meeks, William Law, Barnett Colyer, Wiat Ballard, Humphrey Hariss, Thomas Hill, James Bell, Edward Box, William Harrison, William Burkhollen, Abner Hargiss, John Hargiss, Thomas Hargiss, Abraham Hargiss, Gilliam Jackson, Andrew McGown, Henry Hunt, George Sherell, Nathaniel Hunt, Alexander Brown, William Norman, William Carrell, John Banks, Simon Banks, John McGown, Samuel McGowan, David McGowan, Thomas Littlepage, Leiper Brown, Francis Brown, John Wilkinson, Samuel Sherrill, Elijah Denway, Joseph Cartright, Nevel Leach, Samuel Dunway, William Dunway, Francis Crabb, Thomas Brown, Elias Jorden, Levi Jorden, William Bryan, John Hunt, Nathaniel Hunt, Ser., Robert Frazier, Reubin Jorden, William Davis, Stafford Silman, John Morris, Stewart Cowan, John Crockett, John Tully, John King, Robert Blackwood, Thomas King, James Brandon, Robert Taylor, John Adams, William Northcut, James Meloney, Henry Barrons, Samuel Colquitt, John T. Colquitt, George Swoler, John Wileman, Peter Wileman, James Brandon, David Farmer, Robert Wallace, Benjamin Adkins, Samuel Farmer, Joshua Bryant, William Bryant, Thomas Silman, Richard Bryant, Reuben Embry, Thomas Silmon, Jr., Abner Silmon, Eli Silmon, Jr., Wiley Silmon, Pumfret Herndon, Nathan Reed, William Floyd, Alexander Floyd, Sims Kelly, Durham Kelly, Samuel Bradshaw, Joseph Cowlin, Joseph Blackburn, James McCulluck, Joseph Dunway, Joshua Gotcher, Henry Gotcher, Isaac McElroy, Michael McElroy, Robert Box, Thomas L. Duncan, James Loyd, Owen Loyd, Stephen Box, John Box, David Floyd, William Moore, Thomas Harrison, Sr., William Harrison, Thomas Harrison, Jr., Nicholas Jasper, Obed Powell, Noah Wimberley, Tela Wimpa, Lewis Tarwater, William Noblett, William Cotquill, Daniel A. Perdue, Benjamin Nevill, Joseph Dunn, Thomas Smith, William Burgiss, Jacob Box, James Greenlees, William Greenlees, George Masters, John Thrasher, John Keykendall, James Hunt, Lambert Reid, James Petty, Stephen Fuller, Jesse King, Solomon Dodd, Joseph Langly, John Price, William Rankins, Daniel Roberts, John Long, James Wood, Lephus Condry, Jonathan Woodall, Stephen Thompson, Jeremiah Ratley, Joshua Ratley, Joshua Calahan, Peter Morrison, Alexander McCullock, David Woods, George Tubbs, Sr., James McMistion, Evin Todhunter, Jacob Garner, David McCullock, Mathew Marshal, Burrell Thompson, James McCullock, William Tubb, Moses McBride, David Stamphill,

Samuel Jackson, Moses Morris, Rowlen Lane, John Harris, Anderson Standifer, William Roark, David Wray, William Wileman, Jeremiah Hill, James Harrison, William Wafford, James Charles, Richard Charles, Thomas Davison, Johnston King, Simms Kelly, Jesse Reid, Jesse King, David Hendrick, William McBride, Nathaniel McBride, Jesse Armstrong, Nathan Reid, John Briant, Valentine Colbert, Daniel McBride, George McPherson, Andrew Walker, John Jorden, David Allen, Jeremiah Smith, William Armstrong, William Davison, Alexander Bird, Samuel Roberts, Robert Dunn, William Young, Simon Autry, James Hardcastle, William Hargiss, Abraham Baker, George Garner, Meredith King, Robert Hardcastle, Britain Jones, Willie Tally, William Farmer, Zachariah Farmer, John Bowen, Samuel Vaughn, Lewis Abbet, Turner Sessam, Larkin Bethel, Adma Dunlap, Richard Grant, Eli Selmon, Archilles Foster, Joseph Atkins, John Hooker, Peter Hyles, Moore Henly, Benjamin Camp, William Henly, William Long, Alexander Long, Thomas Briant, Mason Briant, Thomas A. Williams, Philip Jeans, James Lamburth, Steven Adcock, John Lyttleton, William McClendon, Robert Jones, John Kenley, Abner Armstrong, Thomas Mathis, John Mathis, Elisha Floyd, Jones Young, James Beesly, Johnson King, Thomas Clark, Willis Young, Francis Young, Thomas Young, William Vaughn, James Vaughn, Benjamin Johnson, Richard Faris, Ambrose Barker, Johnson King, William Simmons, Jacob Graves, Charles Simmons, Henry Willis, William Crafford, John Shankle, John Kimbrough, Owen Roark, William Graves, Adam Roonel, William Travis, John Loney, Solomon Joiner, Frederick Mayberry, John King, Wiliam Oliver, John Cook, George G. Black, Barney Roark, Martin Antony, John Robertson, Andrew Youngblood, John May David Hunt, Harrison Johnson, Jacob Shakle, George Sparks, John Sparks, John Young, John Biddict, Moses Alexander, Alexander Gray, Peter Write, John Bean, Jesse Johnson, John Hurley, Thomas Hurley, Jesse Bounds, George Bounds, John Smith, Joseph Denson, John Denson, Samuel Parks, Samuel Nelms, Jacob Nelms, John Busby, John Criffin, Jacob Shankle, Robert Travis, Bernard Rowark, James Embry, Britain Embry, William Agill, William Mann, Richard Faris, John Faris, Samuel McCormack, John Smally, Jonah Barker, John Agent, William Edgings, John Travis, Issac Foster, Peter Noah, Richard Forrest, John Silas, John Cook, Sr,, Pleasant Finney, John Riddle, John Smith, John Craton, George Shankle, George Vandiver, Harmon Riddle, James Craton, James Dougan, Thoma Dougan, John Dougan, James Faris, Cornelius Dollarhide, Millenton Ledbetter, Joshua Dean, John Bean, Jr., James Carlile, Benjamin Rice, Samuel Moss, Abraham Womack, Samuel Hillhouse, William Sheals, Jonathan Eaves, Stephen Bab, James McMinn, Thomas Comer, William McBroom, Thomas Gilliam, James Womack, Wyley Davis, William Metcalf, Alexander Standridge, John Gilliam, James Cunningham, Samuel McBee, Edmond McGuffy, William McBee, Ser.,

Joseph Evans, Lemuel Bean, Edward Nichols, John Bean, Jr., Obediah Hensley, Philip Clepper, Abraham Shipman, James Clepper, John Dean, James Walker, William Smith, James McBee, Henry Davis, William Nichols, David Nichols Sr., David Nichols, Jr., John Owins, Thomas Adams, John Patton, John Duke, Martin Franks, Thomas Brookstann, Thomas Stuckey, James Metcalf, Abner Homes, Hugh John Thratcher, Elijah Arnold, Thomas Kenedy, James Sheid, William Jenkins, Jesse Jenkins, William Morrson, Thomas Kennerly, Jr., William Lusk, Jr., John Morrow, Jacob Dean, Alexander Graham, Samuel Henry, Thomas Brandon, William Lusk, Ser., Isaac Henry, James Henry, Josiah Lusk, Simon Keykendall, William Keykendall, Mathew Keykendall, William Hunt, James McKain, William Evans, James Linley, William Bradley, Swift Mullin, Samuel Johnson, David Jay, John Jay, Jonah Leach, William McBee, Jesse McBee, John Haven, Israel Archer, Henry Herriford, Sr., Henry Herriford, Jr., John Herriford, Andrew Herriford, Jonah Womack, Martin Jackson, Richard Jackson, Isaac Cartright, Joseph Gentry, William Walker, Jesse Wilson, Samuel Rhoeds Silas Curtis, David Crawford, George Pea, Joseph Pea, Lewis Hunt, Abraham Hunt, Abraham Box, Henry Davis, Ser., John Moss, William Moss, James Moss, William Keneday, John Coats, Stephen Faris, Smith Faris, John Riggins, William Wallace, Joseph Wood, Philip Taylor, Moris Saylors, Daniel Saylors, Timothy Roark, John McCormick, John Clark, Elisha Mayfield, John Ross, William Carr, Frances Nabours, James McHern, Martin Farrell, Alexander Gillis, Robert Bean, Daniel Morris Groves Morris, Jacob Hays, William Patton, William Elsey, Benjamin Rice, Jr., Daniel Jest, Hyram Womack, Levi Arnold, Jesse Bean, George Winters, James McMinn, Philip Anderson, Alexander Rhymes, John Gilliam, Jr., Jacob Williams, James Standridge, Stephen Babb, John Jones, James McLaughlin, Neffle Leach, James Brandon, Peter Keykendall, George Thratcher, John Arlington, Frederick Clipper, Thomas Pike, William Linley, George Foster, Jonathan Garrett, Thomas Kenedy, Samuel Colquit, Joseph Cartright, Wit McLariton, Joseph Foster, William Bass, Joseph Brown, William Bean, John McBee, Abraham Bledsow, John Holder, Moses Holder, Bledsow Holder, Tassy Holder, Martin Holder, Lewis Bledsoe, Sherod Williams, James Montgomery, John Nelson, Andrew Nelson, Preston Nelson, Robert Bell, George Keith, John Stuard, William Stuard, Abraham Stuart, William Montgomery, James Stuart, Thomas Hamilton, John Hamilton, Thomas Kilgore, George Weir, Thomas Eliot, John Chilcoat, James Chilcoat, James Chilcoat, George Russell, Sr., George Russell, Jr., Samuel Russell, John Russell, Joseph Bullard, Thomas Wiggin, John Wiggin, Peter Harris, William Young, Isaac Young, Clark Thornton, George Johnson, Christopher Bullard, William Bigham, Abner Reaves, William Kavanaugh, Ebenezer Picket, James S. McWhorter, Leonard Tarrants, Samuel Harris,

William Morton, David Love, James Givens, Nathaniel Bigham, Thomas Alexander, William Alexander, James Henderson, William Forbes, John Bell, Thomas Hutson, Benjamin Weir, James Kelly, James Keith, George McClusky, Samuel McCluskey, John Emberson, Daniel Martin, David Robinson, James Robinson, John Robinson, Daniel Harrison, James Donathan, George Gray, William Gray, David Hunt, John Hutchenson, Hann McWhorter, Hezekiah Faris, Lewis Gillaspie, George Hunt, Sampson Read, William Lea, George Faris, William Logan, Silvester Worthem, John Martin, Philip William, Nimrod Harris, John Peck, John King, William Hutton John Hutton James Martin John Brekem, Soloman Holder Robert Whitly Jabez Fitzjerrel William Hutson Solomon Langham Robert Langham Thomas Vanzant George McCarrell William Hughs, Charles Wood, Andra Jr o, John Burton, William Bird, Alexander Bird, James Nelson, Julius Cesar Sims, John Sims, John Montgomery, Elijah Stovall, William Russell, John Russell, Cook Austin, James Taylor, Amon Cox, Isaac Estill, Fall Sullivan, Jesse Vanpelt,, Francis Gholston, Edmond Russell, Nash Sulivan, Frances Jones, Jacob C. Isacks, Joseph Taylor, William Scott, John Henly, Cornelius Dolarhide, John Smith, James Dawnham, Jesse Bounds, George Bounds, William Rily, John May Joseph Denson, Johnson Denson, Martain Riley, John Robinson, Martain Anthony, James Faris, Bolie Emry, Joseph Street, Thomas Evans, Joseph Campbell, Andrew Campbell, John Campbell, Mims Russell, Thomas Russell, Jonathan Spyker, James Evans, James Rusy, Jonah Barker, Ambrose Barker, Samuel Glover, Stephen Peticock, Avery Reaves, John Russell, Sr., Thomas Hurly, William Scott, George Emburson, John Keith, Alexander S. Alkin, James Emberson, John Cowen, Elias Debusk, John Caperton, Thomas Foster, William Russell, Sr., William Russell, Jr., George Russell, Martin Little, Edmond Russell, William Moore, James Cowen, Robert McCamy, Andrew Eastis, John Eastis, Daniel P. McAlister, Mathew McAlister, William McAlister, Samuel Norwood, Robert Bell, Thomas Kerr, Orman Morgan, John Wallace, Isaac Hannah, Richard Martin, James Martin, William Martin, Robert Cowen, Henry Russell, James Russell, Henry Russell, John Russell, Samuel Stephens, William Stuart, John Perry, Jacob Tally, John Tally, Mathew Tally, Robert Hines, Paul Williams, John Williams, Samuel McClellen, Jeremiah Jeffery, Briton Ragsdale, James Dunwody, Henry Hill, Allen Hill, Greenburry Doss, James Wallen, Johnston Sargant, Jonas Hill, William Champion, Evans Richards, Absalom Russell, John Champion, Aaron Sargent, Temple Sargent, William Sargent, Hugh Montgomery, James Montgomery, Robert Brooks, William Brooks, Maclin Cross, William Hall, Thomas Ross, James McCord, William King, James Sargent, John Brewanton, William Moor, James Cowen, William Jennings, Joshua Townsen, Jesse Perkins, William Delany, Martin Jennings, Nathaniel Robertson, James Kelly, John Kelly,

George Stephens, Gideon Walker, Ezekiel Neal, George Soap, John Parish, Archabald Brooks, John McCleherrin, Elijah Williams, Benjamin Riddle, Winkfield Shropshire, James Shropshire, Cornelius Burnett, George Caperton, Jonah Conn, William Wood, Abraham Rutherford, Robert Morris, William Wheeler, James P. Cowen, James Montgomery, Daniel McAlister, Sargent Johnston, Thomas Smily, Thomas Adams, Joseph McClusky, Elias Oldham, William Norton, John Hodges, David Burton, John Burton, Josiah Stephens, Ebenezer Stephens, Sr., James Stephens, Ebenezer Stephens, Jr., William Jennings, Martin Jennings, James King, Edward Finch, Thomas Hurly, John Stamps, George Stamps, James Stamps, James Harrell, William Adams, John Winford, John Dougan, William Stamps, Martin Sims, Allen Sims, William Smith, Leroy May William Witt, Valentine Yates, George Taylor, Archelus Taylor, Lee Taylor, Sylvester Stokes, John Sturdivant, Nathan Davis, William Vernon, William Whitt, John Jones, Martin Wigginton, John Lee, Cader Lee, Reubin Warren, David Warren, John Davis, John Price, James Morrison, Reubin Herndon, Perry Young, Richard Sharp, James Sharp, John Glaco, John Champion, John Shepherd, Daniel Muse, Jedethen Poe, George Miller, John Wyat, Edward Orzburn, Isaac James, Isaac James, Jr., Joseph James, James Brock, James Rossen, Abner Rossen, Isaac Sanders, John Hamilton, John Stags, Asa Hamilton, Thomas Keesee, Richard Wilson, John Fortenbury, Moses Aryes, Thomas Simpson, Fielden McDaniel, Coalman McDaniel, Lot Strickland, Joab Short, James Hoge, Benjamin Thompson, Richard Lacky, Daniel Roland, Ezekiel Stags, James Howard, James Young, Miles Hoge, Stephen Brundridge, Abraham James, Moses Aryes, William Lasater, John Simmons, William Simmons, Samuel Nellums, David Ford, Thomas Muse, Edw. H. Henson, John Poe, Henry Goodwin, Joseph Moore, Abner Lasater, William Oldfield, John Bynum, George Glover, Absalom Faris, Samuel Parks, Benjamin Majors, William Sutton, George Parks, Charles Weeks, Moses Short, Alexander Beryhill, Benjamin Easly, Hezekiah Lasater, Jr., Moris Wood, John King, Daniel Weaver, War Easly, Stephen James, William Berryhill, Rhoden Poe, William Childers, John Wilson, John Easly, Randolph Riddle, John Nelms, Harmon Riddle, Aron Wods, Mathew Stricklin, William Beasly, Benjamin Jones, Britain Jones, Robert Jones, Peter McGee, John Wagner, Isom Wood, John Herrod, Nick Nicholson, James Lewis, David Lowe, John Keeton, Martin Sims, Allen Sims, Stephen Williford, Edward Dickson, William Faris, Charles Faris, William Childers, John Green, John King, Thomas Williford, John Kenly, John H. Aikens, William Darwin, Benjamin Rawlings, Samuel Blan, Richard Hits, Carrel J. Pricherd, Eli Blackard, William Hammons, Joshua Payne, Anual King, Archabald McCown, Edward Norton, James Dotson, Edward Smith, Jesse Embry, William H. Greenwood, George Wagoner, Solomon Wagoner, William Wagoner,

Wallie Barlary, Owen Taylor, Charles M. Boyse, William Boyse, Eliot Boyse, John Hamilton, Philip Yates, John McQueen, Joshua McCarien

Blount County, Tennessee, Marriages, 1795-1839
Abraham Ridge and Elizabeth Johnston, (MD) Mar. 13, 183?
Robert Hooks and Abigail Alexander, (MD) Nov. 27, 1795
Alex McColloch and Margaret McNutt, (MD) Sep. 22, 1795
James McTeer and Martha Ferguson, (MD) Sep. 29, 1795
Willis Moore and Mary Clampet, (MD) Oct. 20, 1795
Hance Russell and Elizabeth McClannahan, (MD) Sep. 21, 1795
Benjamin Tipton and Rebeck Cusic, (MD) Dec. 19, 1795
Jonathan Bazel and Nancy Mills, (MD) Aug. 19, 1796
John Bell and Jane Craig, (MD) Apr. 19, 1796
George Broyles and Cathern Vaut, (MD) Jun. 16, 1796
John Childers and Mary Curtuy, (MD) Nov. 8, 1796
John Coats and Sarah Rogers, (MD) Jan. 12, 1796
Daniel Cochran and Eleanor Moore, (MD) Mar. 1, 1796
James Durnolds and Elizabeth Hendricks, (MD) Sep. 9, 1796
William Ewing and Elizabeth McNutt, (MD) Nov. 9, 1796
Hugh Furgeson and Margaret Craig, (MD) Nov. 10, 1796
John Hanna and Jane Trimble, (MD) Feb. 15, 1796
John Hannah and Martha Miller, (MD) Sep. 5, 1796
James Houston and Mary Gillespie, (MD) Oct. 6, 1796
Josiah Hutton and Isabella McConnal, (MD) Jan. 7, 1796
Jonathan Legg and Mary Hirfley, (MD) Sep. 6, 1796
Isaac McGuire and Martha Jackson, (MD) Jul. 14, 1796
William Nickels and Elizabeth Vaun, (MD) Aug. 19, 1796
John Roberts and Rachel Robenette, (MD) Sep. 12, 1796
Thomas Rogers and Mary McCarter, (MD) Jul. 5, 1796
John Shanklin and Lidda Hart, (MD) Jun. 14, 1796
William Whittenberger and Mary Robbinett, (MD) Jan. 30, 1796
Hugh L. Cochran and Margaret Reagan, (MD) Sep. 4, 1797
Burrell Bell and Sophia Yancey, (MD) Jan. 17, 1797
Saml Bogle and Nelly Williams, (MD) Sep. 14, 1797
James Boyd and Ann Miller, (MD) Jul. 25, 1797
John Cowan and Rosannah Gillespy, (MD) Aug. 23, 1797
Robert Cowan and Nancy Martin, (MD) Aug. 20, 1797
Miles Cunningham and Mary Denney, (MD) May 22, 1797
Adam Dunlap and Margary Porter, (MD) Jan. 31, 1797
David Eagleton and Elizabeth Hook, (MD) Dec. 2, 1797
James Edmiston and Agnis Alexander, (MD) Oct. 7, 1797
Esom Franklin and Rebecca Majors, (MD) Jul. 17, 1797
William Gammel and Ann McGaughy, (MD) Oct. 12, 1797

John Gilmore and Elenor McKinney, (MD) Mar. 13, 1797
Samuel Gold and Mary Jackson, (MD) Sep. 13, 1797
John Hammil and Ann Rowan, (MD) Nov. 9, 1797
Joseph Hanna and Mary Walker, (MD) Mar. 25, 1797
Major Harp and Susana Roberts, (MD) Sep. 5, 1797
Ephraim Howard and Sarah Vaught, (MD) Jun. 23, 1797
Andrew Jackson and Jean Sloan, (MD) Jun. 8, 1797
Samuel King and Agness Hannah, (MD) Aug. 26, 1797
Wm. Lowery and Ann Wallace, (MD) Mar. 17, 1797
James McClure and Margaret Gamble, (MD) Sep. 12, 1797
John McDowell and Phoebe Franland, (MD) Sep. 20, 1797
John Netherton and Elizabeth Hardan, (MD) Aug. 9, 1797
John Stephens and Rebecca Clampet, (MD) Oct. 24, 1797
Samuel Terry and Sarah Hail, (MD) Oct. 3, 1797
James Thompson and Susannah Weir, (MD) Jun. 5, 1797
Hugh Walker and Nancy Cochran, (MD) Jun. 5, 1797
John Weir and Jenny Weir, (MD) Jun. 3, 1797
John Williams and Agness Bogle, (MD) Sep. 7, 1797
Arch D. Lackey and Isabella Trimble, (MD) Dec. 24, 1798
James Berry and Rebeca Regan, (MD) Aug. 20, 1798
Isom Bradley and Susana Matkocks, (MD) May 13, 1798
John Cabe and Margaret Cooper, (MD) Feb. 22, 1798
Joel Copeland and Rebecka Huchison, (MD) Sep. 14, 1798
David Cunningham and Pressy Denney, (MD) Jan. 13, 1798
James Dunlap and Margaret Palmer, (MD) Dec. 26, 1798
James Ewing and Mary Thompson, (MD) Apr. 30, 1798
John Gamble and Sarah Williams, (MD) Nov. 21, 1798
John Garner and Rachel Henry, (MD) Oct. 17, 1798
Wm. Hanna and Mary Moor, (MD) May 1, 1798
Samuel Henry and Elizabeth Garner, (MD) Mar. 26, 1798
Daniel Hoff and Betsey Chisom, (MD) Jan. 9, 1798
Barton Lovelace and Mary Lovel, (MD) Jun. 30, 1798
Thomas Maxwell and Esther Hogg, (MD) Sep. 17, 1798
John McCammon and Elizabeth Upton, (MD) May 14, 1798
James McGaughey and Margaret McCain, (MD) Apr. 12, 1798
Daniel McKenzey and Jenny Tippet, (MD) Dec. 20, 1798
James McTeer and Jenny McTeer, (MD) Aug. 7, 1798
Robert McTeer and Mary Sherrall, (MD) Mar. 22, 1798
John Montgomery and Peggy Alexander, (MD) Nov. 23, 1798
Howard Richardson and Sarah Reed, (MD) Mar. 31, 1798
Samuel Roane and Jean Cowan, (MD) Aug. 7, 1798
Francis Rogers and Magness Teague, (MD) Jan. 2, 1798
Thomas Spilman and Chittlen Jones, (MD) Jul. 24, 1798

Magness Teague and Francis Rogers, (MD) Jan. 2, 1798
David Wallace and Sarah Justice, (MD) Apr. 23, 1798
John Wallace and Jean Blackburn, (MD) May 22, 1798
Jacob Willis and Margret Majors, (MD) Aug. 20, 1798
John Andes and Selain B. Bailess, (MD) May 27, 1799
John B. Cusick and Hulda Durham, (MD) Oct. 9, 1799
Benjamin Alexander and Ruth Wallace, (MD) Sep. 16, 1799
William Blair and Betsey McDowell, (MD) Dec. 2, 1799
James Boyd and Hannah McMurry, (MD) Sep. 3, 1799
John Boyd and Caty Holloway, (MD) Sep. 30, 1799
William Bradley and Mary Murphy, (MD) Jun. 24, 1799
Abraham Byrd and Betsey Gillespie, (MD) Mar. 20, 1799
David Caldwell and Molly Russell, (MD) Jan. 29, 1799
Isaac Cochran and Polly Kelly, (MD) Apr. 10, 1799
Richard Coulter and Meina Ketchens, (MD) Jun. 19, 1799
George Doherty and Nancy McDowell, (MD) Apr. 1, 1799
John Franklin and Polly Irwin, (MD) Aug. 2, 1799
Joseph Galahor and Margaret Gillespie, (MD) Apr. 16, 1799
Andrew Gamble and Elizabeth Davidson, (MD) Apr. 23, 1799
Hugh Gamble and Betsy Whitenbarger, (MD) Dec. 21, 1799
William Gamble and Sarah Gillespie, (MD) Dec. 10, 1799
Alexander Gillespie and Margaret Young, (MD) Aug. 3, 1799
John Gillespie and Patsey Houston, (MD) Feb. 7, 1799
Robert Gillespie and Betsy Houston, (MD) Feb. 7, 1799
Arthur Greer and Jenny Hart, (MD) Aug. 29, 1799
William Griffetts and Mary Mathus, (MD) Jun. 15, 1799
Hugh Hackney and Ann Lambert, (MD) Jun. 15, 1799
John Kelly and Nancy Mayho, (MD) Apr. 9, 1799
William Leatherdale and Elizabeth Willis, (MD) Mar. 16, 1799
John Likens and Isabella Sloan, (MD) Aug. 22, 1799
James McDowell and Nancy Conner, (MD) Sep. 30, 1799
John McRandls and Jane McRandls, (MD) Nov. 27, 1799
David Montgomery and Margate McCameron, (MD) Feb. 7, 1799
Thos Morrison and Francis Beard, (MD) Aug. 13, 1799
David Parkhill and Martha Wassham, (MD) Aug. 2, 1799
John Tedford and Jean Henderson, (MD) Dec. 11, 1799
John Thompson and Margret McConald, (MD) May 30, 1799
John Trias and Tabitha Ewing, (MD) Nov. 11, 1799
John Tubbs and Mary More, (MD) Dec. 30, 1799
William Wallace and Polly Wallace, (MD) Jun. 29, 1799
Samuel Wear and Polly Gellaher, (MD) Sep. 30, 1799
Patrick Woods and Jenney Hanna, (MD) Jun. 12, 1799
Wm. Brown and Polly Ann Moffett, (MD) Apr. 12, 1800

Alex R. Craig and Susanna Logan, (MD) May 23, 1800
Wm. Alexander and Ann Bingham, (MD) Sep. 5, 1800
William Barnes and Jenny Walker, (MD) Oct. 21, 1800
John Beatty and Sally Rider, (MD) Feb. 15, 1800
Richard Blevins and Elizabeth Arintos, (MD) Nov. 5, 1800
Adam Bourden and Betsey Huchison, (MD) Dec. 4, 1800
Michael Bowerman and Caity Bowers, (MD) Feb. 25, 1800
David Brown and Betsey Sloan, (MD) Jun. 16, 1800
David Caldwell and Elizabeth Giffin, (MD) Oct. 25, 1800
John Clark and Letitia Sharp, (MD) Jan. 29, 1800
James Copeland and Ann Cameron, (MD) Sep. 11, 1800
David Copland and Susannah Craig, (MD) Jun. 25, 1800
James Cowan and Mary Montgomery, (MD) Apr. 23, 1800
Joseph Falkner and Martha Franks, (MD) Jul. 21, 1800
John Fisher and Jean Palmer, (MD) Jul. 25, 1800
Joseph Folkner and Martha Franks, (MD) Jul. 21, 1800
Mathew Gillmore and Margaret Lagan, (MD) Feb. 13, 1800
Wm. Hamelton and Elizabeth Rogers, (MD) Aug. 24, 1800
James Hammontree and Nancy Holoway, (MD) Apr. 30, 1800
Baldwin Harle and Isabella Miller, (MD) Feb. 13, 1800
Samuel Jones and Joana Allin, (MD) Nov. 28, 1800
John King and Becky Pride, (MD) Jun. 11, 1800
Andrew Lackey and Esther Johnston, (MD) Dec. 10, 1800
Thomas Lake and Jenney Majors, (MD) Jan. 1, 1800
Jonathan Mathes and Mary Allin, (MD) Nov. 23, 1800
Samuel McColloch and Margaret Porter, (MD) Oct. 22, 1800
James McConnell and Ann McKee, (MD) Aug. 26, 1800
Samuel McCullock and Margaret Porter, (MD) Oct. 22, 1800
Cullinus Miller and Polly Sloan, (MD) Oct. 22, 1800
William Neily and Jane Hogg, (MD) Feb. 7, 1800
Frconco Pinexo and Liddy Casteel, (MD) Mar. 5, 1800
John Rhea and Rebecca Miller, (MD) Mar. 3, 1800
Thomas Richey and Jenney Greenaway, (MD) Feb. 25, 1800
James Rogers and Anna Blair, (MD) Mar. 12, 1800
Bonner Shields and Peggy Weir, (MD) Feb. 5, 1800
Robert Stewart and Elizabeth Hussey, (MD) Dec. 22, 1800
Robert Tedford and Jenney White, (MD) Jul. 4, 1800
Thomas Tedford and Polly Hannah, (MD) Oct. 21, 1800
Christopher Timberman and Mary Forguson, (MD) Oct. 14, 1800
James Upton and Agness Lyons, (MD) Apr. 7, 1800
Andrew Vaut and Susannah Broils, (MD) Dec. 16, 1800
Sherod Washburn and Mary Hutson, (MD) Jan. 26, 1800
Richard Williams and Sally Williams, (MD) Jul. 25, 1800

Edwin Allin and Sarah Allin, (MD) Dec. 23, 1801
Wm. Barnes and Christian Bowerman, (MD) Dec. 26, 1801
John Bell and Nancy Weir, (MD) Mar. 11, 1801
Hugh Bogle and Hannah Caldwell, (MD) Apr. 2, 1801
John Brown and Nancy Allen, (MD) Jul. 30, 1801
Edward Burnette and Rachell Cheetwood, (MD) Jul. 20, 1801
James Culton and Peggy Weir, (MD) Jan. 28, 1801
Samuel Eakin and Polly Walker, (MD) Apr. 30, 1801
Jesse Fain and Jenny Canway, (MD) Oct. 13, 1801
William Francis and Rebecca Miller, (MD) Oct. 19, 1801
James Gilmore and Sarah Glass, (MD) Aug. 30, 1801
Amos Goodman and Sarah Conway, (MD) Aug. 29, 1801
Thomas Hail and Rosanna Denne, (MD) Apr. 23, 1801
Moses Hughes and Mariam Kelsoe, (MD) Apr. 15, 1801
Elijah Hussey and Elizabeth Baker, (MD) Jul. 26, 1801
Joseph Journey and Elizabeth Jackson, (MD) Jun. 2, 1801
Fleet Manuel and Polly Rossom, (MD) Aug. 4, 1801
James May and ????, (MD) Feb. 16, 1801
James McCandlas and Elizabeth Caldwell, (MD) Feb. 10, 1801
Matt McClanahan and Sally Bradley, (MD) May 16, 1801
John McCollom and Elizabeth Bolton, (MD) Feb. 9, 1801
John McComb and Lethia Davis, (MD) May 13, 1801
James McCord and Dorcas Cowan, (MD) May 30, 1801
William McNab and Margret Mitchel, (MD) Jun. 3, 1801
John Miller and Sally Wood, (MD) Aug. 5, 1801
John Montgomery and Patsy McChesney, (MD) Jun. 9, 1801
Cethain Nave and Levan Watson, (MD) Oct. 1, 1801
John Rankin and Margaret Weir, (MD) Feb. 23, 1801
Jessy Ray and Margaret Blair, (MD) Feb. 23, 1801
Peter Roberts and Mary Blevens, (MD) Mar. 9, 1801
John Russell and Jenny McNutt, (MD) Mar. 2, 1801
Robert Sloan and Margaret Cook, (MD) Dec. 29, 1801
John Smith and Sarah Caceper, (MD) May 2, 1801
Marshal Stockton and Mary Kendrick, (MD) Feb. 5, 1801
Abreham Timberman and Nancy Hakins, (MD) Jan. 19, 1801
James Wallace and Sarah Runnils, (MD) Dec. 31, 1801
Jesse Wallace and Margret Isom, (MD) Sep. 7, 1801
Levan Watson and Cethain Nave, (MD) Oct. 1, 1801
Hugh Wear and Jean Wier, (MD) Jan. 26, 1801
Hugh Wilson and Susy Shils, (MD) Feb. 10, 1801
John W. Caughorn and Hanna Johnston, (MD) Mar. 18, 1802
James N. Fox and Prudence Felkner, (MD) Dec. 1, 1802
Sam L. Walker and Rebeckah Davidson, (MD) Mar. 20, 1802

William More, Jr., and Jenney Montgomery, (MD) May 5, 1802
Robt Alisson and Jenny Thompson, (MD) Mar. 22, 1802
Jecheland Barnes and Betsey Walker, (MD) Mar. 2, 1802
Wm. Bradley and Polly Clampet, (MD) Oct. 20, 1802
Jacob Broils and Mary Vaught, (MD) Apr. 19, 1802
Joseph Colville and Martha Smart, (MD) Dec. 21, 1802
James Cooke and Margaret Gould, (MD) Jan. 22, 1802
David Cooper and Kitty Niaman, (MD) Mar. 13, 1802
William Craig and Esther Montgomery, (MD) Jul. 5, 1802
William Deveport and Polly Huckland, (MD) Dec. 26, 1802
John Dickson and Maryan Edmondson, (MD) Oct. 30, 1802
Charles Donahoo and Margaret Weir, (MD) Jan. 8, 1802
Matthew Donald and Agnus Walker, (MD) Dec. 9, 1802
James Fox and Prudence Felkner, (MD) Dec. 1, 1802
Esom Franklin and Lucy Forester, (MD) Feb. 3, 1802
George Franklin and Jenny Shaw, (MD) Sep. 1, 1802
Alexander Gillespie and Sarah Rhodes, (MD) Sep. 28, 1802
John Gillespie and Ann Chamberlin, (MD) Oct. 18, 1802
Zach Gillespie and Elizabeth Roads, (MD) Apr. 16, 1802
Orin Jones and Susannah Rogers, (MD) Nov. 24, 1802
Alex Kelly and, (MD) May 27, 1802
Marvin Kyle and Betsy Possey, (MD) Dec. 28, 1802
Alexander Long and Elizabeth Vicars, (MD) Aug. 24, 1802
James Maxwell and Mary Majors, (MD) Apr. 22, 1802
James Maxwell and Sarah Moore, (MD) Aug. 18, 1802
John McCaughan and Hanna Johnston, (MD) Mar. 18, 1802
William McTeer and Mary McTeer, (MD) Oct. 20, 1802
Jeremiah Meeks and Betsy Blevins, (MD) Feb. 8, 1802
John Mickle and Rebecka Hussey, (MD) Jun. 12, 1802
James Montgomery and Charity Garretson, (MD) Sep. 9, 1802
John Panther and Serah Waters, (MD) Jun. 26, 1802
Jesse Ray and Margaret Blair, (MD) Dec. 7, 1802
James Russell and Mary Hitchcock, (MD) Aug. 3, 1802
William Simpson and Sarah Beaty, (MD) Sep. 21, 1802
Benjamin Stigall and Patsy Denny, (MD) Aug. 20, 1802
Jenny Thompson and Robt Alisson, (MD) Mar. 22, 1802
William Tipton and Peggy Tipton, (MD) Jan. 22, 1802
Betsey Walker and Jecheland Barnes, (MD) Mar. 2, 1802
Abraham Wallace and Wallace, (MD) Sep. 4, 1802
James Wear and Martha Rankin, (MD) Jul. 12, 1802
Jones White and Polly Tool, (MD) Jul. 20, 1802
Henry Williams and Bethsheba James, (MD) Jul. 13, 1802
James Wilson and Elizabeth Weir, (MD) Nov. 10, 1802

Jeremiah Worsham and Jean King, (MD) Sep. 13, 1802
John Hamelton and Elizabeth Baugher, (MD) Jul. 21, 1803
James Major and Margaret Brumley, (MD) Jan. 13, 1803
John Reace and Precilla Kendrick, (MD) Aug. 24, 1803
Isaac Woods and Elizabeth Wetherspoon, (MD) Sep. 7, 1803
Josiah Bell and Sarah Kendrick, (MD) Aug. 12, 1804
Wm. Greene and Jean Lackey, (MD) Sep. 4, 1804
Edward Hart and Nelly White, (MD) Oct. 18, 1804
James Slaltace and Sally Whitenberger, (MD) Aug. 28, 1804
Henry Vaught and Catheren Whitenbarger, (MD) Apr. 25, 1804
Charles Wormack and Nancy Fields, (MD) Sep. 26, 1804
James S. Porter and Jeane Kirby, (MD) Feb. 15, 1805
David Broils and Elly Rooker, (MD) Oct. 24, 1805
John Condron and Rachel Vaught, (MD) Jun. 27, 1805
Thos Darmond and Elizabeth Hair, (MD) Jan. 23, 1805
Nathaniel Ewing and Betsy McColloch, (MD) Oct. 16, 1805
William Miles and Jean Scott, (MD) Mar. 8, 1805
James Pollen and Christiana Taylor, (MD) Sep. 2, 1805
Jacob Vaught and Polly Colbourn, (MD) Apr. 16, 1805
Wm. Irvin and Lovina Jane Jouster, (MD) Jan. 9, 1806
John Trimble and Elisabeth J. Cargo, (MD) May 9, 1806
Joseph Davis and Elizabeth Gillespie, (MD) Apr. 1, 1806
William Montgomery and Phoebe James, (MD) Jul. 17, 1806
Abraham Tipton and Jane Roddy, (MD) Apr. 29, 1806
John Wilkinson and Elizabeth Willis, (MD) Nov. 17, 1806
Benj M. Franks and Elizabeth Vaut, (MD) Feb. 27, 1807
Robert Barnet and Betey Cannon, (MD) Sep. 29, 1807
John Rucker and Isabella Gillespie, (MD) Nov. 16, 1807
Wm. R. Robinson and Sally Witcher, (MD) Sep. 29, 1808
Andrew Carson and Esther Stone, (MD) Aug. 15, 1808
Thomas Colbourn and Issabella Chamberland, (MD) Dec. 15, 1808
Richard Coventon and Rebecka Cain, (MD) Jul. 23, 1808
Philip Gentry and Sally Frazier, (MD) Dec. 16, 1808
James Henderson and Rachel Debausk, (MD) Apr. 28, 1808
Edward Keywood and Jane Duff, (MD) Jan. 5, 1808
Thomas Owens and Rebecky Jordon, (MD) Dec. 22, 1808
Samuel Patterson and Peggy Taylor, (MD) Apr. 30, 1808
David Pearce and Sarah Bartlett, (MD) Mar. 23, 1808
James Singleton and Rebecka Kerbey, (MD) Feb. 15, 1808
George Tucker and Sibi Lackey, (MD) Nov. 16, 1808
David Walker and Jane Johnson, (MD) Dec. 14, 1808
William White and Letty Bruner, (MD) Jul. 6, 1808
Wm. Badgett and Phebe Braze, (MD) Aug. 14, 1809

John Cupp and Sally Baker, (MD) Sep. 26, 1809
John Dunlap and Ann McAllan, (MD) Mar. 22, 1809
Hansil Hix and Lucy Fea, (MD) Sep. 16, 1809
Edmond Hunt and Anne Newman, (MD) Jul. 27, 1809
James Madden and Peggy Vaught, (MD) Aug. 24, 1809
Wm. Maxwell and Hannah Henney, (MD) May 2, 1809
James McCabe and Nelly Woody, (MD) Dec. 30, 1809
Anne Newman and Edmond Hunt, (MD) Jul. 27, 1809
Samuel Oer and Elizabeth Robertson, (MD) May 4, 1809
Josiah Patty and Elizabeth Rooker, (MD) May 25, 1809
John Smith and Rebecah McCay, (MD) Apr. 28, 1809
Jonathan Tharp and Sally Roddy, (MD) Oct. 4, 1809
Chapman Citchens and Sarah Bird, (MD) Jan. 16, 1810
Samuel Cowan and Jane Houston, (MD) Jul. 18, 1810
John Ingram and Martha Tharo, (MD) Oct. 24, 1810
Wm. Iriar and Bessy Jentry, (MD) Sep. 19, 1810
Benjamin James and Elizabeth Gelbreath, (MD) Oct. 2, 1810
Charles Jones and Patsey Durham, (MD) Jul. 28, 1810
Wm. McWhinney and Betsey Kindrick, (MD) Oct. 5, 1810
John Scott and Marybe Ball, (MD) Mar. 6, 1810
John Sharp and Polly Tulloch, (MD) May 21, 1810
George Snider and Isabella White, (MD) Oct. 25, 1810
William Wallace and Polly Chamberlain, (MD) Jun. 27, 1810
Charles Baker and Sally Cabell, (MD) Nov. 25, 1811
William Glass and Agnus McCulloch, (MD) Apr. 2, 1811
John Law and Nancy Greene, (MD) Jul. 24, 1811
William Taylor and Elizabeth Snider, (MD) Jan. 30, 1811
William Thompson and Rebeckah Wallace, (MD) Apr. 24, 1811
William Wheeler and Nancy Watson, (MD) Sep. 2, 1811
Isaac Hicks and Sarah Long Walker, (MD) Oct. 27, 1812
Thomas Barnett and Nancy McKeigg, (MD) Sep. 9, 1812
John Bowman and Catherine Bowerman, (MD) Jun. 29, 1812
Charles Choat and Leties Camron, (MD) Jun. 19, 1812
James Cochran and Polly Reid, (MD) Oct. 8, 1812
Issom Douglas and Nancy Martin, (MD) Aug. 6, 1812
John Ewing and Susanna Minnis, (MD) Sep. 16, 1812
Elijah Farmer and Polly Blankinship, (MD) Aug. 12, 1812
Alexander Glass and Ann McCulloch, (MD) Aug. 26, 1812
John Guinn and Jane Walker, (MD) Apr. 8, 1812
John Harris and Rebecka Paul, (MD) Nov. 26, 1812
Robert Kindrick and Frankey Reeder, (MD) Jan. 20, 1812
David McCamy and Mary Simons, (MD) Sep. 8, 1812
David McCord and Jane McNeily, (MD) Mar. 18, 1812

James McNeeley and Betsy Houston, (MD) Jul. 14, 1812
James Smith and Mary Tedford, (MD) Mar. ??, 1812
David Waid and Mary Vaught, (MD) Dec. 8, 1812
William Billue and Jane James, (MD) Jun. 14, 1813
William Croley and Jane Chamberlain, (MD) Dec. 4, 1813
John Hisks and Catty Simmons, (MD) Dec. 28, 1813
Andrew Miller and Sally Scott, (MD) Sep. 23, 1813
John Smith and Isabell Vincent, (MD) Jul. 18, 1813
Melinda Vaught and Mich L. Ghormley, (MD) Feb. 12, 1814
Beverage Lawrence and Kezia A. Patton, (MD) Dec. 22, 1814
William S. Mason and Isabella Gibbs, (MD) Jun. 29, 1814
Mich L. Ghormley and Melinda Vaught, (MD) Feb. 12, 1814
Richard C. Edmonson and Leah Hickland, (MD) Apr. 6, 1814
Kezia A. Patton and Beverage Lawrence, (MD) Dec. 22, 1814
Isaac Bonine and Sarah Talbert, (MD) Aug. 18, 1814
Amos Boren and Anny Hiles, (MD) Mar. 30, 1814
Edward Hart and Elizabeth Hood, (MD) Feb. 21, 1814
James Henry and Esther Rogers, (MD) Nov. 25, 1814
Abraham Jones and Rebecca Yunt, (MD) Sep. 4, 1814
Alexander Patterson and Betsy Stuard, (MD) Mar. 21, 1814
Joseph Remerton and Polly Johnston, (MD) Jul. 15, 1814
John Roach and Polly Mash, (MD) Aug. 31, 1814
Matthew Samples and Polly Sexton, (MD) Feb. 29, 1814
Eli Tipton and Peggy Walker, (MD) Sep. 16, 1814
Nathan Williams and Rachael Bonine, (MD) Aug. 9, 1814
Robert Wilson and Esther Carrethers, (MD) Feb. 22, 1814
William C. Rankin and Catherine Gault, (MD) Nov. 30, 1815
David Alexander and Elizabeth Conn, (MD) Nov. 28, 1815
Joseph Brown and Catherine Breakbill, (MD) Oct. 9, 1815
Henry Crittington and Polly Bowerman, (MD) Jul. 4, 1815
Adam Cupp and Peggy Capshaw, (MD) Oct. 18, 1815
Frederick Cupp and Nancy Capshaw, (MD) Jul. 27, 1815
Samuel Dugan and Frances Childres, (MD) Sep. 1, 1815
Thomas Gray and Lucinda Berry, (MD) Jun. 19, 1815
Samuel Hackney and Polly Lambert, (MD) Apr. 28, 1815
Edmund Hunt and Floria Houk, (MD) Aug. 28, 1815
Frances Johnston and Jane Ferguson, (MD) Aug. 29, 1815
John Johnston and Kezia Rowan, (MD) May 9, 1815
David Key and Nancy Bright, (MD) Sep. 21, 1815
Nathan Lane and Sussey Manson, (MD) Dec. 27, 1815
John McCartney and Peggy Boyd, (MD) Jul. 30, 1815
John McConnel and Ann Stuart, (MD) Oct. 25, 1815
Joseph McRanalds and Sally McClure, (MD) Nov. 21, 1815

Elisha Moore and Harriott Creswell, (MD) May 15, 1815
William Rasser and Rutha Hix, (MD) Dec. 30, 1815
John Rouse and Lydia Remington, (MD) Jul. 20, 1815
Isaac Vann and Labinia Scripshir, (MD) Aug. 24, 1815
Benjamin Wallace and Rachel Neil, (MD) Dec. 18, 1815
John Wilson and Peggy Jackson, (MD) Oct. 2, 1815
Jeremiah Johnston and Polly R. Kimberl, (MD) Jan. 17, 1816
Joseph Vaught and Eavy P. Ross, (MD) Mar. 16, 1816
Haywood G. Bennett and Esther L. Houston, (MD) Nov. 13, 1816
Andrew Cowan and Esther F. Houston, (MD) Sep. 25, 1816
James Goliher and Lucinda C. Houston, (MD) Dec. 4, 1816
John M. Rankin and Polly Ann Weir, (MD) Aug. 15, 1816
Alexander Logan and Mary A. Edmondson, (MD) Dec. 26, 1816
Samuel M. Lemons and Ann Weldon, (MD) Dec. 16, 1816
Alexander H. Sharp and Susannah Maxwell, (MD) Sep. 10, 1816
Samuel Acklin and Rebecca Hickey, (MD) Jan. 23, 1816
Alexander Aikin and Tempy Crew, (MD) Dec. 24, 1816
Robert Baity and Rebecah Cammil, (MD) Mar. 30, 1816
Uriah Black and Elizabeth Thompson, (MD) Mar. 19, 1816
Michael Bowerman and Nancy Coulbourn, (MD) Jul. 22, 1816
John Boyd and Matilda Loftiss, (MD) Oct. 31, 1816
Jasper Bright and Polly Key, (MD) Apr. 16, 1816
William Campbell and Margaret Sloan, (MD) Oct. 3, 1816
Robert Carson and Patsey Brease, (MD) Oct. 31, 1816
William Carson and Rosannah McCully, (MD) Sep. 5, 1816
Jonathan Cunningham and Betsy Chitty, (MD) Mar. 2, 1816
Moses Davis and Polly Smith, (MD) Jan. 29, 1816
James Douglas and Polly Brown, (MD) Dec. 27, 1816
William Dunlap and Ellenor Ewing, (MD) Sep. 24, 1816
Wm. Dunn and Catherine Pope, (MD) Oct. 12, 1816
William Eagleton and Peggy Ewing, (MD) Apr. 2, 1816
Thomas Eakin and Nancy Crew, (MD) Jun. 7, 1816
Frederick Edmondson and Celia Hickland, (MD) Apr. 23, 1816
William Everett and Polly Gay, (MD) Jul. 18, 1816
John Ewing and Sally McGauhy, (MD) Dec. 12, 1816
James Findley and Margaret Pickens, (MD) Feb. 15, 1816
King Golliher and Peggy McWhinney, (MD) Jun. 22, 1816
Nathan Hargis and Rebecca Tulluch, (MD) Feb. 22, 1816
Tolliver Harris and Patsy Hope, (MD) Jul. 30, 1816
John Hicks and Rebekah Wade, (MD) Mar. 14, 1816
Barnes Holloway and Ruth Wallace, (MD) Jun. 20, 1816
James Houston and Ann Houston, (MD) Oct. 17, 1816
John Huling and Sally Snider, (MD) Jun. 20, 1816

James Jack and Nancy McCallie, (MD) Feb. 6, 1816
James Johnston and Nancy Davis, (MD) Jan. 16, 1816
Felix Kennedy and Betsy Long, (MD) Sep. 15, 1816
George Love and Nancy Whittenbarger, (MD) Sep. 10, 1816
George McClung and Betty Wilson, (MD) Apr. 23, 1816
James McClung and Peggy Montgomery, (MD) Aug. 8, 1816
Samuel McCroskey and Polly McCollom, (MD) Nov. 12, 1816
Alexander McNutt and Polly Singleton, (MD) Sep. 24, 1816
John Minis and Nancy Warren, (MD) Nov. 13, 1816
James Murphy and Mary Walker, (MD) Oct. 2, 1816
John Parks and Ruth Brown, (MD) Aug. 13, 1816
Henry Reagan and Malinda Delosure, (MD) Feb. 29, 1816
Luna Rhea and Peggy Brooks, (MD) May 18, 1816
Vincen Rogers and Abby Hardin, (MD) Sep. 5, 1816
Samuel Roork and Tabitha Phillips, (MD) Sep. 6, 1816
Hezekiah Routh and Elizabeth Posey, (MD) Oct. 3, 1816
Fuller Ryen and Nancy Brakebill, (MD) Sep. 25, 1816
John Simms and Sally McMurry, (MD) Jul. 25, 1816
John Simons and Rutha Carson, (MD) May 10, 1816
Jacob Snider and Susan Elder, (MD) Jan. 25, 1816
Elisha Spragan and Sally Boling, (MD) Jan. 3, 1816
Frederick Thomas and Patsy McFarland, (MD) Feb. 1, 1816
Samuel Utter and Jane Vance, (MD) Sep. 5, 1816
James Walker and Joannah Elliott, (MD) Apr. 4, 1816
Joseph Walker and Polly Boaz, (MD) Jun. 21, 1816
William Wallace and Margaret Chamberlain, (MD) Oct. 17, 1816
Samuel Wheeler and Peggy Cowan, (MD) Sep. 3, 1816
John Yearout and Patsy Roulston, (MD) Oct. 10, 1816
James Young and Sally Wade, (MD) Mar. 14, 1816
Hambright Black and Mary W. Berry, (MD) Feb. 18, 1817
Samuel Glass and Elizabeth M. Glass, (MD) Jan. 21, 1817
Thos. Smith and Jane M. Paul, (MD) Jul. 8, 1817
Thos. S. Smith and Nancy Farmer, (MD) Jan. 2, 1817
Thomas G. Dearmond and Elizabeth Coldwell, (MD) Nov. 6, 1817
John B. Hale and Jane McClung, (MD) Jun. 17, 1817
Thomas B. McHenry and Fanny McMurry, (MD) Jul. 17, 1817
Joseph Balanger and Ann Farmer, (MD) Sep. 11, 1817
James Ballenger and Rebaka Bailess, (MD) Jun. 19, 1817
Samuel Beaty and Sarah Pate, (MD) Jan. 27, 1817
Benjamin Bond and Rosanna Martin, (MD) Dec. 25, 1817
Floyd Bostick and Rosannah Murray, (MD) Jun. 12, 1817
William Braidwell and Ainey Fifer, (MD) May 12, 1817
John Breakbill and Anna Thomas, (MD) Feb. 17, 1817

William Brooks and Polly Wade, (MD) May 30, 1817
William Burns and Patty James, (MD) Mar. 12, 1817
Alexander Cawhorn and Elizabeth Guy, (MD) Feb. 12, 1817
James Coldwell and Nancy Kelly, (MD) Oct. 2, 1817
James Conner and Lucinda McCool, (MD) Feb. 6, 1817
Sirus Curtes and Polly Shook, (MD) Jan. 19, 1817
Quintin Dines and Jane Brannum, (MD) Nov. 7, 1817
Solomon Eakin and Fanny Jenkins, (MD) Sep. 22, 1817
John Edwards and Penelopy Farr, (MD) Dec. 23, 1817
Alexander Ewing and Jane Warren, (MD) Dec. 8, 1817
Samuel Farr and Elizabeth Boren, (MD) Apr. 15, 1817
John Hackney and Rachel Jones, (MD) Aug. 9, 1817
Adly Harris and Rebecca Gracy, (MD) Apr. 29, 1817
James Henderson and Mary Hunter, (MD) Dec. 30, 1817
John Henry and Esther Gamble, (MD) Oct. 8, 1817
John Houston and Patsy Gillespie, (MD) Oct. 16, 1817
David Irwin and Dorcas Wright, (MD) Jul. 16, 1817
William Jackson and Mary Majors, (MD) Aug. 10, 1817
Wm. Jones and Catty Leadbetter, (MD) Mar. 25, 1817
George Martin and Lucy Saunders, (MD) Aug. 23, 1817
Harlan Mathews and Nancy McCaslin, (MD) Apr. 3, 1817
Nicholas McCool and Ellender Conner, (MD) Sep. 17, 1817
William McCullock and Priscilla Cunningham, (MD) Nov. 24, 1817
Frederick McDonald and Lockey Davis, (MD) Sep. 4, 1817
William McMurry and Peggy McKenry, (MD) Mar. 21, 1817
Robert McTeer and Ellen Conner, (MD) Dec. 18, 1817
Samuel Menis and Polly Pickens, (MD) Apr. 7, 1817
Thomas Menis and Pamelia Warren, (MD) Apr. 10, 1817
James Montgomery and Dorcas Russell, (MD) Dec. 30, 1817
Martin Moorefield and Polly Weaver, (MD) Sep. 24, 1817
Joshua Mosses and Sally Samples, (MD) Sep. 16, 1817
Samuel Reagan and Esther Hargis, (MD) Feb. 13, 1817
Joseph Rhea and Amy Allen, (MD) Aug. 21, 1817
Benjamin Robenette and Rebecca Franks, (MD) Dec. 24, 1817
Lewis Ross and Fanny Holt, (MD) Mar. 15, 1817
John Rush and Mary Beaty, (MD) Sep. 19, 1817
William Shook and Patsy Pride, (MD) Jul. 23, 1817
Benjamin Smith and Polly McAlroy, (MD) Feb. 1, 1817
Jacob Smith and Nancy Houk, (MD) Aug. 20, 1817
William Stone and Sally Diddle, (MD) Apr. 24, 1817
David Taylor and Polly Bigbay, (MD) Sep. 9, 1817
Daniel Teefeteller and Patsy Curtis, (MD) Mar. 14, 1817
John Thompson and Elender Malcom, (MD) Sep. 11, 1817

Robert Thompson and Elizabeth Berry, (MD) Sep. 25, 1817
James Torbet and Patsy Hall, (MD) Jun. 19, 1817
Walker Wade and Mary Snider, (MD) Oct. 29, 1817
Willis Webb and Anna Vaught, (MD) Jul. 16, 1817
Joseph Wilson and Jenet Bayless, (MD) Mar. 27, 1817
James Wooddy and Mary Bane, (MD) Sep. 24, 1817
John S. Burnette and Lydia S. Danforth, (MD) Nov. 12, 1818
James McCartney and Jane M. Russell, (MD) Mar. 3, 1818
Wm. J. Byrd and Malinda H. Gillespy, (MD) Mar. 24, 1818
James Ragan and Elizabeth H. Bates, (MD) Nov. 26, 1818
Jacob F. Foute and Martha E. Berry, (MD) Sep. 29, 1818
James Berry and Rebecca C. McChesney, (MD) Aug. 13, 1818
John T. McAffry and Margaret Kile, (MD) Oct. 1, 1818
Caleb M. Norwood and Jane Manson, (MD) Dec. 5, 1818
Jones M. Russell and Nancy Clinton, (MD) Dec. 31, 1818
Thos. L. Reynolds and Nancy Henderson, (MD) Sep. 23, 1818
Blackmore H. Mayo and Grizy Kelso, (MD) Jul. 9, 1818
Wm. G. Wiseman and Polly Kennedy, (MD) Dec. 30, 1818
John D. Boring and Maryan Russell, (MD) Sep. 24, 1818
Job Allen and Margareta McClain, (MD) Sep. 10, 1818
Isaac Anderson and Isabella McMillin, (MD) Mar. 10, 1818
Dempsy Ballenger and Sarah Patty, (MD) Jul. 1, 1818
John Best and Esther McGauhy, (MD) Dec. 12, 1818
Aaron Bond and Sarah Carter, (MD) Dec. 10, 1818
Isaac Boring and Betsy May (MD) Aug. 15, 1818
John Bowerman and Sally McAlroy, (MD) Jan. 20, 1818
William Bradberry and Jenny Brewer, (MD) Dec. 21, 1818
Jesse Briant and Polly Haskelt, (MD) Dec. 12, 1818
Benjamin Brown and Jane White, (MD) Sep. 1, 1818
George Burns and Elizabeth Raper, (MD) Feb. 14, 1818
Martin Caddell and Mary Davis, (MD) Dec. 17, 1818
Isaac Campbell and Betsey George, (MD) May 14, 1818
Joel Campbell and Agnes Sloan, (MD) Feb. 20, 1818
John Campbell and Sally McClure, (MD) Aug. 20, 1818
William Carroll and Sally Tindel, (MD) Jul. 20, 1818
Abram Casteel and Mary Whittenberger, (MD) Aug. 2, 1818
Philip Casteel and Charlotte Franks, (MD) Sep. 29, 1818
James Clifton and Sally Lee, (MD) Dec. 1, 1818
Alexander Cook and Louisa Ball, (MD) Jan. 22, 1818
John Coppenbarger and Matilda Shugart, (MD) Mar. 11, 1818
John Coppock and Patsy Williams, (MD) Mar. 24, 1818
William Cox and Nancy Nicholson, (MD) Sep. 27, 1818
Elias Craft and Polly Kilbourne, (MD) Mar. 6, 1818

Hu Cunningham and Lucinda McGhee, (MD) Jun. 11, 1818
Asa Davis and Rody Read, (MD) Mar. 10, 1818
Peter Davis and Hannah Harris, (MD) Jul. 29, 1818
John Duggan and Mary Pue, (MD) Sep. 7, 1818
Will Farmer and Rebecca Wilson, (MD) Jan. 8, 1818
William Greene and Mary Bonham, (MD) Oct. 15, 1818
Samuel Grigsby and Dorcas Wyly, (MD) Jul. 9, 1818
Alex Hammontree and Rebecca Robinson, (MD) Dec. 22, 1818
William Harmon and Anna Jones, (MD) Aug. 20, 1818
Alexadner Hart and Jemimah Price, (MD) May 22, 1818
Jos Hasket and Patsy Briant, (MD) Dec. 10, 1818
James Henderson and Betsy Reynolds, (MD) Sep. 22, 1818
Thomas Henderson and Cristina Currier, (MD) Mar. 24, 1818
Jacob Huffman and Polly Lawrence, (MD) Dec. 4, 1818
Wm. Irland and Deborah Huffman, (MD) Dec. 14, 1818
Jesse James and Polly Rooker, (MD) Mar. 19, 1818
Samuel Johnston and Margaret Johnston, (MD) Nov. 14, 1818
Samuel Love and Mary Beeler, (MD) Jun. 30, 1818
George Martin and Sally Davis, (MD) Dec. 3, 1818
Moses Martin and Sally Greenway, (MD) Sep. 20, 1818
John McCallon and Polly McCartney, (MD) Mar. 24, 1818
James McCally and Margaret Ferguson, (MD) Dec. 30, 1818
Solomon McCampbell and Nancy Duran, (MD) Mar. 3, 1818
Henry McCurdy and Hannah Stone, (MD) Aug. 23, 1818
David McLanahan and Polly Ingrum, (MD) Sep. 28, 1818
Marshal McNabb and Mary Adams, (MD) Nov. 12, 1818
Kenneday Moffitt and Zalera Witcher, (MD) Oct. 6, 1818
James Page and Jane Brooks, (MD) Dec. 8, 1818
James Parks and Nancy Walden, (MD) Jul. 20, 1818
John Pennel and Jane McClannahan, (MD) Sep. 17, 1818
John Phillips and Sally Whittenberger, (MD) Feb. 10, 1818
John Poland and Emily McCartney, (MD) Mar. 10, 1818
Abraham Powell and Phebe Anderson, (MD) Dec. 12, 1818
Jemimah Price and Alexadner Hart, (MD) May 22, 1818
George Richardson and Ellen McCartney, (MD) Mar. 3, 1818
Julius Robertson and Peggy Reagan, (MD) May 14, 1818
Thomas Roork and Susannah Huffman, (MD) Dec. 15, 1818
John Samples and Elizabeth Kithcart, (MD) Oct. 28, 1818
Wm. Schrimsheer and Rebecka Vann, (MD) ??, ??, 1818
Alfred Scott and Peggy Wines, (MD) Dec. 9, 1818
James Scott and Nancy Hunter, (MD) Oct. 1, 1818
Joseph Shelton and Anne Phillips, (MD) Jul. 30, 1818
Elisha Tallent and Sally Moses, (MD) Dec. 29, 1818

Isaac Tate and Jemimah Brickey, (MD) Apr. 25, 1818
John Wilson and Polly McKamy, (MD) Oct. 13, 1818
Jeremiah Woodard and Charlotte Maroon, (MD) Feb. 14, 1818
John Wooden and Susannah Forester, (MD) Jul. 16, 1818
John Woods and Eliza Young, (MD) Jul. 18, 1818
John Woody and Abbe Turner, (MD) Apr. 13, 1818
Wm. R. White and Mary W. McGee, (MD) Oct. 25, 1819
Joseph B. Woods and Nancy P. Mayo, (MD) Jul. 14, 1819
David H. Burke and Dorcas M. Lowery, (MD) Jul. 15, 1819
John Weir and Polly L. Weir, (MD) Jun. 3, 1819
Andrew McCampbell and Martha G. Steele, (MD) Sep. 23, 1819
Hezekiah Mitchell and Mary D. Houston, (MD) Mar. 18, 1819
James W. Rogers and Peggy White, (MD) Feb. 4, 1819
John T. Adkins and Nancy Luckett, (MD) Jun. 24, 1819
Alexander S. Colter and Betsy Cumming, (MD) Feb. 22, 1819
John R. Jimeson and Elizabeth Tharp, (MD) Dec. 28, 1819
Reuban L. Cates and Amanda Wilkinson, (MD) Jun. 3, 1819
Sam L. Gault and Sally Wallace, (MD) Jan. 7, 1819
James C. Barnett and Tamer Bell, (MD) Jan. 21, 1819
Christopher A. Woods and Jane Thompson, (MD) Oct. 5, 1819
Berry Abernathey and Miry Cobb, (MD) Dec. 18, 1819
John Anderson and Polly Coker, (MD) Jan. 28, 1819
Jonathan Anderson and Julia Farmer, (MD) Jun. 17, 1819
James Balanger and Rhtuey Bayless, (MD) Aug. 12, 1819
William Bane and Polly Stephenson, (MD) Sep. 11, 1819
Peter Bond and Joannah Martin, (MD) Sep. 26, 1819
William Breakbill and Mary Keller, (MD) Oct. 4, 1819
William Brown and Peggy Strain, (MD) Mar. 10, 1819
Samuel Butler and Elizabet Medlock, (MD) Jul. 1, 1819
Charles Carter and Sarah Lowe, (MD) Aug. 3, 1819
Samuel Carter and Sally Campbell, (MD) Jan. 16, 1819
John Cavett and Sally Wiggins, (MD) Oct. 6, 1819
Matthew Chadwick and Charity King, (MD) Mar. 25, 1819
Benjamin Coup and Amy Pitman, (MD) Apr. 3, 1819
William Crush and Jenny Gibbs, (MD) Mar. 9, 1819
Wm. Crush and Jenny Gibbs, (MD) Mar. 9, 1819
Jacob Cupp and Susan Lingumphelter, (MD) Apr. 20, 1819
George Davis and Alsy Rhea, (MD) May 13, 1819
Jesse Fosha and Sally Fosha, (MD) Apr. 7, 1819
John Gardner and Jane Farr, (MD) Mar. 23, 1819
Richard Gay and Catherine Ransbarger, (MD) Jan. 5, 1819
John Goodman and Ruthy Roach, (MD) Jun. 10, 1819
Elijah Hatcher and Rebecca Walker, (MD) Aug. 6, 1819

Joseph Henderson and Jennet McClung, (MD) Apr. 1, 1819
Wm. Henderson and Elizabeth McGill, (MD) Jan. 12, 1819
Frederick Hittle and Polly Edmonds, (MD) Oct. 2, 1819
Thomas Jones and Agnes Lambert, (MD) May 13, 1819
Daniel Lane and Mary Robertson, (MD) Dec. 16, 1819
Middleton Lane and Nancy Forister, (MD) Dec. 30, 1819
Jeremiah Law and Sally Russell, (MD) Jul. 8, 1819
Bartley Lawson and Elizabeth Douherty, (MD) Jul. 14, 1819
James Martin and Jane Glass, (MD) Nov. 9, 1819
Robert McClain and Susannah Casteel, (MD) Nov. 30, 1819
John McClure and Elizabeth Mitchell, (MD) Jan. 28, 1819
Michal McGuire and Polly Forister, (MD) Feb. 18, 1819
Woods McRandals and Polly McClure, (MD) Feb. 18, 1819
William McTeer and Mary Bogle, (MD) Sep. 16, 1819
Joel Morrison and Nancy Low, (MD) Apr. 20, 1819
G. Nemon and Any Thompson, (MD) Jan. 13, 1819
James Rankin and Sarah Gault, (MD) Nov. 4, 1819
George Ray and Elizabeth Hufman, (MD) Mar. 20, 1819
William Redmon and Rebecca Pate, (MD) May 4, 1819
Martin Rhea and Polly Tipton, (MD) Apr. 15, 1819
Charles Richman and Rodah Franks, (MD) Oct. 25, 1819
James Roach and Catherine Clift, (MD) Aug. 1, 1819
George Robenett and Delilah Fosha, (MD) Feb. 16, 1819
James Roper and Peggy McNally, (MD) Dec. 23, 1819
James Rush and Mary Caler, (MD) Dec. 27, 1819
David Scroggs and Margaret Delzell, (MD) Oct. 6, 1819
George Shamblin and Sarah Hicks, (MD) Dec. 29, 1819
Jacob Snider and Anna Neal, (MD) Nov. 1, 1819
Jacob Stuart and Mary Panther, (MD) Oct. 25, 1819
William Tate and Vina Sawyers, (MD) May 20, 1819
Isaias Thompson and Hannah Phillips, (MD) Jan. 13, 1819
Spencer Thompson and Susannah Montgomery, (MD) Apr. 14, 1819
Carey Tuck and Anna Thompson, (MD) Sep. 22, 1819
William Utter and Sarah Alexander, (MD) Aug. 10, 1819
Joseph Weir and Sally Martin, (MD) Nov. 10, 1819
William Welburn and Rebecka Snider, (MD) Jan. 14, 1819
James Wiggins and Elizabeth Swearingen, (MD) Aug. 14, 1819
Josua Williams and Hannah Copeland, (MD) Jun. 24, 1819
Nicholas Williams and Olivia Nance, (MD) Nov. 7, 1819
John Wilson and Caty Freshour, (MD) Jan. 4, 1819
Peter Yount and Nancy Shook, (MD) Sep. 23, 1819
Allen G. Jack and Betsey W. McCallie, (MD) Dec. 14, 1820
Dr Joseph, Reese and Sophia T, Emmerson, (MD) Nov. 1, 1820

Madison Caywood and Catherine T, Sterling, (MD) Aug. 27, 1820
Enoch Robenitt and Tellitha T, Fosha, (MD) Mar. 20, 1820
William S. Blair and Paty Mahala Hall, (MD) Apr. 4, 1820
George Henderson and Nancy Ann Thompson, (MD) May 25, 1820
John McCroskey and Lucinda A. Grant, (MD) Apr. 4, 1820
Allen W. Davis and Mary Houston, (MD) Mar. 7, 1820
Wm. W. Henry and Sarah Utter, (MD) Oct. 7, 1820
Wm. P. Peterson and Elizabeth Brewer, (MD) Nov. 28, 1820
James M. Sappington and Jememah Wimberlee, (MD) Mar. 7, 1820
Dread J. Freeman and Betsy Thompson, (MD) May 2, 1820
Young H. Griffin and Anna Heath, (MD) Feb. 11, 1820
John H. Shaddin and Nancy McMurray, (MD) Nov. 21, 1820
Thomas D. Oconner and Mary McFaddin, (MD) Apr. 24, 1820
Thos D. Oconnor and Mary McFaddin, (MD) Apr. 24, 1820
William Alexander and Margaret Duncan, (MD) Jan. 13, 1820
Adron Ball and Polly Harres, (MD) Oct. 7, 1820
William Barton and Nancy Bradberry, (MD) Jan. 10, 1820
Abednego Biddy and Patsy Carrol, (MD) Dec. 14, 1820
Christian Bird and Catherine Milton, (MD) Mar. 9, 1820
Gilbert Blankenship and Edy Lane, (MD) Aug. 9, 1820
Samuel Brazelton and Jane Frew, (MD) Oct. 26, 1820
Andrew Campbell and Sarah Duncan, (MD) Aug. 31, 1820
Elijah Carroll and Susannah Grisham, (MD) Aug. 28, 1820
Amos Carter and Betsy Rush, (MD) Feb. 26, 1820
Bazel Carter and Elen McCurdy, (MD) Aug. 3, 1820
Joseph Collins and Isabella Haones, (MD) Dec. 14, 1820
William Cunningham and Hannah Torbit, (MD) Jan. 3, 1820
James Duncan and Jane Rankin, (MD) Mar. 30, 1820
William Dunlap and Jean Coldwell, (MD) Jan. 12, 1820
William Dunwoody and Betsy McGinley, (MD) Feb. 29, 1820
William Eakin and Jane Hooks, (MD) Dec. 3, 1820
Jason Eliott and Rebecca Harris, (MD) Oct. 7, 1820
Lewis Farmer and Lydia Snider, (MD) Dec. 19, 1820
Robert Furguson and Ruth Duff, (MD) Apr. 13, 1820
Josiah Gamble and Polly Farmer, (MD) Feb. 3, 1820
Samuel Gay and Elizabeth Milligan, (MD) Nov. 14, 1820
Archibald Gibbs and Margaret Gallion, (MD) May 23, 1820
John Giffin and Hannah Jordon, (MD) Mar. 30, 1820
John Hall and Elizabeth Wyley, (MD) Nov. 6, 1820
Acy Hardwick and Mary Knoblete, (MD) May 18, 1820
William Harper and Polly Kenniman, (MD) Jun. 22, 1820
John Hess and Polly Garner, (MD) Apr. 25, 1820
Elijah James and Malinda Ticker, (MD) Jan. 16, 1820

Robert Johnston and Barby Ormand, (MD) Jan. 27, 1820
David Kerr and Polly Miller, (MD) Oct. 27, 1820
George Madden and Delilah Hartsell, (MD) Nov. 10, 1820
James McClurg and Jane Henderson, (MD) Jun. 3, 1820
Thomas McClurkin and Delina Goodwin, (MD) Jun. 19, 1820
William McKamy and Nancy Coldwell, (MD) Jan. 27, 1820
William Melone and Nancy Hix, (MD) Mar. 14, 1820
John Morton and Mary Wells, (MD) Oct. 3, 1820
Joshua Parks and Elizabeth Vaught, (MD) Jul. 13, 1820
Josiah Phillips and Elizabeth Deen, (MD) Feb. 24, 1820
Jeremiah Plummer and Jane Snider, (MD) Nov. 5, 1820
Thomas Rhyne and Agness Wethers, (MD) Jun. 1, 1820
Jesse Rogers and Celia Kagle, (MD) Jul. 29, 1820
Daniel Shahan and Patsey Hussong, (MD) Aug. 10, 1820
Archebald Sloan and Susan Snider, (MD) Dec. 19, 1820
John Smith and Jane Campbell, (MD) Mar. 14, 1820
Joshua Smith and Peggy Keller, (MD) Jun. 1, 1820
William Snider and Peggy White, (MD) Nov. 7, 1820
Ezekial Starr and Polly Upshaw, (MD) Feb. 29, 1820
Joseph Stephenson and Letitia Payne, (MD) Mar. 28, 1820
John Swanger and Peggy Stephens, (MD) Dec. 19, 1820
William Tucker and Ann James, (MD) Feb. 6, 1820
David Vaught and Nancy Harmon, (MD) Aug. 5, 1820
Benjamin Walker and Anny Caldwell, (MD) Oct. 5, 1820
George Weathers and Reeny Stephens, (MD) Feb. 8, 1820
Thomas Low and Jane M. Maxwell, (MD) Mar. 1, 1821
John Ferguson and Matilda H. Sexton, (MD) Jul. 24, 1821
Jesse Thompson and Elizabeth H. Montgomery, (MD) May 29, 1821
Saml. A. Moore and Eliza Ann Houston, (MD) Jul. 21, 1821
Able Crisp and Polly Ann Porter, (MD) Feb. 22, 1821
Moses Elliott and Mary Ann Divine, (MD) Feb. 19, 1821
John Gault and Jane A. Thompson, (MD) Aug. 29, 1821
James R. Logan and Rachel Philip, (MD) Feb. 8, 1821
John P. Chapman and Sally Maclin, (MD) May 1, 1821
Matthew M. Houston and Mary Gillespie, (MD) Nov. 29, 1821
John L. McKinzie and Mary Grigsby, (MD) Oct. 17, 1821
John Rider, Jr., and Dorcas Thompson, (MD) Mar. 8, 1821
Wm. H. Reagan and Margaret Carnard, (MD) Dec. 7, 1821
Thomas Berry and Cyntha Russell, (MD) Aug. 28, 1821
Wm. Bowers and Lucretia Harris, (MD) Apr. 12, 1821
Milton Bradbury and Susannah Blackwell, (MD) Feb. 13, 1821
Joel Brock and Patsey Sexton, (MD) Nov. 15, 1821
James Carden and Sarah McConnell, (MD) Feb. 28, 1821

James Chormley and Elizabeth Thompson, (MD) Apr. 5, 1821
Wm. Cooper and Catherine David, (MD) Feb. 10, 1821
Richard Cottrell and Matilda Vaught, (MD) Dec. 29, 1821
Miles Cunningham and Betsy Ghormley, (MD) May 23, 1821
William Davis and Sally Bowers, (MD) May 3, 1821
Wm. Deaver and Elizabeth Mackey, (MD) Mar. 1, 1821
Silas Deen and Rebeka Rogers, (MD) Oct. 2, 1821
Edom Dixon and Polly Law, (MD) Feb. 10, 1821
John Dyer and Margaret McCurdy, (MD) Feb. 12, 1821
John Enis and Dorcas Jacobs, (MD) Dec. 20, 1821
William Erwin and Elizabeth Stanton, (MD) Jan. 11, 1821
Isaac Hart and Martha Roddy, (MD) Oct. 9, 1821
Reubin Hatcher and Martha McGill, (MD) Jun. 1, 1821
Jeremiah Hays and Margaret Hood, (MD) May 23, 1821
William Hays and Betsey Brown, (MD) Mar. 29, 1821
Wm. Johnson and Elizabeth Whittenberger, (MD) Aug. 20, 1821
Henry Keller and Mary Barnett, (MD) Jan. 25, 1821
John Kennedy and Nancy Townsley, (MD) Jul. 5, 1821
Thomas Lane and Patsey Kayton, (MD) Mar. 8, 1821
William Little and Susannah Johnson, (MD) Mar. 17, 1821
Alex Lowry and Elizabeth Johnson, (MD) Dec. 13, 1821
Archibald McCallie and Sally Thompson, (MD) Jul. 26, 1821
Patrick McClung and Margaret Cowan, (MD) May 31, 1821
Wm. McDaniel and Matilda Kirkpatrick, (MD) Jan. 16, 1821
Edmund McEldry and Hetty Roddy, (MD) Nov. 15, 1821
John McGhee and Mary White, (MD) May 3, 1821
James McGinley and Margaret Previtt, (MD) Jan. 23, 1821
Samuel McReynolds and Jane Hale, (MD) May 10, 1821
Samuel McTeer and Sally Cummons, (MD) Jul. 19, 1821
James Oliver and Polly White, (MD) Nov. 28, 1821
David Ormand and Zelphy Davis, (MD) Jan. 20, 1821
John Polland and Nansey Davis, (MD) Oct. 12, 1821
Joseph Price and Sarah Bond, (MD) Apr. 26, 1821
John Ramsower and Hannah Danton, (MD) Dec. 29, 1821
Ephtiam Regan and Hannah Harper, (MD) Jan. 2, 1821
John Russell and Rosana Gillespie, (MD) Jun. 14, 1821
Addison Sharp and Susannah Maxwell, (MD) Dec. 26, 1821
William Smith and Rebecah Loftis, (MD) Oct. 12, 1821
John Spradlin and Zelpha Bryant, (MD) Mar. 1, 1821
Wm. Starliens and Ruthy Green, (MD) Sep. 13, 1821
John Stephens and Barbara Yountt, (MD) Dec. 31, 1821
John Tipton and Mary Helton, (MD) Apr. 9, 1821
Low Todd and Polly Simons, (MD) Aug. 15, 1821

Wm. Trotter and Elizabeth Hart, (MD) Oct. 4, 1821
Kinchen Wall and Elizabeth Talent, (MD) Dec. 27, 1821
Hugh Weathers and Maryan William, (MD) May 22, 1821
Thomas Webb and Polly Hill, (MD) Oct. 27, 1821
Thomas Webb and Nancy Samples, (MD) Jun. 6, 1821
Andrew C. Montgomery and Ann M. Houston, (MD) Oct. 24, 1822
Samuel McClure and Elvira M. Douthit, (MD) Jul. 16, 1822
Samuel Steele and Polly M. McClung, (MD) Jul. 18, 1822
John B. Elliott and Elizabeth J. Bell, (MD) Dec. 20, 1822
Robert Carson and Mary J. Seaton, (MD) Jul. 16, 1822
Mathew C. Houston and Esther H. Gillespie, (MD) Aug. 8, 1822
David George and Ann Eliza Edmonston, (MD) Aug. 28, 1822
Thomas Upton and Ann E. Yearout, (MD) Oct. 15, 1822
Alexander O, George and Elizabeth Paul, (MD) Dec. 24, 1822
Charles K. Shedden and Ann Wilson, (MD) Feb. 26, 1822
Robert Jr, Murren and Caty Bowers, (MD) Mar. 7, 1822
John H. Hair and Elizabeth McClure, (MD) Dec. 5, 1822
Wm. H. Hodge and Lucinda Jeffries, (MD) Feb. 14, 1822
Wm. D. Sewell and Susannah Brawn, (MD) Feb. 21, 1822
James Ball and Rebecca Shot, (MD) Mar. 24, 1822
Robert Bohannan and Elizabeth Janes, (MD) Oct. 17, 1822
Joab Brooks and Sally Burton, (MD) Aug. 15, 1822
Christian Cagle and Patience Cardwell, (MD) Dec. 28, 1822
John Caldwell and Cinthia Shadden, (MD) Feb. 22, 1822
Campbell Carver and Polly Davis, (MD) Jul. 30, 1822
John Cochran and Jane Orr, (MD) Aug. 8, 1822
Tarrence Conner and Polly Young, (MD) Jul. 18, 1822
John Davis and Polly Low, (MD) Jan. 3, 1822
William Davis and Ann Conner, (MD) Jun. 5, 1822
John Devor and Eliza Freeman, (MD) May 22, 1822
Jeremiah Duncan and Elizabeth Chandler, (MD) Aug. 8, 1822
Robert Finley and Agnes Edmiston, (MD) Feb. 8, 1822
Frederick French and Polly Hensley, (MD) Apr. 15, 1822
Andrew Furguson and Susan Carson, (MD) Feb. 14, 1822
Moses Gamble and Jane McCallie, (MD) Nov. 28, 1822
Alexander Gay and Jane Aiken, (MD) Sep. 17, 1822
William Gay and Elizabeth Furguson, (MD) Nov. 7, 1822
Atlas Gibson and Orphy Pierce, (MD) Sep. 3, 1822
Jacob Hair and Elizabeth McClain, (MD) Feb. 14, 1822
Harris Hammontree and Sarah Robertson, (MD) Jan. 12, 1822
Nathan Harris and Jane Lowery, (MD) Feb. 27, 1822
William Henderson and Cynthia Walker, (MD) Jul. 23, 1822
James Henry and Sally Walker, (MD) Aug. 22, 1822

David Hickey and Fanny Bohannan, (MD) Mar. 21, 1822
Elise Hitch and Polly Shook, (MD) Dec. 26, 1822
John Jackson and Eliza Brown, (MD) Jul. 4, 1822
Eli Johnston and Polly Winchester, (MD) Feb. 18, 1822
Clemuel Lee and Sally Chammels, (MD) Aug. 23, 1822
Lewis McCroy and Malicia Goodwin, (MD) Mar. 6, 1822
Abraham Miller and Elizabeth Cannada, (MD) Jan. 8, 1822
Wm. Morris and Elizabeth Eanis, (MD) Dec. 1, 1822
Robert Neel and Nancy Henderson, (MD) Jan. 30, 1822
Thomas Norwood and Anna Rice, (MD) Feb. 19, 1822
Wm. Patrick and Polly Williams, (MD) Oct. 20, 1822
Abraham Phillips and Nancy Wheeler, (MD) Nov. 7, 1822
Isaac Phillips and Margaret Plumer, (MD) Dec. 24, 1822
John Raines and Polly Huckaby, (MD) Jul. 20, 1822
John Ramsey and Susannah Griffitts, (MD) Jan. 26, 1822
Josiah Reagan and Elizabeth Henry, (MD) Feb. 14, 1822
Thomas Stanfield and Esther Rice, (MD) Sep. 10, 1822
Thomas Sutherland and Ann Henry, (MD) Apr. 25, 1822
John Thomas and Elizabeth Daniels, (MD) Aug. 3, 1822
William Thomas and Polly Carver, (MD) Nov. 30, 1822
Jesse Upton and Polly Hackney, (MD) Feb. 27, 1822
Vance Walker and Catherine Henry, (MD) Jan. 17, 1822
James Walls and Betsy Cirkland, (MD) Jan. 17, 1822
Notley Warren and Polly Vanpelt, (MD) Mar. 14, 1822
Edward Westmoreland and Rebecca Hackney, (MD) Mar. 17, 1822
George Williams and Nancy Hall, (MD) Aug. 5, 1822
Albert Wiseman and Sinah Ormond, (MD) Nov. 9, 1822
Henry Wooden and Polly Hathway, (MD) Sep. 14, 1822
James Gillespie and Patsy W. Wallace, (MD) Aug. 12, 1823
Delizon W. Clark and Ann J Conger, (MD) Aug. 9, 1823
Ellen Pickens and Francis J. Henderson, (MD) Mar. 11, 1823
George W. Mayo and Polly H. Woods, (MD) Jul. 11, 1823
James Reid and Polly B. Thompson, (MD) Aug. 12, 1823
James Clark and Esther Ann Bell, (MD) Sep. 8, 1823
Will W. Henry and Jane Tulloch, (MD) Dec. 25, 1823
Robert S. Parsons and Nancy Shanks, (MD) Sep. 25, 1823
John P. Kenney and Alley Plumblee, (MD) Apr. 23, 1823
Alfred N. Woods and Margaret Garons, (MD) Sep. 13, 1823
David L. Logan and Peggy Philips, (MD) May 1, 1823
Francis J. Henderson and Ellen Pickens, (MD) Mar. 11, 1823
Caldwell St. Clair and Margaret Montgomery, (MD) Jan. 16, 1823
Joseph C. Kennedy and Ann Thompson, (MD) Jul. 17, 1823
Brain C. Morse and Ann Cope, (MD) Oct. 2, 1823

David B. Tipton and Sally Janes, (MD) Aug. 17, 1823
John Akrige and Sally Akrige, (MD) Oct. 22, 1823
James Alexander and Nancy Ford, (MD) Feb. 4, 1823
Nathaniel Austin and Polly Gaines, (MD) Aug. 24, 1823
James Beard and Jane Ewing, (MD) Aug. 14, 1823
Wm. Beaty and Polly Brickey, (MD) Feb. 10, 1823
Bryant Brandy and Nelly Hix, (MD) Feb. 23, 1823
Wm. Brickey and Abigail Waters, (MD) Jul. 27, 1823
Jesse Campbell and Martha Porter, (MD) Jan. 22, 1823
James Cavin and Elizabeth Toopes, (MD) Apr. 29, 1823
Harden Cunningham and Rachel Harper, (MD) Apr. 9, 1823
John Delzell and Elizabeth Blair, (MD) Oct. 24, 1823
John Eakin and Margaret Houston, (MD) Mar. 11, 1823
William Early and Rebecca Young, (MD) Dec. 2, 1823
David Edmondson and Egny Scott, (MD) Oct. 21, 1823
John Gault and Margaret Weir, (MD) Jun. 5, 1823
John Gillespie and Jane Kilbourn, (MD) Oct. 16, 1823
William Gregsby and Polly Greenway, (MD) Nov. 20, 1823
Michael Hammon and Malinda McCool, (MD) Jul. 30, 1823
Silas Hart and Susan Straine, (MD) Feb. 20, 1823
Daniel Hickey and Betsy Tipton, (MD) Jul. 5, 1823
Jacob Hollingsworth and Jane Crawford, (MD) Apr. 22, 1823
William Inman and Mary Wear, (MD) May 26, 1823
Jeremiah Johnston and Martha Cowan, (MD) Sep. 9, 1823
Hiram Jones and Zenea Hicks, (MD) Dec. 2, 1823
Thomas Keeble and Betsy Smith, (MD) Oct. 14, 1823
David Kennedy and Rebecca Montgomery, (MD) Nov. 20, 1823
Richard Kirby and Polly Trice, (MD) Feb. 8, 1823
Wm. Knight and Priscilla Underwood, (MD) Jan. 16, 1823
Peyton Lane and Peggy Love, (MD) Feb. 4, 1823
Tandy Lane and Jenny Tuck, (MD) Jan. 3, 1823
John Lea and Maryann Evans, (MD) Aug. 27, 1823
Samuel Lee and Mary Hackney, (MD) Aug. 21, 1823
Thomas Lemingham and Betsey Harris, (MD) Dec. 15, 1823
John Marone and Rosanna Roberts, (MD) Mar. 27, 1823
John McCasland and Polly Winter, (MD) Aug. 7, 1823
James McCully and Elizabeth Bond, (MD) Feb. 4, 1823
John McCully and Eleanor Frew, (MD) Aug. 12, 1823
Joseph McGhee and Elizabeth Calor, (MD) Mar. 26, 1823
James McKamy and Sally Julian, (MD) Feb. 18, 1823
Henry Miser and Francis Farmer, (MD) Feb. 4, 1823
John Moore and Elizabeth Tulloch, (MD) Sep. 25, 1823
Thomas Moore and Sally Kilpatrick, (MD) Sep. 8, 1823

John Morris and Elizabeth Key, (MD) Feb. 5, 1823
James Norton and Prudence Seebastain, (MD) May 31, 1823
Nathan Padgett and Eleanor Underwood, (MD) Mar. 13, 1823
Wm. Recempecker and Catherine Abbott, (MD) Apr. 1, 1823
Henry Reynolds and Polly Gault, (MD) Aug. 12, 1823
Charles Rice and Jane Rhea, (MD) Jan. 16, 1823
Nathan Richards and Nelly Gladden, (MD) Aug. 23, 1823
Josiah Roberts and Polly Stone, (MD) Dec. 25, 1823
William Roberts and Sally Crisp, (MD) Nov. 20, 1823
Isaac Robertson and Polly Shell, (MD) May 28, 1823
Francis Rose and Nancy Sexton, (MD) Sep. 19, 1823
Evan Secrest and Mabra Braden, (MD) Mar. 20, 1823
Francis Shaw and Elizabeth Mosher, (MD) Feb. 6, 1823
Azariah Shelton and Matilda Wright, (MD) Jul. 30, 1823
John Shetterly and Caty Miser, (MD) Apr. 10, 1823
William Smith and Christina Fann, (MD) Sep. 14, 1823
William Stinnet and Franky McCallon, (MD) Mar. 12, 1823
John Taylor and Susannah Blair, (MD) Aug. 6, 1823
Hugh Torbet and Margaret Eagleton, (MD) Sep. 5, 1823
John Torbett and Mary Gault, (MD) Mar. 20, 1823
Wm. Watson and Catherine Heniger, (MD) Nov. 27, 1823
Gabriel Wheeler and Sally Childres, (MD) Aug. 28, 1823
Alexander Ewing and Margaret L. McCulloch, (MD) Sep. 14, 1824
Ezekiel Alexander and Elizabeth G. Ewing, (MD) Oct. 12, 1824
Joseph Henderson and Sarah D. White, (MD) Jan. 29, 1824
Mathew Knox and Elizabeth B. Bond, (MD) Jul. 26, 1824
Alexander Rice and Elizabeth B. Cusack, (MD) Sep. 21, 1824
Jeremiah K. Mosier and Mary Ann Wallace, (MD) Jun. 1, 1824
Samuel M. Rankin and Mary A. Duncan, (MD) Jan. 15, 1824
Joseph V. Moser and Sarah Biddle, (MD) May 20, 1824
Joseph P. Ellige and Betsy Garner, (MD) Apr. 4, 1824
Hugh E. Alexander and Sarah Caldwell, (MD) Jan. 29, 1824
Joseph C. Martin and Mary Balling, (MD) Apr. 8, 1824
Jefferson Adams and Rebecca Dailey, (MD) Jun. 17, 1824
Robison Akridge and Lucinda Floyd, (MD) Aug. 6, 1824
John Bailey and Naoma Connor, (MD) Dec. 7, 1824
Andrew Baker and Lydia Davis, (MD) Feb. 21, 1824
Aron Booth and Elizabeth Harvey, (MD) Nov. 25, 1824
Nicholas Boring and Rody Russell, (MD) Jul. 6, 1824
Michael Bowerman and Sarah Blackwell, (MD) Sep. 18, 1824
John Burton and Margaret Simons, (MD) Jul. 8, 1824
Alexander Caldwell and Jane Logan, (MD) Nov. 9, 1824
Joseph Cruise and Mary Johnson, (MD) Jan. 7, 1824

Wm. Cumming and Jane Night, (MD) Jul. 1, 1824
Hugh Cunningham and Marry Morrice, (MD) Mar. 11, 1824
George Cupp and Rebecca Murphy, (MD) Sep. 7, 1824
Edward Delozier and Sarah Davis, (MD) Apr. 22, 1824
Willis Derosset and Doshea Grimmett, (MD) Mar. 9, 1824
Joseph Dunlap and Hannah Keeble, (MD) Oct. 14, 1824
Elisha Dyer and Polly Townesley, (MD) Mar. 25, 1824
Samuel Ewing and Mary McCulloch, (MD) Sep. 4, 1824
Jesse Ginnings and Nancy Pearson, (MD) Feb. 19, 1824
Michael Girdner and Eliza Wear, (MD) Oct. 27, 1824
Wm. Givins and Hannah Thomas, (MD) Mar. 3, 1824
Isaac Glass and Elizabeth Noblet, (MD) Apr. 29, 1824
James Glass and Peggy Noblet, (MD) Oct. 4, 1824
William Goodman and Betsy Samples, (MD) Mar. 5, 1824
William Gossage and Mary Hendrickson, (MD) Aug. 6, 1824
John Griffitts and Mary Lee, (MD) Apr. 25, 1824
Samuel Grimmet and Fanny Rankin, (MD) Feb. 9, 1824
Doshea Grimmett and Willis Derosset, (MD) Mar. 9, 1824
Jeremiah Hammontree and Alcey Wiles, (MD) Jul. 15, 1824
William Hanna and Sally Endsly, (MD) Jul. 22, 1824
Shelton Harris and Lucinda Childres, (MD) Jan. 20, 1824
John Harvey and Elizabeth Dial, (MD) Dec. 12, 1824
William Hedrick and Susana Borden, (MD) Aug. 7, 1824
Robert Hooks and Elizabeth Kilburn, (MD) Sep. 8, 1824
William Hutton and Narcissa Moore, (MD) Nov. 30, 1824
Benj Johnston and Judah May (MD) Dec. 14, 1824
Edward Jones and Jane Brooks, (MD) Jan. 1, 1824
Alexander Kenedy and Hetty Henry, (MD) Jul. 29, 1824
Randell Kidd and Mary Call, (MD) Oct. 22, 1824
William King and Elendor Keller, (MD) May 22, 1824
Joshua Kirby and Jane Singleton, (MD) Jan. 22, 1824
John Lain and Jane Carson, (MD) Dec. 28, 1824
Street Layne and Matilda Blackwell, (MD) Feb. 12, 1824
Henry Lewis and Keziah Perkins, (MD) Jan. 8, 1824
Samuel Maroon and Elizabeth Hannah, (MD) Jun. 28, 1824
James Maxwell and Elizabeth Jenkins, (MD) Aug. 3, 1824
Judah May and Benj Johnston, (MD) Dec. 14, 1824
Benjamin McCale and Margaret Cannon, (MD) Mar. 20, 1824
French McConnell and Jane Everett, (MD) Jan. 27, 1824
Samuel McCulloch and Eleanor Ewing, (MD) Jul. 20, 1824
Silas McGhee and Arminta Carroll, (MD) Oct. 19, 1824
James McKamy and Ann Hanna, (MD) Jun. 8, 1824
Newton McMurry and Elenar Bogle, (MD) Dec. 16, 1824

John McNutt and Elizabeth McCulloch, (MD) Dec. 9, 1824
Samuel Moore and Jane Utter, (MD) Jul. 13, 1824
James Murphy and Mary McCarroll, (MD) Sep. 2, 1824
Jeremiah Murray and Mary Hammontree, (MD) Nov. 16, 1824
Robert Porter and Elizabeth Singleton, (MD) Sep. 9, 1824
Wm. Ramsey and Elizabeth Cunningham, (MD) Mar. 24, 1824
Leonard Ray and Martha Cochran, (MD) Jan. 20, 1824
Shadrick Rennels and Cynthia Garner, (MD) Sep. 21, 1824
John Robertson and Sarah Perkins, (MD) Sep. 30, 1824
Rody Russell and Nicholas Boring, (MD) Jul. 6, 1824
William Russell and Mary Kirby, (MD) Feb. 25, 1824
Daniel Scott and Jenny McBryant, (MD) Sep. 20, 1824
William Scott and Deidamea Davis, (MD) May 18, 1824
John Tate and Elizabeth Farmer, (MD) Mar. 21, 1824
Robert Thompson and Nancy Thompson, (MD) Dec. 23, 1824
Banjamin Tipton and Nancy Brooks, (MD) Oct. 28, 1824
Thomas Tipton and Susana Harris, (MD) May 22, 1824
Noae Waddle and Polly Givins, (MD) Oct. 5, 1824
Eliza Wear and Michael Girdner, (MD) Oct. 27, 1824
James Wear and Winnifred Gardener, (MD) Jul. 27, 1824
William Wear and Teressa Gardiner, (MD) May 18, 1824
Elisha Williams and Nancy Williams, (MD) Mar. 4, 1824
Lemuel Williams and Elizabeth White, (MD) Feb. 19, 1824
William Williams and Trephena Milsapps, (MD) May 15, 1824
Joseph Wilson and Ann Gault, (MD) Dec. 9, 1824
John R. McClure and Mary W. George, (MD) Mar. 11, 1825
Wm. Pugh and Lucretia Valentine Trice, (MD) May 26, 1825
Wm. A. McCampbell and Jane M. Wallace, (MD) Oct. 25, 1825
Solomon McCully and Ann M. Hamill, (MD) Sep. 1, 1825
Robert Tedford and Phoebe M. Houston, (MD) Aug. 10, 1825
John R. Cannon and Patience L. Smith, (MD) Oct. 11, 1825
Will M. Gamble and Dorcas L. Berry, (MD) Jan. 19, 1825
Robert H. Eagleton and Elizabeth G. McCulloch, (MD) Sep. 19, 1825
James Casteel and Mary Ann Williams, (MD) Dec. 22, 1825
William Anderson and Elizabeth A. McChesney, (MD) Sep. 1, 1825
Hiram W. Lambert and Catherine McQuage, (MD) Nov. 16, 1825
John T. Webb and Nancy McCool, (MD) Jan. 20, 1825
Samuel M. Blythe and Polly Montgomery, (MD) Sep. 8, 1825
Andrew L. McCampbell and Jane Caldwell, (MD) Dec. 27, 1825
James K. Raynes and Elizabeth Payne, (MD) Dec. 21, 1825
Wm. H. McClure and Elizabeth Havens, (MD) Nov. 17, 1825
Wm. A. Keltner and Elizabeth Ward, (MD) May 9, 1825
William Alexander and Phebe Ish, (MD) Jan. 6, 1825

Henry Banta and Frances Carless, (MD) Dec. 28, 1825
James Barnett and Polly Dodd, (MD) Apr. 24, 1825
Jacob Bonine and Christena Pesterfield, (MD) Mar. 10, 1825
Daniel Brewer and Elizabeth Hubbard, (MD) Oct. 23, 1825
James Briant and Elizabeth Tucker, (MD) Mar. 17, 1825
Jonathan Brown and Rebeckah Bowers, (MD) Feb. 28, 1825
Wm. Caylor and Rhoda Dunn, (MD) Mar. 3, 1825
Sevier Clark and Elizaeth Ingram, (MD) Jul. 6, 1825
Robert Cochran and Polly Rhea, (MD) Feb. 10, 1825
James Cope and Polly Hutton, (MD) Jan. 20, 1825
Gideon Cruze and Nancy Johnston, (MD) Nov. 3, 1825
Jacob Dailey and Matilda Tucker, (MD) Dec. 15, 1825
Robert Dearmond and Monarky Lucket, (MD) Nov. 8, 1825
Silas Deen and Lucinda Forester, (MD) May 1, 1825
John Denton and Lavenia Tipton, (MD) Oct. 13, 1825
William Dines and Polly Bowers, (MD) Dec. 1, 1825
Josiah Dyer and Mahala King, (MD) May 31, 1825
Alexander Ewing and Isabella McClure, (MD) Feb. 24, 1825
John Finley and Edy Saffell, (MD) Feb. 15, 1825
Joseph Flinn and Leah Rush, (MD) Apr. 10, 1825
Jeremiah Foster and Polly Rhea, (MD) Mar. 8, 1825
James Frew and Jane Scott, (MD) Nov. 10, 1825
Josiah Graston and Ann Hitch, (MD) Nov. 25, 1825
Joseph Hair and Delila Perkins, (MD) Nov. 17, 1825
Joshua Hamilton and Margaret Dearmon, (MD) Dec. 15, 1825
William Harris and Martha Roddy, (MD) Sep. 20, 1825
George Hayse and Avice Greer, (MD) Sep. 15, 1825
Samuel Houston and Ann Huchison, (MD) Feb. 15, 1825
John Jones and Sally Ambrister, (MD) Apr. 7, 1825
James Key and Herserla Greer, (MD) Nov. 18, 1825
James Kinnaman and Talby Dodson, (MD) Aug. 14, 1825
John Langford and Phebe Brooks, (MD) Oct. 27, 1825
Joseph Lawpaser and Jemima Betsaws, (MD) Dec. 22, 1825
Wm. Lowery and Hetty Houston, (MD) Dec. 13, 1825
Wm. McBriant and Mary Scott, (MD) Oct. 27, 1825
Miles McConnell and Martha Scroggs, (MD) Feb. 8, 1825
Henry McCully and Nancy Delzall, (MD) Sep. 5, 1825
Samuel McCully and Betsy Rhea, (MD) Sep. 29, 1825
Wm. McGhee and Maryann Ross, (MD) Sep. 28, 1825
Wm. McMurry and Peggy Malcam, (MD) Sep. 22, 1825
James Melton and Hannah Stallions, (MD) Oct. 6, 1825
Wm. Menis and Catherine Coonse, (MD) Apr. 26, 1825
Wm. Morton and Nancy Mackey, (MD) Feb. 23, 1825

Alex D. Orr and Rebecca McNabb, (MD) Dec. 27, 1825
David Pesterfield and Esther Dunley, (MD) Jan. 2, 1825
Henry Pesterfield and Eleanor Cayton, (MD) May 3, 1825
Hezekiah Privitt and Elizabeth Endsley, (MD) Sep. 10, 1825
Jonathan Pugh and Elizabeth Bingham, (MD) Dec. 15, 1825
Lewis Rice and Eliza Scott, (MD) Sep. 20, 1825
Thomas Robertson and Nancy Dayl, (MD) Dec. 18, 1825
Gideon Roddy and Milly Harris, (MD) Mar. 31, 1825
Shedrich Rogers and Sally Balling, (MD) Jul. 6, 1825
John Slemons and Elizabeth Jones, (MD) Mar. 19, 1825
George Smith and Peggy Bolling, (MD) Apr. 3, 1825
Isaac Smith and Elizabeth White, (MD) Oct. 6, 1825
Conway Stone and Rachel Carter, (MD) Mar. 3, 1825
Joshua Taylor and Mary Brickey, (MD) Aug. 25, 1825
Joseph Tipton and Martha Ingram, (MD) Jan. 20, 1825
Joseph Tipton and Polly Mays, (MD) Jun. 30, 1825
Joseph Tuck and Elizabeth Bond, (MD) Jan. 12, 1825
Hugh Wear and Peggy Chandler, (MD) Oct. 7, 1825
John Welsh and Patsy Burk, (MD) Apr. 5, 1825
Major Wimberly and Adealine Hamentree, (MD) Jun. 29, 1825
Newton Williams and Jane W. Coope, (MD) Aug. 8, 1826
Harvey Thompson and Peggy Thompson Anderson, (MD) Nov. 7, 1826
Lewis Pitman and Pamella L. Warren, (MD) Feb. 28, 1826
John Tedford and Agnes J. Henderson, (MD) Nov. 16, 1826
Richard Lebow and Amy Eliza George, (MD) Sep. 1, 1826
Alexander O. Ayers and Esther D. Johnston, (MD) Mar. 9, 1826
Isaac A Yarnell and Rebecca B. Bonham, (MD) Aug. 11, 1826
Andrew Cole and Mary Ann Robertson, (MD) Dec. 24, 1826
James Gillespie and Hester Ann Talbott, (MD) Mar. 16, 1826
James Montgomery and Polly Ann Thompson, (MD) May 26, 1826
John R. Frew and Jane Hammil, (MD) Jan. 3, 1826
John P. Bonham and Sally Jones, (MD) Feb. 21, 1826
Elijah M. Eagleton and Eleanor Gault, (MD) Sep. 7, 1826
John M. Montgomery and Polly Craft, (MD) Apr. 6, 1826
John L. Aikman and Nancy Paul, (MD) Dec. 7, 1826
Pamella L. Warren and Lewis Pitman, (MD) Feb. 28, 1826
Henry Jr, Bond and Susannah Stanfield, (MD) Jul. 10, 1826
John F. Dearmond and Margaret Hitch, (MD) Sep. 14, 1826
Robert F. Houston and Ann Gillespie, (MD) Apr. 13, 1826
Wm. D. Evans and Elizabeth McMurray, (MD) Nov. 29, 1826
Wm. B. Hudgeons and Rebecca McClure, (MD) Jun. 20, 1826
Henry Baker and Polly Burnes, (MD) Jun. 6, 1826
John Ball and Delila Huffman, (MD) Jan. 4, 1826

Thomas Baucom and Betsey Noble, (MD) Aug. 1, 1826
Silas Bell and Eleanor Wallace, (MD) Jan. 22, 1826
Isaac Bonine and Sally Merrett, (MD) Jan. 26, 1826
John Boring and Rachael Murry, (MD) Dec. 25, 1826
James Boyd and Elizabeth Murry, (MD) Nov. 22, 1826
Alexander Brazelton and Polly Frew, (MD) Nov. 1, 1826
John Brown and Nancy Diamons, (MD) Aug. 17, 1826
Carson Caldwell and Sally Akridge, (MD) Jan. 17, 1826
Silas Campbell and Matilda Todd, (MD) Dec. 25, 1826
Joseph Carson and Elizabeth Samples, (MD) Mar. 23, 1826
Moses Chambers and Dorothy Partin, (MD) May 10, 1826
Robert Clark and Ellender Parker, (MD) Oct. 3, 1826
George Cook and Nancy Craw, (MD) May 8, 1826
Samuel Coope and Clara Williams, (MD) Sep. 8, 1826
Alfred Cowan and Jane Cook, (MD) Mar. 2, 1826
James Davis and Catherine Brewer, (MD) Nov. 14, 1826
Henry Derosset and Eliza Boid, (MD) Jan. 26, 1826
Samuel Dickson and Jane Hammill, (MD) Jul. 20, 1826
William Edmons and Jane Lane, (MD) Oct. 21, 1826
Green Farmer and Jane Waters, (MD) Jan. 28, 1826
Josias Gamble and Polly Henry, (MD) Oct. 31, 1826
William Gault and Peggy Orr, (MD) Oct. 9, 1826
Joel Goodman and Polly Wright, (MD) Apr. 8, 1826
James Hammontree and Nancy Devine, (MD) Dec. 18, 1826
William Hammontree and Jane Carson, (MD) Apr. 20, 1826
James Harrison and Malinda Roddy, (MD) Sep. 14, 1826
William Henderson and Polly Young, (MD) Jul. 27, 1826
Hugh Henry and Nancy Henry, (MD) Oct. 18, 1826
Robert Houston and Dorothy Creswell, (MD) Aug. 9, 1826
Ransom Kerr and Sally Best, (MD) Oct. 10, 1826
Joseph Key and Telitha Haydon, (MD) Mar. 23, 1826
Wm. Laney and Nancy Smith, (MD) Sep. 27, 1826
Elijah Longbottom and Elizabeth Bonham, (MD) Nov. 14, 1826
Jesse Loyd and Fanny Greer, (MD) Feb. 24, 1826
Samuel McCammon and Rachel Inman, (MD) Nov. 24, 1826
Joseph McGhee and Cynthea Murphy, (MD) Jan. 9, 1826
Wm. McQuagus and Jane Hamilton, (MD) Dec. 19, 1826
Jesse Milsaps and Dolly Farmer, (MD) Mar. 2, 1826
Thomas Montgomery and Franky Carter, (MD) Jan. 19, 1826
John Moore and Mary Todd, (MD) Feb. 14, 1826
John Neel and Seelia Rush, (MD) Dec. 17, 1826
Hillery Patrick and Mary Houston, (MD) Jul. 28, 1826
John Pesterfield and Quilla Bonine, (MD) Nov. 2, 1826

John Pigg and Elizabeth Jones, (MD) Mar. 1, 1826
Richard Reagan and Barcella Stallions, (MD) Jul. 24, 1826
James Rhea and Betsy Tipton, (MD) Nov. 1, 1826
Thomas Roach and Rebecca May (MD) Sep. 7, 1826
Archabald Simons and Kitery Moore, (MD) Mar. 21, 1826
Moris Snider and Pheobe Roddy, (MD) Oct. 16, 1826
Nathen Spradlin and Betsey Ridg, (MD) Sep. 26, 1826
Thomas Stewart and Sarah Williams, (MD) Sep. 21, 1826
Johnston Suit and Elizabeth Wilson, (MD) Oct. 19, 1826
James Sutton and Isabella Casteel, (MD) Feb. 2, 1826
Larkin Thompson and Polly Anderson, (MD) Jul. 24, 1826
Wesley Underwood and Mary Brown, (MD) Nov. 21, 1826
Thomas Waddle and Eliza Humphries, (MD) Nov. 21, 1826
Pleasant Walker and Betsy Hedrick, (MD) Jan. 18, 1826
Joseph Weaver and Uny Massy, (MD) Dec. 27, 1826
Philip Wilson and Peggy Dawn, (MD) Aug. 3, 1826
John Woodard and Jane Williams, (MD) Nov. 28, 1826
Creed Fulton and Elizabeth T, Wear, (MD) Aug. 14, 1827
Darius Hoyt and Lucinda M. Bogle, (MD) May 3, 1827
Robert Minis and Margaret G. Steele, (MD) Apr. 10, 1827
Robert Donaldson and Polly D. Kirkpaterick, (MD) Mar. 15, 1827
Joseph V. Sims and Sarah Hooper, (MD) Aug. 22, 1827
Barton S. Warren and Evaline Singleton, (MD) Jan. 16, 1827
Henry R. Swisher and Elizabeth King, (MD) Mar. 18, 1827
Henry P. Tedford and Margaret McClung, (MD) Dec. 18, 1827
Bartley M. Duncan and Rachel Thompson, (MD) Sep. 27, 1827
John L. Sullins and Ann Cook, (MD) Aug. 28, 1827
George Ewing, Jr. and Elenor Parker, (MD) Sep. 13, 1827
John D. Wilson and Eleaner Caldwell, (MD) Nov. 8, 1827
Joseph Ashley and Polly Garner, (MD) Dec. 27, 1827
Boling Brook and Jane Jackson, (MD) Jan. 22, 1827
John Brooks and Betsey Hair, (MD) Feb. 29, 1827
John Cagle and Feruby Rogers, (MD) Feb. 22, 1827
Armstead Carpenter and Nancy McClain, (MD) Aug. 16, 1827
David Carson and Jane Gillespy, (MD) Oct. 9, 1827
James Davis and Cherry Phillips, (MD) Jan. 1, 1827
Morgan Davis and Elizabeth Hammontree, (MD) Feb. 22, 1827
William Davis and Sarah Stewart, (MD) Nov. 28, 1827
William Davis and Susan Taylor, (MD) Feb. 22, 1827
Silas Deen and Kitsay Davis, (MD) Feb. 18, 1827
Parker Edmondson and Jane Long, (MD) Feb. 10, 1827
Andrew Evans and Dorothy McMurry, (MD) Aug. 16, 1827
John Fathy and Patsy Wear, (MD) May 2, 1827

Henry Figinwinger and Sally Renfro, (MD) Jul. 3, 1827
Jonas Finger and Delila Sliger, (MD) Jul. 30, 1827
Brittain Garrard and Hazy Smith, (MD) Oct. 30, 1827
John Gould and Jane Hickey, (MD) Nov. 10, 1827
Arthur Greer and Elizbeth Jones, (MD) Oct. 16, 1827
George Griffitts and Martha Stanfield, (MD) Jul. 14, 1827
David Hamil and Nancy Walker, (MD) Aug. 28, 1827
Oney Harvey and Mariah Huffman, (MD) May 10, 1827
James Henry and Catherine Keamy, (MD) Jan. 7, 1827
Aaron Hodges and Jane Houk, (MD) Oct. 15, 1827
Levi Hollingsworth and Polly Boshears, (MD) Mar. 1, 1827
Thomas Hooper and Margaret Simms, (MD) Sep. 4, 1827
James Jeffries and Elizabeth Bowers, (MD) Nov. 15, 1827
Samuel Keller and Caty Hix, (MD) Mar. 1, 1827
James Lane and Malinda Hollers, (MD) Feb. 8, 1827
Jacob Leinback and Barbara Keller, (MD) Aug. 22, 1827
Adam McCroy and Rebecca Hendrickson, (MD) Jan. 31, 1827
Henry McCully and Rebecca Caldwell, (MD) Sep. 3, 1827
Robert McKamy and Martha Julian, (MD) Mar. 20, 1827
Benjamin Miller and Naoma Lewis, (MD) Jan. 4, 1827
Elijah Mitchell and Polly Campbell, (MD) Sep. 25, 1827
Jefferson Montgomery and Grissey Thompson, (MD) Jun. 8, 1827
Jacob Myers and Matilda Cox, (MD) Mar. 15, 1827
Jacob Neimon and Mary Dugan, (MD) Aug. 18, 1827
Martin Orman and Sally Rogers, (MD) Apr. 4, 1827
Jeremiah Plummer and Rebeccah Gates, (MD) Jun. 17, 1827
George Popland and Nancy Edmons, (MD) Jul. 18, 1827
Hiram Rains and Polly Wooden, (MD) Dec. 20, 1827
Jesse Rains and Maryann Merriet, (MD) Jan. 23, 1827
David Rhea and Polly Akrige, (MD) Jan. 23, 1827
Andrew Roach and Sally Adams, (MD) Feb. 18, 1827
Jacob Rule and Caty Hood, (MD) Oct. 11, 1827
Greenberry Saffell and Jane Scroggs, (MD) Feb. 22, 1827
Matthew Samples and Nancy Carson, (MD) Aug. 17, 1827
Ephiam Sawtell and Mary Yearout, (MD) Jul. 17, 1827
Joseph Scott and Patsy Davis, (MD) Dec. 6, 1827
Robert Shields and Peggy Cayler, (MD) Sep. 23, 1827
Jacob Shook and Peggy Harper, (MD) Mar. 20, 1827
Daniel Smith and Ann Wheeler, (MD) Aug. 28, 1827
Hazy Smith and Brittain Garrard, (MD) Oct. 30, 1827
John Stanfield and Elizabeth Griffitts, (MD) Oct. 9, 1827
Samuel Thompson and Jane Robinson, (MD) Jul. 17, 1827
William Vaughn and Judy Stallions, (MD) Jun. 24, 1827

William Wallace and Mary Briant, (MD) Feb. 16, 1827
Joshua Warren and Nancy Vanpelt, (MD) Mar. 5, 1827
John Wheeler and Milly Maze, (MD) Aug. 2, 1827
Claiborn Young and Mary Russle, (MD) Oct. 2, 1827
Jeremiah Young and Rutha Boring, (MD) Mar. 29, 1827
Wm. A. Spencer and Mary W. Duncan, (MD) Feb. 12, 1828
Joel Stone and Nancy W. Nipper, (MD) Mar. 20, 1828
George Smith and Mahala R. Bledsoe, (MD) Oct. 17, 1828
David Lyre and Martha Malinda Campbell, (MD) Aug. 27, 1828
Alexander Talbott and Margaret L. James, (MD) Dec. 4, 1828
Cornelius L. Howard and Betsy J. Douthet, (MD) Oct. 16, 1828
John McClung and Nancy J. Wilson, (MD) Feb. 5, 1828
Cyrus Smoot and Fanny J. Gamble, (MD) Jan. 3, 1828
John McCullough and Hannah H. Boring, (MD) Jan. 24, 1828
James H. Hooks and Margaret E. McGrew, (MD) Nov. 26, 1828
John Delzell and Louisa B. Anderson, (MD) Feb. 12, 1828
Andrew Coulter and Nancy A. James, (MD) Mar. 27, 1828
Richard S. McCollom and Mary Ellis, (MD) Apr. 14, 1828
James K. Finley and Temperance Kenney, (MD) Aug. 14, 1828
Thomas J. Allen and Ann Brown, (MD) Apr. 24, 1828
James H. Alexander and Teressa Davis, (MD) May 20, 1828
Thomas H. Smith and Margaret Gillespie, (MD) Aug. 8, 1828
John F. Dicson and Mary Kennady, (MD) Apr. 1, 1828
John D. Shaver and Mary Brawner, (MD) May 5, 1828
James D. Swan and Isabella Hood, (MD) Nov. 18, 1828
Martin C. Brown and Nancy Cruse, (MD) Aug. 5, 1828
Lauscin C. Moore and Racheal McFee, (MD) Aug. 12, 1828
Jacob C. Talbert and Ann Johnson, (MD) Jan. 22, 1828
James Anderson and Rebecca George, (MD) Jan. 10, 1828
James Bedford and Betsy Hunt, (MD) Dec. 9, 1828
Cornelius Beesley and Sarah Jackson, (MD) May 14, 1828
Philip Bird and Mary Dunn, (MD) Nov. 11, 1828
Samuel Blair and Rosanna Hall, (MD) Nov. 9, 1828
Gilbert Blankinship and Elizabeth Hughes, (MD) Apr. 10, 1828
Robert Bolin and Sally Clampet, (MD) Apr. 12, 1828
Wm. Bradley and Betsy Hudgeons, (MD) Jan. 22, 1828
Asa Brewer and Leah Brickey, (MD) Feb. 28, 1828
Nicholas Brewer and Elizabeth Dunn, (MD) Dec. 26, 1828
Michael Byerley and Sarah Smith, (MD) Aug. 22, 1828
Henry Cagle and Betsy Hill, (MD) Apr. 3, 1828
John Campbell and Ruth Thompson, (MD) Nov. 13, 1828
Eli Caylor and Susan Thomas, (MD) Dec. 23, 1828
John Coalter and Katherine Kitchen, (MD) May 17, 1828

John Cochran and Betsey Huffman, (MD) Mar. 13, 1828
Josiah Coppock and Diannah Hamer, (MD) Sep. 10, 1828
Thomas Costner and Eliza Haire, (MD) Jan. 22, 1828
Jesse Davis and Elizabeth Garner, (MD) Mar. 27, 1828
Lorenzo Donaldson and Peggy Neyman, (MD) Sep. 20, 1828
Joseph Duncan and Susanna Norwood, (MD) Oct. 14, 1828
Wiott Elliott and Elizabeth Simerly, (MD) Nov. 26, 1828
Peter Emmert and Levina Roddy, (MD) Feb. 10, 1828
James Everett and Abby Waller, (MD) Dec. 28, 1828
William Fann and Polly Bolin, (MD) Feb. 21, 1828
Aaron Felts and Matilda Smith, (MD) May 18, 1828
Hamelton Frazier and Ann Hauter, (MD) Apr. 1, 1828
Wm. Garsuch and Racheal Bovenn, (MD) Dec. 3, 1828
George Graham and Luticia Cowan, (MD) Sep. 11, 1828
Joseph Greene and Nancy Brewer, (MD) Feb. 25, 1828
Joseph Henderson and Nancy Minis, (MD) Jan. 8, 1828
Spencer Henry and Elizabeth Maze, (MD) Jan. 17, 1828
Daniel Hollers and Polly Goodwin, (MD) Jun. 21, 1828
James Humphreys and Nancy McClung, (MD) Jan. 31, 1828
James Langford and Ruthy Gamble, (MD) Jul. 22, 1828
John Logan and Polly McFee, (MD) Jun. 8, 1828
Mark Martin and Cyntha Tucker, (MD) Oct. 2, 1828
James Mathews and Nancy Tuck, (MD) Feb. 20, 1828
William Maxwell and Martha Utter, (MD) Jan. 3, 1828
Wm. McClorg and Elizabeth Henderson, (MD) Dec. 22, 1828
Ebenezer McGinley and Polly Tefetallor, (MD) Aug. 7, 1828
John Noblet and Bethenia Boble, (MD) Feb. 19, 1828
John Plummer and Rachel Davis, (MD) Aug. 7, 1828
John Poplin and Avey Poplin, (MD) Oct. 26, 1828
Hezekiah Privit and Eliza Roberts, (MD) Oct. 30, 1828
James Rice and Sally Hedrick, (MD) Oct. 12, 1828
Eliza Roberts and Hezekiah Privit, (MD) Oct. 30, 1828
Henry Roddy and Peggy Harris, (MD) Nov. 13, 1828
Levina Roddy and Peter Emmert, (MD) Feb. 10, 1828
Andrew Singleton and Sarah Cox, (MD) Mar. 13, 1828
David Spradlin and Matilda Wimberly, (MD) Aug. 13, 1828
Joseph Tate and Elizabeth Waters, (MD) Jan. 9, 1828
Robert Tedford and Rebecka McClurg, (MD) Feb. 7, 1828
Isaac Thompson and Polly Wheeler, (MD) Feb. 6, 1828
Wm. Tuck and Ann Baun, (MD) Dec. 4, 1828
Cyntha Tucker and Mark Martin, (MD) Oct. 2, 1828
George Wells and Catharine Yearout, (MD) Sep. 17, 1828
Jacob Wheeler and Elizabeth Orman, (MD) Jul. 17, 1828

William Wheeler and Ann Phillips, (MD) Oct. 2, 1828
James Williams and Jane Roddy, (MD) Oct. 20, 1828
Robert Woods and Mary King, (MD) Jul. 15, 1828
James Wyley and Mary Whittenberger, (MD) Jan. 15, 1828
Will N. Ewing and Martha M. Steele, (MD) Apr. 26, 1829
John Houston and Ann G. White, (MD) Jul. 16, 1829
John Graham and Elizabeth E. Yearout, (MD) Nov. 17, 1829
Bazel C. Brown and Elizabeth C. Stephenson, (MD) Feb. 10, 1829
John Gamble and Elizabeth C. Reagan, (MD) Apr. 14, 1829
James Anderson and Mary Ann McKaskle, (MD) Feb. 24, 1829
Charles W. Bingly and Sarah Keller, (MD) Jul. 4, 1829
James W. Farmer and Sally Waters, (MD) Nov. 1, 1829
James P. Householder and Betsy Wiginton, (MD) Sep. 17, 1829
John N. Harris and Nancy Gerner, (MD) May 14, 1829
John H. Cook and Nancy Morton, (MD) Dec. 24, 1829
Oran D. Martin and Jane Farmer, (MD) May 5, 1829
Wm. D. Moore and Sarah Hutton, (MD) Nov. 7, 1829
Benj. Derosset and Matilda Henderson, (MD) Jul. 5, 1829
James B. Brady and Lucinda Haynes, (MD) Apr. 15, 1829
David B. Tipton and Rebecca Jones, (MD) Oct. 29, 1829
Joseph A. Hutton and Elizabeth Henry, (MD) Dec. 3, 1829
William Bingham and Glatha Pew, (MD) Mar. 18, 1829
George Cagle and Polly Latham, (MD) Aug. 2, 1829
Robert Caldwell and Sibby Russell, (MD) Jan. 1, 1829
James Coalter and Polly Rhea, (MD) Dec. 31, 1829
Wm. Cochran and Lucy Hammontree, (MD) Nov. 12, 1829
Linnus Crawford and Susan Camp, (MD) Jan. 1, 1829
Andrew Cromwell and Sally Nash, (MD) Jan. 15, 1829
William Dunlap and Rachel Clampet, (MD) Mar. 12, 1829
Eanos Ellis and Sarah Jones, (MD) Mar. 19, 1829
William Flinn and Caty Headrick, (MD) Dec. 24, 1829
Miles Forrester and Amanda Collins, (MD) Mar. 19, 1829
Stephen Graves and Harriet King, (MD) Feb. 28, 1829
George Gregory and Margaret Means, (MD) Nov. 24, 1829
John Hackney and Phebe Perkins, (MD) Apr. 23, 1829
Michael Harvey and Sally Tallent, (MD) Nov. 10, 1829
Henry Hunt and Judy Starky, (MD) Jan. 13, 1829
James Hunt and Freshy Rose, (MD) Apr. 2, 1829
Manly Keeble and Rebecca Rhea, (MD) Aug. 9, 1829
James May and Susan Pugh, (MD) Aug. 18, 1829
Telford McConnell and Nancy Billue, (MD) Dec. 19, 1829
James McGinley and Polly Kenney, (MD) Apr. 21, 1829
James Miller and Scynthia Anderson, (MD) Dec. =, 1829

Wm. Nichols and Sally Norton, (MD) Sep. 15, 1829
Azariah Parks and Jane Golph, (MD) Jul. 29, 1829
William Rhea and Hariet Farmer, (MD) Apr. 21, 1829
Willis Rogers and Sally Ingram, (MD) Dec. 30, 1829
Thomas Ross and Elizabeth McTeer, (MD) Jul. 22, 1829
Martin Stewart and Polly Blair, (MD) Apr. 7, 1829
Aaron Tallent and Bethena Anderson, (MD) Apr. 14, 1829
Enoch Tallent and Lucinda Wiggington, (MD) Jul. 30, 1829
John Thompson and Maglothel Stone, (MD) Feb. 5, 1829
William Thurman and Betsy Snider, (MD) May 11, 1829
Muse Vinyard and Elizabeth Dearmond, (MD) Dec. 24, 1829
Joel Williams and Susannah Yearout, (MD) Jul. 27, 1829
George S. Gilbert and Nancy M. Saffell, (MD) Dec. 21, 1830
Samuel Tulloch and Catherine M. Caldwell, (MD) Oct. 21, 1830
Hampton Morris and Polly Leuisa Smoot, (MD) Aug. 4, 1830
James Thompson and Sarah J. Brook, (MD) Feb. 27, 1830
Jackson C. Plumlee and Mary Ann Rogers, (MD) Dec. 24, 1830
John Brown and Mary Ann Bright, (MD) Oct. 12, 1830
James Davis and Betty Ann Macafee, (MD) Mar. 2, 1830
James W. Logan and Mary A. Henry, (MD) Dec. 30, 1830
Westley Williams and Eliza A. Wallace, (MD) Jun. 27, 1830
Daniel W. Latimore and Margaret McCall, (MD) Feb. 28, 1830
Thos. S. Cromwell and Sally Nash, (MD) Nov. 16, 1830
John M. Hieskell and Elizabeth Leeper, (MD) Nov. 14, 1830
Moses L. Swan and Isabella Gillespie, (MD) Mar. 9, 1830
Thomas Henry, Teefateller and Teressa Everett, (MD) Mar. 5, 1830
Lee M. Hanson and Martha Cates, (MD) Oct. 23, 1830
Moses H. Hughes and Polly Duncan, (MD) Oct. 7, 1830
James H. McConnell and Phebe McClung, (MD) Dec. 2, 1830
Roger E. Cresap and Angeline Thompson, (MD) Jul. 20, 1830
Samuel E. Rowan and Katherine Hanley, (MD) Mar. 12, 1830
Robert B. Kennaman and Sally Snider, (MD) Feb. 4, 1830
John B. Say and Margaret Hart, (MD) Oct. 22, 1830
Thomas A. Briant and Betsey Singleton, (MD) Apr. 2, 1830
Russell Allen and Luisa Rose, (MD) Aug. 25, 1830
William Bearden and Joicy Rudder, (MD) Aug. 20, 1830
John Best and Betsy Anderson, (MD) Nov. 25, 1830
Joseph Black and Mary Hammontree, (MD) Oct. 24, 1830
Thomas Bohannan and Nancy Morgan, (MD) Feb. 24, 1830
Lewis Burns and Nancy Vaught, (MD) Aug. 26, 1830
Isaac Cole and Rebecca Keltner, (MD) Sep. 25, 1830
Wm. Coulburn and Caty Kee, (MD) Sep. 28, 1830
Charles Coulter and Isabella Tipton, (MD) Oct. 20, 1830

Richard Davis and Betsey Murray, (MD) Jun. 28, 1830
Elix Dixon and Charity Jones, (MD) Jun. 2, 1830
Marvel Duncan and Mary Kirkpatrick, (MD) Apr. 29, 1830
Alex Eanos and Elizabeth Winchester, (MD) Oct. 14, 1830
James Hamilton and Terressa Berry, (MD) Apr. 27, 1830
James Hanes and Mariah Henley, (MD) Feb. 8, 1830
William Haskew and Talletha Gourly, (MD) Jun. 17, 1830
Enoch Hollingsworth and Sally Burk, (MD) Jul. 21, 1830
Alexander Hood and Sarah Frow, (MD) Mar. 30, 1830
Samuel Hudson and Britann Bowerman, (MD) Mar. 7, 1830
Wm. Hutcheson and Nelly Brewer, (MD) Aug. 26, 1830
Francis Johnston and Polly Bond, (MD) Mar. 20, 1830
Hiram Lebow and Sarah Bledsoe, (MD) Dec. 24, 1830
John Matthews and Elizabeth Lain, (MD) Dec. 20, 1830
David Maze and Luscinda Tipton, (MD) Jul. 15, 1830
Joseph McReynolds and Eleanor Edmonson, (MD) Jan. 21, 1830
Henry Menifold and Rebecca Scott, (MD) Nov. 11, 1830
Robert Murren and Sally Davis, (MD) Jun. 26, 1830
Thomas Newberry and Mary Patrick, (MD) Feb. 21, 1830
Sanders Noble and Mary Robenitt, (MD) Oct. 7, 1830
Hezekiah Pacely and Jane Samples, (MD) Mar. 24, 1830
Lorenzo Perkins and Mahala Key, (MD) Nov. 12, 1830
Charles Richards and Patsy Boren, (MD) Jun. 29, 1830
Moses Scruggs and Elizabeth Dunkan, (MD) Apr. 23, 1830
Robert Sloan and Elizabeth Ross, (MD) Oct. 28, 1830
James Stinnet and Patsy Hinton, (MD) Oct. 7, 1830
Richard Stone and Catherine Snider, (MD) Sep. 9, 1830
Calvin Tally and Jane Black, (MD) Dec. 8, 1830
Abraham Taylor and Jane Barns, (MD) Oct. 19, 1830
Pleasant Taylor and Elizabeth Waters, (MD) Jan. 7, 1830
James Thompson and Polly Carson, (MD) Dec. 10, 1830
John Tipton and Jane Clark, (MD) Aug. 8, 1830
Garret Toney and Margaret Francis, (MD) May 2, 1830
Carey Tuck and Ann McMenas, (MD) Sep. 8, 1830
John Wallace and Hannah Hartsell, (MD) Sep. 16, 1830
Henry Waller and Elizabeth Yates, (MD) Jan. 11, 1830
James Way and Susan Danley, (MD) Nov. 6, 1830
Wm. Weaver and Ann Adams, (MD) Apr. 1, 1830
James Wilson and Jane Hutten, (MD) Oct. 30, 1830
Joseph Wilson and Lucinda Cook, (MD) Aug. 10, 1830
Thomas J. Young and Rebeckah R. Houston, (MD) Jul. 21, 1831
Lewis Neyman and Rachel M. Logan, (MD) Jun. 20, 1831
James Hamil and Jane L. Simms, (MD) Feb. 22, 1831

John Taylor and Mary Ann Diddle, (MD) Apr. 6, 1831
Thomas Wooden and Malinda Ann Rains, (MD) Oct. 23, 1831
Thos McCallie and Mary A. Hook, (MD) Dec. 26, 1831
George W. Ackridge and Elizabeth French, (MD) Oct. 4, 1831
James W. Lee and Melvina Wear, (MD) Jul. 18, 1831
Samuel W. Rankin and Isabella Ewing, (MD) Jan. 27, 1831
George W. Tipton and Nancy Jones, (MD) Apr. 20, 1831
E. S. Blair and Jane Henry, (MD) Jul. 28, 1831
Ephriam P. Noel and Jane Fleshart, (MD) Mar. 29, 1831
Issac M. Hair and Lucinda Coston, (MD) Feb. 12, 1831
James M. Kerr and Betsey Best, (MD) Dec. 26, 1831
John L. Henderson and Esther Allen, (MD) Sep. 20, 1831
Samuel J. Gould and Jane Maxwell, (MD) Oct. 11, 1831
Christopher J. Whittenberger and Polly Whittenberger, (MD) Sep. 22, 1831
Edward H. Nichols and Hetty Houston, (MD) Feb. 17, 1831
Emanuel Best and Susan Taylor, (MD) Dec. 15, 1831
Shadrick Boling and Patsy Rogers, (MD) Feb. 2, 1831
Nathaniel Brewer and Isabella Davis, (MD) Jul. 28, 1831
John Campbell and Sibby Ewing, (MD) May 12, 1831
John Campbell and Margaret Thompson, (MD) Jul. 26, 1831
David Conger and Elizabeth Young, (MD) Mar. 22, 1831
John Davis and Elizabeth Kiser, (MD) Aug. 2, 1831
Richard Dearmond and Cynthia Hix, (MD) Feb. 10, 1831
William Dixon and Eliza Cook, (MD) Jan. 27, 1831
Madison Douglas and Sarah Bonham, (MD) Dec. 29, 1831
Berry Duncan and Winney Brickey, (MD) Dec. 22, 1831
Avery Ellis and Elizabeth Divine, (MD) May 5, 1831
Samuel Ellis and Abigail Kee, (MD) Feb. 24, 1831
John Evens and Elisabeth Halpain, (MD) Dec. 26, 1831
Jonas Fronabarger and Missouri Davis, (MD) Dec. 26, 1831
John Fultner and Rhody Ross, (MD) Mar. 3, 1831
John Glass and Rachel Vickers, (MD) Mar. 31, 1831
Martin Harper and Betsy McConnell, (MD) Dec. 9, 1831
Andrew Harris and Maria Harris, (MD) Dec. 6, 1831
Avice Hayse and Peter Key, (MD) Oct. 18, 1831
Peter Hedrick and Polly Stinson, (MD) Jun. 28, 1831
Andrew Hook and Betsey Jinkens, (MD) Jan. 27, 1831
John Jones and Isabella Roulston, (MD) Sep. 8, 1831
Lewis Jones and Sarah Simons, (MD) May 1, 1831
John Julian and Sally Murphy, (MD) Aug. 5, 1831
William Kanard and Elizabeth McKaskel, (MD) Sep. 17, 1831
Richard Keeble and Betsy Rhea, (MD) Nov. 17, 1831

Stephen Kerrick and Mariah Hayden, (MD) Aug. 30, 1831
Peter Key and Avice Hayse, (MD) Oct. 18, 1831
Wm. Kidd and Tennessee Hafley, (MD) Jul. 17, 1831
John Latham and Beedy Rogers, (MD) Nov. 27, 1831
Silas Leverter and Katy Greenfield, (MD) Feb. 23, 1831
Wm. McCerg and Melinda Hooper, (MD) Nov. 22, 1831
Sam McGill and Sally Leventer, (MD) Dec. 23, 1831
Andrew McRoberts and Susannah Bond, (MD) Dec. 12, 1831
Benjamin Merone and Mary Nolen, (MD) May 24, 1831
James Moore and Hapy Caldwell, (MD) Oct. 21, 1831
John Moore and Sarah Mackey, (MD) Apr. 13, 1831
James Murphy and Mary Smith, (MD) Feb. 13, 1831
George Patterson and Susannah Garren, (MD) Aug. 13, 1831
Joseph Reed and Jane Reed, (MD) Feb. 8, 1831
John Rhea and Jane Cameron, (MD) Jan. 5, 1831
Thomas Rice and Eliza Daneson, (MD) Feb. 10, 1831
John Rose and Sally Halpain, (MD) Aug. 25, 1831
Edward Sharp and Malinda Malcum, (MD) Feb. 2, 1831
Roberson Snider and Ritter Staunlor, (MD) Mar. 3, 1831
Daniel Spencer and Vina Wheeler, (MD) Oct. 11, 1831
Ritter Staunlor and Roberson Snider, (MD) Mar. 3, 1831
Jehu Stephens and Anny Tipton, (MD) Nov. 26, 1831
David Thompson and Lucinday Hutchison, (MD) Sep. 15, 1831
Isaac Thompson and Ann Roan, (MD) Aug. 20, 1831
Anny Tipton and Jehu Stephens, (MD) Nov. 26, 1831
Edward Tuck and Sarah McMenus, (MD) Apr. 19, 1831
Daniel Ward and Sally Melton, (MD) Dec. 29, 1831
Robert Wear and Margaret Wilkinson, (MD) Apr. 14, 1831
Absolom Wiseman and Nancy Davis, (MD) Oct. 7, 1831
Jonathan Wright and Sarah King, (MD) Dec. 13, 1831
George McCoy and Jane S. Duncan, (MD) Apr. 17, 1832
Wm. McFee and Eliza R. Davis, (MD) Aug. 2, 1832
Harvey H. Caruthers and Nancy M. Sterling, (MD) Jul. 19, 1832
Joseph Curler and Nancy M. Cannon, (MD) Sep. 27, 1832
Aaron Grigsby and Eliza M. Maclin, (MD) Sep. 26, 1832
John Hammontree and Rhody M. Griffin, (MD) Jul. 25, 1832
Alexander Moore and Eliza M. Montgomery, (MD) Jan. 17, 1832
Harvey B. McClurg and Nancy L. Dixon, (MD) Feb. 2, 1832
William Martin and Susan J. Montgomery, (MD) Apr. 26, 1832
James Shadden and Sarah H. Russell, (MD) Jan. 21, 1832
Alexander Copeland and Ann Eliza Low, (MD) Aug. 6, 1832
Thomas Edmonson and Jane E. Keys, (MD) Feb. 9, 1832
Abraham M. Wallace and Mary Ann Hartsell, (MD) Sep. 27, 1832

Cassweek Hall and Mary Ann Thompson, (MD) Sep. 6, 1832
James McIlheron and Betsy Ann Bilderbea, (MD) Jan. 5, 1832
Joseph Neyman and Thirzee Ann Clark, (MD) Mar. 20, 1832
Daily W. Hood and Nancy Tipton, (MD) Jul. 19, 1832
Pleasant M. Tipton and Mary Davis, (MD) Jan. 18, 1832
James H. Rowan and Margaret Berry, (MD) Sep. 19, 1832
Wm. G. Brooks and Margaret Wheeler, (MD) May 26, 1832
Jessee D. Robison and Elizabeth Tolly, (MD) Feb. 21, 1832
Joseph B. Logan and Sarah Coham, (MD) Aug. 21, 1832
Alyhew Alexander and Nancy Smith, (MD) Jan. 12, 1832
Martin Best and Polly Martin, (MD) Oct. 4, 1832
Robert Bogle and Ann Boyd, (MD) May 17, 1832
George Bond and Nancy Singleton, (MD) Jan. 3, 1832
Calloway Brewer and Barbara Shields, (MD) Oct. 13, 1832
Elisha Briant and Susan Jones, (MD) Apr. 12, 1832
Joseph Brown and Nancy Kirkpatrick, (MD) Dec. 13, 1832
Lenoir Bryant and Nancy Blair, (MD) Nov. 20, 1832
Josiah Carter and Jane Trent, (MD) Dec. 13, 1832
Stephen Colter and Hannah Caylor, (MD) Jul. 26, 1832
John Coslon and Sally Noblet, (MD) Sep. 26, 1832
Samuel Cowden and Nancy Keller, (MD) Mar. 4, 1832
Willoughby Davis and Polly Ormond, (MD) Nov. 1, 1832
Levi Dunn and Betsy Walker, (MD) Jan. 26, 1832
John Eakin and Sarah Greer, (MD) Nov. 10, 1832
William Ellis and Rachel Tucker, (MD) Sep. 11, 1832
Thomas Enis and Barbara Jacobs, (MD) Apr. 17, 1832
John Everett and Susan Shook, (MD) Oct. 10, 1832
Nathan Farmer and Sussanna Dever, (MD) Dec. 9, 1832
Albert Finley and Betsy Kennedy, (MD) Sep. 27, 1832
Edward George and Dorcas Chandler, (MD) May 3, 1832
Wm. Graston and Catherine Hich, (MD) Oct. 25, 1832
Miles Griffin and Nancy Hammontree, (MD) Jul. 12, 1832
Archibald Grisham and Polly McRanalds, (MD) Mar. 21, 1832
Wm. Haddon and Nancy Vineyard, (MD) Mar. 8, 1832
Abraham Hickman and Betsa Blair, (MD) Nov. 8, 1832
John Hood and Polly Dyer, (MD) Feb. 16, 1832
Baxter Ivey and Susana Ellidge, (MD) Oct. 23, 1832
William James and Margaret Jones, (MD) Oct. 30, 1832
John Keller and Jane McKaskele, (MD) Oct. 30, 1832
John Kerr and Ann Cowden, (MD) Mar. 22, 1832
Maclin Kerr and Lucinda Davis, (MD) Mar. 6, 1832
Thomas Lyon and Susan Legg, (MD) Jul. 21, 1832
Wm. Mancoosky and Winafred McConel, (MD) Oct. 27, 1832

John Maxwell and Eliza Love, (MD) Oct. 30, 1832
John McClain and Ann Duncan, (MD) Oct. 23, 1832
John McClanehan and Polly Snider, (MD) Mar. 22, 1832
Charles McGill and Peggy Barnett, (MD) Jan. 21, 1832
Lewis McMelloon and Margaret Hamontree, (MD) Jul. 24, 1832
Richard Mills and Dillily Cross, (MD) Jul. 24, 1832
Clinton Milsaps and Polly Tipton, (MD) Mar. 1, 1832
Samuel Montgomery and Mary Montgomery, (MD) Aug. 7, 1832
Blount Morres and Mary Browner, (MD) Feb. 29, 1832
Samuel Parks and Serene Cook, (MD) Jun. 19, 1832
Matthew Roach and Susannah Hunt, (MD) Jan. 11, 1832
James Russell and Sally McCallie, (MD) Aug. 14, 1832
John Russell and Rebecca Snider, (MD) Jan. 27, 1832
Bedford Ryland and Francis Tucker, (MD) Nov. 22, 1832
Kerneleus Shaver and Jane Moore, (MD) Oct. 16, 1832
Lewis Swain and Jane Hackney, (MD) Nov. 6, 1832
George Thompson and Polly Neal, (MD) Nov. 29, 1832
James Thompson and Polly Brotherton, (MD) Feb. 23, 1832
William Thompson and Katharine Smith, (MD) Dec. 27, 1832
Francis Tucker and Bedford Ryland, (MD) Nov. 22, 1832
Newton Wilson and Lavinia Frow, (MD) Aug. 16, 1832
Samuel Winters and Polly Jackson, (MD) Oct. 5, 1832
Peter Yount and Mary Pain, (MD) Mar. 29, 1832
Redden S. Taylor and Nancy W. Warren, (MD) Sep. 24, 1833
Franklin Grubb and Teressa W. Douthit, (MD) Sep. 12, 1833
Samuel M. Creswell and Catherine S. Williams, (MD) Apr. 5, 1833
John B. Webster and Margaret L. Foute, (MD) Mar. 12, 1833
William Boyd and Eliza J. Anderson, (MD) Nov. 12, 1833
Wayne Gedions and Mary J. Hitch, (MD) Jul. 15, 1833
Mat M. Alexander and Eliza H. Thompson, (MD) Feb. 12, 1833
Joseph H. Pritchard and Polly H. Williamson, (MD) Jan. 5, 1833
John Gault and Susan H. Culton, (MD) Apr. 11, 1833
Andrew C. Montgomery and Evelinea C. Green, (MD) Mar. 28, 1833
Campbell Gillespie and Hannah C. Wallace, (MD) Dec. 3, 1833
George Moorelock and Jane C. Richey, (MD) Nov. 28, 1833
Jefferson Reagan and Fanny C. Johnson, (MD) Oct. 17, 1833
John Kerr and Jane B. McClure, (MD) Oct. 8, 1833
Alexander McGhee and Ann B. McLin, (MD) Mar. 26, 1833
Joseph M. Roarex and Rossy Ann Harris, (MD) Dec. 5, 1833
George D. Herrole and Sarah Ann Hale, (MD) Sep. 26, 1833
John Delzell and Philena A. Parker, (MD) Dec. 24, 1833
Wm. W. Bayless and Sarah Black, (MD) May 28, 1833
Joseph W. Finley and Polly Nicholson, (MD) Jan. 1, 1833

Moses W. McMahan and Mary Taylor, (MD) Mar. 21, 1833
James R. Sexton and Polly Paul, (MD) Jun. 4, 1833
James N. Harvey and Elizabeth Birdwell, (MD) Dec. 17, 1833
David Maclin, Kerr and Elizabeth Thompson, (MD) Aug. 13, 1833
John M. Bonham and Lucinda Vanpsett, (MD) Feb. 19, 1833
David M. Wear and Lovicy Poland, (MD) Oct. 10, 1833
John Fagg, Jr., and Jane White, (MD) Dec. 31, 1833
John Griffith, Jr., and Margaret Lea, (MD) May 21, 1833
Andrew H. King and Terrissa Lorence, (MD) Mar. 20, 1833
Andrew F. Hannah and Cynthia Hitch, (MD) Nov. 6, 1833
Wm. B. Bird and Susan Campbell, (MD) Jan. 27, 1833
John A. D. Carter and Nancy Irick, (MD) Aug. 15, 1833
James A. McClure and Sarah Ferguson, (MD) Oct. 8, 1833
John A. D. Miller and Dorcas Hammintree, (MD) Sep. 20, 1833
James Aiken and Nancy McClure, (MD) Jan. 16, 1833
James Baty and Ann Spradling, (MD) Apr. 21, 1833
Benjamin Bond and Martha McClure, (MD) Jul. 14, 1833
John Boyd and Caty Shell, (MD) Apr. 2, 1833
Michael Bright and Isabella Bonham, (MD) Feb. 14, 1833
David Caldwell and Sarah Yearout, (MD) Apr. 22, 1833
Joseph Caldwell and Anny Maize, (MD) May 16, 1833
James Coach and Defeny Hendrixson, (MD) Nov. 13, 1833
Tarrence Conner and Eveline McWilliams, (MD) Oct. 8, 1833
David Crye and Elizabeth Tuck, (MD) Jan. 2, 1833
John Davis and Becky Tipton, (MD) Apr. 18, 1833
Leander Duncan and Rebecca Wimberley, (MD) Aug. 7, 1833
William Dunn and Mary Shields, (MD) Jan. 27, 1833
Samuel Ferguson and Betsy Patterick, (MD) Apr. 12, 1833
Henry Finger and Catherine Hoatsell, (MD) Sep. 16, 1833
David Fox and Mary Greene, (MD) Jul. 13, 1833
Joseph French and Sarah Casteel, (MD) Dec. 3, 1833
Wm. Gormly and Mary Milsaps, (MD) Mar. 9, 1833
William Graves and Mary Holloway, (MD) Apr. 25, 1833
Addison Hannah and Margaret Scott, (MD) Aug. 29, 1833
Abram Hendrickson and Polly Parkins, (MD) Jan. 22, 1833
James Henry and Elizabeth Gamble, (MD) Jan. 31, 1833
James Jones and Polly Miser, (MD) Feb. 21, 1833
Joseph Jones and Tamer Bryant, (MD) Oct. 22, 1833
Wm. Kerr and Letitia Wear, (MD) Mar. 28, 1833
Middleton Lane and Nancy Winters, (MD) Dec. 22, 1833
John Long and Agnes Finley, (MD) Aug. 22, 1833
Stephen Lute and Elizabeth Dillard, (MD) Jun. 8, 1833
James McCauly and Mahaley Shook, (MD) Feb. 23, 1833

Alexander McCollom and Pheby Hammontree, (MD) Jul. 11, 1833
Newton McConnell and Nancy Brody, (MD) Apr. 12, 1833
James McNutt and Susanah McCulloch, (MD) Nov. 29, 1833
Robert McReynolds and Sarah Wear, (MD) Feb. 20, 1833
James Mitchell and Rebecca Sharp, (MD) Oct. 29, 1833
Wm. Perry and Nancy Strain, (MD) Jul. 23, 1833
Wm. Pleming and Susan Smith, (MD) Feb. 26, 1833
Samuel Prater and Mary Wright, (MD) Apr. 29, 1833
Wm. Price and Mary Bearden, (MD) Mar. 19, 1833
Jacob Ridg and Delila Russell, (MD) Feb. 24, 1833
Thomas Rogers and Leona Garner, (MD) Mar. 28, 1833
James Ross and Sally Cook, (MD) Jan. 26, 1833
Peter Rule and Mary McTeer, (MD) Aug. 8, 1833
James Scott and Elizabeth Lambert, (MD) Feb. 21, 1833
James Simpson and Hannah Webster, (MD) Jul. 1, 1833
Preasent Spradlin and Rosanah McCool, (MD) Jan. 31, 1833
Jesse Swisher and Rebecca King, (MD) Mar. 21, 1833
Jonathan Tallent and Polly French, (MD) Aug. 1, 1833
Daniel Taylor and Elinor Ewing, (MD) Jan. 29, 1833
Caswell Tipton and Lucinda Brooks, (MD) Feb. 17, 1833
James Trice and Mary Arnett, (MD) Feb. 5, 1833
Aaron White and Lydia Davis, (MD) Apr. 18, 1833
Alexr Williams and Polly Hamill, (MD) Feb. 21, 1833
Presley Williams and Ann Norse, (MD) Dec. 21, 1833
Richard Williams and Minervy Criswell, (MD) Jan. 1, 1833
Wm. Wilson and Isabella Carson, (MD) Aug. 1, 1833
Isaac Wright and Susan Brown, (MD) Apr. 18, 1833
Josiah Balinger and Rebeca M. George, (MD) Sep. 19, 1834
John Tipton and Charlotte M. Hollingsworth, (MD) Nov. 16, 1834
Leonard Woods and Jane M. Ewing, (MD) Nov. 4, 1834
Zebulon B. Wallace and Catherine L. Foute, (MD) May 13, 1834
John Davis and Martha Jane Maxwell, (MD) Sep. 11, 1834
Wm. H. McNeely and Mary G. Luster, (MD) Oct. 30, 1834
Morgan Maupin and Polly Elmyra Barnes, (MD) Aug. 12, 1834
James Reed and Harriet Elizbeth Cashon, (MD) May 13, 1834
Nathan Thompson and Ann Eliza Alexander, (MD) Feb. 5, 1834
James S. Rea and Evaline E. Keith, (MD) Feb. 18, 1834
James W. Caven and Elizabeth C. Murphy, (MD) Feb. 27, 1834
Alfred Copeland and Nich Bledsoe Thomas, (MD) Sep. 17, 1834
Jesse Kerr, Jr., and Polly Ann Henry, (MD) Apr. 3, 1834
Harvey Hammontree and Hetty Ann McCroskey, (MD) Sep. 9, 1834
Joseph W. Duncan and Sarah Hudson, (MD) Mar. 4, 1834
John W. Parkes and Sarah Sharp, (MD) Feb. 25, 1834

Matthew W. Thompson and Jane Bogle, (MD) Oct. 15, 1834
Joseph V. Armstrong and Nancy Cunningham, (MD) Mar. 25, 1834
Danl S. Casey and Sally Boyd, (MD) Apr. 7, 1834
Amos R. Trotter and Mary Gamble, (MD) Oct. 23, 1834
James M. Booth and Margaret McReynolds, (MD) Jan. 9, 1834
Robert J. Allen and Eleanor Harmon, (MD) Dec. 23, 1834
H. J. Davis and Susannah Best, (MD) Aug. 10, 1834
John J. Hoover and Sarah Bowerman, (MD) Sep. 4, 1834
Miles H. Bailey and Nancy Ewing, (MD) Feb. 25, 1834
Johnston H. Campbell and Patsey Andrews, (MD) Oct. 7, 1834
William H. Dearmond and Mary Childres, (MD) Dec. 30, 1834
Ralph E. Thompson and Jane Earwood, (MD) Jun. 5, 1834
Joseph C. Bogle and Minerve Green, (MD) Feb. 25, 1834
Jonas B. Frost and Ursula Cox, (MD) Oct. 19, 1834
Thomas Alexander and Mary Greer, (MD) Dec. 4, 1834
John Anderson and Mary Dunn, (MD) Aug. 24, 1834
Frederick Best and Susannah Williamson, (MD) Dec. 23, 1834
Thomas Caton and Francis Young, (MD) Jan. 23, 1834
Hobbs Crowder and Ann Kounse, (MD) Dec. 24, 1834
Elijah Davis and Hannah Whitehead, (MD) Sep. 25, 1834
Philip Davis and Mary Law, (MD) Dec. 14, 1834
Wm. Ewing and Jane Tucker, (MD) Apr. 22, 1834
Charles Fisher and Elizabeth Hamilton, (MD) Sep. 17, 1834
Lewis Forrester and Ann Vineyard, (MD) Jul. 24, 1834
John Gault and Polly Logan, (MD) Jun. 17, 1834
Andrew Gould and Jane Early, (MD) Oct. 30, 1834
George Haddon and Jane McWilliams, (MD) Nov. 6, 1834
Zepheniah Harris and Jude Kidd, (MD) Feb. 27, 1834
Abraham Hartsell and Louisa Rankin, (MD) Sep. 4, 1834
Elijah Hix and Sarah Starkey, (MD) Mar. 13, 1834
Andrew Howel and Amanda McCallie, (MD) Feb. 10, 1834
Jones Jenkins and Eleanor Craig, (MD) Dec. 30, 1834
Robert Johnston and Sarah Steele, (MD) Sep. 8, 1834
David Kerr and Martha Henry, (MD) Apr. 5, 1834
Jude Kidd and Zepheniah Harris, (MD) Feb. 27, 1834
Samuel Kinnaman and Jane Reed, (MD) Mar. 25, 1834
James Kirkpatrick and Elizabeth Shadden, (MD) Sep. 24, 1834
Silvester Law and Nancy Williams, (MD) Jan. 22, 1834
Joseph McGill and Susan Barnett, (MD) Sep. 7, 1834
John McKamy and Elizabeth Shaver, (MD) Mar. 16, 1834
Stephen McReynolds and Eleanor Tedford, (MD) Feb. 6, 1834
Alexander Neal and Sarah Hix, (MD) Dec. 2, 1834
Mitchel Reed and Mary Harden, (MD) Jun. 3, 1834

John Ricket and Sussannah Hannah, (MD) Sep. 11, 1834
John Roop and Isabel Davis, (MD) Jul. 31, 1834
James Rose and Neomi Davis, (MD) Jun. 8, 1834
Joshua Shields and Sarah Johnston, (MD) Feb. 7, 1834
James Stanfield and Elizabeth Bond, (MD) Mar. 13, 1834
Joseph Stewart and Elizabeth Cannon, (MD) Feb. 20, 1834
Calvin Sutton and Clarranday Wood, (MD) May 1, 1834
William Teefateller and Sarah McClure, (MD) May 28, 1834
Joel Tharp and Jane Crawley, (MD) Feb. 27, 1834
James Tucker and Sally Phillips, (MD) Jan. 23, 1834
Thomas Vickers and Charity Hendrichson, (MD) Sep. 26, 1834
James Walker and Jane Lambert, (MD) Oct. 19, 1834
John Walker and Esther Henderson, (MD) Feb. 7, 1834
Abel Wheeler and Charlotte Hinson, (MD) Sep. 16, 1834
Thomas Wheeler and Elizabeth Hitch, (MD) Nov. 6, 1834
John Wilburn and Sarah Davis, (MD) Aug. 27, 1834
Sterling Winter and Dicy Birdwell, (MD) Jan. 12, 1834
James H. Montgomery and Martha W. Frow, (MD) Oct. 1, 1835
Montgomery McTeer and Martha W. Bogle, (MD) Mar. 12, 1835
James K. Duncan and Sarah S. Dunlap, (MD) Jan. 15, 1835
Samuel Anderson and May R. Thompson, (MD) Sep. 10, 1835
John C. Richey and Elizabeth N. Duncan, (MD) Nov. 12, 1835
Rhadamanthus Montgomery and Harriet N. Bogle, (MD) May 26, 1835
David Morton and Margaret M. Delzell, (MD) Feb. 19, 1835
Peter Breakbill and Leah L. Reagan, (MD) Jan. 6, 1835
Ruth McMahan and Lewis L. Spilman, (MD) Jan. 22, 1835
Andrew McClain and Susan E. Sawtell, (MD) Jan. 15, 1835
Robert S. Cumming and Ann C. McMahan, (MD) Nov. 30, 1835
John H. Edmondson and Margaret C. Dunlap, (MD) Feb. 19, 1835
Jefferson P. Brown and Hester Ann Cox, (MD) Mar. 4, 1835
John Ellis and Mary Ann McCroy, (MD) Feb. 23, 1835
Wm. P. Logan and Uterpe A. Earley, (MD) Oct. 27, 1835
James Conner and Harriett A. Ewing, (MD) Nov. 5, 1835
Jesse Watkins and Martha A. Cunningham, (MD) Oct. 27, 1835
David S. Delzell and Ann Morton, (MD) Sep. 24, 1835
Thomas P. Headrick and Selethia Bryant, (MD) Jul. 23, 1835
Robert P. McCulloch and Christina Caldwell, (MD) Oct. 8, 1835
John M. Barnes and Myra Bryant, (MD) Jul. 28, 1835
James M. Evans and Susannah Tipton, (MD) Feb. 12, 1835
Thomas L. Lucket and Jane Martin, (MD) Apr. 30, 1835
Leah L. Reagan and Peter Breakbill, (MD) Jan. 6, 1835
Lewis L. Spilman and Ruth McMahan, (MD) Jan. 22, 1835
Alfred L. Wright and Jane Howard, (MD) Dec. 31, 1835

Jacob Bird, Jr., and Nancy Brickey, (MD) Mar. 29, 1835
Jacob J. Brown and Margaret McAfee, (MD) Mar. 30, 1835
Samuel F. Williams and Martha Maupin, (MD) Jul. 24, 1835
David E. McCallie and Nancy Hart, (MD) Sep. 26, 1835
Wm. C. Regans and Loisa Tuck, (MD) Jul. 23, 1835
Joel B. Reagan and Aley Tuck, (MD) Jul. 4, 1835
David B. Tipton and Rachel Henry, (MD) Feb. 9, 1835
Larkin Biby and Elvira Sanders, (MD) Jun. 14, 1835
David Caldwell and Elizabeth Russell, (MD) Feb. 19, 1835
Matthew Collins and Rachel Hendrixson, (MD) Oct. 18, 1835
John Colter and Elizabeth McBrient, (MD) Aug. 14, 1835
Nathan Cox and Frances Tuck, (MD) Nov. 13, 1835
David Cusick and Elinor Williams, (MD) Mar. 4, 1835
James Dunlap and Mary Harris, (MD) Dec. 3, 1835
William Dunlap and Elizabeth Cavett, (MD) Feb. 10, 1835
William Edmunds and Charlotte Roach, (MD) Nov. 21, 1835
Asbury Fuquay and Sydney Gamble, (MD) Jan. 7, 1835
William Garner and Elthey Garner, (MD) Feb. 19, 1835
David Hamelton and Katherine Potter, (MD) Jun. 4, 1835
John Henderson and Nancy Tuck, (MD) Aug. 13, 1835
John Henley and Aley Privet, (MD) Jan. 6, 1835
John Houston and Elinor Wilson, (MD) Dec. 17, 1835
John Hunt and Nancy Patrick, (MD) Dec. 17, 1835
John Kidd and Mary Harris, (MD) Mar. 27, 1835
Adam Kuns and Rachel Logan, (MD) Feb. 25, 1835
David Logan and Margaret Conner, (MD) Aug. 27, 1835
Nelson Low and Semanthe Yearout, (MD) Oct. 22, 1835
Wm. McMahan and Elizabeth Taylor, (MD) Nov. 10, 1835
Elijah Nelson and Nancy Kinneman, (MD) Sep. 8, 1835
George Pesterfield and Tempy Caton, (MD) Jan. 27, 1835
Moses Ragan and Rachel Bonoin, (MD) Aug. 25, 1835
William Smith and Ann Greer, (MD) Jun. 18, 1835
William Smith and Salena Law, (MD) Sep. 24, 1835
Charles Spilman and Ferrybe Bell, (MD) Dec. 2, 1835
Joseph Tate and Sarah Tipton, (MD) Apr. 30, 1835
John Taylor and Elizabeth Maxwell, (MD) Nov. 2, 1835
Edward Thomas and Melvina Cowden, (MD) Feb. 14, 1835
Isaac Tipton and Dama Jones, (MD) Nov. 19, 1835
Granville Waddy and Rachel Tarbet, (MD) Aug. 26, 1835
Davis Ward and Susannah Downey, (MD) Oct. 27, 1835
Merry Webb and Fanny Couch, (MD) Apr. 2, 1835
Wm. Webster and Nancy Holcomb, (MD) Mar. 5, 1835
John Wethers and Nancy Sutten, (MD) Dec. 25, 1835

Semanthe Yearout and Nelson Low, (MD) Oct. 22, 1835
Jesse Wallace and Rosanna M. Gamble, (MD) Sep. 15, 1836
William Williams and Sarah M. Steel, (MD) Oct. 27, 1836
Samuel Clemens and Martha L. Teafateller, (MD) May 18, 1836
Preston Cartwright and Susan Jane Brotherton, (MD) Sep. 25, 1836
John C. Duncan and Sarah J. Martin, (MD) Oct. 8, 1836
Ralph E. Tedford and Malinda G. Houston, (MD) Apr. 12, 1836
Willis Hendrickson and Nancy Elvina Maze, (MD) Feb. 9, 1836
Carson Caldwell and Polly E. Barrett, (MD) Dec. 13, 1836
Tomas Downey and Matilda Caroline Briant, (MD) Oct. 13, 1836
Ake Henry and Sarah B. Green, (MD) Mar. 15, 1836
Wm. Prater and Mary B. Leeper, (MD) Jul. 28, 1836
Abijah W. Emmitt and Betsy Ann Cameron, (MD) Apr. 14, 1836
Samuel S. Finley and Betsey Ann Delaney, (MD) Oct. 27, 1836
Robert Bowman and Nancy Ann Sloan, (MD) Dec. 8, 1836
Matthew W. Edmondson and Martha A Duncan, (MD) Nov. 4, 1836
Pleasent W. Gentry and Jane Cottrell, (MD) Mar. 18, 1836
Abraham N. Low and Arah Bonham, (MD) Sep. 22, 1836
Wm. M. Brickell and Sarah Hix, (MD) Jul. 19, 1836
James M. Tulloch and Mary Best, (MD) Nov. 17, 1836
Wm. Jr, Samples and Katherine Kerr, (MD) Feb. 25, 1836
John J. Alexander and Matilda Bustle, (MD) Dec. 15, 1836
Walter H. Keeble and Polly White, (MD) Aug. 15, 1836
Robert H. McReynolds and Dicy Brown, (MD) Sep. 8, 1836
Alfred C. Cunningham and Isabel Hutton, (MD) Aug. 31, 1836
John C. Greenway and Rebecca McLain, (MD) Sep. 29, 1836
Wm. C. Hunt and Patsey McDaniel, (MD) Jul. 7, 1836
George A. Mathes and Nancy Hart, (MD) Apr. 7, 1836
Francis Alexander and Margaret Vickers, (MD) Oct. 14, 1836
Samuel Alexander and Ann Morelock, (MD) Dec. 8, 1836
Nelson Alloway and Jane Cannon, (MD) Feb. 18, 1836
Larkin Anderson and Kesiah Hix, (MD) Mar. 31, 1836
William Anderson and Jane Houston, (MD) Oct. 11, 1836
George Best and Jane Roach, (MD) Mar. 7, 1836
James Black and Nancy Bogle, (MD) Feb. 10, 1836
Robert Caldwell and Lavenia McGhee, (MD) Apr. 14, 1836
George Caylor and Nancy Briant, (MD) Nov. 5, 1836
Henry Clemens and Elizabeth Everett, (MD) Aug. 18, 1836
James Dunn and Anna Briant, (MD) Jul. 26, 1836
Jackson Garner and Elizabeth Palmer, (MD) Jun. 5, 1836
Leander Garren and Savillar Hobbs, (MD) Apr. 21, 1836
Thomas Goodman and Mary Hix, (MD) Sep. 4, 1836
John Gray and Malinda Wallace, (MD) Mar. 1, 1836

Engle Griffitts and Eleanor Vanderpool, (MD) Oct. 4, 1836
John Hammontree and Mary Murry, (MD) Aug. 8, 1836
Mathew Hannah and Margaret Weir, (MD) Apr. 29, 1836
Evan Hinshaw and Nancy Hackney, (MD) Feb. 11, 1836
Benjamin Hitch and Eliza Jones, (MD) Sep. 22, 1836
Kesiah Hix and Larkin Anderson, (MD) Mar. 31, 1836
Savillar Hobbs and Leander Garren, (MD) Apr. 21, 1836
Alfred Hook and Elizabeth Howell, (MD) Jun. 12, 1836
Christian Kagle and Nancy Wheeler, (MD) Aug. 14, 1836
John Kizer and Malinda Cope, (MD) Sep. 15, 1836
Abraham Lane and Delila Williams, (MD) May 26, 1836
Samuel Lane and Elizabeth Williams, (MD) Apr. 27, 1836
John Long and Jane Low, (MD) Oct. 6, 1836
Moses Martin and Celia Kerr, (MD) Apr. 28, 1836
James Matson and Lavenia Hart, (MD) Sep. 13, 1836
Fleming Maze and Jane Shirrell, (MD) Aug. 2, 1836
John McBriant and Sarah Scott, (MD) Nov. 31, 1836
Joseph McClure and Elizabeth Greenway, (MD) Oct. 20, 1836
John McKinley and Sarah Lane, (MD) Feb. 25, 1836
James McKinly and Sally Stewart, (MD) Jun. 8, 1836
James McTeer and Martha Gardner, (MD) Dec. 22, 1836
Wiley Medlock and Nancy Kirtis, (MD) Aug. 8, 1836
George Mizer and Elizabeth Pickering, (MD) Oct. 14, 1836
Daniel Nichalson and Mary Talent, (MD) Jan. 15, 1836
Edward Obriant and Elizabeth Jones, (MD) Jul. 26, 1836
Spencer Ogle and Viney Davis, (MD) Jan. 26, 1836
Reed Oneal and Maria Denison, (MD) Nov. 7, 1836
John Palmer and Sarah McFee, (MD) Dec. 22, 1836
James Reed and Lucinda Austin, (MD) Nov. 14, 1836
Harrison Roach and Patsy Bryant, (MD) Apr. 11, 1836
Alexander Ross and Margaret Best, (MD) Jan. 28, 1836
Ezekiel Stanbury and Matilda Mulvanis, (MD) Dec. 29, 1836
Michael Teefateller and Jane Cumming, (MD) Oct. 6, 1836
Jacob Tipton and Dotia Halcom, (MD) Feb. 29, 1836
Eleanor Vanderpool and Engle Griffitts, (MD) Oct. 4, 1836
Lewis West and Martha Ragan, (MD) Aug. 25, 1836
Jacob Tipton and Martha R. Henry, (MD) Aug. 8, 1837
James Griffitts and Mary P. Scott, (MD) Feb. 28, 1837
Wm. A. Matthews and Margaret M. Hart, (MD) Dec. 5, 1837
George Grigsby and Nancy L. Whittenbarger, (MD) Jan. 5, 1837
Alexander S. Armstrong and Mary Jane Henry, (MD) Nov. 2, 1837
Alexander M. Wilson and Mary Jane Rankin, (MD) Mar. 9, 1837
Anderson Downey and Lucinda Jane Anderson, (MD) Jun. 22, 1837

Samuel Edmondson and Eliza Jane Duncan, (MD) Aug. 17, 1837
Wm. McTeer and Margaret Jane Tedford, (MD) May 25, 1837
Stephen Warren and Ann Eliza Wiseman, (MD) Sep. 27, 1837
Joseph B. Houston and Huldah D. Cusick, (MD) Dec. 6, 1837
Robert Everette and Mary Ann Clemens, (MD) Sep. 7, 1837
Samuel Haddox and Eleanor Ann Jones, (MD) Nov. 30, 1837
Wm. Y. Warren and Mary Tarbet, (MD) May 2, 1837
James W. Craig and Jane Torbet, (MD) Mar. 27, 1837
William R. Adams and Nancy Burchfield, (MD) Dec. 14, 1837
James M. Shields and Celia Jones, (MD) Jun. 1, 1837
James Irvin, Rudd and Elizabeth Keeling, (MD) Aug. 31, 1837
Charles G. Stranahan and Uphama Hale, (MD) Feb. 2, 1837
Charles A. Irwin and Margaret Hamil, (MD) Apr. 18, 1837
Wm. Badgett and Polly Farmer, (MD) Nov. 23, 1837
Joel Barnes and Elizabeth Gamble, (MD) Jul. 16, 1837
Wm. Breazeal and Margaret Phillips, (MD) May 30, 1837
David Bright and Jane Key, (MD) Jul. 26, 1837
John Brooks and Harriet Hayden, (MD) Jun. 14, 1837
Enoch Brown and Nancy Vineyard, (MD) Dec. 14, 1837
George Cailor and Ann Dunn, (MD) Nov. 29, 1837
Philip Costner and Polly Hays, (MD) Nov. 9, 1837
Jabez Coulson and Jane Jones, (MD) Jul. 20, 1837
Nathaniel Ewing and Margaret Caldwell, (MD) Mar. 16, 1837
Joseph Farmer and Betsy Garner, (MD) Sep. 28, 1837
Eli Garner and Elizabeth Rogers, (MD) Jan. 12, 1837
William Goddard and Margaret Hitch, (MD) Nov. 7, 1837
Wm. Goen and Patsy Hix, (MD) Dec. 31, 1837
John Haffley and Elizabeth Kirkpatrick, (MD) Nov. 30, 1837
Robert Hooks and Susan Roach, (MD) Oct. 3, 1837
John Hunt and Polly Odear, (MD) Jan. 27, 1837
Solomon Ivins and Maryann Moore, (MD) Oct. 5, 1837
Russell Jones and Jane Carver, (MD) Dec. 26, 1837
Robert Kidd and Esther Neiman, (MD) Oct. 3, 1837
Aaron Lambert and Eliza Jones, (MD) Oct. 17, 1837
John Law and Malyssa McGinley, (MD) Oct. 24, 1837
James Logan and Lourinda Dyke, (MD) Dec. 19, 1837
Samuel Logan and Martha Strain, (MD) Oct. 3, 1837
John Malcom and Jane Henry, (MD) Aug. 17, 1837
Wm. McGhill and Polly Macklin, (MD) Feb. 22, 1837
John McNabb and Elizabeth McConnel, (MD) Feb. 2, 1837
Samuel McTeer and Isabella Cooper, (MD) Sep. 20, 1837
Isaac Medlock and Margaret Lea, (MD) Mar. 30, 1837
Wm. Payne and Susan Hitch, (MD) Mar. 21, 1837

James Price and Nancy Wilson, (MD) Aug. 26, 1837
Thomas Russell and Sydney Ogle, (MD) Nov. 4, 1837
Jesse Scoggins and Sarah Owens, (MD) Sep. 21, 1837
Benjamin Smith and Sarah Campbell, (MD) Nov. 18, 1837
George Snider and Susan Hanley, (MD) Feb. 5, 1837
James Tedford and Jane Ferguson, (MD) May 2, 1837
David Thompson and Mary Kerr, (MD) Jan. 31, 1837
James Thompson and Margaret Smith, (MD) Dec. 26, 1837
Joseph Thompson and Eliza Cathcart, (MD) Nov. 11, 1837
Jonathan Tipton and Margaret Singleton, (MD) Oct. 5, 1837
Mashack Tipton and Elizabeth McReynolds, (MD) Nov. 16, 1837
Green Vineyard and Polly Ingram, (MD) Mar. 28, 1837
Lindsey Vineyard and Aggrippina Sherrill, (MD) Dec. 29, 1837
John Walker and Polly Mires, (MD) Jan. 19, 1837
William Watkins and Margaret Byerly, (MD) Mar. 21, 1837
George Wilson and Mary Moore, (MD) Jan. 2, 1837
Samuel Yates and Elizabeth Kinneman, (MD) Apr. 13, 1837
Samuel Yearout and Rusinah Early, (MD) Sep. 12, 1837
William Allen and Janet S. Duncan, (MD) Jan. 10, 1838
Rufus Pate and Eliza S. Brown, (MD) Dec. 13, 1838
Banjamin Tipton and Maulkem Mary Haulkner, (MD) Nov. 20, 1838
Lynnville Gibbs and Elizabeth Mahaley Speers, (MD) Apr. 1, 1838
Esther Davis and Pleasant M. Boling, (MD) Apr. 27, 1838
John M. Coffin and Mary K. Wilson, (MD) Mar. 1, 1838
Elijah R. Snider and Barbary Jane Curtis, (MD) Jul. 18, 1838
James D. Harrelson and Martha Jane Deroney, (MD) Feb. 28, 1838
Joseph Harris and Martha Jane Stinnett, (MD) Mar. 22, 1838
Stephen Porter and Margaret Jane McNutt, (MD) Jan. 23, 1838
James Tipton and Mary Jane Henderson, (MD) Dec. 18, 1838
Samuel Wallace and Martha Jane Wallace, (MD) Oct. 16, 1838
Albert P. Early and Eliza J. Miller, (MD) Aug. 16, 1838
Thomas J. Lea and Eliza J. Rankin, (MD) Feb. 14, 1838
George McConnell and Mary J. Adams, (MD) Nov. 15, 1838
John Minnis and Elizabeth J. Debusk, (MD) Oct. 11, 1838
Joseph V. Cumming and Malinda H. Hafley, (MD) Jul. 6, 1838
Daniel L. Trundle and Mary Elizabeth Trundle, (MD) Jan. 9, 1838
William Dunn and Ann Eliza Boyd, (MD) Mar. 8, 1838
Saml. Cook and Jane C. Robbins, (MD) Sep. 3, 1838
Robert Anderson and Nancy B. Harris, (MD) Nov. 15, 1838
Adam W. Caldwell and Nancy Waters, (MD) Oct. 18, 1838
John W. Gay and Branham, (MD) Dec. 27, 1838
Wm. W. Glass and Malinda Miller, (MD) Jan. 4, 1838
George W. Hiatt and Mary Jones, (MD) Aug. 5, 1838

Mitchell W. Porter and Susannah Foute, (MD) Jul. 26, 1838
John S. Henderson and Winneford Davis, (MD) Dec. 20, 1838
James P. Allen and Nancy Jones, (MD) Apr. 29, 1838
John P. Brewer and Judah Poindexter, (MD) Oct. 17, 1838
Wm. P. Cummings and Mary Bogle, (MD) Mar. 20, 1838
Pleasant M. Boling and Esther Davis, (MD) Apr. 27, 1838
James M. Crews and Katherine Brakebill, (MD) Jan. 16, 1838
Andrew L. Rambo and Susan Wright, (MD) Oct. 8, 1838
Wm. J. Hackney and Martha Dunlap, (MD) Dec. 27, 1838
James H. Donaldson and Lucinda Mathews, (MD) Jan. 23, 1838
Joseph H. More and Cinthy Seals, (MD) Oct. 1, 1838
Albert G. Henry and Maryann Henry, (MD) Aug. 7, 1838
Willie B. Wright and Elizabeth Henry, (MD) Sep. 21, 1838
James A. Cathcart and Cyntha Hammontree, (MD) Jan. 15, 1838
John Anderson and Mary White, (MD) Dec. 4, 1838
Robert Anderson and Sally Hix, (MD) Mar. 12, 1838
Madison Arwood and Louiza Rudd, (MD) Nov. 13, 1838
John Best and Katherine Best, (MD) Apr. 5, 1838
Levi Bird and Rachel Brickey, (MD) Jul. 19, 1838
Henry Brakebill and Anna David, (MD) Oct. 30, 1838
Lawson Carpenter and Sarah Costner, (MD) Jan. 25, 1838
Wm. Chambers and Rhody Dunn, (MD) Jun. 7, 1838
John Clark and Matilda Thompson, (MD) Nov. 1, 1838
Wm. Claybo and Elizabeth Henley, (MD) Sep. 23, 1838
John Davis and Sally Hix, (MD) Apr. 8, 1838
Stephen Davis and Mary Keeble, (MD) Apr. 5, 1838
William Davis and Mahala Goodman, (MD) Feb. 8, 1838
James Dunaway and Tempy Brickle, (MD) Nov. 15, 1838
William Gardner and Mary Thompson, (MD) Mar. 22, 1838
Samuel Gibson and Ruthy Hall, (MD) Nov. 6, 1838
David Giffin and Malvina Roddy, (MD) Aug. 14, 1838
Wm. Goen and Rachel Rudd, (MD) Sep. 7, 1838
Francis Hackney and Ann Miser, (MD) Nov. 22, 1838
Thomas Hawkins and Sally Wimberly, (MD) Aug. 13, 1838
John Hedrick and Susannah Long, (MD) Oct. 21, 1838
Andrew Hix and Sarah Brickey, (MD) Jun. 22, 1838
John Kerr and Juliann Townsley, (MD) Aug. 14, 1838
Adrian Martin and Sarah Kerr, (MD) Apr. 26, 1838
James Martin and Rosannah Low, (MD) Dec. 6, 1838
James McCully and Margaret Dixon, (MD) Dec. 19, 1838
Andrew McHaffy and Nancy Kilburn, (MD) Jul. 7, 1838
Guilford McReynolds and Permalia Gamble, (MD) Oct. 5, 1838
George Mizer and Sarah Brooks, (MD) Nov. 6, 1838

Samuel Murrin and Margaret Knight, (MD) Oct. 13, 1838
Daniel Myers and Matilda Cable, (MD) Aug. 19, 1838
Elijah Nelson and Martha Nuchols, (MD) Jun. 5, 1838
Martin Newman and Hannah Logan, (MD) Dec. 25, 1838
Jonathan Parsons and Nancy Jenkins, (MD) Mar. 7, 1838
Titus Pendergraft and Elizabeth Alloway, (MD) Nov. 15, 1838
Lot Rogers and Rebecah Boling, (MD) Feb. 25, 1838
John Rose and Rebecca Haynes, (MD) Sep. 27, 1838
Wm. Rossin and Sarah Thomas, (MD) Mar. 15, 1838
Louiza Rudd and Madison Arwood, (MD) Nov. 13, 1838
Alexander Scott and Lucinda Maxwell, (MD) Mar. 28, 1838
Fredrick Shields and May Oliver, (MD) Oct. 25, 1838
Alexander Smith and Sarah Johnson, (MD) Mar. 8, 1838
John Sneed and Mary Simerley, (MD) Apr. 3, 1838
John Stallions and Isabella Thomason, (MD) Nov. 1, 1838
Lewis Stinnett and Nancy Forester, (MD) Mar. 22, 1838
John Tuck and Clementine McRoy, (MD) Aug. 23, 1838
Nathaniel Winder and Lucinda Daniels, (MD) Jan. 16, 1838
John Woody and Jane Forister, (MD) Aug. 16, 1838
Nathan Ragan and Nancy S. Heartsell, (MD) Sep. 5, 1839
Barckly M. Irwin and Elizabeth M. Cummings, (MD) Sep. 26, 1839
George W. Cowan and Mary L. Clark, (MD) Dec. 2, 1839
John Davis and Nancy Jane Cunningham, (MD) Aug. 20, 1839
Christopher C. Hamby and Juliett E. Cox, (MD) Feb. 7, 1839
James E. Bright and Nancy D. King, (MD) Sep. 10, 1839
Benjamin D. Brabson and Elizabeth B. Toole, (MD) Sep. 5, 1839
Joseph Hutsell and Mary Ann Long, (MD) Aug. 23, 1839
Andrew Vance and Nancy Ann Wilson, (MD) Mar. 10, 1839
Gould Wilson and Martha Ann Cook, (MD) Mar. 21, 1839
John P. Sterling and Elizabeth Bell, (MD) May 20, 1839
Wm. M. Biggs and Nancy Carson, (MD) Sep. 29, 1839
Wm. M. Burnett and Laticia Sharp, (MD) Mar. 15, 1839
Reps J. Davis and Malinda Singleton, (MD) Dec. 24, 1839
Andrew J. Smith and Mahala Vineyard, (MD) Apr. 4, 1839
J. J. Walker and Rachel McGhee, (MD) Nov. 28, 1839
Robert H. Bowen and Anna Henry, (MD) Mar. 26, 1839
James F. Early and Sarah Divine, (MD) Jan. 22, 1839
Franklin D. Conner and Jane Greer, (MD) Jul. 25, 1839
Stephen C. Newberry and Barbary Rose, (MD) Aug. 6, 1839
John Bird and Elizabeth Shields, (MD) Sep. 19, 1839
George Blair and Isabella Hix, (MD) Mar. 25, 1839
George Bledsoe and Famy Bledsoe, (MD) Dec. 31, 1839
John Bogle and Nancy Henderson, (MD) Aug. 29, 1839

Washington Bradley and Margaret Hitch, (MD) Aug. 15, 1839
James Briant and Maryann Roach, (MD) Mar. 31, 1839
Adam Carpenter and Isabella Melson, (MD) Nov. 12, 1839
John Caylor and Martha Briant, (MD) Jul. 28, 1839
Thomas Chambers and Rebecca Frazier, (MD) Sep. 21, 1839
Isaiah Dotson and Isabel Means, (MD) Mar. 31, 1839
John Duncan and Mary Delzell, (MD) Dec. 12, 1839
Daniel Dunn and Amanda Cameron, (MD) Feb. 14, 1839
Thomas Elliott and Margaret Snider, (MD) Jan. 3, 1839
James Endsley and Jane Jones, (MD) Sep. 25, 1839
John Ewing and Margaret Conner, (MD) Jan. 17, 1839
Benjamin Hampton and Cintha Haze, (MD) Sep. 21, 1839
John Harrison and Mary Dills, (MD) Sep. 29, 1839
William Harvey and Carsa Hunt, (MD) Jul. 11, 1839
James Henry and Ann Hutton, (MD) Nov. 19, 1839
John Hood and Susan Barnett, (MD) Feb. 7, 1839
John Huckaby and Adeline Ruston, (MD) Oct. 2, 1839
Joseph Kizer and Mary Tucker, (MD) Jan. 25, 1839
Moses McConnell and Jane Rensbarger, (MD) Apr. 1, 1839
Isabel Means and Isaiah Dotson, (MD) Mar. 31, 1839
Levi Patterson and Emeline Patty, (MD) Apr. 27, 1839
Uriah Phillips and Jane McMurray, (MD) Nov. 28, 1839
Alfred Roddy and Elizabeth Cook, (MD) Feb. 28, 1839
Drury Rose and Susan Tuck, (MD) Mar. 21, 1839
Henry Russell and Margaret White, (MD) Jan. 11, 1839
Isaac Russell and Penelope White, (MD) Sep. 30, 1839
John Simerly and Lydia McDaniel, (MD) May 5, 1839
Alexander Soults and Perneaty Waters, (MD) Jan. 14, 1839
Wm. Sparks and Nancy Tate, (MD) Feb. 26, 1839
Christian Vineyard and Ann Haddox, (MD) Jul. 11, 1839

Henry County, Tennessee, Persons Mentioned in the Sale of the Estate of Jacob Meek, dec., Dec. 7, 1824

Henry Meek, Abner Pearce, Mary Meek, Joh Witt, Saml. Hankins, George H. Young, Bartley Fry, John Hickey, William Felps, Wiley Taylor, William Caldwell, William Barker, Augustin Berry, James Barton, John Overton, Benjamin Coats, James Miller, Harris Berry, Martin Winset, Philip halter, James Wright, Scarborough Pentecost, Abner Pearce, Adam Perkins, Hiram Langston, James Dunlap, John Will, Danl. Bagby, Bennett Trainer, George Young, Jesse Strickland, Jacob W. Meek, Robert Allen, Oran D. Watson, Bennett Jones, Lucy Ross, Allen Dunlap, Benjamin Yeargin, James Flack, Hosea H. League, Thomas Shaw, John L. Allen, W. G. Dewitt, James Harper, William McFarland, Merit Searcy, William

Chance, Gilbert Hart, James Brackin, Willie Taylor, William Campbell, John Lilly, Moses Dunlap, Isaac Cruse, Joseph Caruthers, Maberry cox, R. E. C. Daugherty, Jones L. Belote, Rich N. Woodson, John Studdurt, Andrew Miller, Robert Hays, Henry Matthew, John Dunlap, Matthew H. Harris, Thos. A. Slaughter, E. H. Tarrant.

Sevier County, Tennessee, Tax List 1832
Absalom Abbot, Absalom Abbot, Jr., Catherine Abbot, James Adair, Johnson Adams, Christopher Aden, Samuel Agnew, Martin Alehty, Charles Alfred, William Alfred, Alfred Allen, John Allen, John R. Allen, Sandford Allen, Bautlett Anderson, James Anderson, Joseph Anderson, Joseph Anderson, Sr., Alexander Andes, John Andes, Solomon Andes, Benjamin Atchley, Daniel Atchley, Isaac Atchley, Joseph Atchley, Joshua Atchley, Noah Atchley, Thomas Atchley, Jr., Thomas Atchly, Jr., William Atchly, Felis Auley, Nathaniel Austin, Caleb Babb, Caleb Bailes, Robert Bailes, Samuel Baily, James Baker, Joseph Baker, Martin Baker, Samuel Baker, Betsey Ballard, Henry Baller, Blackburn Barnet, Coonrod Barnhart, Armstad Barns, Allen Bryan, Jr., David D. Beagles, Elisabeth Beasly, James Beasly, Isaac Been, James Benson, John Benson, John Benyes, Andrew Bird, Jacob Bird, John Bird, Lewis Bird, Jerril Birrur, Griffie Black, Benjamin Blackburn, Hugh Blair, James Blair, Sr., Nathaniel Blair, Samuel Blair, Jr., Jeremiah Blalock, Francis Bodine, Henry Bohannon, Burrel Boomfield, Elisha Borden, Clark Botton, Agustin Bowers, Anderson Bowers, Polly Bowman, Ahaz Brayn, David Bricker, William Brimer, John Brown, Nancy Brown, Samuel Brown, Bryant Bruden, John Bruden, Hanah Brudin, William Brudin, James Bruster, Allen Bryan, Sr., Thomas Bryan, William Bryan, Harry Buchhannon, John Buckner, Thomas Buckner, Patsey Budin, Jacob Bun, Joseph Burk, Moses Burnine, Adam Burns, James Burns, Mary Burns, Wilson Burns, Andrew Bush, George Bush, Henry Butler, Horatio Butler, William Butler, Thomas Byron, Elijah Cagle, Henry Cagle, John Cagle, John N.C. Cagle, William Cagle, Thomas Caldwell, Jane Campbell, John Cannon, William Cannon, William Canterbury, James Carmon, John Carringen, Robert Carson, Elisabeth Castle, Elisha Cate, Joshua Cate, Thomas Cate, Elijah Cati, Benjamin W. Catle, Samuel Catlett, John Catters, Richard Catters, Andrew Chambers, Catherine Chandler, George Chandler, James Chandler, John Chandler, Andrew Chane, Thomas Christian, William Claber, J. Cunberland Clabough, John Clabough, Samuel Clabough, Spencer Clack, Danice Clarck, John Clarck, Amos Clark, Isom Clark, James Clark, John S. C. Clark, Joseph Clark, Silva Clark, William Clifer, Patsey Cliffin, John Clinton, William Clinton, James Cole, Aron Collier, Cyrus Compton, Jeremiah

Compton, Joseph Compton, William M. Compton, William Cotten, John Cotton, John Covington, Hugh Cowan, Martha Cowan, Mary Cowan, Lynn Cowden, Henry Cox, John Cox, Nathan Cox, Andrew Criswell, William Crouch, Elisabeth Crow, Moses Crow, Aron Crowson, James Cummings, David Cuningham, John Cuningham, Moses Cuningham, Christopher Cunningham, David Cusick, Joseph Cusick, Samuel Cusick, Jesse Davis, Sarah Davis, Washington Decke, Asa Delosure, Owen C. Dennis, Jonas Derick, Jacob Derrick, John Devenport, Mary Dickerson, Rebecca Dickey, John Dicky, Isaac Dison, Alfred Dixon, Johnson Dobbins, Benjamin Dockery, Allexander Douglas, John Douglas, Samuel Douglas, Thomas Douglas, Samuel Dowdle, Daniel Duggan, Hugh Duggan, Robert Duggan, Adam Dunlap, John Dunn, Richard Dunn, Hanah Earnest, James Earnest, John Elliad, Christopher Ellice, James W. Ellice, William Ellice, James Ellige, Johnathan Ellison, James Emery, Daniel Emmet, Elisabeth Emmit, Alexander England, William Etherton, Bartholomew Evans, Daniel Evans, Jacob Evans, John Evans, Richard Evans, Adam Fagala, Michael Fagala, John Fann, William Fann, William Fannon, David Fanshire, John Fanshire, Samuel Fanshire, James Farr, John Feazle, John Fergason, Samuel Fergason, James Ferguson, Richard Ferguson, William Ferguson, Betsey Floyd, Burgess Floyd, Jonathan Floyd, George Flynn, George Follet, Frank Foster, James Foster, Enoch Fowler, Richard Fowler, Abraham Fox, Adam Fox, George Fox, John Fox, Mark Fox, William Fox, Mary Fraim, Joseph Francis, John Franklin, Willis Franklin, David Frazier, Joseph French, Catherine Gabbla, Amos Gabble, Russel Gaforth, Amos Gallion, Gilbert Gallion, Thomas Gallion, Charles George, Nathan Gibson, John Gilbert, Richard Gilbert, Atlap Gipson, Stephen Gipson, Lewis Glap, Hugh Goforth, Atchley Haggard, James Haggard, Martin Haggard, Elizabeth Hale, Guy Hale, James Hamilton, Catherine Hardin, Thomas Hardin, James Harper, William Harper, James Harris, Jeremiah Harrison, John Hatcher, John R. Hatcher, Mary Hatcher, Reuben Hatcher, Adam Haun, Henry Hederick, Mary Henderson, William Henderson, James Henly, Polly Henly, Samuel Henny, Aikman Henry, Benjamin Henry, Hugh Henry, John Henry, Robert Henry, William Henry, William Henry, Jr., James Hess, John Hichols, James Hickman, Sally Hickman, Thomas Hickman, William Hickman, Elisbeth Hicks, Alfred Higgins, Isaac Hill, John Hill, Randal Hill, Thomas Hill, Tibny Hill, Riley Hinet, Thomas Hinly, Owen Histen, Charles Hodges, Edmund Hodges, Henry Hodges, John Hodges, William Hodges, Benjamin Holland, Jacob Holland, Sally Holms, Jacob Hoofs, Benjamin Hooft, John Hooft, William Hooft, Drury Hooker, Hiram Hooper, Isaac Hooper, Jacob Hooper, John Hooper, Thomas Hooper, Adam Houk, Henry

Houk, John Houk, Jordon Houk, Martin Houk, Barbary Howard, John Howard, Jacob Huber, George Hudson, Leonard Huff, George L. Huffaker, Wesley Huffaker, John Huffs, Joseph Huffs, Atchly Huggard, John Hunter, Betsey Hurst, George Hurst, George Hurst, Jr., Henry Hurst, John Hurst, Nancy Hurst, Sevier Hurst, William Hurst, Isaac Husky, Jr., Albert Husky, Isaac Husky, Sr., John Husky, John Husky, Stephen Husky, Stephen Husky, William Husky, Thomas Ireland, Armstrong G. Irvin, Joel Ivy, William Ivy, Milly James, Randall James, James Jenkins, John Jenkins, John G.C. Jenkins, Polly Jenkins, Thomas Johnson, Solomon Johnston, Alston Jones, John Jones, Layman Jones, Polly Kagle, William Kagle, Hubbard Karnes, Joseph Keeler, George Keener, William P. Keener, Andrew Kelly, John Kelm, Matthew Kelson, Andrew Kenathin, Reuben Kenester, Daniel Kero, Amy Kerr, James Kerr, James Kerr, Sr. John Kerr, John A. Kerr, John Kerr, Jr., John M. Kerr, William Kerr, Jacob Kifer, John inester, George King, William King, Willie King, Asa Knight, Thomas Knight, James Langston, Jesse Langston, John Laning, Mary Laning, Isaac Large, James Large, John Large, Robert Large, Samuel Large, Robert Lavedy, Andrew Lawson, Anthony Lawson, Reynolds Lawson, Daniel Layman, Jacob Layman, Jacob Layman, Jr., John Layman, Michael Layman, Augustin B. Lea, David Legerwood, Samuel Leverwill, Allen Lewelling, Alexander Lewilling, James Lewilling, Margaret Lewilling, Martha Lewilling, David Lewis, Levi Lewis, Samuel Lewis, George Lindly, Jessee Lindsy, John Lindsy, George Long, James Long, Maples Long, Moses Long, Reuben Long, Isaac Love, Edward Lovedy, Henry Lovedy, Amos Lovelady, Jacob W. Low, Jefferson Low, Morris Lusk, Peggy Malcomb, William Malcomb, Jacob Manes, Samuel Manes, Joseph Mangrum, Henry Maning, Honor Maning, Joab Mning, Thomas Maning, Amos Manis, Elijah Manis, William Manis, Joseph Mann, Richard Many, Elijah Maples, Ephraim Maples, James Maples, Jessee Maples, Josiah Maples, Peter Maples, Sarah Maples, Thomas Maples, William Maples, John Marshall, Robert Marshall, Abner Martin, William Martin, James Mason, Jesser Mason, William Matthew, Jeremiah Matthews, Robert Matthews, William Mattocks, David McAnahan, Spencer McBrian, William McBryan, Alexander McCally, John McCarty, Joseph McCarty, William McCarty, Roysel McChandler, Joseph McClary, Georg McCown, David McCrosky, Jane McCrosky, John McCrosky, Robert McCrosky, Wm. McCrosky, Sarah McDaniel, Peggy McGaughy, William McGaughy, Betsey McHess, Elijah McHew, John McKinan, Ann McKinly, Peter cKinly, Charles McKinsey, John McKinsey, Kneel McKinsey, Roger McKinsey, John McKisick, William McKisick, Archibald McMahan, Ely McMahan, George McMahan, James McMahan, James McMahan, Jr., Redman McMahan, Robert

McMahan, William McMahan, Archibald McMurry, John McMurry, Elijah Mehur, Jr., Fergason Melelelan, William Merrit, William Meslvany, Isaac A. Miller, Joseph Miller, Curtis Mills, James Mills, Dennis M.B. Mitchell, John Mitchell, Philip Mock, Cyrus Montgaue, Robert Montgomery, William Montgomery, John Moon, John Moon, Jr., William Moon, John Moore, Morgan G. Mopin, Jordon Morgan, Willis Morgan, George Morping, Jessee Morris, Jessee Morris, John Mullendove, John Mullendove, Abraham Mullindore, Edward Murphy, Elizabeth Murphy, Samuel Murphy, Joseph Murphy, Christopher Nations, Isaac Newman, John J. Nichols, Edward Nichols, John Nichols, Robert Nichols, William Nichols, James Norton, William Norton, William O'connel, Hercules Ogle, Isaac Ogle, John Ogle, Thomas Ogle, William Ogle, William Ogle, Jr., William Ogle, Sr., Allen Owens, Jacob Owens, John Ownsly, Peter Panbean, Martin Parker, John Parmer, George Parsons, Charles Pate, Samuel Pate, Christina Paterson, Caleb Patterson, Charles Patterson, Cornelius Patterson, George Patterson, Samuel Patterson, Meady Pearson, Elisabeth A. Perryman, James Perryman, James P.H. Pertin, Horation Petty, James Petty, John Petty, John Pharis, Samuel Pharris, Samuel Pickens, John Pierce, Mary Pierce, Adam Pitner, John Pitner, Sr., Nancy Pitts, Jeremiah M. Plummer, George W. Porter, John W. Porter, Mitchel Porter, Nichalos Porter, William Porter, William Porter, Jr., William Porter, Sr., James Price, Alexander Priston, Josiah Priswood, Benjamin Prophet, Casper Rader, Isaac Rains, James Rains, John N. Rainwater, Moses Rainwater, Allen Rainwaters, Polly Rainwaters, Samuel Ramsey, John Randales, William Randales, Rhody Randalls, Andrew Randles, Richard Randles, Daniel Reagan, Joshua Reagan, Richard Reagan, Timothy Reagan, Thomas Redings, Nancy Reece, James Rence, Jesse Renfro, John Renfro, Mark Renfro, Jeremiah Riagan, James Rice, John Rice, Isaac Richards, Jacob Richards, John Richards, Robert Richards, William Richardson, William Ridings, Ignatius Riggin, Mary Riggin, Lewis Rineari, Susanah Ringan, John Rinier, Charles Rird, John Rird, William Rird, Aron Roberts, Benjamin Roberts, Bennet Roberts, Elisha Roberts, Ely Roberts, Isaac Roberts, John Roberts, Mark Roberts, William Roberts, Clison Robertson, Elijah Robertson, Isbel Robertson, Mark B. Robertson, Samuel Robertson, William Robertson, James Rodings, Elijah Rogers, George Rogers, Josiah Rogers, Micaja C. Rogers, Henry Romines, John Romines, Latin Romines, Benjamin Romins, Jacob Romland, Elisha Rose, Hosea Rose, John Rose, Sampson Rouhooft, James Routh, Jeremaih Routh, Jeremiah Routh, Jr., Zechariah Routh, Burdenham Rudd, Aron Runyan, John Runyan, Hanah Rustin, John Rustin, Morgan Sage, Samuel Sage, Joseph Sallens, Lewis Sampson, John Saunders, William Scott, Archibald

Scruggs, Jacob Seaton, James Seaton, Philip Seaton, John Shahan, Judea Shahan, John Shamblin, Lot Shamblin, William Shamblin, John Sharp, Willis B. Sharp, Robert Shewbird, Charles Shewbread, Robert Shield, Sr., Barbary Shields, Hackton Shields, Richard Shields, Robert Shields, Samuel Shields, William Shields, Philip Shoulds, Jacob Shoutts, Martin Shoutts, Christopher Shrader, Jacob Shrader, Joseph Shrader, Matthias Sink, John Smallwood, William Smallwood, Betsey Smith, Epter Smith, Jamsey Smith, Thomas B. Smith, William Smith, George Snapp, George Snapp, Joseph Snapp, Joseph Snapp, Peter Snapp, William Sneed, Thomas Sow, William Spencer, Henry Stafford, Matthew Stallions, Nathan Stanley, Solomon Stansbury, Joel Starkey, Elisabeth Staver, William Steaty, John Steel, Andrew Stephens, Nehemiah Stephens, Alexander Stiner, John Stinett, Patience Stockton, Daniel Supataller, Silas Suvely, William Swoddy, Thomas Talbot, Zechinah Taliver, John Tanner, Goerge Taylor, Isaac Taylor, Peter Taylor, Matthias Teage, Absalom Thompson, Antipart Thomas, Benjamin Thomas, David Thomas, Dennis M. Thomas, Henry M. Thomas, Isaac Thomas, John Thomas, Johnathan Thomas, William Thomas, William N.C. Thomas, Dorias Thompson, Eizabeth Thompson, Joseph Thompson, William Thornbury, James Toomy, John Toomy, Eliza Towls, William Trenthorn, Jr., Archibald Trotter, Clabourn Trotter, John Trotter, John Trotter, Jr., William Trotter, William Tunis, Henry Turner, Stephen Underdown, Benjamin Underwood, Enoch Underwood, George Underwood, John Underwood, Billy Unknown, Richard Varneli, Jessee Varnell, Lyda Varnell, Thomas Varnill, Josiah Varrnell, William Vaun, Betsy Waddle, John Walker, Polly Walker, Absalom Wall, Thomas Ward, Collin Warren, Sally Watson, Ezekiel Watters, Lewis Wayland, John Wear, John Wear, Jr., Mary Wear, P. M. Wear, Elizabeth Webb, Joseph Webb, Thomas Webb, Andrew Wells, Jr., Andrew Wells, Sr., Middleton Whealy, William Wheyby, William White, William M. C. White, Campbell Whittle, George Whittle, Levi Whittle, Elisabeth Wilcox, John William, Joshua William, Catherine Williams, David Williams, John Williams, Polly Williams, John Williamson, Nelson Williamson, William Williamson, James Wilson, John B. Wilson, Susan Wilson, Samuel Wist, William Witerner, Elijah Wood, Joseph Wood, Richard Wood, Jr., Jane Woods, John York.

Douglas County, Washington Territory, Tennesseans on the 1885 Territorial Census

    Smith Harding: (A) 52, (OC) Farmer, (BP) Tennessee
    D. H. Ford: (A) 63, (OC) Farmer, (BP) Tennessee

Houston Morning Star Obituary, March 25, 1841
Died, in this city, on Monday, 22d inst. of consumption, Mr. Ewing H. Crockett, in the 25th year of his age. He was a native of Robertson County, Tennessee

Tennesseans on the Brazos County, Texas, 1850 Federal Census
Henry G. Hudson: (LN) 8, (HN) 31, (FN) 31, (A) 50, (SEX) M. (RACE) W. (OC) Gunsmith, (BP) TN, (B) 1800 ca
Alexander Spencer: (LN) 26, (HN) 78, (FN) 78, (A) 30, (SEX) M. (RACE) W. (OC) Farming, (BP) TN, (B) 1820 ca
Thomas C. Bowman: (LN) 23, (HN) 35, (FN) 35, (A) 43, (SEX) M. (RACE) W. (OC) Farming, (BP) TN, (B) 1807 ca
Charles Clayton: (LN) 7, (HN) 3, (FN) 3, (A) 26, (SEX) M. (RACE) W, (OC) Farming, (BP) TN, (B) 1824 ca
William C. Walker: (LN) 32, (HN) 28, (FN) 28, (A) 40, (SEX) M. (RACE) W. (OC) Farming, (BP) TN, (B) 1810 ca
Gilbert H. Love: (LN) 25, (HN) 54, (FN) 54, (A) 29, (SEX) M. (RACE) W. (OC) Farming, (BP) TN, (B) 1821 ca
James P. Bowman: (LN) 19, (HN) 34, (FN) 34, (A) 50, (SEX) M. (RACE) W. (OC) Farming, (BP) TN, (B) 1800 ca
Richard Carter: (LN) 3, (HN) 66, (FN) 66, (A) 72, (SEX) M. (RACE) W, (OC) Farming, (BP) TN, (B) 1778 ca
Wilson Reed: (LN) 5, (HN) 67, (FN) 67, (A) 39, (SEX) M. (RACE) W, (OC) Farming, (BP) TN, (B) 1811 ca
William Havens: (LN) 40, (HN) 22, (FN) 22, (A) 35, (SEX) M. (RACE) W. (OC) Farming, (BP) TN, (B) 1815 ca
Isabella Ellison: (LN) 38, (HN) 50, (FN) 50, (A) 40, (SEX) F. (RACE) W. (OC) Farming, (BP) TN, (B) 1810 ca
Mary F. Richerson: (LN) 1, (HN) 1, (FN) 1, (A) 27, (SEX) M. (RACE) W. (OC) Farming, (BP) TN, (B) 1823 ca
Joseph Webb: (LN) 4, (HN) 1, (FN) 1, (A) 27, (SEX) M. (RACE) W. (OC) Farming, (BP) TN, (B) 1823 ca
William Webb: (LN) 5, (HN) 1, (FN) 1, (A) 18, (SEX) M. (RACE) W, (OC) Farming, (BP) TN, (B) 1832 ca
Crystopher C. Collins: (LN) 6, (HN) 2, (FN) 2, (A) 33, (SEX) M. (RACE) W. (OC) Farming, (BP) TN, (B) 1817 ca
William King: (LN) 37, (HN) 43, (FN) 43, (A) 35, (SEX) M. (RACE) W, (OC) Farming, (BP) TN, (B) 1815 ca
Stephen Sparkes: (LN) 10, (HN) 51, (FN) 51, (A) 26, (SEX) M. (RACE) W. (OC) Farming, (BP) TN, (B) 1824 ca
Thomas McCuny: (LN) 12, (HN) 52, (FN) 52, (A) 50, (SEX) M. (RACE) W. (OC) Farming, (BP) TN, (B) 1800 ca
John McDonald: (LN) 29, (HN) 55, (FN) 55, (A) 25, (SEX) M.

(RACE) W. (OC) Farming, (BP) TN, (B) 1825 ca
William King: (LN) 41, (HN) 58, (FN) 58, (A) 45, (SEX) M. (RACE) W, (OC) Farming, (BP) TN, (B) 1805 ca
Marshall Payne: (LN) 4, (HN) 59, (FN) 59, (A) 23, (SEX) M. (RACE) W. (OC) Farming, (BP) TN, (B) 1827 ca
Mathew McDonald: (LN) 18, (HN) 61, (FN) 61, (A) 28, (SEX) M. (RACE) W. (OC) Farming, (BP) TN, (B) 1822 ca
Benjamin Higgs: (LN) 3, (HN) 74, (FN) 74, (A) 24, (SEX) M. (RACE) W. (OC) Farming, (BP) TN, (B) 1826 ca
James Higgs: (LN) 4, (HN) 74, (FN) 74, (A) 20, (SEX) M. (RACE) W, (OC) Farming, (BP) TN, (B) 1830 ca
Thomas Higgs: (LN) 5, (HN) 74, (FN) 74, (A) 19, (SEX) M. (RACE) W, (OC) Farming, (BP) TN, (B) 1831 ca
William Higgs: (LN) 6, (HN) 74, (FN) 74, (A) 17, (SEX) M. (RACE) W, (OC) Farming, (BP) TN, (B) 1833 ca
William Bowman: (LN) 22, (HN) 34, (FN) 34, (A) 18, (SEX) M. (RACE) W , (BP) TN, (B) 1832 ca
George Higgs: (LN) 12, (HN) 74, (FN) 74, (A) 23, (SEX) M. (RACE) W , (BP) TN, (B) 1827 ca
Virginia Richerson: (LN) 2, (HN) 1, (FN) 1, (A) 24, (SEX) F. (RACE) W. (BP) TN, (B) 1826 ca
Mary Midleton: (LN) 13, (HN) 24, (FN) 24, (A) 62, (SEX) F. (RACE) W. (BP) TN, (B) 1788 ca
Elizabeth Hudson: (LN) 9, (HN) 31, (FN) 31, (A) 48, (SEX) F. (RACE) W. (BP) TN, (B) 1802 ca
Mary Bowman: (LN) 24, (HN) 35, (FN) 35, (A) 41, (SEX) F. (RACE) W. (BP) TN, (B) 1809 ca
Parlee Bowman: (LN) 25, (HN) 35, (FN) 35, (A) 19, (SEX) F. (RACE) W. (BP) TN, (B) 1831 ca
Susan Bowman: (LN) 26, (HN) 35, (FN) 35, (A) 15, (SEX) F. (RACE) W. (BP) TN, (B) 1835 ca
Mary Warren: (LN) 9, (HN) 39, (FN) 39, (A) 35, (SEX) F. (RACE) W, (BP) TN, (B) 1815 ca
Minerva Nevill: (LN) 28, (HN) 41, (FN) 41, (A) 20, (SEX) F. (RACE) W. (BP) TN, (B) 1830 ca
Sarah Seale: (LN) 29, (HN) 49, (FN) 49, (A) 48, (SEX) F. (RACE) W , (BP) TN, (B) 1802 ca
Jane Sparkes: (LN) 3, (HN) 51, (FN) 51, (A) 44, (SEX) F. (RACE) W. (BP) TN, (B) 1806 ca
Matilda McCuny: (LN) 13, (HN) 52, (FN) 52, (A) 45, (SEX) F. (RACE) W. (BP) TN, (B) 1805 ca
Elizabeth Lines: (LN) 23, (HN) 53, (FN) 53, (A) 19, (SEX) F. (RACE) W. (BP) TN, (B) 1831 ca

Mary Payne: (LN) 5, (HN) 59, (FN) 59, (A) 29, (SEX) F. (RACE) W. (BP) TN, (B) 1821 ca
Ofelia Payne: (LN) 6, (HN) 59, (FN) 59, (A) 14, (SEX) F. (RACE) W. BP) TN, (B) 1836 ca
Cain Payne: (LN) 7, (HN) 59, (FN) 59, (A) 11, (SEX) M. (RACE) W. (BP) TN, (B) 1839 ca
Permelia Payne: (LN) 8, (HN) 59, (FN) 59, (A) 8, (SEX) F. (RACE) W, (BP) TN, (B) 1842 ca
Richard Payne: (LN) 9, (HN) 59, (FN) 59, (A) 5, (SEX) M. (RACE) W, (BP) TN, (B) 1845 ca
John McDonald: (LN) 20, (HN) 61, (FN) 61, (A) 8, (SEX) M. (RACE) W. (BP) TN, (B) 1842 ca
Elizabeth McDonald: (LN) 21, (HN) 61, (FN) 61, (A) 5, (SEX) F. (RACE) W. (BP) TN, (B) 1845 ca
Pegy Foley: (LN) 30, (HN) 63, (FN) 63, (A) 43, (SEX) F. (RACE) W. (BP) TN, (B) 1807 ca
John Foley: (LN) 31, (HN) 63, (FN) 63, (A) 14, (SEX) M. (RACE) W, (BP) TN, (B) 1836 ca
Josephine Johnson: (LN) 1, (HN) 65, (FN) 65, (A) 20, (SEX) F. (RACE) W. (BP) TN, (B) 1830 ca
Elizabeth Carter: (LN) 4, (HN) 66, (FN) 66, (A) 59, (SEX) F. (RACE) W. (BP) TN, (B) 1791 ca
Maryann Reed: (LN) 6, (HN) 66, (FN) 66, (A) 33, (SEX) F. (RACE) W, (BP) TN, (B) 1817 ca
Caroline Berton: (LN) 14, (HN) 68, (FN) 68, (A) 34, (SEX) F. (RACE) W. (BP) TN, (B) 1816 ca
Tabithia McMilan: (LN) 25, (HN) 70, (FN) 70, (A) 27, (SEX) F. (RACE) W. (BP) TN, (B) 1823 ca
Victor Higgs: (LN) 7, (HN) 74, (FN) 74, (A) 15, (SEX) M. (RACE) W, (BP) TN, (B) 1835 ca
Mary Wilson: (LN) 21, (HN) 76, (FN) 76, (A) 20, (SEX) F. (RACE) W, (BP) TN, (B) 1830 ca

Pendleton County, Kentucky, Delinquent Tax List, 1807
Francis Crabb: Removed to Tennessee

Pendleton County, Kentucky, Delinquent Tax List, 1808
Francis Crabb: Removed to Tennessee
John Buckley: Removed to Tennessee State
Robert Riddle: Removed to Tennessee State

Pendleton County, Kentucky, Delinquent Tax List, 1809
Robert Riddle: Removed to Tennessee

John Buckley: Removed to Tennessee

Washington County, Tennessee, Captain Greer's Company Taxable Property for 1790

Name	Acres	Free Poles	Black Poles
Richd Kite	150	1	
Solomon Hollit	283	1	
Capt Alexd Greer		1	1
Jno. Gillam		1	0
Saml Tate			
John Kerr		1	0
William Duggard	200	1	
Teter Nave	350	1	
Jeremiah Bass		1	8
Thos Duncan		1	
Richd Cox		1	
Jacob Heathrick	300	1	
Thos Miller	200	1	
Isaac Tipton	200	1	
Leonard Bowers	50	1	
Jas Ivy	50	1	
Abraham Cox		1	
Joseph Heathrick		1	
John Greer		1	
John Parker Moore		1	
Nicholas Carriger		1	
Isaac Lincoln	500	1	
Jno. Arendel	100	1	
Godfrey Carriger Sr.	2167	1	
John H? Lacy		1	
William Murray		1	
Elisha Humphrey		1	
Valentine Sevier Sr.	360		
Joseph Greer	400	1	1
John Michael Smithpeter	375	1	
Andrew Greer Sr.	216	1	2
Abraham Sevier			
Joseph Sevier		1	
Samuel Tipton	744	1	

Wilson County, Tennessee, Marriages, 1806-1830
Sam Stockard and Polly Thomas, (MD) May 20, 1806
Anthony Winston and Sally Ann Watson, (MD) Aug. 27, 1806

John B. Bedford and Ruth Brown, (MD) Jul. 7, 1806
Elijah Gwyn and Sarah Idlett, (MD) Jan. 3, 1806
John Phillips and Elizabeth Scott, (MD) Jan. 6, 1806
John Fergeson and Patsey Harris, (MD) Jan. 18, 1806
John Scobey and Ann Spears, (MD) Jan. 21, 1806
Lucy Patterson and Hardy Peneel, (MD) Jan. 31, 1806
Thomas Dill and Agness Hopson, (MD) Feb. 3, 1806
Julius Alford and Ann Hays, (MD) Feb. 18, 1806
James Johnson and Elizabeth Nixon, (MD) Feb. 18, 1806
Phillip Anderson and Polly Macnatt, (MD) Feb. 24, 1806
Leven Macnatt and Nancy Smith, (MD) Feb. 24, 1806
Anthony Copland and Nancy Craig, (MD) Mar. 24, 1806
George Lockmiller and Polly Porter, (MD) Apr. 3, 1806
George Brown and Polly Thompson, (MD) Apr. 10, 1806
Peter Cotton and Lebenah Tucker, (MD) May 20, 1806
Phillip Hintson and Elizabeth Tucker, (MD) May 20, 1806
Edward James and Margret Thomas, (MD) Jun. 6, 1806
John Pankey and Peggy Smith, (MD) Jun. 15, 1806
Lear Herrod and Stephen Lankford, (MD) Jul. 5, 1806
Benjamin Alexander and Sarah Cloyd, (MD) Jul. 21, 1806
Joseph Jadwin and Mary Vanhooser, (MD) Jul. 26, 1806
Wyall Bettis and Milly Powers, (MD) Aug. 7, 1806
Robert Boyd and Elizabeth Gardner, (MD) Aug. 11, 1806
Alexander Steele and Lucy Compton, (MD) Aug. 11, 1806
Patrick Youree and Respey Chapman, (MD) Aug. 11, 1806
Levi Holland and Nancy Siddle, (MD) Aug. 25, 1806
John Afflack and Nancy Taylor, (MD) Aug. 27, 1806
Hugh McCoy and Caty Wilson, (MD) Aug. 27, 1806
George Allin and Sally Johnson, (MD) Aug. 28, 1806
Hugh McElyea and Polly McElyea, (MD) Sep. 2, 1806
Peter Walker and Drucilla Hendrick, (MD) Sep. 2, 1806
Andrew Morrison and Jane Robertson, (MD) Sep. 6, 1806
Avery Brown and Sarah Marlow, (MD) Sep. 22, 1806
William Holland and Fannie Still, (MD) Nov. 14, 1806
Bailory Pitner and Samuel Thomas, (MD) Dec. 21, 1806
Thomas Clifton and Letty Rogers, (MD) Dec. 22, 1806
Leeroy Lact and Rebecca Williamson, (MD) Dec. 22, 1806
James Newby and Sally Batley, (MD) Dec. 22, 1806
Jacob Baring and Ann Ray, (MD) Jan. 4, 1807
Joshua Barnes and Nancy Reiff, (MD) Jan. 10, 1807
John Bettis and Sally Bradley, (MD) Jan. 10, 1807
James Broadaway and Elizabeth Forbes, (MD) Jan. 14, 1807
Moses Carter and Polly Davidson, (MD) Jan. 23, 1807

Thomas Bowen and Lucy Drew, (MD) Jan. 24, 1807
John Smith and Polly Warmack, (MD) Jan. 24, 1807
Adam Barns and Polly Leonard, (MD) Feb. 1, 1807
John Braddock and Nelly Leonard, (MD) Feb. 9, 1807
Buster Alford and Mary Bryant, (MD) Feb. 21, 1807
William Anderson and Nancy Greenwood, (MD) Mar. 14, 1807
James Carruth and Sally Williams, (MD) Mar. 20, 1807
John Jennings and Fanny Word, (MD) Mar. 21, 1807
James Byrns and Rebecca Ward, (MD) Mar. 23, 1807
Edward Bruce and Nelly Burns, (MD) Mar. 30, 1807
Joshua Anderson and Sally Patton, (MD) Apr. 4, 1807
John Brown and Patty Bumpass, (MD) Apr. 10, 1807
David London and Polly Parten, (MD) Apr. 10, 1807
William Thompson and Rebecca Wilson, (MD) Jun. 2, 1807
John Morris and Nancy Walls, (MD) Jun. 13, 1807
John Keeling and Polly Manning, (MD) Jul. 13, 1807
Ezekiel Lindsey and Elizabeth McNeeley, (MD) Jul. 22, 1807
Samuel Dickings and Nancy Heflin, (MD) Jul. 28, 1807
Dread Bass and Nancy Brean, (MD) Aug. 7, 1807
Middleton Bell and Rebecah Gibson, (MD) Aug. 11, 1807
James Anderson and Elizabeth Chapman, (MD) Aug. 13, 1807
John Ashford and Jinsey King, (MD) Aug. 26, 1807
John Barnet and Polly McAdow, (MD) Sep. 23, 1807
David Burton and Ann Davis, (MD) Oct. 8, 1807
Abner Stuart and Nancy Gray, (MD) Oct. 8, 1807
Zebulom Baird and Clevy Hunt, (MD) Nov. 14, 1807
John Nicks and Anna Richards, (MD) Dec. 8, 1807
Willsher Bandy and Nancy Johnson, (MD) Jan. 6, 1808
Dabney Tatum and Polly Whitson, (MD) Jan. 9, 1808
Milbrey Hearn and Hestey Mickle, (MD) Jan. 18, 1808
Humphrey Donalson and Sally Kelly, (MD) Feb. 17, 1808
Bennajah Gray and Elenor Warmack, (MD) Mar. 1, 1808
Jeney Cooksey and Luke Tippit, (MD) Mar. 12, 1808
John Davis and Polly McAlpin, (MD) Mar. 14, 1808
John Green and Nancy Myrick, (MD) Apr. 25, 1808
Robert Bogle and Sally Brison, (MD) Jun. 2, 1808
William Adamson and Demorris Bledsoe, (MD) Jun. 7, 1808
Joshua Brown and Prudence McAllen, (MD) Jun. 27, 1808
James Cropper and Peggy Poviance, (MD) Aug. 17, 1808
Hezekiel Cartwright and Elizabeth Maholland, (MD) Sep. 2, 1808
John Clemment and Jane Pullin, (MD) Sep. 29, 1808
John Bond and Sarah Cummings, (MD) Oct. 15, 1808
Thomas Telford and Elizabeth Chawning, (MD) Oct. 15, 1808

John Cambell and Pheby Cassady, (MD) Nov. 2, 1808
Graham Jackson and Betsey Smith, (MD) Nov. 5, 1808
Robert Harris and Elizabeth McCowen, (MD) Nov. 6, 1808
Henry Cocke and Elizabeth Tipton, (MD) Nov. 21, 1808
James Crator and Jenny Warmack, (MD) Dec. 31, 1808
Isham F. Davis and Rachel S Hays, (MD) Oct. 1, 1809
Joshua Anderson and Peggy H Thomas, (MD) Feb. 1, 1809
James E. Davis and Polly Taylor, (MD) Apr. 1, 1809
John Baker and Genny Bearding, (MD) Feb. 13, 1809
Spencer Edwards and Sally Wilson, (MD) Feb. 21, 1809
Sion Bass and Polly Perry, (MD) Feb. 25, 1809
George Whitson and Polly Meridith, (MD) Feb. 25, 1809
Simon Adamson and Susannah Hopkins, (MD) Feb. 29, 1809
John Robertson and Elizabeth Williamson, (MD) Mar. 9, 1809
Joseph Hubbard and Susannah Wamack, (MD) Mar. 22, 1809
Soloman Bell and Nancy Jacobs, (MD) Mar. 25, 1809
Nathaniel Wade and Polly Melton, (MD) Mar. 27, 1809
William Porterfield and Myrandy Young, (MD) Mar. 29, 1809
Andrew Morrison and Lyda Alexander, (MD) Apr. 1, 1809
John Rieff and Hannah Ross, (MD) Apr. 19, 1809
Daniel McCoy and Jane ?????, (MD) Apr. 27, 1809
Lewis McCartney and ????, (MD) May 8, 1809
Gabriel Anderson and Polly Scaret, (MD) May 23, 1809
William Cartwright and Patsey Fuller, (MD) Jun. 3, 1809
John Leech and Jensey Stuart, (MD) Jun. 20, 1809
Richard Talley and Sally Taylor, (MD) Jul. 25, 1809
Josiah Impson and Polly Smith, (MD) Aug. 26, 1809
John Anglin and Elizabeth Carver, (MD) Sep. 1, 1809
Robert Morrison and Edy Sharpe, (MD) Sep. 2, 1809
Richardson Carr and Mily Sawyers, (MD) Sep. 6, 1809
Benjamin Castleman and Polly McFarland, (MD) Sep. 7, 1809
Bryant Ward and Polly Wynne, (MD) Sep. 23, 1809
Jonathon Eatherly and Jenny Thompson, (MD) Sep. 27, 1809
Eli Donnell and Peggy Logue, (MD) Sep. 30, 1809
John Berry and Elizabeth Campbell, (MD) Oct. 12, 1809
Robert Campbell and Tilly Stuart, (MD) Nov. 3, 1809
John Jones and Frances Knight, (MD) Nov. 7, 1809
Thomas Carver and Margret Donelson, (MD) Dec. 4, 1809
Roland Gipson and Betsey Rather, (MD) Dec. 10, 1809
Jesse Bloodworth and Narcissa Gibson, (MD) Dec. 11, 1809
John Brown and Rachel Lomax, (MD) Dec. 16, 1809
Jas. Horton and Rebecca White, (MD) Dec. 21, 1809
Parron Bandy and Lytia Rice, (MD) Dec. 25, 1809

John McNeely and Belinda W. Carson, (MD) Mar. 8, 1810
David W. Breedlove and Nancy Breedlove, (MD) Feb. 10, 1810
Isaac B. Eslick and Jencey George, (MD) Apr. 30, 1810
William Mann and Frances Turner, (MD) Jan. 4, 1810
David Johnson and Elizabeth Walker, (MD) Jan. 8, 1810
John Walker and Nancy Nelson, (MD) Jan. 8, 1810
Nathaniel Brown and Sally Scott, (MD) Jan. 24, 1810
Justis Rulmon and Ruth Standford, (MD) Jan. 25, 1810
Edward Lawrence and Delilah Woodward, (MD) Jan. 29, 1810
Obediah Woodrum and Dolley Bradberry, (MD) Jan. 29, 1810
Gabrial Chandler and Jensey Thomas, (MD) Jan. 30, 1810
Jensey Brannon and Francis Woodward, (MD) Feb. 21, 1810
James Dickings and Mary McWhirter, (MD) Feb. 27, 1810
James Hicks and Lobithia Standeford, (MD) Mar. 2, 1810
James Hollard and Elizabeth Walker, (MD) Mar. 4, 1810
John Travillian and Mary Carson, (MD) Mar. 8, 1810
Leeroy Bradley and Sally McSpadden, (MD) Mar. 14, 1810
Josiah Jackson and Nancy Clampit, (MD) Mar. 17, 1810
John Thompson and Peggy Wilson, (MD) Mar. 27, 1810
William Hollandworth and Jensey Walker, (MD) Apr. 7, 1810
Merrel Elkins and Thankful Maddox, (MD) Apr. 16, 1810
Miles Gray and Rhody Harkins, (MD) Apr. 19, 1810
Daniel Baker and Sally Woodward, (MD) May 4, 1810
George Donnell and Armela Shanks, (MD) May 14, 1810
John Hubbard and Elizabeth Jennings, (MD) Jun. 11, 1810
Tryry Laine and Nancy Ligon, (MD) Jul. 17, 1810
Moses Sterrett and Sarah Witherspoon, (MD) Aug. 11, 1810
James Shorter and Margret Smith, (MD) Aug. 18, 1810
Thomas Bormer and Polly Granade, (MD) Oct. 1, 1810
Ezekiel Alexander and Polly Cooper, (MD) Oct. 8, 1810
Rezon Byrn and Frances Craddock, (MD) Oct. 13, 1810
Jesse Bowers and Nancy Mann, (MD) Nov. 8, 1810
Henry Dameron and Sally Wright, (MD) Dec. 5, 1810
Robert Anderson and Nancy Sands, (MD) Dec. 13, 1810
Samuel Alsup and Elizabeth Jennings, (MD) Dec. 25, 1810
William Nicks and Sally Pugh, (MD) Dec. 31, 1810
Isiah Cox and Patsey P. Rather, (MD) Aug. 1, 1811
Robert Irwin and Mary Luch ????, (MD) Feb. 23, 1811
James Laceter and Susannah Allen Cetchern, (MD) Dec. 4, 1811
Robert W. Ppool and Polly Cartwright, (MD) Mar. 16, 1811
Saml. R. Anderson and Fanny Parish, (MD) Feb. 20, 1811
Johnson J. Birch and Sally Caldwell, (MD) Sep. 13, 1811
Morris G. Burton and Polly Reading, (MD) Feb. 13, 1811

Abraham Adams and Nansey Adams, (MD) Jan. 7, 1811
Jency Howell and Samuel Irwin, (MD) Jan. 14, 1811
Eddins Chandler and Huldy Sherrool, (MD) Jan. 16, 1811
George McWhorter and Patsey Mitchell, (MD) Jan. 19, 1811
Frances Adams and Lewis Hancock, (MD) Jan. 21, 1811
Reubin Allin and Jemima Lewis, (MD) Jan. 21, 1811
Lewis Hancock and Frances Adams, (MD) Jan. 21, 1811
Jemima Lewis and Reubin Allin, (MD) Jan. 21, 1811
James Mays and Polly Tucker, (MD) Jan. 21, 1811
Stephen Medlock and Sarah Tucker, (MD) Jan. 23, 1811
Henry Robertson and Polly Lambert, (MD) Feb. 20, 1811
Thomas Bogle and Rachel Brison, (MD) Feb. 26, 1811
John Cartwright and Polly Dillard, (MD) Mar. 16, 1811
John Blurton and Sally McMennaway, (MD) Mar. 27, 1811
John Davis and Theodelia Marton, (MD) Apr. 16, 1811
Nathaniel Davis and Elizabeth McFarland, (MD) Apr. 16, 1811
Randal Carter and Polly Johnson, (MD) May 11, 1811
Pitts Chandler and Pernelia Henderson, (MD) May 11, 1811
Mathew East and Jinsey McPeak, (MD) Jun. 4, 1811
Beuriah Bateman and Sally Magness, (MD) Jun. 17, 1811
Stephen Cloyd and Polly Wilson, (MD) Jun. 28, 1811
Sampson Allen and Polly Somers, (MD) Jul. 10, 1811
Hugh Henry and Phebe Oneal, (MD) Jul. 10, 1811
Jacob Casselenor and Anne Moore, (MD) Aug. 29, 1811
James Bass and Kissiah Rowland, (MD) Sep. 10, 1811
Thomas Barton and Tabitha Hodges, (MD) Oct. 6, 1811
David Barton and Sarah Borum, (MD) Oct. 7, 1811
Kenneth Bethoson and Delilah Ragsdale, (MD) Oct. 12, 1811
Samuel Bettis and Achaza Chapman, (MD) Oct. 12, 1811
James Crawford and Amy Thrower, (MD) Dec. 4, 1811
Lewis Clark and Patsey Doak, (MD) Dec. 26, 1811
James McDaniel and Amy B Vaughn, (MD) Feb. 10, 1812
William Wood and Elizabeth B Harris, (MD) Oct. 5, 1812
Eli T. Hunt and Sarah Webb, (MD) Jul. 11, 1812
Joseph Humphries and Nancy Brown, (MD) Jan. 4, 1812
Lewis Howel and Polly Jennings, (MD) Jan. 7, 1812
Elijah Armstrong and Peggy Higgins, (MD) Jan. 18, 1812
Aaron Romine and Polly Wells, (MD) Jan. 21, 1812
Jesse Brinson and Susannah Moss, (MD) Jan. 29, 1812
William Terry and Betsey Marton, (MD) Jan. 29, 1812
John Blackburn and Caty Carver, (MD) Feb. 3, 1812
Arden Somers and Nancy Tucker, (MD) Feb. 16, 1812
William Benson and Fanny Dodd, (MD) Feb. 22, 1812

James Drew and Rebecca Brown, (MD) Feb. 22, 1812
Lemuel Brichan and Polly Logan, (MD) Feb. 28, 1812
William Bettis and Minny Lamberth, (MD) Mar. 17, 1812
Dempsy Lambuth and Hicksy Bettis, (MD) Mar. 17, 1812
Martin Frankling and Nelly Watson, (MD) Mar. 21, 1812
William McHaney and Sally Word, (MD) Mar. 23, 1812
John Kimbro and Nancy Bearden, (MD) Mar. 30, 1812
Alexander Rutledge and Nancy Cox, (MD) Mar. 30, 1812
Luke Kent and Polly Mann, (MD) Apr. 2, 1812
Patrick Anderson and Fanny Chandler, (MD) May 13, 1812
John Eagan and Margret Wray, (MD) May 16, 1812
Dudley Brown and Edness Henderson, (MD) May 30, 1812
John Compton and Lucinda Treavillian, (MD) Jun. 9, 1812
Henry Blackwell and Patsy Brown, (MD) Jun. 14, 1812
Theodore Ross and Peggy Garmany, (MD) Jun. 23, 1812
David Williams and Betsey Hoozer, (MD) Jun. 23, 1812
James McAdow and Judith Smith, (MD) Jul. 4, 1812
John Caplinger and Catharine Harpole, (MD) Jul. 24, 1812
Robert Mitchel and Agey Moore, (MD) Jul. 28, 1812
Overton Harlen and Betsy Hart, (MD) Aug. 1, 1812
Carter Marlow and Gerlates Bryant, (MD) Aug. 1, 1812
McKinsey Marlow and Nancy McMillin, (MD) Aug. 1, 1812
Benjamin Bonner and Lucy Locke, (MD) Aug. 10, 1812
Hugh Bradly and Patsey Hunter, (MD) Aug. 13, 1812
William Hancock and Neely West, (MD) Aug. 22, 1812
Joseph Bridges and Elizabeth Gill, (MD) Aug. 24, 1812
Charles Golston and Elizabeth Neel, (MD) Aug. 28, 1812
Jesse Dickins and Polly McDerment, (MD) Sep. 10, 1812
Lewis Johnson and Elly Wright, (MD) Sep. 10, 1812
Elly Wright and Lewis Johnson, (MD) Sep. 10, 1812
Robert Eason and Lidiah Hariss, (MD) Sep. 16, 1812
Samuel Realy and Cinthia Marler, (MD) Sep. 28, 1812
Isiah Tribble and Patience Pemberton, (MD) Sep. 28, 1812
James Cawthon and Sally Peak, (MD) Sep. 29, 1812
William Jewell and Annie Thomas, (MD) Oct. 2, 1812
Joseph Hays and Susannah Adams, (MD) Oct. 5, 1812
Pleasant Irby and Kezia Lamburt, (MD) Oct. 5, 1812
David Smith and Priscilla Bennett, (MD) Oct. 5, 1812
Joseph Phillips and Martha Williams, (MD) Oct. 14, 1812
Thomas Robertson and Betsey Wooten, (MD) Oct. 17, 1812
Norman McDaniel and Mildred Perrywood, (MD) Oct. 21, 1812
Nicholas Edwards and Milly Powers, (MD) Oct. 24, 1812
Smith Belote and Nancy Gill, (MD) Nov. 2, 1812

James Calhoun and Winney Woodward, (MD) Nov. 7, 1812
Thomas Calleway and Alice Griffin, (MD) Nov. 25, 1812
Thomas Knight and Ally Martin, (MD) Dec. 24, 1812
Wiley Whitley and Polly ????, (MD) Dec. 24, 1812
James Irwin and Elizabeth D Robb, (MD) Dec. 15, 1813
James Adams and Jenny B Thomas, (MD) Sep. 10, 1813
William McNeely and Grace Shaw, (MD) Jan. 3, 1813
John Clopton and Matilda Drake, (MD) Mar. 25, 1813
Jeremiah Jedwin and Elsey Rogers, (MD) Jun. 24, 1813
Moses Brooks and Nancy Tait, (MD) Jul. 14, 1813
Elijah Currey and Margaret Law, (MD) Jul. 16, 1813
William George and Catlincey Hunt, (MD) Jul. 19, 1813
John Berry and Elvira Harris, (MD) Aug. 13, 1813
John Foster and Elizabeth Rogers, (MD) Sep. 21, 1813
Robert Jennings and Polly Word, (MD) Sep. 21, 1813
Simpson Organ and Sina Wilson, (MD) Oct. 4, 1813
Joshua Dillard and Catharine Quinn, (MD) Oct. 9, 1813
Dillard Beasley and Sally Harris, (MD) Oct. 25, 1813
Robert Baskin and Rachel Ricketts, (MD) Nov. 3, 1813
Burwell Kemp and Elizabeth Romling, (MD) Nov. 3, 1813
John Bachelor and Nancy Clackston, (MD) Nov. 17, 1813
John Cooper and Piney Rogers, (MD) Dec. 6, 1813
John Little and Betsey Reynold, (MD) Dec. 18, 1813
Anderson Freeman and Delila Yearnell, (MD) Dec. 22, 1813
A. W. Huddleston and Elizabeth Lewis, (MD) Aug. 15, 1814
Richard . McNight and Permelia Woodward, (MD) Aug. 9, 1814
Andrew Baird and Patsey Hunt, (MD) Jan. 8, 1814
William Bennett and Elly Tippet, (MD) Jan. 31, 1814
Eli Allen and Elizabeth Lasater, (MD) Feb. 25, 1814
Lewis Land and Nancey Bethume, (MD) Feb. 28, 1814
John Williams and Elizabeth Browning, (MD) Feb. 28, 1814
James Bates and Sally Stephenson, (MD) Mar. 5, 1814
James Ewing and Nancy Smith, (MD) Mar. 7, 1814
Green Cooke and Polly Nicholson, (MD) Apr. 11, 1814
Nathaniel Parker and Polly Thomas, (MD) Apr. 20, 1814
William McElyea and Jenney Sutton, (MD) May 10, 1814
Elisha Hodges and Milly Ward, (MD) Jul. 23, 1814
William Gleeves and Polly Wilson, (MD) Aug. 22, 1814
Charles Golston and Elizabeth Neel, (MD) Aug. 28, 1814
Samuel Crutchfield and Nancy Mahaland, (MD) Aug. 29, 1814
Bradford Edwards and Jenney Bond, (MD) Aug. 29, 1814
William Roach and Ann Sparrow, (MD) Sep. 3, 1814
William Reese and Livena Scobey, (MD) Sep. 10, 1814

Reddley Blouston and Brittain Odum, (MD) Sep. 12, 1814
Solomon Deloach and Rachal Searcy, (MD) Sep. 12, 1814
Brittain Odum and Reddley Blouston, (MD) Sep. 12, 1814
Josiah Rogers and Peggy McElyea, (MD) Sep. 12, 1814
Hallam Sullivan and Polly Osment, (MD) Sep. 12, 1814
Aaron Climer and Rebecca Sullivan, (MD) Sep. 20, 1814
James Griffin and Sally Woodward, (MD) Oct. 10, 1814
William Handsbrough and Elizabeth Marshall, (MD) Nov. 10, 1814
Isaac Griffin and Ibby Wiley, (MD) Nov. 14, 1814
William Green and Polly Hooker, (MD) Nov. 23, 1814
Morris Brewer and Sally Shannon, (MD) Dec. 6, 1814
William Hall and Martha Willard, (MD) Dec. 19, 1814
Joseph Greenwood and Elizabeth ---, (MD) Dec. 20, 1814
Brinkley Bridges and Nancy McWhirter, (MD) Dec. 28, 1814
John Medlin and Susanah Lantin, (MD) Dec. 28, 1814
George W. Still and Polly L Wynn, (MD) Nov. 9, 1815
Wm. L. Smith and Fanny Wooldridge, (MD) Aug. 16, 1815
George H. Bullard and Elizabeth Spradlen, (MD) Mar. 2, 1815
George D. Summers and Polly Jennings, (MD) Jul. 22, 1815
Henry B. Maxey and Peggy Taylor, (MD) Feb. 14, 1815
John B. Parker and Ellenor Tipton, (MD) Oct. 7, 1815
Josiah Brichun and Sally Logan, (MD) Jan. 2, 1815
Andrew Finney and Nansy Phillips, (MD) Jan. 13, 1815
John Harpole and Elisabeth Swingley, (MD) Jan. 26, 1815
John Boon and Cloe Garrison, (MD) Feb. 8, 1815
William Pugh and Jenny Donelson, (MD) Feb. 14, 1815
Henry Akins and Sally Still, (MD) Feb. 23, 1815
William Lawrence and Elizabeth Neil, (MD) Feb. 28, 1815
Julius Sanders and Penney Fields, (MD) Feb. 28, 1815
Aquilla Greer and Elizabeth Welch, (MD) Mar. 21, 1815
Fany Edwards and Seth Hackney, (MD) Apr. 22, 1815
Littleberry Madlock and Phebee Sharp, (MD) Apr. 25, 1815
Eli Harris and Cinthia Moore, (MD) Apr. 26, 1815
Abraham Jones and Cela Rogers, (MD) May 18, 1815
George Marlow and Elizabeth Terry, (MD) Jun. 1, 1815
John Johnson and Nancy Young, (MD) Jun. 7, 1815
Jemison Bandy and Elizabeth Taylor, (MD) Jul. 8, 1815
Smidley Lynch and Elizabeth Robertson, (MD) Jul. 22, 1815
Archabald Shannon and Matilda Allen, (MD) Jul. 25, 1815
Joseph Smart and Polly Burnett, (MD) Jul. 25, 1815
John Cross and Elizabeth West, (MD) Jul. 31, 1815
Peter Sullivan and Sally Avary, (MD) Jul. 31, 1815
Owen Quinley and Polly Sullivan, (MD) Aug. 3, 1815

Micajah Joiner and Patsey Wood, (MD) Aug. 4, 1815
Edward Estes and Nancy Lewis, (MD) Aug. 19, 1815
John Roach and Polly Kirkpatrick, (MD) Aug. 19, 1815
Jacob Bennett and Ceta Bonds, (MD) Sep. 27, 1815
James Basford and Mary Bradshaw, (MD) Oct. 7, 1815
Hallen Brinson and Arthur McSpaden, (MD) Oct. 7, 1815
Frances Alsup and Soloman Bond, (MD) Oct. 9, 1815
William Boyd and Faithy Lawrence, (MD) Oct. 9, 1815
Harrison Harris and Priscilla Brown, (MD) Oct. 9, 1815
Alexander McNeely and Fanny Hamilton, (MD) Oct. 9, 1815
William Buchanon and Nancy Worthan, (MD) Oct. 11, 1815
Robertson Wright and Sally Golston, (MD) Oct. 18, 1815
Samuel McDaniel and Jane McKnight, (MD) Oct. 21, 1815
Richard Cartwright and Anne Waters, (MD) Nov. 6, 1815
Zachariah Davis and Elizabeth Hill, (MD) Nov. 30, 1815
Francis Wynn and Susannah Cavis, (MD) Dec. 2, 1815
Lot Joiner and Polly Jones, (MD) Dec. 7, 1815
Henry Rice and Nancy Cawthon, (MD) Dec. 19, 1815
Samuel Braly and Peggy McSpaden, (MD) Dec. 20, 1815
Phillip Hass and Gracy McNeely, (MD) Dec. 20, 1815
William Anglen and Elizabeth Sheppard, (MD) Dec. 21, 1815
Thomas Bennett and Elizabeth Bond, (MD) Dec. 21, 1815
Thomas Grissom and Margery Robertson, (MD) Dec. 30, 1815
David McKnight and Patsey M McWhirter, (MD) Dec. 10, 1816
George W. Still and Polly L Wynne, (MD) Nov. 9, 1816
Archibald Ray and Lou Ellen Thompson, (MD) Dec. 26, 1816
Thomas T. Hays and Sally Drake, (MD) Nov. 27, 1816
John P. Maddox and Polly Jones, (MD) Mar. 28, 1816
Drury Hall and Sally Thrower, (MD) Jan. 4, 1816
Moses Owen and Jenny Reeves, (MD) Jan. 13, 1816
Tazwell Mitchell and Sally Stuart, (MD) Jan. 16, 1816
Charles Harrington and Visey Johnson, (MD) Feb. 3, 1816
Houston Alexander and Abby Vernatta, (MD) Feb. 23, 1816
Jacob McDerment and Ruby Trusty, (MD) Feb. 25, 1816
Benjamin Cox and Nancy Bean, (MD) Mar. 14, 1816
John Phelp and Sally Carlin, (MD) Mar. 14, 1816
Edmund Proctor and Judith Dill, (MD) Mar. 14, 1816
George Sands and Cassey Green, (MD) Mar. 14, 1816
James Cravens and Charity Tait, (MD) Mar. 28, 1816
Absolon Lasater and Elizabeth Rainey, (MD) Mar. 28, 1816
Josiah Brinson and Betsy Modglin, (MD) Apr. 7, 1816
Ransom King and Addy Rogers, (MD) Apr. 9, 1816
Elijah Parsons and Polly Turner, (MD) Apr. 13, 1816

Moses Barret and Rebecca Fisher, (MD) May 9, 1816
David Arnold and Susannah Bryson, (MD) May 16, 1816
James Dooley and Nancy Woodward, (MD) Jun. 5, 1816
Henry Moser and Elizabeth Oneal, (MD) Jun. 25, 1816
Joseph Lawrence and Polly Neil, (MD) Jun. 27, 1816
Jeminiah Collins and Amos Gibson, (MD) Jul. 3, 1816
Banister Anderson and Betsey Anderson, (MD) Jul. 11, 1816
James Howard and Elizabeth Collings, (MD) Jul. 25, 1816
Owen Quinley and Polly Sullivan, (MD) Aug. 4, 1816
James Carruth and Polly Donnell, (MD) Aug. 29, 1816
Fanny Miles and Ridley Wynne, (MD) Sep. 5, 1816
Mercer Morriss and Rebecca Wright, (MD) Sep. 10, 1816
William Reese and Levina Scoby, (MD) Sep. 11, 1816
William Roach and Ann Sparrow, (MD) Sep. 14, 1816
Hallan Sullivan and Polly Ozment, (MD) Sep. 14, 1816
David Estes and Hannah Jackson, (MD) Oct. 4, 1816
Butler Arnold and Rachel Hudson, (MD) Nov. 7, 1816
John Campbell and Mary Dodds, (MD) Nov. 21, 1816
William Modglin and Nelly Dukes, (MD) Nov. 27, 1816
Elisha Dismukes and Fany Petty, (MD) Dec. 8, 1816
Solomon Gibson and Tempa Modglin, (MD) Dec. 8, 1816
William Hollinsworth and Phebe Owen, (MD) Dec. 10, 1816
David Bradshaw and Tempa Casson, (MD) Dec. 29, 1816
John McAffry and Patsey W Hunt, (MD) Mar. 26, 1817
Joseph Cocke and Sarah W Winston, (MD) Dec. 16, 1817
William Altman and Susannah R Mitchell, (MD) Dec. 4, 1817
James Braden and Betsey M Merritt, (MD) Apr. 12, 1817
Zuritha Allcorn and Harry L Douglas, (MD) Aug. 19, 1817
Jordan Chandler and Elizabeth L Avery, (MD) Dec. 16, 1817
James McDonald and Anne L Moore, (MD) Dec. 30, 1817
Ephriam G. Harris and Isabella H Miller, (MD) Jul. 16, 1817
James Bunten and Sindy H Thomas, (MD) Jan. 9, 1817
John Cocke and Elizabeth H Williams, (MD) Feb. 25, 1817
John F. Brown and Margret F Seawell, (MD) Sep. 16, 1817
Daniel Aston and Jane D Bell, (MD) Aug. 5, 1817
William C. Collins and Sarah B Wortham, (MD) Jul. 2, 1817
Elijah Rew and Saly A. Brown, (MD) Jun. 19, 1817
John W. Greer and Rachel Thomas, (MD) Mar. 19, 1817
William S. New and Sally Hancock, (MD) Nov. 29, 1817
Enoch P. Hannah and Elizabeth Phillips, (MD) Jan. 21, 1817
James M. Hurt and Martha Marshall, (MD) Mar. 26, 1817
Benjamin M. Davis and Casander Taylor, (MD) Aug. 6, 1817
Thomas L. Hill and Ann Lansden, (MD) Sep. 6, 1817

William F. Jones and Lucy Warmack, (MD) Sep. 23, 1817
John F. Porter and Josaphine Whitworth, (MD) Dec. 24, 1817
Ira E. Eason and Dolly Vaughan, (MD) Jan. 9, 1817
John E. Warren and Sally Jennings, (MD) Sep. 2, 1817
John C. Jones and Elizabeth Lane, (MD) Mar. 24, 1817
Mathias B. Click and Nancy Moss, (MD) May 6, 1817
William A. Langston and Rebecca Sutton, (MD) Dec. 30, 1817
William Wray and Ann Wright, (MD) Jan. 9, 1817
Green Tucker and Priscilla Williams, (MD) Jan. 12, 1817
Joseph Casky and Caty Scobey, (MD) Jan. 15, 1817
Joseph Eddings and Parthena Henderson, (MD) Jan. 18, 1817
John Ellis and Mary Sandford, (MD) Jan. 18, 1817
Bennett Babb and Abegale Guthrie, (MD) Jan. 21, 1817
Miller Carter and Pheby Phillips, (MD) Jan. 21, 1817
John Preston and Rachel Bond, (MD) Jan. 21, 1817
Zachariah Rickets and Sally May (MD) Jan. 22, 1817
William Setter and Sally Ray, (MD) Jan. 22, 1817
Thomas Ames and Elizabeth Aust, (MD) Jan. 27, 1817
William Melton and Lucinda Wilmath, (MD) Feb. 5, 1817
Samuel Parker and Maude Shaw, (MD) Feb. 12, 1817
Petterson Burge and Elizabeth Palmer, (MD) Feb. 26, 1817
Green Flowers and Mary Sypert, (MD) Feb. 26, 1817
Aaron Cluck and Marenda Howel, (MD) Mar. 7, 1817
Edmund York and Nancy Bass, (MD) Mar. 7, 1817
Rhody Goodman and Turner Perry, (MD) Mar. 17, 1817
William Baskins and Rebecca Belt, (MD) Apr. 19, 1817
William Coats and Patsey Trasy, (MD) Apr. 19, 1817
John Patton and Elizabeth Shoras, (MD) Apr. 26, 1817
Leaven Rusell and Anna Alsup, (MD) May 7, 1817
George Webb and Nancy Cross, (MD) May 7, 1817
Joseph Moore and Lydia Adams, (MD) May 13, 1817
Edmond Jones and Elizabeth Shoras, (MD) Jun. 13, 1817
Israel Moore and Sally Roach, (MD) Jun. 16, 1817
Eli Edwards and Milly Hancock, (MD) Jun. 19, 1817
Mellen Carter and Pheby Phillips, (MD) Jun. 21, 1817
James Godphrey and Frances Rogers, (MD) Jul. 12, 1817
James Ozment and Elizabeth Eddings, (MD) Jul. 16, 1817
John Hogdwood and Rhody Pemberton, (MD) Aug. 3, 1817
Boze Jacobs and Nancy Jennings, (MD) Aug. 23, 1817
Phillip Smart and Abigale Wright, (MD) Aug. 29, 1817
James Goodrich and Patsey Taylor, (MD) Aug. 30, 1817
William Bilbro and Margret McFarland, (MD) Sep. 3, 1817
James Turner and Kiziah Hunter, (MD) Sep. 9, 1817

Sutton Belcher and Abigale Ellis, (MD) Sep. 16, 1817
Daniel Jackson and Sally Jackson, (MD) Sep. 24, 1817
Samuel Speed and Patsy Archer, (MD) Sep. 24, 1817
William Chison and Patsy Griffin, (MD) Sep. 27, 1817
Absolom Smith and Lydia Beard, (MD) Sep. 27, 1817
Isaac Carver and Mary Hugels, (MD) Oct. 11, 1817
John Davidson and Elizabeth Brown, (MD) Oct. 11, 1817
John Starnes and Elizabeth Chandler, (MD) Oct. 11, 1817
Allen Fuller and Nancy Harris, (MD) Oct. 28, 1817
Alvis Sellars and Jane Cumings, (MD) Oct. 29, 1817
John Bradberry and Bershaba Golston, (MD) Nov. 2, 1817
Wright Hickman and Sarah Tucker, (MD) Nov. 20, 1817
Thomas Davis and Elizabeth Robertson, (MD) Nov. 25, 1817
Levi Knotts and Eliza Young, (MD) Nov. 29, 1817
Sterling Harrison and Elizabeth Jones, (MD) Dec. 1, 1817
William Chenney and Elizabeth Fassey, (MD) Dec. 12, 1817
Benjamin Clayton and Luckey Quarles, (MD) Dec. 15, 1817
William Avery and Permelia Sparry, (MD) Dec. 16, 1817
John Qualls and Lockey Quarles, (MD) Dec. 17, 1817
Allen Avery and Polly Wynne, (MD) Dec. 29, 1817
Adam Cowger and Kizziah Davis, (MD) Dec. 29, 1817
Isaac W. Brooks and Martha Huddleston, (MD) Feb. 2, 1818
Thomas W. Ellis and Caroline Glanton, (MD) May 23, 1818
Patrick R. Puckett and Martha Cocke, (MD) Dec. 23, 1818
Milton P. Brittle and Winney Spring, (MD) Dec. 21, 1818
Samuel M. McCorkle and Polly Priestly, (MD) Apr. 8, 1818
James M. Sisk and Nancy Blair, (MD) Aug. 25, 1818
James H. Liggon and Elizabeth Thompson, (MD) Jul. 28, 1818
William G. Wood and Polly Davis, (MD) Jun. 4, 1818
Benjamin F. Stevenson and Elizabeth Rutland, (MD) May 28, 1818
William E. McSpadden and Margaret Miller, (MD) Sep. 16, 1818
Jose C. Dew and Nancy Hunter, (MD) Oct. 20, 1818
Edward B. Wheeler and Elizabeth Young, (MD) Sep. 22, 1818
George A. Evans and Thussey Hegarty, (MD) Nov. 17, 1818
Wm. A. Langstone and Rebecca Sutton, (MD) Dec. 30, 1818
Elijah Jennings and Elizabeth Rogers, (MD) Jan. 6, 1818
Green Tucker and Priscilla Williams, (MD) Jan. 12, 1818
Mosses Harris and Sally Dillard, (MD) Jan. 17, 1818
Hansel Trusty and Nancy Welch, (MD) Jan. 27, 1818
Jesse Eagan and Narcissa Ruff, (MD) Jan. 29, 1818
Jeremiah Brooks and Rachel Spring, (MD) Feb. 2, 1818
Reuben Sullivan and Polly Climer, (MD) Feb. 7, 1818
Moses Woollen and Elizaeth Stokes, (MD) Feb. 7, 1818

Haily Patterson and Redding Wright, (MD) Feb. 11, 1818
Redding Wright and Haily Patterson, (MD) Feb. 11, 1818
Soloman Corder and Martha Brown, (MD) Feb. 12, 1818
James Bowman and Elizabeth Taylor, (MD) Feb. 14, 1818
John Cocke and Elizabeth Harris, (MD) Feb. 17, 1818
Josiah McGehee and Scoty Mitchell, (MD) Feb. 24, 1818
Wilson Mosley and Sally Sands, (MD) Mar. 19, 1818
John Owens and Dolley Waters, (MD) Mar. 19, 1818
Thomas Breedlove and Sally Travilian, (MD) Mar. 24, 1818
James Moore and Margaret Road, (MD) Mar. 24, 1818
Thomas Horn and Louisa Woollard, (MD) Mar. 30, 1818
Thomas Marlow and Lucy Hull, (MD) Apr. 8, 1818
Littleton Benthal and Susannah Stanley, (MD) Apr. 9, 1818
Anthony Settle and Nancy Higgins, (MD) Apr. 27, 1818
Isaac Green and Elizabeth Eagan, (MD) Apr. 28, 1818
Peter Harvell and Sally Watkins, (MD) May 11, 1818
William Cox and Evelina Reese, (MD) May 16, 1818
George Cooper and Martha Dillard, (MD) May 26, 1818
William Stafford and Martha Cartwright, (MD) May 26, 1818
William Dilliard and Elizabeth Carley, (MD) Jun. 15, 1818
Nathan Bundy and Absilla Johnson, (MD) Jun. 18, 1818
William Adams and Doratha Richardson, (MD) Jul. 7, 1818
Anderson Friece and Elizabeth Hickman, (MD) Jul. 7, 1818
Zilphy Midget and Hiram Russell, (MD) Jul. 7, 1818
Hiram Russell and Zilphy Midget, (MD) Jul. 7, 1818
Anderson Trice and Elizabeth Hickman, (MD) Jul. 7, 1818
Nobles Cannon and Annis Chandler, (MD) Jul. 11, 1818
Jonathan Fuston and Rebecca Stanley, (MD) Jul. 15, 1818
Jonathon Fuston and Rebecca Stanley, (MD) Jul. 15, 1818
Miles Fuller and Charity Seals, (MD) Jul. 26, 1818
Reuben Dial and Zilphy Medlin, (MD) Aug. 1, 1818
Zilphy Medlin and Reubin Dial, (MD) Aug. 1, 1818
Benjamin Wilson and Charlotte Adamson, (MD) Aug. 6, 1818
Jasper Ashworth and Cassandra Berry, (MD) Aug. 8, 1818
Archibald Allen and Matilda Lambert, (MD) Aug. 30, 1818
Benjamin Davis and Nancy Mitchell, (MD) Sep. 1, 1818
Kdder White and Betsey Liggon, (MD) Sep. 3, 1818
John Garrett and Ann McWhirter, (MD) Sep. 9, 1818
Hezekiah Archer and Patsey Mitchell, (MD) Sep. 19, 1818
Arden Somers and Sally Walker, (MD) Sep. 22, 1818
Willis Caraway and Susanna Clemmons, (MD) Sep. 25, 1818
Elisha Brien and Elizabeth Johnson, (MD) Sep. 26, 1818
James Mitchell and Susan Owen, (MD) Sep. 29, 1818

Stephen Brooks and Mariah Swiney, (MD) Sep. 30, 1818
James Davis and Penelope Drake, (MD) Oct. 10, 1818
William Carlin and Sarah Johnson, (MD) Oct. 13, 1818
John Cox and Elizabeth Palmer, (MD) Oct. 13, 1818
Stephen Hampton and Elizabeth Williams, (MD) Oct. 20, 1818
Hiram Howard and Cinthia Bennett, (MD) Oct. 20, 1818
Dolphen Bass and Frances Gaddy, (MD) Oct. 23, 1818
John Campbell and Judah Lambert, (MD) Oct. 23, 1818
Frances Gaddy and Dolphen Bass, (MD) Oct. 23, 1818
James Scot and Sally Jones, (MD) Oct. 24, 1818
Robert Boothe and Minerva Payne, (MD) Nov. 2, 1818
James Scott and Fannie Coe, (MD) Nov. 5, 1818
Joseph Underwood and Elizaeth Adamson, (MD) Nov. 10, 1818
Humphrey Chappell and Charity Johnson, (MD) Nov. 13, 1818
William Baily and Sally Tally, (MD) Nov. 14, 1818
James Frazer and Hannah Shelby, (MD) Nov. 17, 1818
Mark Joplin and Malome Maxwell, (MD) Nov. 21, 1818
Malone Maxwell and Mark Joplin, (MD) Nov. 21, 1818
Kendred Tucker and Darcus King, (MD) Nov. 25, 1818
Johns Hornsberry and Elizabeth Martin, (MD) Nov. 27, 1818
Elisha Bryson and Polly Ward, (MD) Dec. 8, 1818
Robert Jennings and Hannah Ward, (MD) Dec. 18, 1818
Milton Brittles and Winnie Spring, (MD) Dec. 21, 1818
Samuel Dickings and Ann Enoch, (MD) Dec. 21, 1818
James Stuart and Sarah Smith, (MD) Dec. 21, 1818
Michael Harris and Nancy Talley, (MD) Dec. 22, 1818
Michael Harris and Nancy Tally, (MD) Dec. 22, 1818
Thomas Proctor and Anne Dickins, (MD) Dec. 26, 1818
William Adkinson and Araminta Reed, (MD) Dec. 27, 1818
Robert Bone and Polly S Gwin, (MD) Nov. 24, 1819
James Berry and Mary Ann Taylor, (MD) Feb. 2, 1819
Isaac W. Brook and Martha Huddleston, (MD) Feb. 2, 1819
William W. Hearn and Susannah Tarver, (MD) Aug. 6, 1819
Anthony W. Huddleston and Elizabeth Lewis, (MD) Aug. 18, 1819
Benjamin T. Bell and Charlott ---, (MD) Jan. 30, 1819
Elliott T. Hollomon and Rachel Williams, (MD) Feb. 26, 1819
John R. Eatherly and Polly Williams, (MD) Feb. 22, 1819
Moody P. Harris and Susannah Caplinger, (MD) Aug. 6, 1819
Daniel H. Mabies and Sally Williams, (MD) Apr. 24, 1819
John H. Briant and Elizabeth Puckett, (MD) Dec. 28, 1819
John C. Collings and Mahaly Wortham, (MD) Mar. 20, 1819
William Norman and Elizabeth Pursley, (MD) Jan. 1, 1819
Jesse Clifton and Sally Smith, (MD) Jan. 4, 1819

James Thompson and Peggy Williams, (MD) Jan. 9, 1819
Edmund Collins and Delsha Drennon, (MD) Jan. 13, 1819
Solomon Kemp and Hollon Ray, (MD) Jan. 21, 1819
William Goodall and Elizabeth Phelps, (MD) Jan. 22, 1819
Aaron Anglin and Hannah McGee, (MD) Jan. 26, 1819
John Edwards and Mary Rich, (MD) Jan. 28, 1819
Richardson Rowling and Polly Neal, (MD) Jan. 28, 1819
John Smith and Lettie Brown, (MD) Jan. 28, 1819
James Andrews and Elizabeth McDonell, (MD) Jan. 29, 1819
Vincen Cawthon and Rasannah Irwin, (MD) Feb. 1, 1819
Stephen Cavley and Patsy Tally, (MD) Feb. 8, 1819
Drury Joyner and Polly Wood, (MD) Feb. 9, 1819
William Brown and Delila Pate, (MD) Feb. 11, 1819
Joseph Wray and Elizabeth Moore, (MD) Feb. 12, 1819
Redding Wright and Haity Patterson, (MD) Feb. 12, 1819
Thomas Gains and Lucindy Smith, (MD) Feb. 15, 1819
Azariah Corda and Viney Shaw, (MD) Feb. 25, 1819
Abram Prim and Nancy Cook, (MD) Feb. 25, 1819
Viney Shaw and Azariah Corda, (MD) Feb. 25, 1819
Joseph Neal and Sally Smith, (MD) Mar. 4, 1819
John Woolard and Levina Meagle, (MD) Mar. 4, 1819
William Babb and Nancy Ross, (MD) Mar. 6, 1819
James Payne and Elizabeth Williams, (MD) Mar. 19, 1819
John Gun and Malinda Bryant, (MD) Mar. 20, 1819
David Bond and Lydia Jones, (MD) Mar. 26, 1819
Aline Dillard and Shadrick Owens, (MD) Mar. 27, 1819
Mathew Hancock and Elizabeth Mills, (MD) Mar. 30, 1819
James Baird and Elizabeth Richmond, (MD) Apr. 22, 1819
William Grier and Polly Ricketts, (MD) Apr. 24, 1819
Thomas Babb and Polly Powel, (MD) Apr. 29, 1819
Josiah Kirkpatrick and Nancy Tilford, (MD) Apr. 29, 1819
Hugh Carlen and Patsey Pemberton, (MD) May 4, 1819
David Cloyd and Nane Wilson, (MD) May 22, 1819
Atkinson Johnson and Sally Martin, (MD) May 31, 1819
Solomon Beardon and Rebecca Woodrum, (MD) Jun. 12, 1819
Anderson Cox and Sally Palmer, (MD) Jun. 17, 1819
Leonard Hathehaway and Barthery West, (MD) Jun. 18, 1819
Howel Horn and Rebecca Stone, (MD) Jun. 22, 1819
Richard Jones and Rebecca Martin, (MD) Jun. 24, 1819
William Morton and Nancy Walker, (MD) Jul. 5, 1819
Elijah Foster and Polly Taylor, (MD) Jul. 10, 1819
William Shanks and Patsey Wormack, (MD) Jul. 10, 1819
William Allen and Eliza Marshall, (MD) Jul. 19, 1819

Ishmeal Bradshaw and Lucinda McWhirter, (MD) Jul. 20, 1819
Charles Horn and Rachel Swindle, (MD) Jul. 23, 1819
Benjamin Hobson and Elizabeth Murry, (MD) Aug. 2, 1819
James Edwards and Sally Jones, (MD) Aug. 3, 1819
Thomas McGriff and Sally Mitchel, (MD) Aug. 5, 1819
Stephen Deury and Elizabeth Allen, (MD) Aug. 6, 1819
James Edwards and Sally Jones, (MD) Aug. 11, 1819
William Brown and Mary Johnson, (MD) Aug. 12, 1819
William Phillips and Nancy Waters, (MD) Aug. 12, 1819
John Weir and Elizabeth Chandler, (MD) Aug. 12, 1819
John Shane and Nancy Drennon, (MD) Aug. 18, 1819
Gerald Link and Sally Harrison, (MD) Sep. 2, 1819
William Prim and Ann Johnson, (MD) Sep. 2, 1819
Stealey Hager and Polly Whitley, (MD) Sep. 7, 1819
Benjamin Beasley and Mary Jackson, (MD) Sep. 13, 1819
John Byates and Elizabeth Talley, (MD) Sep. 16, 1819
Richard Hudson and Polly Smith, (MD) Sep. 23, 1819
Daniel Wilkerson and Rebecca Massey, (MD) Sep. 23, 1819
William Adams and Charlott Ward, (MD) Sep. 30, 1819
James Nettles and Tempy Bettes, (MD) Oct. 7, 1819
John Potts and Cynthia Jones, (MD) Oct. 7, 1819
Thomas Atkinson and Elizabeth Lambert, (MD) Oct. 9, 1819
Robert Sweatt and Elizabeth Glenn, (MD) Oct. 9, 1819
Isaac Turnage and Patsey Bell, (MD) Oct. 9, 1819
James Griffin and Sally Woodward, (MD) Oct. 10, 1819
James Henry and Rebecca Mitchell, (MD) Oct. 13, 1819
Nicholas Edwards and Milly Powers, (MD) Oct. 24, 1819
James Guthrie and Teracy McElroy, (MD) Oct. 26, 1819
John Conyer and Susanah Spadlen, (MD) Oct. 30, 1819
George Miller and Mary Sellers, (MD) Nov. 1, 1819
Charles Seay and Mary Beard, (MD) Nov. 1, 1819
Robert Boethe and Minerva Payne, (MD) Nov. 2, 1819
Thomas Cartwright and Patsey Davidson, (MD) Nov. 2, 1819
Henry Wrye and Sally Frout, (MD) Nov. 2, 1819
Zadock Mulison and Polly Talley, (MD) Nov. 10, 1819
William Bailey and Sally Talley, (MD) Nov. 14, 1819
Mark Jackson and Mary Ramsey, (MD) Nov. 20, 1819
David McKnight and Patsy McWhirter, (MD) Nov. 20, 1819
Jesse Shaw and Mary Pack, (MD) Nov. 20, 1819
John Edwards and Mary Richmond, (MD) Nov. 25, 1819
Josiah Beasley and Elizabeth Tarpley, (MD) Dec. 7, 1819
Ira Barber and Nancy Leith, (MD) Dec. 10, 1819
Skeen Hancock and Nancy Hearn, (MD) Dec. 20, 1819

Benjamin Barkley and Lydia Reader, (MD) Dec. 23, 1819
Jesse Goldman and Susannah Sullivan, (MD) Dec. 23, 1819
Gabriel Barton and Jane Johnson, (MD) Dec. 28, 1819
William Chandler and Rachel Shannon, (MD) Dec. 28, 1819
William Cobb and Catharine Jackson, (MD) Dec. 28, 1819
James Murry and Cassa Yarnell, (MD) Dec. 28, 1819
William Reed and Rachel Pentecost, (MD) Dec. 28, 1819
John Cook and Anna S Mathay, (MD) Dec. 4, 1820
Franky Shaw and Silas M Williams, (MD) Sep. 5, 1820
Wm. Hartsfield and Frances H Anderson, (MD) Nov. 18, 1820
Alfred McClain and Harriet F Robinson, (MD) Feb. 10, 1820
Jas. C. Carruth and Molly C Davis, (MD) Aug. 14, 1820
Thos. Standle and Mary Ann Huggins, (MD) Dec. 19, 1820
Jno. Caraway and Narcissa A. Rogers, (MD) Oct. 10, 1820
Jas. W. Hodge and Polly Pucket, (MD) Mar. 8, 1820
Jno. P. Campbell and ???? Lambut, (MD) Oct. 17, 1820
Robt. Goodman, Jr. and Martha Richardson, (MD) Feb. 20, 1820
Jno. H. Cawthon and Nancy Rice, (MD) Aug. 9, 1820
Wm. H. Buckley and Rebecca Johnson, (MD) Aug. 21, 1820
L. D. Crabtree and Winney Medling, (MD) Apr. 3, 1820
Thos. C. Hoskins and Jane Simpson, (MD) Dec. 12, 1820
Jno. A. Criswell and Martha Mays, (MD) Jun. 13, 1820
Wm. A. Johnson and Lucentia Asby, (MD) Oct. 10, 1820
Ira Jacobs and Solomon Sugg, (MD) Jan. 2, 1820
Willsher Bandy and Nancy Johnson, (MD) Jan. 6, 1820
Reuben Davenport and Susan Richardson, (MD) Jan. 13, 1820
Ivy Gibson and Sally Aytes, (MD) Jan. 15, 1820
Jno. Lasiter and Lucy Edwards, (MD) Jan. 15, 1820
Eaton Edwards and Alston Morgan, (MD) Jan. 19, 1820
Joel Swindle and Nancy Hudson, (MD) Jan. 20, 1820
Johathan Doak and Isabel Donnell, (MD) Jan. 25, 1820
Sampson Knight and Nancy Robertson, (MD) Jan. 25, 1820
Littleberry Freeman and Elizabeth Young, (MD) Jan. 26, 1820
Wm. Satterfield and Ann Tally, (MD) Jan. 29, 1820
Thos. Hill and Elizabeth Johnson, (MD) Feb. 10, 1820
Phillip Grissim and Sally Spring, (MD) Feb. 14, 1820
Jas. McCollin and Elizabeth ????, (MD) Feb. 15, 1820
Humphrey Donalson and Sally Kelly, (MD) Feb. 17, 1820
Alexander McKnight and Anne Grier, (MD) Feb. 17, 1820
Jesse Berry and Milly Shanks, (MD) Feb. 18, 1820
Robert Ellis and Prudence Belcher, (MD) Feb. 19, 1820
Julius Williams and Margaret Cason, (MD) Feb. 19, 1820
Wm. McKnight and Elizabeth McWherter, (MD) Feb. 24, 1820

Payton Marlow and Elizabeth Smith, (MD) Feb. 25, 1820
Wm. Chappell and Elizabeth ????, (MD) Mar. 1, 1820
Zachariah Keeton and Margret Walker, (MD) Mar. 8, 1820
Zachariah Evans and Cynthia Sweat, (MD) Mar. 10, 1820
Jenney Cooksey and Luke Tippit, (MD) Mar. 12, 1820
Jesse Wright and Mary Young, (MD) Mar. 13, 1820
John Davis and Polly McAlpin, (MD) Mar. 14, 1820
Wm. Hutcherson and Jensy Williams, (MD) Mar. 18, 1820
Jno. Smith and Mary Cloyd, (MD) Mar. 24, 1820
Alfred Bryant and Nancy Hickman, (MD) Mar. 30, 1820
Robertson Crooks and Selery Eathridge, (MD) Apr. 5, 1820
John Conrod and Catey Morris, (MD) Apr. 22, 1820
Wm. Chappell and Elizabeth Redding, (MD) May 5, 1820
Robert Bogle and Sally Brison, (MD) Jun. 2, 1820
Jesse Tally and Margret Wynn, (MD) Jun. 10, 1820
Midget Brooks and Rebecca Oneal, (MD) Jun. 24, 1820
Joshua Brown and Prudence McAllen, (MD) Jun. 27, 1820
Jesse Sullivan and Elizabeth Carter, (MD) Jul. 13, 1820
Joseph Williams and Jenny Patterson, (MD) Jul. 13, 1820
Alexander Periman and Sally Baskins, (MD) Jul. 17, 1820
Philip Periman and Hannah Forch, (MD) Jul. 17, 1820
John Dillard and Sarah Jacob, (MD) Jul. 18, 1820
John Dortch and Cynthia Walker, (MD) Jul. 31, 1820
Jno. Sauls and Fany Davenport, (MD) Aug. 2, 1820
Martin Douglass and Nancy Massey, (MD) Aug. 3, 1820
Joseph Barbee and Rachel Compton, (MD) Aug. 7, 1820
Wiley Bodin and Nancy Rutchledge, (MD) Aug. 20, 1820
Herzekiel Cartwright and Elizabeth Maholland, (MD) Sep. 2, 1820
Epenetus Carlock and Nancy Pimberton, (MD) Sep. 5, 1820
James Dunsmore and Delilah Gowen, (MD) Sep. 21, 1820
Anthony Gaines and Temple Scott, (MD) Sep. 28, 1820
Ellender Jones and Alygood Woollard, (MD) Sep. 30, 1820
Henry Leeman and Kesiah Warren, (MD) Oct. 4, 1820
Robert Guthrie and Aseneth Motheral, (MD) Oct. 11, 1820
Alfred Sherrill and Peggy Sherrill, (MD) Oct. 12, 1820
John Bond and Sarah Cummings, (MD) Oct. 15, 1820
Thomas Telford and Elizabeth Chawning, (MD) Oct. 15, 1820
Paskel Callico and Janny Wheeler, (MD) Oct. 17, 1820
Wm. Davis and Elizabeth Webb, (MD) Oct. 17, 1820
John Stevenson and Nancy Tristy, (MD) Oct. 17, 1820
Janny Wheeler and Paskel Callico, (MD) Oct. 17, 1820
Wm. Alsup and Polly Lane, (MD) Oct. 25, 1820
Jubal Grant and Nancy Hightower, (MD) Oct. 28, 1820

Francis Cooper and Ann Thomas, (MD) Oct. 31, 1820
Ransom Ward and Patsy Rogers, (MD) Oct. 31, 1820
Hazel Butt and Cynthia Hunt, (MD) Nov. 1, 1820
John Campbell and Pheby Casady, (MD) Nov. 2, 1820
Graham Jackson and Betsey Smith, (MD) Nov. 5, 1820
Jas. Osment and Levena Osment, (MD) Nov. 6, 1820
Wm. Hudson and Sally Tracy, (MD) Nov. 10, 1820
Presby Edwards and Mary Sims, (MD) Nov. 13, 1820
Wayne Thomas and Anne Barton, (MD) Nov. 13, 1820
Byrd Wall and Fanny Johnson, (MD) Nov. 13, 1820
Presley Edwards and Mary Sims, (MD) Nov. 15, 1820
James Chance and Mary Nichols, (MD) Nov. 18, 1820
Henry Coke and Elizabeth Tipton, (MD) Nov. 21, 1820
Wm. Todd and Elizabeth Steele, (MD) Nov. 21, 1820
Lemuel Nicholson and Lavena Young, (MD) Nov. 25, 1820
Wm. Sutherland and Polly Hobb, (MD) Dec. 1, 1820
Edward Trier and Lilly Smith, (MD) Dec. 1, 1820
Andrew Ward and Sally Rice, (MD) Dec. 1, 1820
Allen Smith and Frances Woods, (MD) Dec. 4, 1820
James Dyer and Lucy Howe, (MD) Dec. 6, 1820
David Phillips and Polly Waters, (MD) Dec. 11, 1820
Wm. Drennan and Kitty Eddins, (MD) Dec. 14, 1820
Garrett Mansfield and Lydia Sullivan, (MD) Dec. 14, 1820
Lemuel Nickings and ????, (MD) Dec. 19, 1820
Jas. Sommuns and Anne McFarland, (MD) Dec. 19, 1820
James Burton and Nancy Edwards, (MD) Dec. 29, 1820
Burrel Wall and Sally M Johnson, (MD) Jan. 19, 1821
Lem Hickman, Jr. and Susannah H Trice, (MD) Jul. 11, 1821
Absolom Ellis and Elender C Jones, (MD) Mar. 17, 1821
Jacob B. Lassiter and Levena B McMinn, (MD) Aug. 7, 1821
Arthur W. Dew and Nancy Hallum, (MD) Jul. 4, 1821
John W. Evans and Catherine Davis, (MD) Jul. 14, 1821
Thomas W. Ellis and Sally Wright, (MD) Sep. 10, 1821
William R. Phipps and Elizabeth Cummings, (MD) May 22, 1821
Eliza M. Beard and Samuel Bell, (MD) Oct. 10, 1821
George J. Cain and Chisteaince Jones, (MD) Sep. 22, 1821
Owen C. Dennis and Deborah Green, (MD) Jun. 20, 1821
Joseph B. Heflin and Emassy Ward, (MD) Jun. 11, 1821
Green B. Edwards and Martha Howard, (MD) Jul. 21, 1821
Ryal Atkinson and Rebecca Hoak, (MD) Dec. 20, 1821
Mathew Gibson and Mary Jariman, (MD) Jan. 10, 1821
Pryor Tyrell and Elizabeth Collings, (MD) Jan. 10, 1821
Benj Standley and Patsey Carter, (MD) Jan. 18, 1821

Benj Stanly and Patsey Carter, (MD) Jan. 18, 1821
Samuel Patterson and Jane Smith, (MD) Jan. 19, 1821
William Horn and Celia Wollard, (MD) Jan. 27, 1821
Enoch Henry and Jane Massey, (MD) Feb. 14, 1821
William Hickman and Equlla Swingle, (MD) Feb. 15, 1821
David Cole and Diley Pike, (MD) Feb. 21, 1821
Charles Collings and Elizabeth Sanders, (MD) Mar. 10, 1821
Reuben Dockings and Rhody Hankins, (MD) Mar. 14, 1821
Willie Dockings and Fanny Goodall, (MD) Mar. 14, 1821
Peledge Swingle and Nancy Hickman, (MD) Mar. 17, 1821
Peter Hollansworth and Polly Miller, (MD) Mar. 19, 1821
Hardy Youbanks and Nancy Arnold, (MD) Mar. 19, 1821
Snoden Hickman and Milly Richardson, (MD) Mar. 29, 1821
Edward White and Rachael Williamson, (MD) Mar. 30, 1821
Thomas Babb and Hicksy Hunt, (MD) Apr. 2, 1821
Edward Denton and Rebecah Dillard, (MD) Apr. 2, 1821
John Cowger and Musey Hill, (MD) Apr. 3, 1821
Anderson Evans and Mely Stuart, (MD) Apr. 8, 1821
Wallace Caldwell and Abigail Nicholson, (MD) Apr. 11, 1821
David Martin and Martha Weir, (MD) Apr. 12, 1821
Lumsford Bagwell and Rispa Truett, (MD) Apr. 14, 1821
Rispa Truett and Lumsford Bagwell, (MD) Apr. 14, 1821
Joshua Bradberry and Susan Wright, (MD) Apr. 26, 1821
John Wilson and Nancy Koonce, (MD) May 22, 1821
John Bradford and Matilda Ray, (MD) May 24, 1821
Johathan Baker and Sally Eagan, (MD) May 26, 1821
Mathew Hunt and Elizabeth Moore, (MD) May 31, 1821
Josiah Ely and Jane Lawrence, (MD) Jun. 2, 1821
Cela Barton and Joab Sullivan, (MD) Jun. 9, 1821
John Lankford and Lacey Martin, (MD) Jun. 11, 1821
Robt Creedop and Polly Guylle, (MD) Jun. 19, 1821
Robert Martin and Fanny Coe, (MD) Jul. 2, 1821
Stephen McDaniel and Jane Williams, (MD) Jul. 14, 1821
William Cox and Holland Greer, (MD) Jul. 25, 1821
Peter Sullivan and Polly Tarver, (MD) Jul. 26, 1821
William Blackburn and Lucy Clark, (MD) Aug. 14, 1821
Samuel Bichen and Elizabeth Morriss, (MD) Aug. 22, 1821
Andrew Gwyn and Esther Rice, (MD) Aug. 25, 1821
Herod Lassiter and Polly Patterson, (MD) Aug. 25, 1821
Halem Creswell and Elizabeth Johnson, (MD) Aug. 29, 1821
Laly Chambers and Littleberry Stevens, (MD) Sep. 12, 1821
Littleberry Stevens and Laly Chambers, (MD) Sep. 12, 1821
Archibald Wilson and Cynthia Johnson, (MD) Sep. 12, 1821

George Collings and Nancy Renshaw, (MD) Sep. 15, 1821
Alfred Mount and Mary Thomas, (MD) Sep. 18, 1821
Dandridge Moss and Sally Richmond, (MD) Sep. 22, 1821
Pernal Bennet and Annis Williams, (MD) Oct. 9, 1821
Willis Coferld and Maria McDonald, (MD) Oct. 10, 1821
Barbary Boon and Marmaduke Mitchener, (MD) Oct. 13, 1821
John Furgasen and Barbary Harpall, (MD) Oct. 14, 1821
Philip Howill and Cynthia Willis, (MD) Oct. 22, 1821
James Lowery and Sally Wetherly, (MD) Nov. 5, 1821
Anderson Webb and Susanah Lester, (MD) Nov. 5, 1821
William Corder and Martha Stone, (MD) Nov. 10, 1821
James Mitchell and Eliza Reese, (MD) Dec. 12, 1821
Solomon Caplinger and Martha Massey, (MD) Dec. 18, 1821
Jonas Livinglay and Martha Curd, (MD) Dec. 18, 1821
Thomas Taylor and Polly Garner, (MD) Dec. 18, 1821
Jacob Woodrum and Nancy Miles, (MD) Dec. 18, 1821
Shadrach Moore and Nancy Swaney, (MD) Dec. 26, 1821
Lemuel Loyd and ????, (MD) Dec. 29, 1821
George Cato and Eupenia Rife, (MD) Dec. 31, 1821
Allen R. Dillard and Emma D Taylor, (MD) Jan. 3, 1822
Geo S. Avery and Judia Chandler, (MD) Mar. 9, 1822
Mathew R. Gibson and Ester Campbell, (MD) Feb. 6, 1822
Jno. F. Doak and Elizabeth Hunter, (MD) Jan. 10, 1822
Noah A. Suggs and Nancy Tarver, (MD) Mar. 18, 1822
Nathaniel Sanders and Naomi Summers, (MD) Feb. 2, 1822
Jas. Cason and Jane McKnight, (MD) Feb. 6, 1822
Perrigrim Taylor and Mary Williams, (MD) Feb. 7, 1822
Reuben Jackson and Levina Miller, (MD) Feb. 11, 1822
Jas. Wright and Rebecca Kirkpatrick, (MD) Feb. 11, 1822
Enoch Hugle and Polly Walker, (MD) Feb. 14, 1822
Jas. Knight and Nancy Merritt, (MD) Feb. 19, 1822
Allen Dennis and Polly Tipton, (MD) Feb. 21, 1822
Eli Thrower and Rebecca Wall, (MD) Feb. 22, 1822
Thos. Burk and Fanny Robertson, (MD) Feb. 26, 1822
Isham Baker and Sally Caldwell, (MD) Mar. 2, 1822
Alford Bettes and Margaret Conyer, (MD) Mar. 3, 1822
Theophilus Lambert and Charlotte Reynolds, (MD) Mar. 9, 1822
Ambrose Holland and Rhody Winters, (MD) Mar. 16, 1822
Jno. Medlin and Fanny Sands, (MD) Mar. 20, 1822
Israel Moore and Susannah Hunt, (MD) Mar. 20, 1822
Geo Phillips and Lucinda Turner, (MD) Mar. 29, 1822
Brantley Burns and Cela Harrington, (MD) Apr. 2, 1822
William Coonrood and Patsey Rogers, (MD) Apr. 2, 1822

Elijah Adamson and Susanah Hathway, (MD) Apr. 24, 1822
Samuel Conyer and Elizabeth Kenedy, (MD) Apr. 25, 1822
Franklin Bartlett and Polly Meaks, (MD) Apr. 30, 1822
Wm. Boas and Harriet Simpson, (MD) Apr. 30, 1822
Jas. Mason and Olive Petty, (MD) May 2, 1822
Pleasant Arnold and Synthea Barns, (MD) May 6, 1822
John Harrel and Sally Hutson, (MD) May 7, 1822
Jno. Greer and Lidia Sands, (MD) May 21, 1822
Archalack Bass and Rachal Phillips, (MD) Jun. 18, 1822
Wm. Bryson and Elizabeth Richardson, (MD) Aug. 22, 1822
???? Hancock and Fountain Owen, (MD) Nov. 19, 1822
Archibald Gibson and Fanny Mosely, (MD) Nov. 27, 1822
Henry Hobson and Lucy S Tarver, (MD) Oct. 3, 1823
Jno. Craddock and Ruth E Hicks, (MD) Jun. 14, 1823
Knox Armstrong and Nancy C Green, (MD) Aug. 16, 1823
Jno. Simpson and Polly Ann Teague, (MD) Dec. 27, 1823
Joseph G. Clendenin and Hannah Kirkpatrick, (MD) Jun. 11, 1823
Jno. C. Gibson and Sally Ratterce, (MD) Jul. 16, 1823
Jas. C. Wier and Mary Wier, (MD) Nov. 6, 1823
George Blaze and Elizabeth Loyd, (MD) Jan. 17, 1823
Wm. Garret and Sarah Welch, (MD) Jan. 22, 1823
Benj Carver and Nancy Lumpkin, (MD) Feb. 3, 1823
Oliver Oneil and Elizabeth Taylor, (MD) Feb. 11, 1823
Jas. Clemmons and Elizabeth Lee, (MD) Feb. 26, 1823
David King and Lucy Peniel, (MD) Mar. 30, 1823
Jno. Estes and Scynthia McDaniel, (MD) Apr. 25, 1823
Benjamin Clifton and Hannah Clifton, (MD) Jun. 30, 1823
Burwell Reeves and Maria Wilson, (MD) Jul. 11, 1823
Leon Bass and Sally Philips, (MD) Aug. 2, 1823
Wm. Colewick and Margaret Steele, (MD) Aug. 7, 1823
Henry Ligon and Martha Shephard, (MD) Aug. 7, 1823
Henry Brown and Rebecca Mitchell, (MD) Aug. 17, 1823
Wm. Ferrill and Elizabeth Wilson, (MD) Aug. 22, 1823
Greenberry Eaton and Jinsey McKinney, (MD) Aug. 24, 1823
Henry Hancock and Priscilla Hancock, (MD) Aug. 25, 1823
Wm. Bryant and Cely Higdon, (MD) Aug. 27, 1823
Henry Hull and Lucy Wright, (MD) Sep. 2, 1823
Willie Davenport and Lucinda Ward, (MD) Sep. 8, 1823
Joseph Cuthrel and Margaret Spring, (MD) Sep. 12, 1823
Wyat Parkman and Patsy Sims, (MD) Sep. 12, 1823
Richard Dortch and Susan Hunt, (MD) Sep. 16, 1823
Jas. Godfrey and Nancy Whitlock, (MD) Sep. 22, 1823
Dandridge Moss and Catharine Avans, (MD) Oct. 2, 1823

Henry Fite and Mary Grandstaff, (MD) Oct. 6, 1823
Hope Hancock and Patsey Rogers, (MD) Oct. 13, 1823
Allen Clemmons and Jincey Young, (MD) Oct. 14, 1823
Watkins Owen and Peggy Rias, (MD) Oct. 18, 1823
Elly Jones and Hiram Pursley, (MD) Oct. 22, 1823
Perry Adle and Elizabeth Joiner, (MD) Oct. 23, 1823
John Anderson and Jane Roane, (MD) Oct. 23, 1823
Ashley Neil and Elizabeth Water, (MD) Oct. 24, 1823
Robt. Sypert and Priscilla Davis, (MD) Dec. 4, 1823
Watkins Johnson and Patsy Edwards, (MD) Dec. 10, 1823
Chas McWhirter and Nancy Griffin, (MD) Dec. 10, 1823
Benjamin Hunt and Lucy Mayo, (MD) Dec. 16, 1823
Azor Bone and Hulda Sherrill, (MD) Dec. 18, 1823
Jefferson Bodin and Peggy Furgason, (MD) Dec. 22, 1823
Diana Carter and Peter Myers, (MD) Dec. 22, 1823
Wm. Leeth and Olive Fields, (MD) Dec. 22, 1823
Peter Myers and Diana Carter, (MD) Dec. 22, 1823
James C. Bond and Mary W Smith, (MD) Nov. 26, 1824
James Arnold and Sarah T Mitchell, (MD) Dec. 22, 1824
William Chester and Sophie M Hogg, (MD) Feb. 12, 1824
Robert N. Colso and Frances J Walters, (MD) Jun. 27, 1824
Goodrich Andrews and Aley B Tarrer, (MD) Jul. 20, 1824
John W. Avory and Malinda Ann Tarver, (MD) Jan. 23, 1824
Jonathan Baker and Lucy Ann Foster, (MD) Nov. 21, 1824
James W. Harris and Catsey Smith, (MD) Aug. 30, 1824
Isaac T. Stephenson and Minerva Norris, (MD) Dec. 21, 1824
James S. Odom and Mary Francis, (MD) Sep. 14, 1824
William M. Crook and Rebecca Lassiter, (MD) Nov. 23, 1824
Young L. Herndon and Sally Kelly, (MD) Dec. 8, 1824
Saml . Calhoun, Jr. and Martha Figars, (MD) Jul. 15, 1824
Orang D. Beardin and Margaret Woodvill, (MD) Apr. 30, 1824
Robert D. Reed and Sally Reed, (MD) Dec. 8, 1824
James C. Bradshaw and Charlotte Organ, (MD) Mar. 1, 1824
Ezekiel C. Green and Jane Linch, (MD) Nov. 7, 1824
Ansil B. Jolly and Patsey Wright, (MD) Feb. 2, 1824
Benjamin B. Coaper and Rebecca Owen, (MD) Dec. 11, 1824
Ila Douglass and Elizabeth Harris, (MD) Jan. 5, 1824
Green Chandler and Betsey Lumpkin, (MD) Jan. 6, 1824
Newton Cloyd and Elizabeth Williamson, (MD) Jan. 7, 1824
Robert Furgason and Nancy Organ, (MD) Jan. 9, 1824
Samuel Quarls and Parthenia Hines, (MD) Jan. 14, 1824
Martin Wadkins and Sally Hopkins, (MD) Jan. 14, 1824
Eden Donnell and Eliza Garmony, (MD) Jan. 19, 1824

Talbot Jones and Anny Saterfield, (MD) Jan. 19, 1824
Samuel Jones and Lucy Winston, (MD) Jan. 31, 1824
John Cluck and Mary Martin, (MD) Feb. 4, 1824
Frederick Rotramble and Celia Maddocks, (MD) Feb. 4, 1824
Obediah Freeman and Elizabeth Hancock, (MD) Feb. 12, 1824
Jesse Bloodworth and Celia Tucker, (MD) Feb. 14, 1824
Elisha Bonds and Elizabeth Truett, (MD) Feb. 18, 1824
Alexander Kirkpatrick and Lucy Smith, (MD) Feb. 19, 1824
Gardner Morgan and Polly Chaver, (MD) Feb. 23, 1824
David Kincade and Sally McWhirter, (MD) Feb. 24, 1824
William Lawness and Nancy Curd, (MD) Feb. 24, 1824
Elijah Hodges and Hannah Hubbard, (MD) Feb. 25, 1824
Benjamin Sullivan and Polly Sullivan, (MD) Mar. 1, 1824
Wilson Bradshaw and Polly Shickord, (MD) Mar. 2, 1824
William Reese and Martha Taylor, (MD) Mar. 2, 1824
Robert Cox and Rebecca Routon, (MD) Mar. 20, 1824
William Mosely and Jemima Turner, (MD) Apr. 7, 1824
Willis Booker and Sally Joplin, (MD) Apr. 15, 1824
William Knight and Lavina Redding, (MD) May 3, 1824
Jeney Anderson and Elisha Cole, (MD) May 25, 1824
Enos Bone and Lucy Hern, (MD) May 27, 1824
Isham Johnson and Susan Smith, (MD) Jun. 8, 1824
Lesley Hancock and Nancy Smith, (MD) Jun. 27, 1824
Joseph Drennon and Lucinda Drennon, (MD) Jun. 28, 1824
Hezekiah Brown and Betsey Collings, (MD) Jun. 30, 1824
Jeremiah Garner and Fanny Tracy, (MD) Jun. 30, 1824
John Bitts and Milly Jolly, (MD) Jul. 13, 1824
Anderson Turpin and Corlin Buck, (MD) Jul. 15, 1824
Thomas Copeland and Elizabeth Mount, (MD) Jul. 16, 1824
Soloman Allman and Elizabeth Puckett, (MD) Jul. 28, 1824
Henry Vivrett and Polly Hickman, (MD) Jul. 28, 1824
Nathaniel Corley and Nancy Turner, (MD) Jul. 30, 1824
Josiah Chandler and Annie Heraldson, (MD) Jul. 31, 1824
William Campbell and Polly Warren, (MD) Aug. 10, 1824
Willis Allen and Elizabeth Joyner, (MD) Aug. 12, 1824
John Cox and Betsey Edwards, (MD) Aug. 26, 1824
John Seatt and Abslay Bond, (MD) Sep. 4, 1824
Nelson Owen and Peggy Duggan, (MD) Sep. 7, 1824
John Rogers and Lucy Goard, (MD) Sep. 14, 1824
Joseph Jinkins and Mary Vantreese, (MD) Sep. 18, 1824
Rodey Hathaway and Jessey Pue, (MD) Sep. 20, 1824
Alexander Penny and Kitty Harrison, (MD) Sep. 20, 1824
Jessey Pue and Rodey Hathaway, (MD) Sep. 20, 1824

Asa Graves and Sally Jones, (MD) Sep. 22, 1824
Isaac Sparks and Orpha Thompson, (MD) Sep. 27, 1824
Thomas Almond and Polly Ellison, (MD) Sep. 28, 1824
James Baker and Levina Donnell, (MD) Oct. 4, 1824
Abram Lassiter and Nancy Puckett, (MD) Oct. 8, 1824
Jefferson Bell and Leathy Johnson, (MD) Oct. 11, 1824
John Lacky and Jane White, (MD) Oct. 11, 1824
John Baird and Elenor Bild, (MD) Oct. 19, 1824
Hezekiah Davis and Nancy Wilson, (MD) Oct. 23, 1824
Charles Bradberry and Nancy Fields, (MD) Oct. 24, 1824
John Hutcherson and Nancy Harvey, (MD) Oct. 25, 1824
Baily Hutcheson and Betsey Harvy, (MD) Oct. 25, 1824
William Johns and Mary Major, (MD) Nov. 1, 1824
Jordan Robertson and Mary Peacock, (MD) Nov. 3, 1824
Baker Woodward and Martha Pearcy, (MD) Nov. 3, 1824
Saml. Doake and Nancy Word, (MD) Nov. 7, 1824
Robert Bondurant and Permelia Moseley, (MD) Nov. 10, 1824
Zacheriah Wortham and Sally Gun, (MD) Nov. 10, 1824
Hugh Hays and Sally Durk, (MD) Nov. 15, 1824
Thomas Hearn and Elizabeth Nettles, (MD) Nov. 29, 1824
Peter Goard and Dice Smith, (MD) Dec. 1, 1824
James Hays and Polly Thomas, (MD) Dec. 15, 1824
Jonathan Turner and Nancy Sneed, (MD) Dec. 15, 1824
James Spradlin and Margaret Spradlin, (MD) Dec. 20, 1824
Richard Bass and Emily Duke, (MD) Dec. 28, 1824
James Bond and Sarah Clemmons, (MD) Dec. 28, 1824
Elijah Clae and Patsey Lane, (MD) Dec. 28, 1824
James Cropper and Rhody Holland, (MD) Dec. 28, 1824
Jacob Furgerson and Mary Furgerson, (MD) Dec. 28, 1824
Jesse Gibson and Susan T Hollman, (MD) Jan. 15, 1825
Stephen H. Coleman and Nancy P Harrison, (MD) Aug. 29, 1825
Jno. Bass and Elizabeth G Remon, (MD) Feb. 1, 1825
Jonathan Drenan and Lucy G Liggon, (MD) Nov. 14, 1825
David Lane and Lucy E Lane, (MD) Dec. 3, 1825
George D. Cummings and Martha D Cummings, (MD) Apr. 13, 1825
James T. Carruth and Nancy Williams, (MD) Jan. 26, 1825
Wm. S. Carruth and Elizabeth Davis, (MD) Apr. 21, 1825
John S. Patterson and Harriet Reynolds, (MD) Oct. 6, 1825
James M. Brown and Celia Roach, (MD) Jul. 28, 1825
Alfred M. Hite and Mary Lassiter, (MD) Aug. 31, 1825
Joseph L. Wilson and Margret Barton, (MD) Jul. 5, 1825
Daniel J. Gutherie and Mary White, (MD) Dec. 20, 1825
Wm. H. Blackburn and Sarah Fletcher, (MD) Jun. 16, 1825

James H. Barr and Eliza Miller, (MD) Sep. 22, 1825
Benjamin H. Dennis and Rhody Sanders, (MD) Sep. 25, 1825
Hardy H. Baird and Nancy Baird, (MD) Sep. 30, 1825
John G. Brown and Sarah Scott, (MD) Mar. 23, 1825
Benjamin F. Stepenson and Elizabeth Willis, (MD) Apr. 5, 1825
Benjamin F. Stevenson and Elizabeth Willis, (MD) Apr. 5, 1825
Samuel F. Patterson and Lucy Waters, (MD) Sep. 20, 1825
Lewis D. Yarnell and Ann Arnald, (MD) Jan. 18, 1825
John D. Taylor and Nancy Williams, (MD) Aug. 31, 1825
Joel B. Holbert and Tursey Sherrill, (MD) May 3, 1825
Isham Butterworth and Elizabeth Ross, (MD) Jan. 1, 1825
Hiram Bryant and Mary Wray, (MD) Jan. 3, 1825
Thomas Alexander and Nancy Jennings, (MD) Jan. 11, 1825
William Joiner and Polly Coe, (MD) Jan. 11, 1825
Thos. Scurlock and Jane Compton, (MD) Jan. 11, 1825
James Bond and Ruth Florady, (MD) Feb. 1, 1825
Isaac Hollingsworth and Alliminta Justin, (MD) Feb. 12, 1825
Granville Mansfield and Frances Scurlock, (MD) Feb. 15, 1825
Moses Brown and Tabitha Gardner, (MD) Feb. 16, 1825
James Hays and Malindey Night, (MD) Feb. 23, 1825
Warren Davenport and Susey Whitlock, (MD) Feb. 25, 1825
David Briant and Mary Land, (MD) Mar. 1, 1825
Jas. Campbell and Polly Prichard, (MD) Mar. 7, 1825
George Benthall and Sally Brown, (MD) Mar. 8, 1825
Brooking Burnett and Lithe Moss, (MD) Mar. 10, 1825
Lovet Caroway and Peggy Schannon, (MD) Mar. 13, 1825
James Martin and Mary Eason, (MD) Mar. 15, 1825
Caleb Taylor and Margaret Glanton, (MD) Mar. 15, 1825
Locky Organ and Gabriel Shaw, (MD) Mar. 17, 1825
Thomas Ames and Sally Ray, (MD) Mar. 18, 1825
Isaac Brune and Midy Hefton, (MD) Mar. 21, 1825
Logan Linch and Elizabeth Wier, (MD) Mar. 21, 1825
Flemming Cocke and Martha Williams, (MD) Mar. 23, 1825
Ezekiel Holloway and Jane Shannon, (MD) Mar. 23, 1825
Gideon Carter and Martha Dvualt, (MD) Mar. 28, 1825
Whaley Newby and Elizabeth Cooksey, (MD) Mar. 28, 1825
John Brown and Sarah Williams, (MD) Apr. 16, 1825
Allen Hill and Sarah Peace, (MD) Apr. 25, 1825
Jonathan Patton and Ruth Godfrey, (MD) May 3, 1825
James Clemmons and ????, (MD) May 7, 1825
Simeon Horse and Sally Sneed, (MD) May 9, 1825
William Stuart and Mary Tooly, (MD) May 13, 1825
Aaron McCrary and Mary Oliver, (MD) May 23, 1825

Moses McCrary and Elizabeth Witherly, (MD) May 23, 1825
Thomas Martin and Thursey Richardson, (MD) Jun. 3, 1825
Joel Fragon and Mary Gilbert, (MD) Jun. 15, 1825
Greenbury Adams and Sally Periman, (MD) Jun. 23, 1825
Wm. Brison and Sally Debenport, (MD) Jul. 2, 1825
John Hankins and Elizabeth Routen, (MD) Jul. 7, 1825
Ezekiel Cloyd and Nancy White, (MD) Jul. 18, 1825
George Brison and Ester Read, (MD) Jul. 21, 1825
Mark Leeke and Elizabeth Lewis, (MD) Jul. 29, 1825
John Cunningham and Sally Warren, (MD) Jul. 30, 1825
Zacariah Keeton and Nancy Redigo, (MD) Aug. 3, 1825
Wm. Baird and Lucinda Bennet, (MD) Aug. 22, 1825
John Palmer and Margaret Reese, (MD) Aug. 22, 1825
Samuel Baxter and Frances Irby, (MD) Aug. 27, 1825
Jas. Cunningham and Elizabeth Patterson, (MD) Aug. 31, 1825
John Campbell and Melinda Bore, (MD) Sep. 6, 1825
Thomas Clifton and Mansey Seat, (MD) Sep. 7, 1825
Jas. Irby and Sarah Kindred, (MD) Sep. 20, 1825
William Ames and Ann Eagon, (MD) Sep. 24, 1825
Berry Grier and Catherine Myres, (MD) Sep. 27, 1825
John Adamson and Polley Davis, (MD) Oct. 3, 1825
Jas. Devenport and Nancy Mobey, (MD) Oct. 5, 1825
William Adkins and Mahala Stublefield, (MD) Oct. 13, 1825
Maben Anderson and Mary McMurray, (MD) Nov. 10, 1825
Benjamin Bell and Polly Spring, (MD) Nov. 22, 1825
Alfred Clemmons and Elizabeth Young, (MD) Nov. 23, 1825
Charles Bradley and Polly Bradley, (MD) Nov. 28, 1825
James Faweal and Sally Faweal, (MD) Dec. 2, 1825
Larkin Keeton and Mary Willerd, (MD) Dec. 8, 1825
John Haywood and Lucy Wynne, (MD) Dec. 10, 1825
Silas Hedgepath and Rebecca Rice, (MD) Dec. 10, 1825
Absolom Knight and Pernella Dodd, (MD) Dec. 10, 1825
William Williams and Rebecca Jackson, (MD) Dec. 15, 1825
Jno. Brown and Beedy Vivrett, (MD) Dec. 29, 1825
Washington Robertson and Barshaba Williford, (MD) Dec. 31, 1825
Edward Dillard and Martha S Gold, (MD) Dec. 11, 1826
Wm. T. Sherrell and Elener M Thomas, (MD) Dec. 20, 1826
Drury Mays and Susan M Williams, (MD) May 17, 1826
William McCowen and Mary M Moseley, (MD) Sep. 20, 1826
Horatio Bernard and Margarett M Williamson, (MD) Oct. 11, 1826
Edwin McCorkle and Jane M Thomas, (MD) Nov. 25, 1826
Thos. Y. Banks and Ann Riddle, (MD) May 23, 1826
John W. Beauchamp and Mary Wilson, (MD) Sep. 12, 1826

Caswell S. Sims and Nancy Carter, (MD) Mar. 13, 1826
James S. Bailey and Lucy Puckett, (MD) Dec. 4, 1826
Henry R. Cox and Purlena Shorter, (MD) Nov. 11, 1826
John P. Johnson and Eliza Mitchell, (MD) Sep. 15, 1826
Francis P. Davidson and Sarah Hearn, (MD) Dec. 18, 1826
John N. Taylor and ????, (MD) Nov. 20, 1826
Turner M. Johnson and Elizabeth Taylor, (MD) Feb. 15, 1826
John K. Parker and Elizabeth Tipton, (MD) Feb. 1, 1826
Alanson F. Doak and Adaline Donnell, (MD) Jul. 11, 1826
Robert D. Bell and Elizabeth Roane, (MD) Dec. 13, 1826
Thomas C. Hudson and Cintha McLeroy, (MD) Jan. 5, 1826
John C. Mondine and Maria Youree, (MD) Jan. 12, 1826
John B. Lane and Nancy Arnold, (MD) Jul. 11, 1826
Wm. B. Gleevs and Harriet Lumpkins, (MD) Nov. 20, 1826
Charles Blalock and Palny Tucker, (MD) Jan. 5, 1826
Henry Burnett and Parthena Moss, (MD) Jan. 9, 1826
James Cowan and Nancy Walker, (MD) Jan. 12, 1826
William Vantreece and ????, (MD) Jan. 28, 1826
Samuel Bryson and Mary Millegan, (MD) Feb. 3, 1826
Nathaniel Bell and Lusinda Smith, (MD) Feb. 4, 1826
Harris Campbell and Sarena Hambleton, (MD) Feb. 8, 1826
John Gunn and Polley Sims, (MD) Feb. 10, 1826
William England and Seluda Fergerson, (MD) Feb. 16, 1826
John Paisley and Martha Thrower, (MD) Mar. 13, 1826
David Hodges and Mary Rolls, (MD) Mar. 18, 1826
Leeman Hancock and Caty Moxley, (MD) Apr. 1, 1826
Nathan Wheeler and Catharine Grandstaff, (MD) Apr. 1, 1826
Andrew Thorn and ????, (MD) May 1, 1826
Isaac Barnett and Nancy Long, (MD) May 13, 1826
Mark Nickings and Penny Osbrooks, (MD) Jun. 5, 1826
James Daniel and Eliza Smith, (MD) Jun. 17, 1826
David Grindstaff and Margaret Phillips, (MD) Jul. 22, 1826
Hardin Goodall and Polly Scoby, (MD) Jul. 29, 1826
James Lanns and Susan Moser, (MD) Aug. 4, 1826
Joseph Bell and Jane Donnell, (MD) Aug. 24, 1826
Samuel Harlin and Susanna Bradley, (MD) Aug. 24, 1826
Simpson Bennett and Nancy Jackson, (MD) Aug. 26, 1826
Montgomery Pitner and Jane Wray, (MD) Aug. 31, 1826
William Cason and Mary McKnight, (MD) Sep. 2, 1826
Charles Ferris and Susanna Mason, (MD) Sep. 5, 1826
John Cloyd and Elizabeth Griffet, (MD) Sep. 11, 1826
Edmund Simpson and Rachel Whitton, (MD) Sep. 18, 1826
John Webber and Elizabeth Etherly, (MD) Sep. 30, 1826

Anderson Walker and Elizabeth Bradley, (MD) Oct. 21, 1826
Edmund Rucker and Lousasa Winchester, (MD) Oct. 26, 1826
Henry Southern and Bathsheba ????, (MD) Oct. 26, 1826
Charles Hicks and Clanpa Webb, (MD) Oct. 28, 1826
Benjamin Spring and Catherine Spring, (MD) Oct. 30, 1826
Asa Ragsdale and Rhoda Ragsdale, (MD) Nov. 1, 1826
Loven Clifton and Hannah Skean, (MD) Nov. 8, 1826
James Cox and Lucy Cox, (MD) Nov. 11, 1826
Richard Lyon and Ann Swann, (MD) Nov. 14, 1826
Thompson Glenn and Julia Scurlock, (MD) Nov. 21, 1826
William Alsup and Morning Hill, (MD) Nov. 29, 1826
Henry Mathews and Sally Seat, (MD) Dec. 2, 1826
Thomas Barbee and Hester Taylor, (MD) Dec. 4, 1826
Nathan Dillon and Sarah Greer, (MD) Dec. 9, 1826
James Melton and Nancy Palmer, (MD) Dec. 20, 1826
Jesse Johnson and Rebeccah Stuart, (MD) Dec. 22, 1826
Thos. B. Applack and Martha W Warren, (MD) Dec. 28, 1827
John F. Doak and Colan Q Harrison, (MD) Apr. 4, 1827
George Donnell and Elizabeth E McMurry, (MD) Jun. 11, 1827
Conrad Carpenter and Eliza Ann Quarles, (MD) Mar. 5, 1827
Beverly W. Seay and Mary Bowers, (MD) Jan. 29, 1827
Thomas W. Harney and Cynthia Bay, (MD) Mar. 5, 1827
Thomas W. Tarpley and Susannah Harvey, (MD) Mar. 5, 1827
Cornelius W. Bailey and Rebecah Patterson, (MD) Jun. 9, 1827
James W. Booth and Sarah Eaby, (MD) Jun. 15, 1827
James W. Booth and Sarah Ealey, (MD) Jun. 15, 1827
James R. Allen and Lusinda Smart, (MD) Mar. 13, 1827
John P. Carter and Mary Lacking, (MD) Apr. 28, 1827
John L. Allison and Margarett Bond, (MD) Mar. 16, 1827
Wm. L. Martin and Emily Allcorn, (MD) Sep. 3, 1827
Henry K. Dice and Elizabeth Spring, (MD) Dec. 13, 1827
Beverly J. Miller and Saluda Stovall, (MD) Apr. 25, 1827
Alexander J. Compton and Martha Wood, (MD) Sep. 4, 1827
Allen H. Bridgers and Sarah Hancock, (MD) Nov. 28, 1827
Edward G. Campbell and Seanath Maxwell, (MD) Dec. 21, 1827
John D. Morris and Mary Morris, (MD) Feb. 27, 1827
Harry B. Williams and Nancy Copeland, (MD) Dec. 24, 1827
Robert Elliott and Ann Thorn, (MD) Jan. 1, 1827
Wyatt Ramsey and Peggy Rice, (MD) Jan. 4, 1827
Jacob Keeton and Sally Panter, (MD) Jan. 5, 1827
William Barnett and Peggy Gunn, (MD) Jan. 9, 1827
George Crutchfield and Amy Hancock, (MD) Jan. 9, 1827
Walter Carruth and Nancy Keath, (MD) Jan. 10, 1827

Thomas Furgerson and Rebecah Furguson, (MD) Jan. 16, 1827
Richardson Carr and Jemimah Glenn, (MD) Jan. 27, 1827
Briant McDeamon and Elizabeth McDornart, (MD) Feb. 1, 1827
John Perkins and Renanna Sherrill, (MD) Feb. 8, 1827
George Barnfield and Polly Williams, (MD) Feb. 24, 1827
John Escue and Sarah Lumpkins, (MD) Mar. 7, 1827
William Johnson and Mary Rice, (MD) Mar. 9, 1827
Jesse Bond and Sarah Sypert, (MD) Mar. 15, 1827
John Reynolds and Abigail Baskins, (MD) Mar. 15, 1827
William Smith and Liddy Turner, (MD) Mar. 15, 1827
John Maxwell and Catherine Williams, (MD) Mar. 29, 1827
James Merritt and Sally Ferrington, (MD) Apr. 4, 1827
James Booth and Lousiah Graves, (MD) Apr. 14, 1827
Elisha Crudup and Lousiance Alford, (MD) Apr. 14, 1827
Isaac Dorch and Martha Allen, (MD) Apr. 25, 1827
Josiah Kirkpatrick and Nancy Tilford, (MD) Apr. 27, 1827
George Apperson and Eliza Cole, (MD) May 9, 1827
Barna Tipton and Harriet Bridges, (MD) May 9, 1827
Davis Crowder and Elizabeth Pugh, (MD) May 14, 1827
Arnold Burke and Margarett Smith, (MD) May 18, 1827
Joab Heflin and Margarett Moore, (MD) May 21, 1827
Benjamin Andrews and Polly Parker, (MD) May 22, 1827
Thomas Tracy and Rutha Hearn, (MD) May 22, 1827
William Houston and Mary Mann, (MD) Jun. 18, 1827
Samuel Sperry and Mourning Wright, (MD) Jun. 18, 1827
Robert Foster and Margaret Rea, (MD) Jun. 26, 1827
Jesse Bloodworth and Jane Tucker, (MD) Jun. 28, 1827
Edmund Burton and Amanda Jones, (MD) Jun. 30, 1827
Rody Cunningham and Jefferson Hamilton, (MD) Jun. 30, 1827
Martin Rogers and Tempy Warren, (MD) Jul. 3, 1827
Jesse Joynel and ????, (MD) Jul. 13, 1827
James Belcher and Rebeckey Talley, (MD) Jul. 20, 1827
Mekin Ship and Mary Warren, (MD) Jul. 21, 1827
Samuel Bond and Elizabeth Milton, (MD) Jul. 24, 1827
Henry Gilliam and Fanny Shaw, (MD) Jul. 28, 1827
Achilles Chandler and Cloe Dew, (MD) Jul. 31, 1827
Allen Hunt and Rebecah Sanders, (MD) Aug. 1, 1827
Joel Fusten and Ranney Hollingsworth, (MD) Aug. 6, 1827
George Hunter and Jane Winset, (MD) Aug. 22, 1827
Daniel McKee and Sarah Thomas, (MD) Aug. 22, 1827
Benjamin Belt and Sally Reed, (MD) Aug. 25, 1827
David Bass and Harriet Harris, (MD) Aug. 27, 1827
John Beard and Margaret Cloyd, (MD) Aug. 27, 1827

William Hunter and Elizabeth Drake, (MD) Aug. 27, 1827
Merritt Lyon and Nancy Astin, (MD) Aug. 29, 1827
William Batey and Sarah Grissum, (MD) Sep. 3, 1827
William Bilbro and Elizabeth Johnson, (MD) Sep. 3, 1827
Jesse Grimes and Tempey Murry, (MD) Sep. 3, 1827
Samuel Creswell and Sarah Mays, (MD) Sep. 5, 1827
Hicks Ellis and Lucy Jones, (MD) Sep. 25, 1827
Hardy Manning and Lissa Robertson, (MD) Oct. 5, 1827
Thomas Branch and Jane Moon, (MD) Oct. 13, 1827
Hezekiah Cartwright and Sally Mallan, (MD) Oct. 16, 1827
John Summers and Elizabeth Loash, (MD) Oct. 16, 1827
George Tucker and Abagill Hartsfield, (MD) Oct. 16, 1827
James Walton and Mary Mosier, (MD) Oct. 16, 1827
Joseph Thompson and Elizabeth Dodds, (MD) Oct. 23, 1827
James Warren and Ceila Organ, (MD) Oct. 23, 1827
Samuel Capslinger and Rebecca Maricle, (MD) Oct. 29, 1827
William Thompson and Mirandy Kelly, (MD) Oct. 29, 1827
Isaac Ellis and Nancy Jinnings, (MD) Oct. 31, 1827
John Mitchell and Elizabeth Crocker, (MD) Oct. 31, 1827
Milly Johnson and Hose Ward, (MD) Nov. 10, 1827
Chestley Wynn and Martha Whitson, (MD) Nov. 17, 1827
Samuel Allison and Malinda Florida, (MD) Nov. 20, 1827
Lindley Baird and Lewarken Mealley, (MD) Nov. 23, 1827
Lewarken Mealley and Lindley Baird, (MD) Nov. 23, 1827
Mayfield Johnson and Mandane Rutland, (MD) Nov. 24, 1827
Robert Law and Ann Telford, (MD) Nov. 26, 1827
Thomas Hearn and Sarah Sillaman, (MD) Dec. 1, 1827
Joseph Rutland and Margaret Thompson, (MD) Dec. 5, 1827
Anderson Wright and Sina Eagan, (MD) Dec. 5, 1827
Bracston Hill and Polly Tarpley, (MD) Dec. 11, 1827
Abraham Massey and Tabitha Hearn, (MD) Dec. 11, 1827
William Williams and Nancy Crutchfield, (MD) Dec. 11, 1827
Thomas Davis and Jane Donnell, (MD) Dec. 15, 1827
James Hays and Sally Night, (MD) Dec. 16, 1827
Lynus Armstrong and Jane Maxwell, (MD) Dec. 20, 1827
Jeremiah Murry and Rhunry Hesson, (MD) Dec. 20, 1827
Henry Cooley and Malinda Lunce, (MD) Dec. 22, 1827
Sterling Edwards and Mahala Puckett, (MD) Dec. 24, 1827
Claibourn Baily and Frances Philips, (MD) Dec. 27, 1827
Charles W. Cummings and Eliza W Foster, (MD) Nov. 19, 1828
John A. Dods and Marget M Thomison, (MD) Mar. 7, 1828
Asa Mosley and Frances M Snoddy, (MD) Feb. 19, 1828
Allen Blankenship and Eliza J Spinks, (MD) Jul. 4, 1828

John Meak and Charlotte J. Morris, (MD) Nov. 14, 1828
David Fillops and Anney France Hart, (MD) Mar. 22, 1828
Abner Jennings and Cloey F. Lester, (MD) Oct. 13, 1828
Littleberry E. Williamson and Rebecca E. Powell, (MD) Oct. 18, 1828
Alexander Roach and Elizabeth E. Wright, (MD) Jul. 1, 1828
Wm. W. Huddleston and Mary B. Tarver, (MD) Jan. 16, 1828
John Booker and Lusinda B. Griffin, (MD) Feb. 18, 1828
Obediah V. Rogers and Sarah Underwood, (MD) Jun. 14, 1828
John T. Lee and Louiza Murry, (MD) Jul. 26, 1828
Wm. S. Scott and Sally Sneed, (MD) Jun. 8, 1828
H. R. Shembridge and Selina Smith, (MD) Jul. 2, 1828
Edmond R. Harrison and Rebecca Hawkins, (MD) Nov. 11, 1828
William M. Andrews and Elizabeth Silloman, (MD) Mar. 19, 1828
Hall J. Winsett and Elizabeth Jarman, (MD) Feb. 18, 1828
William J. Goodwin and Mary McHenry, (MD) Oct. 22, 1828
Samuel H. Lasater and Salley Barker, (MD) Feb. 23, 1828
Nelson G. Allexander and Mary Patterson, (MD) May 13, 1828
Coston F. Ballentine and Nancy Taylor, (MD) Nov. 26, 1828
Nelson D. Hancock and Margaret Woodrum, (MD) Jan. 19, 1828
Michael D. Henderson and Elizabeth Wiley, (MD) Jul. 19, 1828
David C. Jackson and Mary Wood, (MD) Feb. 23, 1828
John B. Arnold and Frances Young, (MD) Jul. 29, 1828
Wm. B. Drake and Ann Robertson, (MD) Aug. 14, 1828
John B. Holman and Lavina Randolph, (MD) Sep. 18, 1828
Wm. A. Vowel and Caraline Camell, (MD) Mar. 18, 1828
William A. Thompson and Artemisia ????, (MD) Jul. 4, 1828
John Ingram and Eliza Todd, (MD) Jan. 3, 1828
Alfred Dukes and Nancy Bradshaw, (MD) Jan. 9, 1828
Sanders Stephens and Nelly Chambers, (MD) Jan. 9, 1828
Ruffin Capel and Lucinda Edins, (MD) Jan. 13, 1828
Charles George and Fassti Hughs, (MD) Jan. 13, 1828
Allen Nelson and Sarah Pugh, (MD) Jan. 28, 1828
Michael Bond and Elizabeth King, (MD) Feb. 8, 1828
Rawlings Henderson and Minerva Kennedy, (MD) Feb. 18, 1828
Thomas Fillops and Cassey Jonslan, (MD) Feb. 19, 1828
Macom Smith and Elizabeth Young, (MD) Feb. 22, 1828
Jideon Carter and Lydia Case, (MD) Mar. 10, 1828
Samuel Coles and Calista Walker, (MD) Mar. 10, 1828
Abner Weatherly and Jane Sims, (MD) Mar. 18, 1828
Pleasant Belcher and Sally Belcher, (MD) Mar. 19, 1828
Joseph Moore and Susannah Wood, (MD) Mar. 19, 1828
Jacob Holdefield and Elizabeth Horn, (MD) May 3, 1828
William Climer and Jane Lane, (MD) May 8, 1828

William Barker and Martha Winston, (MD) May 13, 1828
John Cates and Ally Johnson, (MD) Jun. 1, 1828
Baxter Bennett and Elizabeth Chandler, (MD) Jun. 3, 1828
Hezekiah Cartwright and Delila Searcy, (MD) Jun. 6, 1828
William Dotson and Elizabeth Heflig, (MD) Jul. 9, 1828
Henry Cluck and Mary Robinson, (MD) Jul. 19, 1828
James Smith and Gilley Stewart, (MD) Jul. 26, 1828
John McDaniel and Elizabeth Moore, (MD) Jul. 29, 1828
Matthew Brown and Elizabeth Walker, (MD) Jul. 30, 1828
Clabourne Clark and Sarah Neal, (MD) Aug. 2, 1828
Daniel Smith and Amy Neal, (MD) Aug. 2, 1828
Wm. Eddins and Sarah Hooker, (MD) Aug. 10, 1828
William England and Candis Trovilion, (MD) Aug. 11, 1828
Albert Foster and Lucinda Major, (MD) Aug. 12, 1828
Slith Harrison and Harriet Wood, (MD) Sep. 3, 1828
Wilee McDonald and Mary Yandle, (MD) Sep. 15, 1828
William Edwards and Patsy Maning, (MD) Sep. 23, 1828
Samuel Patton and Elenor Compton, (MD) Sep. 23, 1828
William Patrick and Pheby Smith, (MD) Sep. 24, 1828
Willey Medling and Alsay Reese, (MD) Oct. 2, 1828
James Haleam and Rebecca Underhill, (MD) Oct. 18, 1828
Lewis Patterson and Martha Ward, (MD) Oct. 23, 1828
William Carter and Izabella Roan, (MD) Nov. 20, 1828
Peter Patterson and Sarah Patterson, (MD) Nov. 29, 1828
Thomas Mitchell and Jane Southworth, (MD) Dec. 1, 1828
James Coner and Sarah Elliston, (MD) Dec. 2, 1828
Alexander Michaels and Elira Powell, (MD) Dec. 11, 1828
Sneed Harris and Fany Tilford, (MD) Dec. 13, 1828
Wilson Hearn and Elizabeth Winford, (MD) Dec. 22, 1828
Ferrell Davis and Frances J Joplin, (MD) Nov. 2, 1829
James M. Cloyd and Margaret C Sharpe, (MD) Oct. 18, 1829
James M. Coppage and Elizabeth Miller, (MD) Feb. 3, 1829
Robert H. Edwards and Minerva Robertson, (MD) Jan. 24, 1829
James H. Dickens and Lydia Pitner, (MD) Sep. 19, 1829
John H. Dorch and Winny Todd, (MD) Dec. 30, 1829
L. D. Crabtree and Winney Medling, (MD) Apr. 3, 1829
John Collins and Nancy Drew, (MD) Apr. 2, 1829
Christopher Cobb and Sally Underhill, (MD) Apr. 21, 1829
William Dunn and Sealy Jones, (MD) May 11, 1829
Wilson Coapland and Milly Rhea, (MD) Jun. 17, 1829
John Cox and Zeda Edwards, (MD) Jun. 20, 1829
Samuel Corley and Esther Priestly, (MD) Jul. 13, 1829
Edmant Crawford and Elizabeth Smith, (MD) Dec. 16, 1829

Elisha Clower and Martha Tucker, (MD) Dec. 24, 1829
William Coppage and Mary T Davis, (MD) Dec. 1, 1830
Josiah Donnell and Nancy P Thompson, (MD) May 17, 1830
Abraham Greer and Mary Ann Bollard, (MD) May 1, 1830
Edward P. Faulkner and Rebecca New, (MD) Jun. 4, 1830
James M. Boyd and Martha Thomas, (MD) Sep. 11, 1830
John B. Forester and Elizabeth Hall, (MD) Jun. 17, 1830
James B. Goodwin and Mildred Powell, (MD) Dec. 18, 1830
Nelson Doak and Jane Smith, (MD) Jan. 20, 1830
Littleberry Freeman and Elizabeth Young, (MD) Jan. 26, 1830
John Clopton and Matilda Drake, (MD) Mar. 25, 1830
Addison Eskins and Caroline Harrison, (MD) Apr. 2, 1830
Henry Devault and Susan Jackson, (MD) May 1, 1830
Jonathan Hendrixon and Clarisa Lermon, (MD) May 1, 1830
James Gibson and Rachel Bowers, (MD) May 17, 1830
Hickerson Barksdale and Harriet Lowe, (MD) Jun. 23, 1830
George Dooley and Emily Jackson, (MD) Aug. 11, 1830
Francis Eubank and Fanny Harland, (MD) Aug. 17, 1830
William Davis and Lucy Stewart, (MD) Sep. 7, 1830
Henry Collis and Elizabeth Farrington, (MD) Sep. 23, 1830
Jefferson Baxter and Rebecca Wynn, (MD) Sep. 27, 1830
Elijah Clower and Nicy Sutton, (MD) Oct. 4, 1830
Midget Cutrall and Fanny Swan, (MD) Oct. 16, 1830
Thomas Dillon and Harriet Roane, (MD) Oct. 18, 1830
James Clary and Penny Stephens, (MD) Nov. 25, 1830
Robert Donnell and Cleopatra Hearn, (MD) Dec. 2, 1830
McCoy Moore and Ovalina Williams, (MD) Dec. 18, 1830

Bedford County Tennessee, Power of Attorney of Benjamin Coats, Polk County, Missouri

State of Tennessee Bedford County. I Benjamin Coats of Polk County State of Missouri do hereby nominate and appoint either James Coats or John Reed or both of them as the case may be my attorney in fact for me and in my name to sell and convey to any person or persons their heirs and assigns forever who will purchase the same by general warranty deed in one or more tracts as they may think best my proportional part of lot no. 10 in the State of Tennessee county of Bedford formerly owned by Baity W. Coats deceased and now owned by the heirs of said Baity Coats Beginning at a hickory south west corner of lot no. 9 running thence south 23 4/10 poles to an elm and red oak thence east 96 poles to an Ironwood hickory and elm. Thence North 28 4/10/ poles to two Elms thence West to the Beginning containing seventeen acres---and take and receive the consideration money or to take notes for the same at their discretion they may also bring suit in my name if necessary to gain possession of or establish my title to the same, employ such counsel or other aid as they may need at my expense and charge and I do hereby ratify and confirm any act or thing they may lawfully do in the premises as fully as if I were present and doing the same myself, this the 7th day of Nov 1838.

Signed: Benjamin Coats (seal), Wit: Thomas Davis, William Brown, Certification by Bedford County Court Clerk 7th day of November 1838, Registered January 31st 1839

Tennesseans on the 1870 Census of Morgan County, IN
Andrew Adams: (A) 37, (BP) TN, (TWP) Harrison, (P) 419, (B) 1833ca
James Adams: (A) 41, (BP) TN, (TWP) Clay, (P) 372, (B) 1829ca
Madison Adams: (A) 33, (BP) TN, (TWP) Clay, (P) 367, (B) 1837ca
George Bailey: (A) 69, (BP) TN, (TWP) Green, (P) 392, (B) 1801ca
Joseph Bailey: (A) 68, (BP) TN, (TWP) Green, (P) 393, (B) 1802ca
Wm.Barnes: (A) 40, (BP) TN, (TWP) Washington, (P) 511, (B) 1830ca
Esther Barrickman: (A) 71, (BP) TN, (TWP) Washington, (P) 531, (B) 1799ca
Alfred Bates: (A) 50, (BP) TN, (TWP) Madison, (P) 467, (B) 1820ca
Christopher Bolen: (A) 82, (BP) TN, (TWP) Washington, (P) 502, (B) 1788ca
Priscila Bouman: (A) 57, (BP) TN, (TWP) Adams, (P) 325, (B) 1813ca
William J. Bragg: (A) 55, (BP) TN, (TWP) Jefferson, (P) 447, (B) 1815ca
James Bray: (A) 60, (BP) TN, (TWP) Gregg, (P) 405, (B) 1810ca
Henry Brewer: (A) 59, (BP) TN, (TWP) Monroe, (P) 487, (B) 1811ca
Richard Brown: (A) 47, (BP) TN, (TWP) Green, (P) 385, (B) 1823ca
Jesse Bryant: (A) 31, (BP) TN, (TWP) Washington, (P) 535, (B) 1839ca
Alexanderca ldwell: (A) 43, (BP) TN, (TWP) Green, (P) 389, (B) 1827ca
Mary A.ca natsdey: (A) 42, (BP) TN, (TWP) Jackson, (P) 432, (B) 1828ca
John Champlain: (A) 89, (BP) TN, (TWP) Madison, (P) 459, (B) 1781ca
William Childers: (A) 32, (BP) TN, (TWP) Baker, (P) 343, (B) 1838ca
John F. Clary: (A) 61, (BP) TN, (TWP) Green, (P) 389, (B) 1809ca
John Cline: (A) 38, (BP) TN, (TWP) Adams, (P) 316, (B) 1832ca
Peter Cline, Jr.: (A) 36, (BP) TN, (TWP) Adams, (P) 316, (B) 1834ca
W. Colensworth: (A) 57, (BP) TN, (TWP) Adams, (P) 313, (B) 1813ca
Nancy Collins: (A) 62, (BP) TN, (TWP) Washington, (P) 535, (B) 1808ca
Moss Crawford: (A) 39, (BP) TN, (TWP) Monroe, (P) 482, (B) 1831ca
Henry D. Culley: (A) 60, (BP) TN, (TWP) Brown, (P) 359, (B) 1810ca
Matthew Dean: (A) 44, (BP) TN, (TWP) Ray, (P) 498, (B) 1826ca
Samuel Denny: (A) 56, (BP) TN, (TWP) Washington, (P) 506, (B) 1814ca
Jonathon Doan: (A) 69, (BP) TN, (TWP) Monroe, (P) 483, (B) 1801ca
Wm. Dunavent: (A) 39, (BP) TN, (TWP) Washington, (P) 530, (B)

1831ca
Priscilla Durham: (A) 62, (BP) TN, (TWP) Jefferson, (P) 447, (B) 1808ca
Wm.Dyke: (A) 45, (BP) TN, (TWP) Clay, (P) 374, (B) 1825ca
Thomas Edwards: (A) 62, (BP) TN, (TWP) Washington, (P) 508, (B) 1808ca
Wm. Edwards: (A) 44, (BP) TN, (TWP) Washington, (P) 508, (B) 1826ca
Thomas Farley: (A) 48, (BP) TN, (TWP) Washington, (P) 514, (B) 1822ca
Mary Fletcher: (A) 82, (BP) TN, (TWP) Gregg, (P) 407, (B) 1788ca
Matilda Graves: (A) 54, (BP) TN, (TWP) Harrison, (P) 416, (B) 1816ca
Reuben Griffit: (A) 73, (BP) TN, (TWP) Jackson, (P) 430, (B) 1797ca
John Hale: (A) 59, (BP) TN, (TWP) Harrison, (P) 419, (B) 1811ca
Wm.Hardwick: (A) 62, (BP) TN, (TWP) Clay, (P) 369, (B) 1808ca
Elizabeth Hardy: (A) 55, (BP) TN, (TWP) Ashland, (P) 334, (B) 1815ca
Wm. Harrison: (A) 47, (BP) TN, (TWP) Washington, (P) 534, (B) 1823ca
Wallace W. Helton: (A) 62, (BP) TN, (TWP) Jackson, (P) 439, (B) 1808ca
Thompson Hendricks: (A) 56, (BP) TN, (TWP) Washington, (P) 525, (B) 1814ca
Andrew S. Hickey: (A) 45, (BP) TN, (TWP) Jackson, (P) 427, (B) 1825ca
James Hickey: (A) 46, (BP) TN, (TWP) Jackson, (P) 429, (B) 1824ca
James Holloway: (A) 43, (BP) TN, (TWP) Adams, (P) 317, (B) 1827ca
Jeremiah Jackson: (A) 55, (BP) TN, (TWP) Washington, (P) 524, (B) 1815ca
Alexander Kelso: (A) 62, (BP) TN, (TWP) Jackson, (P) 432, (B) 1808ca
John J. Kelso: (A) 59, (BP) TN, (TWP) Jackson, (P) 435, (B) 1811ca
Mahaly Kemp: (A) 64, (BP) TN, (TWP) Jackson, (P) 442, (B) 1806ca
Ruth Kemp: (A) 55, (BP) TN, (TWP) Jackson, (P) 440, (B) 1815ca
Elizabeth Kirkendoll: (A) 46, (BP) TN, (TWP) Clay, (P) 378, (B) 1824ca
David Kitchen: (A) 54, (BP) TN, (TWP) Clay, (P) 370, (B) 1816ca
James Lake: (A) 39, (BP) TN, (TWP) Jackson, (P) 437, (B) 1831ca
William Lankford: (A) 41, (BP) TN, (TWP) Jefferson, (P) 448, (B) 1829ca
Lemuel Lennear: (A) 43, (BP) TN, (TWP) Washington, (P) 510, (B) 1827ca
Rena Lipsay: (A) 56, (BP) TN, (TWP) Jackson, (P) 429, (B) 1814ca
William M. Macy: (A) 50, (BP) TN, (TWP) Brown, (P) 355, (B) 1820ca
Nancy McClung: (A) 66, (BP) TN, (TWP) Washington, (P) 522, (B) 1804ca
John McGuire: (A) 35, (BP) TN, (TWP) Jackson, (P) 439, (B) 1835ca
Thomas F. Merriman: (A) 41, (BP) TN, (TWP) Jackson, (P) 434, (B) 1829ca
Thomas Mitchell: (A) 73, (BP) TN, (TWP) Harrison, (P) 418, (B) 1797ca
Thomas Morgan: (A) 59, (BP) TN, (TWP) Clay, (P) 368, (B) 1811ca
Joseph Morrison: (A) 41, (BP) TN, (TWP) Jefferson, (P) 451, (B) 1829ca
Wm.H. Mull: (A) 51, (BP) TN, (TWP) Monroe, (P) 472, (B) 1819ca

Joseph T. Norman: (A) 46, (BP) TN, (TWP) Jackson, (P) 440, (B) 1824ca
Wm. Norman: (A) 53, (BP) TN, (TWP) Jackson, (P) 440, (B) 1817ca
Wm. B. Norman: (A) 41, (BP) TN, (TWP) Jackson, (P) 435, (B) 1829ca
John Oliver: (A) 41, (BP) TN, (TWP) Washington, (P) 502, (B) 1829ca
John Oneal: (A) 72, (BP) TN, (TWP) Jefferson, (P) 448, (B) 1798ca
Benjamin Overton: (A) 44, (BP) TN, (TWP) Clay, (P) 380, (B) 1826ca
Wiley Peyton: (A) 60, (BP) TN, (TWP) Baker, (P) 340, (B) 1810ca
Hiram Pogue: (A) 59, (BP) TN, (TWP) Jackson, (P) 428, (B) 1811ca
Margaret Preston: (A) 72, (BP) TN, (TWP) Washington, (P) 535, (B) 1798ca
Ishmael Rains: (A) 64, (BP) TN, (TWP) Madison, (P) 460, (B) 1806ca
Elbert Rariden: (A) 43, (BP) TN, (TWP) Brown, (P) 350, (B) 1827ca
Newel Rariden: (A) 50, (BP) TN, (TWP) Brown, (P) 352, (B) 1820ca
James Redford: (A) 40, (BP) TN, (TWP) Monroe, (P) 479, (B) 1830ca
Hiram Reeder: (A) 48, (BP) TN, (TWP) Jackson, (P) 436, (B) 1822ca
Wm.Reeder: (A) 50, (BP) TN, (TWP) Jackson, (P) 435, (B) 1820ca
James Rhea: (A) 28, (BP) TN, (TWP) Adams, (P) 324, (B) 1842ca
George Rhule: (A) 68, (BP) TN, (TWP) Jackson, (P) 425, (B) 1802ca
Joshua Richards: (A) 35, (BP) TN, (TWP) Monroe, (P) 480, (B) 1835ca
Wm.Robison: (A) 58, (BP) TN, (TWP) Jackson, (P) 434, (B) 1812ca
Jesse Rogers: (A) 52, (BP) TN, (TWP) Ashland, (P) 327, (B) 1818ca
Isaac Rooker: (A) 63, (BP) TN, (TWP) Brown, (P) 352, (B) 1807ca
Samuel W./M. Rooker: (A) 70, (BP) TN, (TWP) Brown, (P) 346, (B) 1800ca
Jackson Russell: (A) 50, (BP) TN, (TWP) Clay, (P) 371, (B) 1820ca
Wm. Ryan: (A) 44, (BP) TN, (TWP) Adams, (P) 314, (B) 1826ca
Mary A. Shell: (A) 50, (BP) TN, (TWP) Jackson, (P) 430, (B) 1820ca
Tolbert Shipley: (A) 67, (BP) TN, (TWP) Jefferson, (P) 443, (B) 1803ca
Wm.R. Smithers: (A) 42, (BP) TN, (TWP) Madison, (P) 468, (B) 1828ca
John H. Stephens: (A) 36, (BP) TN, (TWP) Ashland, (P) 328, (B) 1834ca
Andrew Stine: (A) 55, (BP) TN, (TWP) Washington, (P) 514, (B) 1815ca
George Stout: (A) 32, (BP) TN, (TWP) Washington, (P) 525, (B) 1838ca
Evan Tooma: (A) 53, (BP) TN, (TWP) Ashland, (P) 330, (B) 1817ca
Ervin Townsend: (A) 50, (BP) TN, (TWP) Washington, (P) 515, (B) 1820ca
Andrew Troxel: (A) 47, (BP) TN, (TWP) Jackson, (P) 424, (B) 1823ca
Wm. H. Troxel: (A) 42, (BP) TN, (TWP) Jackson, (P) 428, (B) 1828ca
James Wallace: (A) 32, (BP) TN, (TWP) Adams, (P) 318, (B) 1838ca
Daniel Walling: (A) 39, (BP) TN, (TWP) Ray, (P) 491, (B) 1831ca
Eli B. Warren: (A) 34, (BP) TN, (TWP) Madison, (P) 461, (B) 1836ca
Mary A. Watson: (A) 64, (BP) TN, (TWP) Madison, (P) 465, (B) 1806ca
Silas Wells: (A) 49, (BP) TN, (TWP) Jackson, (P) 433, (B) 1821ca
Joel Williams: (A) 44, (BP) TN, (TWP) Baker, (P) 341, (B) 1826ca

Louis Williams: (A) 65, (BP) TN, (TWP) Green, (P) 388, (B) 1805ca
Angeline Winchester: (A) 50, (BP) TN, (TWP) Jackson, (P) 432, (B) 1820ca
Benjamin Woodward: (A) 64, (BP) TN, (TWP) Monroe, (P) 483, (B) 1806ca
Ruth Wright: (A) 67, (BP) TN, (TWP) Brown, (P) 362, (B) 1803ca

Sumner County, Tennessee, Stock Marks and Brands, 1787-1818

April, 1787

Simon Kuykendall, Ephraim Payton, John Norris, John Hardin, Edward Hogan, Elmore Douglass, George Mansco, Edward Douglass, John Brigance, Thomas Mastin, John Hambleton, Abner Bush, John Hardin

July, 1787

Thomas Billew, Duke Hannah, Ezekiel Douglass, Peter Looney, Matthew Anderson, Kasper Mansker, William Hacker, Anthony Bledsoe, Isaac Bledsoe, Danl, Smith, Jas McKeen, David Shelley, Peter Looney, Charles Morgan, Charles Carter, John Donohoo.

July, 1788

Geo D. Blackemore, David Wilson

Jan., 1789

Alex Neeley, George Ridley, Thankfull Peele, James Adam

April, 1789

Jno. Hutchison, Abraham Sanders, Joseph Dixon

1789

Richard Hogan

July, 1789

John Roberts, Lewis Crane

July, 1790

William Edwards, John Cotton, Joseph Kuykendall, Anthony Sharp, William Cage, Robert Desha, Jo McElwrath, David Wilson

April, 1791

Robert Payton, William Neeley, Benjamin Williams

July, 1791

James Clendening, James Haw

Oct., 1791

Robert Shaw, Anthony Sharp

Jan., 1792

William Parmer, George Blackemore, William Dillard, Lazarus Cotton, Sion Perry, Edward Douglass, William Brigance, Hugh Crafford, Richard Cavit, Amos Smith, John Steel, Joseph Latimore, Nathaniel Latimore

April, 1792

Edward Williams, Richard Stroder, William Gillespie, John Williams,

Mathew Pain
John Young

July, 1792

Jan., 1793
Thomas Eskew

April, 1793
Robert Steel, Archibald Fisher, Wm.Douglass, Francis Cantron
July, 1793
Rhody Allen

Oct., 1793
John Carr, William Wilson, James Wilson, son of David Wilson; William Maney

Jan., 1794
Thomas Blackemore, James Williams
April 1794
Wilson Cage

July, 1794
Nathaniel Latimer

April, 1795
Theophilus Allen, Robert Latimer, James McKain
Oct., 1795
Orman Allen, John Hamilton

Apr., 1796
Wm. Lauderdale, Christopher Cooper, James Wilson, Lacheus Wilson, Joseph Steel, James Trousdale, Samuel Wilson, John Wilson
July, 1796
James Farr, Thomas Donnell

Oct., 1796
John Wilson, William Thomas

Jan., 1797
Danl. Rogers, Pearce Wall, Wm. Alexander, Henry Lyon, James Morrison, David White

April, 1797
John Hamilton, Matthew Cartwright, William Wyer
Oct., 1797
Andrew Blythe, James Blythe, Jonathan Hannun, Wm. Cartwright
Jan., 1798
Wm. Beard, James Winchester, John Patterson, Isaac Towell
April, 1798
Jacob Thomas, James Lane, Wm. Reed
July, 1798
Thadwick Nye

Oct., 1798
William Phipps, Isaac Lane, Edward Hudson
April, 1799
James Brown, James Harrison, Samuel Elliot
April, 1800
David Echols, John Echols
July, 1800
Henry Harrison
Oct., 1800
John Hassell
April, 1801
Micajah House
July, 1801
Joseph Motherall, Ann Greer
April, 1802
Charles Latimer, Lynde Latimer
July, 1803
Abraham Hassell, Henry Belote, Lynde Latimer
March, 1804
Jesse Hainey, Redmond D. Barry
June, 1804
Thomas Gregory, Joshua Cherry
Dec., 1804
John Giles
March, 1805
Henry Miller, John Miller, Heli Herring, George Duty, Solomon Duty, Joseph Clark
June, 1805
John Lauderdale, Joel Hart, John Young
Dec., 1805
Joseph McGlothlin, Bartholomew Stoval
March, 1806
William White, William Duty
March, 1807
John McMurry
Sept., 1807
James Smothers, Redmond D. Barry, Joseph Sebastian
Dec., 1809
Jas Rankin, Henry Bledsoe, Will Trigg, John L Swainy, Ben Hudson
Dec., 1811
Jesse Sheen, Joshua Cloaton
Aug., 1817
John Hanson, Mary Mayfield

Redmond D. Barry   Feb., 1818

              May 1818
Joseph Jackson, Christopher Woodall, George Hall

SURNAME INDEX

ABBET, 101
ABBOT, 156
ABBOTT, 56 95 127
ABERNATHEY, 119
ABERNATHY, 56
ACILLIS, 56
ACKLIN, 114
ACKRIDGE, 140
ACOR, 56
ACRE, 56
ACREE, 56
ACTON, 2
ACUFF, 26
ADAIR, 55 84 90 93 156
ADAM, 34 202
ADAMS, 2 56-57 91 97
　100 102 104 118 127
　134 139 151-152 156
　169-171 175 177 180
　191 199
ADAMSON, 166-167 177-
　178 186 191
ADCOCK, 57 77 101
ADDAMS, 56
ADEN, 156
ADKERSON, 98
ADKINS, 1 97 119 191
ADKINSON, 178
ADLE, 187
ADONES, 74
ADWELL, 2
AFFLACK, 165
AGENT, 101
AGILFRY, 71
AGILL, 101
AGNEW, 156
AHART, 98
AIKEN, 2 4 11 45 57 84
　124 144
AIKENS, 104

AIKIN, 114
AIKMAN, 131
AILESWORTH, 57
AKENS, 95-96
AKER, 46
AKINS, 90 97 172
AKRIDGE, 127 132
AKRIGE, 126 134
ALBERTSON, 57
ALEGER, 50
ALEHTY, 156
ALEXANDER, 9 16-17 36
　44 54 57 72 79 87 91 95
　101 103 105-108 113
　120-121 126-127 129
　135 142-143 145-146
　149 165 167-168 173
　190 203
ALEY, 98
ALFORD, 57 85 165-166
　194
ALFRED, 156
ALISON, 27
ALISSON, 110
ALKIN, 103
ALLAN, 96 98
ALLAY, 57
ALLCORN, 174 193
ALLEN, 1-3 30 34 57-58
　72 88 101 109 116-117
　135 138 140 146 152-
　153 155-156 169 171-
　172 177 179-180 188
　193-194 203
ALLEXANDER, 196
ALLEY, 58
ALLGOOD, 58
ALLIN, 108-109 165 169
ALLISON, 3 14 37 44-45
　49 58 85 90 193 195

ALLMAN, 3 188
ALLMOND, 58
ALLON, 3 31
ALLOWAY, 149 154
ALLRED, 1
ALMON, 55
ALMOND, 189
ALREAD, 56
ALSABROOKS, 82 90
ALSUP, 168 173 175 193
ALTMAN, 174
ALVIN, 91
ALVIS, 93
AMBRISTER, 130
AMBROSE, 3 8
AMES, 175 190-191
ANDERS, 3 6 77
ANDERSON, 1-3 10 16 20
　29 55 58 86 102 117-
　119 129 131 133 135
　137-138 143 146-147
　149-150 152-153 156
　165-168 170 174 181
　187-188 191 202
ANDES, 3 9 15 20 25 41
　51 107 156
ANDREW, 3 46
ANDREWS, 4 7 58 82 146
　179 187 194 196
ANGLEN, 173
ANGLIN, 167 179
ANGSLEY, 97
ANTHONY, 103
ANTONY, 101
APPERSON, 3 194
APPLACK, 193
ARCHER, 3 48 102 176-
　177
AREHART, 98
ARENDEL, 164

ARINTOS, 108
ARLINGTON, 102
ARMFIELD, 93
ARMSTRONG, 3 58 62 93
  100-101 146 150 169
  186 195
ARNALD, 190
ARNETT, 145
ARNOLD, 55 86 88 102
  174 184 186-187 192
  196
ARRENDUFFS, 47
ARRERWOOD, 37
ARRINGTON, 3
ARTHUR, 1
ARTHURBURN, 3
ARWOOD, 153-154
ARYES, 99 104
ASBY, 181
ASHER, 44 79
ASHFORD, 166
ASHLEY, 133
ASHLIN, 87
ASHWORTH, 177
ASLIN, 92
ASTEN, 3
ASTIN, 30 195
ASTON, 174
ATCHLEY, 95 98 156
ATCHLY, 156
ATKENSON, 90
ATKINS, 101
ATKINSON, 3 18 39 180
  183
AULEY, 156
AUST, 175
AUSTIN, 1 3 103 126 150
  156
AUSTON, 97
AUTRY, 101
AVANS, 186
AVARY, 172
AVERY, 75 78 82 93 174
  176 185
AVORY, 187
AYERS, 131
AYTES, 181
BAB, 101
BABB, 3 60 78 86 102 156
  175 179 184
BABER, 87
BACCHUS, 60
BACHELOR, 171
BACK, 96
BACON, 2-6 16-18 20 22-
  23 28 31 33 36-37 41

BACON (cont)
  47 49
BADGER, 55
BADGETT, 111 151
BAGBY, 155
BAGGATT, 4
BAGGEL, 60
BAGGET, 100
BAGWELL, 184
BAILES, 4 48 156
BAILESS, 107 115
BAILEY, 60 79 93 127 146
  180 192-193 199
BAILS, 4 14 28 37 42
BAILY, 79 156 178 195
BAIN, 26 75
BAINS, 3-4
BAIRD, 4 166 171 179
  189-191 195
BAITY, 114
BAKELEY, 30
BAKER, 4 29 41 45 51 60
  74-76 79 82 97 101 109
  112 127 131 156 167-
  168 184-185 187 189
BALAH, 9
BALANGER, 115 119
BALCH, 60
BALDERSON, 55
BALDRIDGE, 82
BALDWIN, 4 72
BALES, 4 18
BALEY, 74 80-81
BALINGER, 145
BALL, 4 30 34 37 112 117
  121 124 131
BALLARD, 60 96 100 156
BALLENGER, 13 115 117
BALLENTINE, 196
BALLER, 156
BALLEU, 88
BALLEW, 60
BALLING, 127 131
BALLINGER, 4
BALLINTINE, 88
BALSTON, 13
BANDY, 60 166-167 172
  181
BANE, 72-73 76 117 119
BANISTER, 82
BANKS, 60 69 90 100 191
BANNER, 4 22
BANTA, 130
BARBEE, 182 193
BARBER, 180
BARCKLEY, 4

BARCLAY, 35 60
BARCROFT, 14
BARFIELD, 61
BARGER, 4 45 52
BARHAM, 92
BARING, 165
BARINGER, 4
BARKELEY, 13
BARKER, 61 101 103 155
  196-197
BARKLEY, 4 8 23 45 61
  181
BARKSDALE, 73 198
BARKSDEL, 95 98
BARLARY, 105
BARLOW, 4 61
BARLY, 8
BARNARD, 61
BARNER, 2
BARNES, 4-5 13 21-22 28
  30 32 35 37 61 86 91
  108-110 145 147 151
  165 199
BARNET, 5 17 61 111 156
  166
BARNETT, 61 99 112 119
  123 130 143 146 155
  192-193
BARNFIELD, 194
BARNHART, 156
BARNON, 18
BARNS, 5 80 91 95 139
  156 166 186
BARR, 61 190
BARREN, 4 29
BARRET, 174
BARRETT, 149
BARRICKMAN, 199
BARRON, 5 17 43 61 84
BARRONS, 100
BARROTT, 93
BARROW, 95
BARRY, 9 204-205
BARTLETT, 61 94 111 186
BARTLEY, 18
BARTLY, 33
BARTON, 81 88 92 121
  155 169 181 183-184
  189
BASER, 5
BASFORD, 173
BASHAM, 2
BASHAW, 61
BASHOR, 5
BASINGER, 86
BASKET, 5 9 12 26 37

BASKETT, 5 24
BASKIN, 171
BASKINS, 175 182 194
BASS, 5 20 55 61 86 102
  164 166-167 169 175
  178 186 189 194
BASSFORD, 61
BASWELL, 62
BATEMAN, 169
BATES, 62 81 88-89 94
  96-97 117 171 199
BATEY, 195
BATLEY, 165
BATTLE, 89
BATY, 144
BAUCOM, 132
BAUGHER, 111
BAUN, 136
BAXTER, 1 5 79 191 198
BAY, 62 193
BAYLES, 2 5 10 17 22 24
  27 34 41 47 51-52
BAYLESS, 5 9 24 37 42
  117 119 143
BAYLEY, 5
BAYLIS, 62
BAYLISS, 62
BAYLY, 49
BAYNE, 74
BAYSINGER, 50 75 78 85
  90
BAZEL, 105
BEACHAM, 90
BEAGLES, 5 156
BEALS, 5-6
BEAM, 15
BEAN, 3 6 9 12 15 21 25-
  26 37 40 46 86-87 97-
  98 100-102 173
BEANE, 6
BEARD, 2 5-6 16 22 41 52
  54 62 71 107 126 176
  180 183 194 203
BEARDEN, 62 138 145
  170
BEARDIN, 187
BEARDING, 167
BEARDON, 179
BEASLEY, 99 171 180
BEASLY, 104 156
BEATTY, 62 108
BEATY, 6 62 110 115-116
  126
BEAUCHAMP, 191
BEAVER, 84
BEAVERS, 45

BEAVERT, 62
BEAZLEY, 90
BEAZLY, 82
BECK, 99-100
BECKHAM, 6 84
BECTON, 81 85 89
BEDFORD, 135 165
BEDSALLS, 6
BEDSAULS, 6
BEDSOL, 45
BEDWELL, 95-96
BEELER, 62 118
BEEN, 156
BEESLEY, 135
BEESLY, 101
BELCHER, 6 62 176 181
  194 196
BELEW, 93
BELL, 2-3 6 11 33 35 39
  55 62-63 71-72 77 79
  81 83 86 93 99-100
  102-103 105 109 111
  119 124-125 132 148
  154 166-167 174 178
  180 183 189 191-192
BELLAMY, 6
BELLEW, 88-89
BELLIEU, 99
BELLUE, 88
BELOTE, 156 170 204
BELT, 175 194
BENDER, 63
BENGE, 99
BENLEY, 31
BENNER, 45
BENNET, 1 15 185 191
BENNETT, 98 114 170-
  171 173 178 192 197
BENSON, 63 98 156 169
BENTHAL, 177
BENTHALL, 190
BENTLEY, 63
BENTON, 63 95 98
BENYES, 156
BERGE, 86
BERKLEY, 6
BERNARD, 191
BERRY, 63 79 88 99 106
  113 115 117 122 129
  139 142 155 167 171
  177-178 181
BERRYHILL, 55 63 104
BERTON, 163
BERYHILL, 104
BESSET, 6 25
BEST, 117 132 138 140

BEST (cont)
  142 146 149-150 153
BETHEL, 63 101
BETHELL, 90
BETHOSON, 169
BETHUME, 171
BETNER, 6
BETS, 95
BETSAWS, 130
BETTES, 180 185
BETTIS, 165 169-170
BETTS, 75
BEWLEY, 29
BHASS, 80
BIARD, 90
BIBEE, 63
BIBEL, 98
BIBY, 148
BICHEN, 184
BICKLEY, 6
BIDDICT, 101
BIDDILL, 6
BIDDLE, 6 23 49 127
BIDDY, 121
BIDE, 18
BIFFLE, 63
BIGBAY, 116
BIGGER, 63
BIGGS, 75 78 87 97 154
BIGHAM, 63 82 102-103
BILBRO, 175 195
BILD, 189
BILDERBEA, 142
BILLEU, 72
BILLEW, 202
BILLINGLY, 6
BILLINGSLEY, 3 6 14 74
  91 96
BILLINGSLY, 75 82
BILLINGTON, 63
BILLUE, 113 137
BINGHAM, 63 108 131
  137
BINGLY, 137
BIRCH, 168
BIRD, 6 32-33 101 103 112
  121 135 144 148 153-
  154 156
BIRDWELL, 6-7 22 144
  147
BIRRUR, 156
BISHOP, 2
BITNER, 7 48
BITSON, 1
BITTS, 188
BLACK, 1 7 81 96 101

BLACK (cont)
114-115 138-139 143
149 156
BLACKARD, 104
BLACKBURN, 33 55 63
100 107 156 169 184
189
BLACKEMORE, 72 202-203
BLACKLEY, 88-89
BLACKMAN, 2
BLACKMOORE, 32
BLACKMORE, 64
BLACKWELL, 64 75 94
122 127-128 170
BLACKWELLS, 97
BLACKWOOD, 100
BLAIR, 5-7 11 14 35-36
47-49 51 64 73 78 82
84 90 95 107-110 121
126-127 135 138 140
142 154 156 176
BLAKELY, 7 51
BLAKEMORE, 72-73 82
86
BLAKLEY, 7 16
BLALACK, 64
BLALOCK, 64 156 192
BLAN, 104
BLANCKINGSHIP, 96
BLANKENSHIP, 121 195
BLANKINSHIP, 112 135
BLANN, 79
BLANTON, 64
BLARE, 96
BLAZE, 186
BLEAKLEY, 7 25 51
BLEDSOE, 64 72 75-76
79-82 84 87 89-91 93
102 135 139 154 166
202 204
BLEDSOW, 102
BLETCHER, 64
BLEVENS, 64 97 109
BLEVIN, 43
BLEVINS, 108 110
BLIVIN, 64
BLOODWORTH, 167 188
194
BLOUSTON, 172
BLOYS, 77
BLURTON, 64 169
BLYTHE, 7 129 203
BOALS, 75
BOAS, 186
BOAZ, 115

BOBBETT, 82 90
BOBBITT, 90
BOBLE, 136
BODIN, 182 187
BODINE, 156
BODKIN, 84
BODKINS, 81
BOETHE, 180
BOGARD, 7 42
BOGART, 7 23 35
BOGLE, 105-106 109 120
128 133 142 146-147
149 153-154 166 169
182
BOHANNAN, 125 138
BOHANNON, 124 156
BOID, 132
BOIN, 64
BOISSEAU, 64
BOLAND, 76
BOLE, 64
BOLEN, 64 199
BOLES, 76 78
BOLIN, 13 135-136
BOLING, 1 65 72-73 115
140 152-154
BOLLANGER, 95
BOLLARD, 198
BOLLING, 131
BOLTON, 109
BONAR, 65
BOND, 65 115 117 119
123 126-127 131 139
141-142 144 147 166
171 173 175 179 182
187-190 193-194 196
BONDS, 173 188
BONDURANT, 189
BONE, 87 92 178 187-188
BONHAM, 118 131-132
140 144 149
BONINE, 113 130 132
BONNER, 65 100 170
BONOIN, 148
BOOKER, 97 188 196
BOOKOUT, 98
BOOMFIELD, 156
BOON, 80 85 90 92 98 172
185
BOOTH, 7 65 127 146 193-194
BOOTHE, 7 24 31 178
BOOYLE, 35
BORDEN, 95 128 156
BORDERS, 13
BORE, 191

BOREING, 73
BOREN, 7 14 24 28 31-32
48 53 113 116 139
BORIN, 30 32
BORING, 7 32 50 117 127
129 132 135
BORMER, 168
BORRAN, 93
BORRIN, 91
BORRING, 40
BORUM, 169
BOSHEARS, 134
BOSTICK, 115
BOSTON, 65
BOSWELL, 78 88
BOTTLES, 7
BOTTOM, 65
BOTTON, 156
BOUMAN, 199
BOUN, 87
BOUNDS, 101 103
BOURDEN, 108
BOVELL, 7
BOVENN, 136
BOWAN, 71
BOWARS, 65
BOWDEN, 65
BOWEN, 80 89 101 154
166
BOWERMAN, 108-109
112-114 117 127 139
146
BOWERS, 7-8 65 75 81 84
108 122-124 130 134
156 164 168 193 198
BOWLEN, 93
BOWLIN, 8
BOWLING, 84
BOWMAN, 1 5 8 13 15 29
41 55-56 65 72 88 112
149 156 161-162 177
BOWSER, 8 29
BOX, 1 65 99-100 102
BOY, 66
BOYD, 4 8 10 13 19 28 37-38 54 66 83 105 107
113-114 132 142-144
146 152 165 173 198
BOYDSTON, 66
BOYDSTUN, 55
BOYER, 9
BOYERS, 66
BOYETT, 77
BOYLE, 2
BOYLES, 84
BOYLS, 81

210

BOYSE, 105
BOYT, 76 78-79 87
BOYTT, 76
BRABSON, 154
BRACKIN, 156
BRADBERRY, 74 81 83 85 117 121 168 176 184 189
BRADBURY, 122
BRADDOCK, 166
BRADEN, 16 95 127 174
BRADFORD, 18 55 66 72 76 91 184
BRADLEY, 8 29 66 80 95 102 106-107 109-110 135 155 165 168 191-193
BRADLY, 170
BRADSHAW, 100 173-174 180 187-188 196
BRADY, 137
BRAGG, 66 199
BRAIDWELL, 115
BRAKEBILL, 115 153
BRALY, 173
BRAN, 86
BRANCH, 91 195
BRANDEN, 95
BRANDON, 11 55 66 100 102
BRANDY, 126
BRANHAM, 1 152
BRANNAM, 96
BRANNEN, 8
BRANNON, 8-9 66 168
BRANNUM, 116
BRANSTUTTER, 49
BRANUM, 8
BRASHEARS, 66
BRASSFIELD, 76
BRATCHER, 66
BRATTON, 78 81-82
BRAWLEY, 66
BRAWN, 124
BRAWNER, 135
BRAY, 199
BRAYN, 156
BRAZE, 111
BRAZELTON, 8 95 121 132
BREADSHAW, 55
BREAKBILL, 113 115 119 147
BREAKKILL, 67
BREAN, 166
BREARLY, 8

BREASE, 114
BREAZEAL, 151
BRECHEN, 66
BREDEN, 66-67
BREDON, 97
BREEDLOVE, 168 177
BREKEM, 103
BRENT, 67
BRESER, 43
BREVARD, 67
BREWANTON, 103
BREWER, 67 88 117 121 130 132 135-136 139-140 142 153 172 199
BRIANT, 4 19 29 52 76 86 101 117-118 130 135 138 142 149 155 178 190
BRICHAN, 170
BRICHUN, 172
BRICKELL, 149
BRICKER, 6 8 28 47 156
BRICKEY, 119 126 131 135 140 148 153
BRICKLE, 153
BRIDGEMON, 90
BRIDGERS, 193
BRIDGES, 84 92 170 172 194
BRIDWELL, 67
BRIEN, 177
BRIGANCE, 202
BRIGGANCE, 2
BRIGGS, 67
BRIGHAM, 72
BRIGHT, 8 67 113-114 138 144 151 154
BRIMER, 67 156
BRIMLET, 95
BRINSON, 169 173
BRISCOE, 99
BRISON, 166 169 182 191
BRIT, 8 24
BRITENHAM, 92
BRITINGHAM, 75
BRITNER, 9
BRITT, 8 67 75
BRITTAIN, 67
BRITTAN, 8
BRITTEN, 8-9 13
BRITTLE, 176
BRITTLES, 178
BRITTON, 67
BRIZELY, 9
BRIZENDINE, 67
BROADAWAY, 165

BROADWAY, 67
BROCHUS, 67
BROCK, 104 122
BRODY, 145
BROILES, 9
BROILS, 108 110-111
BROMMIT, 9
BROOK, 67 133 138 178
BROOKS, 67-68 95 100 103-104 115-116 118 124 128-130 133 142 145 151 153 171 176 178 182
BROOKSTANN, 102
BROTHERTON, 68 97 143 149
BROTT, 95
BROWN, 1-2 4-6 9-13 18-20 22 25-27 29-30 33 35 38 42 44-51 54-55 68-69 73-74 92 95 97 99-100 102 107-109 113-115 117 119 123 125 130 132-133 135 137-138 142 145 147-149 151-152 156 165-170 173-174 176-177 179-180 182 186 188-191 197 199 204
BROWNER, 143
BROWNING, 10 89 171
BROYLES, 5-6 8 10 13 20-21 23 30 33-34 39 41-43 45 69 105
BRUCE, 55 69 166
BRUDEN, 156
BRUDIN, 156
BRUFF, 76 85-86
BRUMFIELD, 97
BRUMIT, 47
BRUMLEY, 111
BRUMMET, 10 69 74
BRUMMETT, 12
BRUMMIT, 10 20 40
BRUMMITT, 12
BRUMSENT, 100
BRUNDIDGE, 104
BRUNE, 190
BRUNER, 69 111
BRUNSON, 91
BRUS, 60 69
BRUSTER, 156
BRUTON, 1 95
BRYAN, 2 69 100 156
BRYANT, 69 76-78 82 88-89 100 123 142 144 147

BRYANT (cont)
150 166 170 179 182
186 190 199
BRYSON, 70 174 178 186
192
BUCHANAN, 14
BUCHANON, 173
BUCHEIGHAN, 37
BUCHHANNON, 156
BUCK, 8 10 188
BUCKINGHAM, 10 17
BUCKLEY, 70 163-164
181
BUCKNER, 97 156
BUDIN, 156
BULL, 10 36
BULLARD, 70 102 172
BULLINGTON, 89
BUMPASS, 166
BUN, 156
BUNCH, 1
BUNDY, 177
BUNKER, 10
BUNTEN, 174
BUNTING, 83
BURCH, 95
BURCHFIELD, 151
BURDON, 1
BURDSONG, 1
BURFORD, 70
BURGE, 175
BURGISS, 100
BURGNER, 52
BURK, 10 55 70 94 96 98
131 139 156 185
BURKE, 10-11 70 119 194
BURKES, 70
BURKET, 10
BURKETT, 70
BURKHART, 89
BURKHOLLEN, 100
BURNAM, 89
BURNES, 131
BURNETT, 97 104 154
172 190 192
BURNETTE, 109 117
BURNINE, 156
BURNITT, 70
BURNS, 10 45 70 116-117
138 156 166 185
BURRESS, 10
BURRIS, 16 20 50 70 99-
100
BURROW, 82-83
BURROWS, 100
BURT, 10

BURTON, 1 10 55 70 87
103-104 124 127 166
168 183 194
BURTS, 10
BURWICK, 98
BUSBY, 70 101
BUSH, 70 77 156 202
BUSHAM, 1
BUSHONG, 70
BUSKILL, 10
BUSSELL, 71
BUSTER, 96 98
BUSTLE, 149
BUTCHER, 97
BUTH, 27
BUTLER, 10-11 71 79 119
156
BUTRAM, 91
BUTT, 183
BUTTERWORTH, 190
BYANT, 71
BYATES, 180
BYERLEY, 135
BYERLY, 10-11 27 50 71
152
BYERS, 71
BYLER, 11
BYLES, 71
BYNUM, 71 104
BYRD, 107 117
BYRN, 2 168
BYRNE, 82
BYRNS, 2 166
BYRON, 156
BYSINGER, 83
CABE, 106
CABELL, 112
CABLE, 154
CABLER, 87 89-90
CACEPER, 109
CADDELL, 117
CADE, 11 23
CAGE, 202-203
CAGLE, 124 133 135 137
156
CAILOR, 151
CAIN, 111 183
CAIRY, 46
CALAHAN, 100
CALDWELL, 55 107-109
122 124 127 129 132-
134 137-138 141 144
147-149 151-152 155-
156 168 184-185
CALER, 120
CALHOUN, 89 171 187

CALL, 128
CALLAM, 11
CALLAN, 11
CALLAWAY, 99
CALLEWAY, 171
CALLICO, 182
CALLON, 98
CALLUMS, 1
CALOR, 126
CALUM, 55
CALVERT, 9
CAMBELL, 167
CAMELL, 196
CAMERON, 108 141 149
155
CAMIL, 97
CAMMIL, 114
CAMP, 101 137
CAMPBELL, 6 8-9 11-13
17-18 20 25 28 31 35
40 71-72 77 80 87 94
97 103 114 117 119
121-122 126 132 134-
135 140 144 146 152
156 167 174 178 181
183 185 188 190-193
CAMPBLE, 11
CAMRON, 112
CANADAY, 90
CANADEY, 89
CANADY, 89
CANATSDEY, 199
CANNADA, 125
CANNON, 6 11 45 55 111
128-129 141 147 149
156 177
CANTERBURY, 156
CANTRELL, 2 78
CANTRON, 203
CANWAY, 109
CAPEL, 196
CAPERTON, 99 103-104
CAPLINGER, 170 178 185
CAPP, 39
CAPPS, 8
CAPSHAW, 113
CAPSLINGER, 195
CAR, 40
CARATHERS, 11 19
CARAWAY, 177 181
CARBURY, 52
CARDEN, 122
CARDER, 11 27 35
CARDWELL, 124
CARE, 87 89
CAREATHERS, 19

CARETHERS, 19
CAREY, 11
CARGO, 111
CARIGER, 24
CARITHERS, 11
CARLEN, 179
CARLESS, 130
CARLEY, 177
CARLILE, 101
CARLIN, 173 178
CARLOCK, 94 182
CARMICHAEL, 11 51
CARMON, 156
CARNAHAM, 99
CARNAHAN, 84
CARNARD, 122
CARNEY, 23
CAROTHERS, 4-5 55
CAROWAY, 190
CARP, 42
CARPENTER, 133 153 155 193
CARR, 1 8 11 24 30 32 41 71 79 85 96-97 102 167 194 203
CARRADINE, 80
CARRAHAN, 82
CARRAY, 91
CARREATHERS, 7 11
CARRELL, 11 100
CARRETHERS, 113
CARRIGER, 11 14 164
CARRINGEN, 156
CARROL, 14 121
CARROLL, 11 78-79 82 93 117 121 128
CARRUTH, 166 174 181 189 193
CARRY, 84
CARSON, 11-12 17 20-22 26 29 34 43 53 96-97 99 111 114-115 124 128 132-134 139 145 154 156 168
CARTEN, 88
CARTER, 11 25 37 71 82 86 92-93 95 117 119 121 131-132 142 144 161 163 165 169 175 182-184 187 190 192-193 196-197 202
CARTRIGHT, 100 102
CARTWRIGHT, 149 166-169 173 177 180 182 195 197 203
CARUTHERS, 11 18 26 33

CARUTHERS (cont) 141 156
CARVER, 124-125 151 167 169 176 186
CASADAY, 2 11-12
CASADY, 21 183
CASE, 24 196
CASEL, 96
CASEY, 12 97 146
CASH, 12 31
CASHEDY, 41 54
CASHON, 145
CASKY, 175
CASNER, 51
CASON, 181 185 192
CASS, 12
CASSADY, 8 10 25 167
CASSELENOR, 169
CASSEN, 18
CASSIDY, 12
CASSON, 12 24 174
CASTEEL, 108 117 120 129 133 144
CASTIEL, 33
CASTLE, 156
CASTLEMAN, 167
CASTLES, 74
CATE, 96 156
CATES, 95-96 119 138 197
CATHCART, 152-153
CATHEY, 97
CATI, 156
CATLE, 156
CATLETT, 156
CATO, 185
CATON, 146 148
CATRON, 97
CATTERS, 156
CAUGHORN, 109
CAUSEY, 95
CAVEN, 145
CAVETT, 119 148
CAVIN, 126
CAVIS, 173
CAVIT, 72 202
CAVLEY, 179
CAWHORN, 116
CAWTHON, 173
CAWTHORN, 170 179 181
CAYLER, 134
CAYLOR, 130 135 142 149 155
CAYTON, 131
CAYWOOD, 121
CAZIA, 12
CCOLLIER, 12

CEBLER, 27
CELLERS, 12
CELSO, 15
CERLY, 2
CESSNA, 12
CETCHERN, 168
CHADWICK, 119
CHAFERO, 90
CHAMBERLAIN, 22 112-113 115
CHAMBERLAND, 111
CHAMBERLIN, 110
CHAMBERLING, 84
CHAMBERS, 73 98 132 153 155-156 184 196
CHAMMELS, 125
CHAMPAIN, 76
CHAMPION, 103-104
CHAMPLAIN, 199
CHANCE, 155-156 183
CHANDLER, 12 21 23 28 51 124 131 142 156 168-170 174 176-177 180-181 185 187-188 194 197
CHANDLEY, 19
CHANE, 156
CHANEY, 1 12
CHANLER, 12 24
CHANY, 42
CHAPION, 97
CHAPMAN, 12 19 122 165-166 169
CHAPPELL, 178 182
CHARLES, 101
CHARLETON, 4
CHARLITON, 52
CHARLTON, 12 74
CHARTON, 12
CHASE, 12 23
CHATON, 96
CHAVER, 188
CHAWNING, 166 182
CHEATHAM, 55
CHEATS, 12
CHEETWOOD, 109
CHELTON, 2
CHENNEY, 176
CHERRY, 83 204
CHESTER, 12 20 33 44 95 187
CHILCOAT, 102
CHILDERS, 97-98 104-105 199
CHILDRAS, 76
CHILDRES, 113 127-128

CHILDRES (cont)
146
CHILDRESS, 73
CHILERTT, 96
CHINNOTH, 12
CHINOUTH, 12 46
CHINUTH, 12
CHISOM, 106
CHISON, 176
CHISUM, 1
CHITTY, 114
CHOAT, 112
CHOOKSON, 96-97
CHOOPER, 96 98
CHORMLEY, 123
CHRISLEY, 12
CHRISTIAN, 3 156
CHRISTIE, 31
CHRISTMAS, 55
CHRONISTER, 81
CILTY, 4
CIRKLAND, 125
CITCHENS, 112
CITTY, 52
CLABAUGH, 48
CLABER, 156
CLABOO, 98
CLABORN, 95
CLABOUGH, 156
CLACK, 96 156
CLACKSTON, 171
CLAE, 189
CLAIBORNE, 73-74 77
CLAK, 53
CLAMPET, 105-106 110 135 137
CLAMPIT, 168
CLARCK, 156
CLARK, 1 6-7 12 18 20 24 36 39 45 48 81 95-96 101-102 108 125 130 132 139 142 153-154 156 169 184 197 204
CLARKE, 37 89
CLARY, 198-199
CLAUSE, 13
CLAY, 87-88
CLAYBO, 153
CLAYPOLE, 1
CLAYTON, 161 176
CLEEK, 13
CLEM, 13
CLEMENS, 149 151
CLEMENTS, 83
CLEMMENT, 166
CLEMMONS, 177 186-187

CLEMMONS (cont)
189-191
CLEMMONT, 93
CLEMONS, 84
CLENDENIN, 186
CLENDENING, 202
CLEPPER, 36 102
CLICK, 8 13 24 38 54 175
CLIFER, 156
CLIFFIN, 156
CLIFFORD, 45
CLIFT, 120
CLIFTON, 117 165 178 186 191 193
CLIMER, 172 176 196
CLINE, 13 199
CLINGAN, 98
CLINGER, 13
CLINTON, 117 156
CLIPPER, 13 102
CLOATON, 204
CLOPTON, 171 198
CLOUSE, 13 29 50 52
CLOWER, 198
CLOWS, 9
CLOYD, 5-6 11 13 40 165 169 179 182 187 191-192 194 197
CLUCK, 175 188 197
COACH, 144
COALTER, 135 137
COAPER, 187
COAPLAND, 197
COATS, 102 105 155 175 198-199
COBB, 1 13 119 181 197
COBINGER, 23
COBLER, 55
COBURN, 55
COCHRAN, 13 105-107 112 124 129-130 136-137
COCK, 73
COCKE, 74 167 174 176-177 190
COE, 178 184 190
COFERLD, 185
COFF, 22
COFFEE, 2
COFFEL, 98
COFFIN, 152
COFFITT, 98
COFFMAN, 2 13 46
COFFY, 95
COGDIN, 1
COGGBURN, 13

COHAM, 142
COKE, 183
COKER, 119
COLBERT, 101
COLBOURN, 111
COLDWELL, 13 115-116 121-122
COLE, 4 13 73 75 78 80 83 87 89-90 131 138 156 184 188 194
COLEMAN, 13 94 189
COLENSWORTH, 199
COLES, 196
COLEWICK, 186
COLLAM, 13
COLLAN, 98
COLLEN, 96
COLLET, 9 13 52
COLLETT, 7 9
COLLIER, 13 53 156
COLLINGS, 174 178 183-185 188
COLLINGSWORTH, 13
COLLINS, 5 12-13 38 41 53 95 99 121 137 148 161 174 179 197 199
COLLIS, 198
COLLOR, 13
COLQUIT, 102
COLQUITT, 100
COLSO, 187
COLSON, 14 48
COLSTEN, 14
COLTER, 119 142 148
COLVELLE, 97
COLVILLE, 110
COLYAR, 14
COLYEAR, 74
COLYER, 14 48 83 97 100
COMBS, 14 40 49
COMBY, 14 28
COMER, 101
COMPTON, 156-157 165 170 182 190 193 197
CONDRON, 111
CONDRY, 100
CONE, 18
CONELL, 82
CONER, 197
CONGER, 2 125 140
CONKIN, 14
CONKLIN, 14
CONLEE, 73 80 83 87 92-93
CONLEY, 14 35
CONN, 104 113

CONNELL, 73 83 89
CONNER, 107 116 124
    144 147-148 154-155
CONNOR, 127
CONROD, 182
CONVILL, 87
CONWAY, 46 109
CONWELL, 73
CONYER, 71 180 185-186
COOK, 14 53 77 79 91 99
    101 109 117 132-133
    137 139-140 143 145
    152 154-155 179 181
COOKE, 110 171
COOKSEY, 166 182 190
COOLEY, 195
COON, 44
COONROOD, 185
COONSE, 130
COOP, 78
COOPE, 85 131-132
COOPER, 14 18 41 73 106
    110 123 151 168 171
    177 183 203
COPAS, 14
COPASS, 25
COPE, 1 125 130 150
COPELAND, 14 94 106
    108 120 141 145 188
    193
COPLAND, 2 108 165
COPP, 21 42
COPPAGE, 197-198
COPPECK, 14
COPPENBARGER, 117
COPPENGER, 14
COPPICK, 11
COPPINGER, 37
COPPOCK, 117 136
COPS, 21
CORDA, 179
CORDER, 14 177 185
CORLEY, 188 197
CORNETT, 14
CORRINGTON, 78
COSIAH, 9
COSLON, 142
COSNER, 14
COSTNER, 136 151 153
COSTON, 140
COTQUILL, 100
COTTEN, 157
COTTON, 2 7 157 165 202
COTTRELL, 123 149
COUCH, 42 97 148
COUGHFMAN, 49

COUGHMAN, 14 31
COULBOURN, 114
COULBURN, 138
COULSON, 151
COULTER, 1-2 107 135
    138
COUNTS, 85 99
COUP, 119
COVENTON, 111
COVINGTON, 2 157
COWAN, 14 28 33 96 99-
    100 105-106 108-109
    112 114-115 123 126
    132 136 154 157 192
COWDEN, 142 148 157
COWEN, 1 96 103-104
COWGER, 176 184
COWLIN, 100
COWPENGER, 37
COWSON, 55
COX, 1 14-16 21 24 55 78
    98 103 117 134 136
    146-148 154 156-157
    164 168 170 173 177-
    179 184 188 192-193
    197
COZBY, 2
CRABB, 99-100 163
CRABTREE, 14 181 197
CRADDICK, 7 14
CRADDOCK, 80 168 186
CRADOCK, 34
CRADY, 72
CRAFFERD, 72
CRAFFORD, 101 202
CRAFT, 117 131
CRAFTON, 73 76 83-84
CRAGE, 95
CRAIG, 73-74 78 80 105
    108 110 146 151 165
CRAIGE, 90 93
CRAIN, 94
CRANE, 71 76 78 202
CRATON, 101
CRATOR, 167
CRAVENS, 173
CRAVINS, 71
CRAW, 132
CRAWFORD, 14-15 44
    102 126 137 169 197
    199
CRAWLEY, 147
CREAMER, 15
CREEDOP, 184
CRESAP, 138
CRESSALEUS, 51

CRESSEALEAS, 31
CRESWELL, 114 132 143
    184 195
CREW, 114
CREWS, 90-91 153
CRIBBS, 72-74 76 78
CRIDER, 82-83 90 92
CRIDLEY, 99
CRIFFIN, 101
CRISELUS, 15
CRISP, 88 122 127
CRISWELL, 145 157 181
CRITTINGTON, 113
CRITZELUS, 39
CROCKER, 90 195
CROCKETT, 73 76 81-83
    85-86 92-93 100 161
CROCKSELL, 29
CROGGINS, 15
CROLEY, 113
CROMES, 76
CROMWELL, 137-138
CRONELL, 15
CRONWELL, 15
CROOK, 187
CROOKS, 182
CROOKSHANKS, 53
CROPPER, 166 189
CROSS, 72 77 88-89 103
    143 172 175
CROUCH, 6 8 10 15-16
    23-24 26-27 30 33 52
    157
CROW, 15 28 55 157
CROWDER, 146 194
CROWLEY, 1
CROWN, 15
CROWSON, 157
CRUDUP, 194
CRUISE, 127
CRUMPARKER, 36
CRUMWELL, 96
CRUMWILL, 96
CRUSE, 135 156
CRUSH, 119
CRUTCHFIELD, 171 193
    195
CRUZE, 130
CRYE, 144
CULBERTSON, 25
CULLEY, 199
CULP, 79
CULTON, 109 143
CUMINGS, 176
CUMMING, 119 128 147
    150 152

CUMMINGS, 38 51 82 153-154 157 166 182-183 189 195
CUMMINS, 15
CUMMONS, 123
CUNINGHAM, 157
CUNNINGHAM, 1 5 7 15 34-35 89 101 105-106 114 116 118 121 123 126 128-129 146-147 149 154 157 191 194
CUPP, 112-113 119 128
CURD, 185 188
CURLER, 141
CURMUSS, 97
CURREY, 44 171
CURRIER, 118
CURTES, 116
CURTICE, 72
CURTIS, 76 78 86 91 102 116 152
CURTUY, 105
CUSACK, 127
CUSIC, 105
CUSICK, 107 148 151 157
CUTBERT, 53
CUTHREL, 186
CUTRALL, 198
DAIL, 97
DAILEY, 127 130
DALE, 97
DAMERON, 168
DANESON, 141
DANFORTH, 117
DANIEL, 2 55 90 192
DANIELS, 29 42 47 125 154
DANLEY, 139
DANTON, 123
DARMER, 95
DARMOND, 111
DARWIN, 104
DASSET, 2
DAUGHERTY, 77 97 156
DAUSSON, 79
DAVAULT, 15 17
DAVENPORT, 15 95 181-182 186 190
DAVID, 123 153
DAVIDSON, 55 76 79 82 84-85 88 90-92 107 109 165 176 180 192
DAVIDSSON, 75 80
DAVIS, 1 10 15 24 38 53 55 72-74 78-79 86 92 94-98 100-102 104 109

DAVIS (cont)
111 114-119 121 123-124 127-129 132-136 138-142 144-147 150 152-154 157 166-167 169 173-174 176-178 181-183 187 189 191 195 197-199
DAVISON, 15-16 26 31 55 101
DAVOTT, 16
DAWN, 133
DAWNHAM, 103
DAWSON, 75
DAY, 16 95
DAYL, 131
DEADERICK, 16 55
DEADRICK, 3 16 32
DEAKEN, 26
DEAKENS, 16
DEAKINS, 9 11 16 26 33 37 46
DEAN, 16 100-102 199
DEARIN, 95
DEARMAN, 97
DEARMON, 130
DEARMOND, 16 115 130-131 138 140 146
DEASON, 56
DEAVER, 123
DEBAUSK, 111
DEBENPORT, 191
DEBORD, 16
DEBUSK, 103 152
DECKE, 157
DEEN, 41 122-123 130 133
DEFOOR, 96
DELANEY, 16 26 36 149
DELANY, 14 16 36 47 103
DELASHMET, 16
DELASHMONT, 31
DELOACH, 99 172
DELOSURE, 115 157
DELOZIER, 128
DELPH, 78
DELZALL, 130
DELZELL, 120 126 135 143 147 155
DENISON, 150
DENNE, 109
DENNEY, 105-106
DENNIS, 17 88 157 183 185 190
DENNY, 110 199
DENSON, 101 103
DENTON, 15-16 20-21 26

DENTON (cont)
42 49 130 184
DENWAY, 100
DEPEW, 16 32 38
DERICK, 157
DERONEY, 152
DEROSSET, 128 132 137
DERRICK, 157
DESHA, 72 202
DEUGGEN, 97
DEUGIN, 97
DEURY, 180
DEVAULT, 16 30 36 43 198
DEVENPORT, 157 191
DEVEPORT, 110
DEVER, 142
DEVINE, 132
DEVOR, 124
DEW, 176 183 194
DEWALT, 16
DEWITT, 155
DEWOODY, 16
DIAL, 74 76 84 86 128 177
DIAMONS, 132
DIBRILL, 82
DICE, 193
DICKASON, 86
DICKENS, 35 197
DICKERSON, 157
DICKEY, 75 78 99 157
DICKINGS, 166 168 178
DICKINS, 170 178
DICKSON, 72-73 77 79 87 96 104 110 132
DICKY, 157
DICSON, 135
DIDDLE, 116 140
DIGGINS, 78 83
DILL, 73 84 86 165 173
DILLARD, 11 32 73 144 169 171 176-177 179 182 184-185 191 202
DILLIARD, 177
DILLINGHAM, 16
DILLON, 193 198
DILLS, 155
DINES, 116 130
DINKENS, 16
DINKIN, 16
DINWIDDIE, 16
DISKILL, 88
DISMUKES, 174
DISON, 157
DIVINE, 122 140 154
DIXON, 74 79 123 139-141

DIXON (cont)
153 157 202
DOAK, 7 16 33 43 51 169
    181 185 192-193 198
DOAKE, 189
DOAN, 53 199
DOBBINS, 55 157
DOBS, 99
DOCKERY, 157
DOCKINGS, 93 184
DODD, 96 100 130 169
    191
DODDS, 174 195
DODS, 195
DODSON, 1 96 130
DOHERTY, 17 107
DOLARHIDE, 103
DOLLARHIDE, 101
DONAHOO, 110
DONALD, 17 110
DONALDSON, 84 87-88
    91-92 133 136 153
DONALSON, 166 181
DONATHAN, 103
DONEL, 85
DONELSON, 167 172
DONNELL, 167-168 174
    181 187 189 192-193
    195 198 203
DONOHOO, 202
DOOLEY, 174 198
DORCH, 194 197
DORSET, 91
DORTCH, 182 186
DOSS, 103
DOSSER, 12 17
DOTSON, 17 44 98 104
    155 197
DOUGAN, 99 101 104
DOUGHERTY, 1 82
DOUGLAS, 17 112 114
    140 157 174
DOUGLASS, 2 17 71 182
    187 202-203
DOUHERTY, 120
DOUTHER, 1
DOUTHET, 135
DOUTHIT, 124 143
DOWDLE, 157
DOWELL, 78 82 89
DOWLAND, 79
DOWLY, 99
DOWNEY, 83 148-150
DOWNING, 99
DOXEY, 91
DOZER, 89 91-92

DRAKE, 17 55 99 171 173
    178 195-196 198
DRENAN, 189
DRENNAN, 183
DRENNON, 179-180 188
DREW, 166 170 197
DRUNDEN, 1
DRYDEN, 92
DRYMAN, 29
DUCKETT, 98
DUFF, 2 111 121
DUFFY, 93
DUGAN, 113 134
DUGAR, 2
DUGGAN, 118 157 188
DUGGARD, 17 164
DUGGER, 2 17
DUGLASS, 72 99
DUGLES, 17
DUKE, 36 102 189
DUKES, 174 196
DULANEY, 17 19
DUNAGAN, 75-76
DUNAHOO, 97
DUNAVENT, 199
DUNAWAY, 153
DUNCAN, 7-8 17 23 34 38
    40 43 48-49 52 74 99-
    100 121 124 127 133
    135-136 138-141 143-
    145 147 149 151-152
    155 164
DUNCOME, 40
DUNHAM, 17 28
DUNIHOO, 72
DUNKAN, 139
DUNKIN, 17 26 53
DUNLAP, 17 75 101 105-
    106 112 114 121 128
    137 147-148 153 155-
    157
DUNLEY, 131
DUNN, 96 100-101 114
    130 135 142 144 146
    149 151-153 155 157
    197
DUNNEGAN, 75
DUNNING, 91
DUNSMORE, 182
DUNWAY, 100
DUNWOODY, 83 103 121
DUNWORTH, 17
DURAN, 118
DURHAM, 1 107 112 200
DURK, 189
DURLEY, 81-82 89

DURNOLDS, 105
DUTY, 204
DUVALT, 1
DVUALT, 190
DWIGGINS, 2
DYER, 75 80 123 128 130
    142 183
DYKE, 7 151 200
DYKES, 7 17
DYSON, 87
EABY, 193
EAGAN, 170 176-177 184
    195
EAGIN, 17
EAGLETON, 105 114 127
    129 131
EAGON, 191
EAKIN, 109 114 116 121
    126 142
EALEY, 193
EANIS, 125
EANOS, 139
EANS, 99
EARLEY, 147
EARLY, 126 146 152 154
EARNEST, 17 41 95 157
EARWOOD, 146
EASLEY, 41
EASLY, 104
EASON, 15 32 170 175
    190
EAST, 169
EASTEP, 36
EASTERWOOD, 89
EASTIS, 103
EATHERLY, 167 178
EATHRIDGE, 182
EATON, 186
EAVES, 101
EBERLY, 18
ECHOLS, 204
EDDEN, 31
EDDINGS, 175
EDDINS, 183 197
EDGEMON, 18
EDGINGS, 101
EDGMAN, 40
EDINS, 196
EDMISTON, 105 124
EDMONDS, 120
EDMONDSON, 110 114
    126 133 147 149 151
EDMONS, 132 134
EDMONSON, 81 113 139
    141
EDMONSTON, 124

EDMUNDS, 148
EDMUNDSON, 91 93
EDMUNDSTON, 76 91
EDNEY, 84
EDWARDS, 2 4-5 9-10 18 29 73-74 84 88 96 116 167 170-172 175 179-181 183 187-188 195 197 200 202
EGEMAN, 18
EGNEW, 72
EIDSON, 2
ELAERADGE, 95
ELAM, 1
ELDER, 74-75 78 82 94 115
ELHERTON, 18
ELIOT, 102
ELIOTT, 121
ELISON, 97
ELKINS, 168
ELLEN, 88
ELLIAD, 157
ELLICE, 157
ELLIDGE, 97 142
ELLIGE, 127 157
ELLINGTON, 84
ELLIOT, 2 11 42 204
ELLIOTT, 24 115 122 124 136 155 193
ELLIS, 2 8 12-13 15 18 23 26-27 31 33 43 135 137 140 142 147 175-176 181 183 195
ELLISON, 18 157 161 189
ELLISTON, 197
ELSEY, 12 14 18 28 102
ELY, 86 184
EMBERSON, 103
EMBREE, 4 10 17-18 35 53
EMBRY, 38 100-101 104
EMBURSON, 103
EMERSON, 18
EMERT, 18 32
EMERY, 157
EMMERSON, 18 39 120
EMMERT, 136
EMMET, 18 157
EMMIT, 157
EMMITT, 149
EMRY, 103
ENDSLEY, 131 155
ENDSLY, 128
ENGLAND, 73-74 157 192 197

ENGLE, 8 18 24
ENGLISH, 3 14 41
ENIS, 123 142
ENOCH, 178
ENSOR, 18 41
EPERSON, 96
EPPERSON, 15 18
ERBY, 97
ERSPY, 71
ERVIN, 81 98
ERWIN, 4 18 41 73 78 123
ESCUE, 194
ESKEW, 203
ESKINS, 198
ESLICK, 168
ESTES, 55 79 173-174 186
ESTILL, 99 103
ETHERAGE, 91
ETHEREDGE, 81
ETHERIDGE, 85
ETHERLY, 192
ETHERTON, 157
EUBANK, 198
EVANS, 18 22 80 83 102-103 126 131 133 147 157 176 182-184
EVENS, 97 140
EVERETT, 114 128 136 138 142 149
EVERETTE, 151
EWING, 18 105-107 111-112 114 116 126-128 130 133 137 140 145-147 151 155 171
FAGALA, 157
FAGG, 144
FAIN, 15 18 28 109
FALKNER, 108
FALLS, 18 48
FANN, 48 127 136 157
FANNEN, 18
FANNON, 157
FANSHIRE, 157
FARIS, 101-104
FARLAN, 18
FARLEY, 200
FARMEAR, 98
FARMER, 100-101 112 115 118-119 121 126 129 132 137-138 142 151
FARNSWORTH, 18
FARR, 116 119 157 203
FARRELL, 102
FARRINGTON, 198
FARRIS, 88

FASSEY, 176
FASTHING, 76
FATHY, 133
FAUBUSH, 19 25 32 35-36
FAULKNER, 198
FAWBUSH, 3 15 19 37 45 48
FAWEAL, 191
FEA, 112
FEAZLE, 157
FEBRUARY, 19
FEEZLE, 19
FELKNER, 109-110
FELLERS, 19 37
FELLOWS, 22
FELPS, 155
FELTS, 19 50 136
FENCHUM, 19
FENNER, 55
FERGASON, 157
FERGERSON, 192
FERGESON, 165
FERGUSON, 6 19 21 25 38 73 75 78 81 91 105 113 118 122 144 152 157
FERJER, 19
FERNSWORTH, 23
FERREL, 19
FERRIL, 94
FERRILL, 186
FERRINGTON, 194
FERRIS, 192
FIELDER, 76 82 89-90
FIELDING, 82
FIELDS, 82 85 93 111 172 187 189
FIFER, 115
FIGARS, 187
FIGINWINGER, 134
FILLOPS, 196
FINCH, 5 75 104
FINDLEY, 2 114
FINE, 11 15 17 19 44
FINEY, 87
FINGER, 134 144
FINK, 19
FINLEY, 1 85 95 124 130 135 142-144 149
FINNEY, 101 172
FISHER, 13 19 76-77 81 88 90 96 108 146 174 203
FITE, 73 75 84-85 96 187
FITSGERAL, 97-98
FITZGERALD, 14-15
FITZJARELL, 95
FITZJERREL, 103

FITZPATRICK, 19
FITZSIMMON, 19
FLACK, 155
FLAER, 5
FLEMMING, 17
FLENN, 19
FLESHART, 140
FLETCHER, 19 50 73 75-78 81 83-84 87 91 97 189 200
FLINN, 130 137
FLINTER, 79 81
FLIPPIN, 55 81
FLORADY, 190
FLORIDA, 195
FLOWERS, 76 79 84-86 91-92 175
FLOYD, 19 100-101 127 157
FLY, 73 77 82 87-88 90
FLYNN, 157
FOGG, 97
FOLEY, 163
FOLKNER, 108
FOLLET, 157
FOLLON, 51
FON, 19
FONDWELL, 19
FONVILLE, 74 77 90
FORBES, 10 103 165
FORBUSH, 19 34 54
FORCH, 182
FORD, 8 14-15 19-20 24 38 49 75-77 95 104 126 160
FOREN, 83 86
FOREST, 75 83
FORESTER, 76 78 82-83 95 110 119 130 154 198
FORGUSON, 20 30 39 108
FORISTER, 120 154
FORRAN, 87
FORREST, 101
FORRESTER, 74-75 93 137 146
FORSYTH, 99
FORTENBURY, 104
FOSHA, 119-121
FOSTER, 7 20 76 95 97 101-103 130 157 171 179 187 194-195 197
FOUS, 95
FOUTE, 117 143 145 153
FOWLER, 20 80-81 84 93 157
FOX, 15 20 73-74 76 78 89

FOX (cont)
91 109-110 144 157
FRAGON, 191
FRAIM, 157
FRAKE, 48
FRAKER, 20
FRAKES, 20
FRANCE, 20
FRANCES, 42
FRANCIS, 29 109 139 157 187
FRANKLIN, 1 9 21 42 74 105 107 110 157
FRANKLING, 170
FRANKS, 102 108 111 116-117 120
FRANLAND, 106
FRAZER, 20 78 178
FRAZIER, 20 71 99-100 111 136 155 157
FREEMAN, 4 20 29 50 78 80 83 85-87 121 124 171 181 188 198
FREMAN, 20
FRENCH, 20 44 124 140 144-145 157
FRESHOUR, 120
FREW, 121 126 130-132
FREY, 96
FRIECE, 177
FRIERSON, 55
FRONABARGER, 140
FROST, 146
FROTER, 24
FROUT, 180
FROW, 139 143 147
FRY, 155
FRYER, 20 27
FUDGE, 55
FUEL, 74
FULERTON, 78
FULGHUM, 74
FULK, 20
FULKERSON, 20 54
FULKES, 48
FULKS, 96
FULLEN, 20 56
FULLER, 20 79 86-87 100 167 176-177
FULLERTON, 75 77
FULMAN, 12
FULTNER, 140
FULTON, 95 133
FULYERS, 100
FUNDERBULK, 95
FUQUA, 83

FUQUAY, 148
FURGARSON, 93
FURGASEN, 185
FURGASON, 187
FURGERSON, 189 194
FURGESON, 39 42 105
FURGUSON, 121 124 194
FUSTEN, 194
FUSTON, 177
GABBERT, 20
GABBLA, 157
GABBLE, 157
GADDY, 178
GADY, 95
GAFORTH, 157
GAILARD, 86
GAINES, 20 41 126 182
GAINS, 179
GALAHAN, 96
GALAHOR, 107
GALLAWAY, 38
GALLION, 121 157
GALLOWAY, 20
GAMBELL, 75
GAMBLE, 106-107 116 121 124 129 132 135-137 144 146 148-149 151 153
GAMBUL, 72
GAMMEL, 105
GAMMIL, 11 20
GAMMON, 2 20-21
GANN, 20 24 39 41 51-52
GANNS, 21
GANT, 82
GARBER, 25 29 32 45-46
GARDENER, 129
GARDINER, 129
GARDNER, 20 45 119 150 153 165 190
GARIN, 20
GARLAND, 21 32 40
GARMANY, 170
GARMONY, 187
GARNER, 21 97 100-101 106 121 127 129 133 136 145 148-149 151 185 188
GARNS, 21
GARONS, 125
GARRARD, 134
GARREN, 141 149-150
GARRET, 10 186
GARRETSON, 110
GARRETT, 55 102 177
GARRISON, 172

GARSUCH, 136
GARVIN, 21
GASKINS, 79 81
GASSAWAY, 97
GASTON, 96
GATELY, 85
GATES, 21 134
GATHER, 95
GAULT, 113 119-120 122 126-127 129 131-132 143 146
GAY, 114 119 121 124 152
GEAHL, 21
GEARIN, 95
GEDIONS, 143
GEE, 90
GELBREATH, 112
GELLAHER, 107
GENEST, 90
GENKINS, 21
GENT, 98
GENTRY, 77 83 86 102 111 149
GEORGE, 9 98-99 117 124 129 131 135 142 145 157 168 171 196
GERNER, 137
GERREL, 97
GERUIN, 36
GERVIN, 8 20
GESEL, 99
GEYLARD, 74
GHOLSTON, 103
GHORMLEY, 113 123
GIBBONS, 1
GIBBS, 76 113 119 121 152
GIBSON, 1 16 19 21 29 33 35 72 85 89 91 95 124 153 157 166-167 174 181 183 185-186 189 198
GIESLER, 5
GIFFIN, 108 121 153
GIFFORD, 20 99
GIGER, 14 21
GILBERT, 55 138 157 191
GILBRETH, 95
GILCHRIST, 77 79 83 88
GILES, 204
GILL, 170
GILLAM, 164 194
GILLAND, 81
GILLASPIE, 103
GILLES, 11 21
GILLESPIE, 8 21 53 105

GILLESPIE (cont) 107 110-111 116 122-126 131 135 138 143 202
GILLESPY, 105 117 133
GILLEY, 21
GILLIAM, 101-102
GILLILAND, 83 88 92
GILLINWATTERS, 97
GILLIS, 21 102
GILLMORE, 108
GILLUM, 77
GILMAN, 21
GILMORE, 39 106 109
GINKENS, 21
GINN, 99
GINNINGS, 128
GIPSON, 72 96 157 167
GIRDNER, 128-129
GIST, 67
GITTSON, 43
GIVANS, 99
GIVENS, 103
GIVINS, 128-129
GLACO, 104
GLADDEN, 127
GLANTON, 176 190
GLAP, 157
GLASCOCK, 21 23 87 90
GLASE, 21
GLASGOW, 71 88
GLASON, 77
GLASS, 6 9 12 88 109 112 115 120 128 140 152
GLASSCOCK, 6 36 74 77 83 85-87
GLAVES, 95
GLAZE, 53-54
GLEASON, 86 91
GLEEVES, 171
GLEEVS, 192
GLENN, 21 41 95 180 193-194
GLIDWELL, 84
GLOVER, 21 103-104
GOARD, 188-189
GOBSON, 55
GODDARD, 151
GODFREY, 186 190
GODPHREY, 175
GOEN, 151 153
GOFF, 21 85 94
GOFORTH, 5 21 157
GOIN, 21
GOINS, 16-17 21
GOLD, 106 191

GOLDEN, 21
GOLDING, 56
GOLDMAN, 181
GOLIHER, 114
GOLLIHER, 114
GOLPH, 137-138
GOLSTON, 170-171 173 176
GOOD, 21-22 36 38 45 52
GOODALL, 179 184 192
GOODEN, 1 87
GOODLOE, 55
GOODLOW, 87
GOODMAN, 16 46 77-78 80 86 93 109 119 128 132 149 153 175 181
GOODNER, 95
GOODRICH, 92 175
GOODWIN, 99 104 122 125 136 196 198
GORDON, 73
GORGE, 98
GORMLY, 144
GOSEY, 83
GOSSAGE, 128
GOTCHER, 99-100
GOTHERD, 98
GOTT, 20 22-23
GOULD, 110 134 140 146
GOURLY, 139
GOWEN, 96 182
GOWING, 96
GRACY, 116
GRADY, 74 86
GRAHAM, 1 10 14 22 28 48 99 102 136-137
GRANADE, 168
GRANDSTAFF, 187 192
GRANT, 95 101 121 182
GRASTON, 130 142
GRAVES, 22 101 137 144 189 194 200
GRAY, 4 7 14 22 26 36 42-43 75 101 103 113 149 166 168
GRAYHAM, 6 20 22 48 54
GRAYNN, 22
GRAYOR, 78
GRAYSON, 1-2 94
GREEN, 7 10 22 72 97 104 123 143 146 149 166 172-173 177 183 186-187
GREENAWAY, 108
GREENE, 18 22 43 54 111-112 118 136 144

GREENFIELD, 141
GREENLEES, 100
GREENWAY, 22 35-36 51
  118 126 149-150
GREENWOOD, 104 166
  172
GREER, 31 34 48 107 130
  132 134 142 146 148
  154 164 172 174 184
  186 193 198 204
GREGGORY, 93
GREGORY, 79 137 204
GREGSBY, 126
GREMITT, 96
GRESHAM, 22
GRICE, 91
GRIEN, 43
GRIER, 22 179 181 191
GRIFFEE, 78
GRIFFET, 192
GRIFFETTS, 107
GRIFFIN, 83 85-87 92 121
  141-142 171-172 176
  180 187 196
GRIFFIT, 200
GRIFFITH, 144
GRIFFITS, 128
GRIFFITTS, 125 134 150
GRIFFY, 80
GRIGSBY, 95-96 118 122
  141 150
GRILLS, 19 46
GRIMES, 48 195
GRIMLEY, 5
GRIMMET, 128
GRIMMETT, 95 128
GRIMSLEY, 22
GRIMSLY, 28
GRINDSTAFF, 192
GRISHAM, 22 121 142
GRISSAM, 95
GRISSIM, 181
GRISSOM, 173
GRISSUM, 195
GROGEN, 97
GROSS, 98
GROVE, 22
GRUBB, 143
GRUNDY, 77
GUESS, 93
GUIN, 22 55
GUINN, 97 112
GULLET, 55
GUN, 179 189
GUNN, 192-193
GUTHERIE, 189

GUTHRIE, 175 180 182
GUY, 116
GUYLLE, 184
GUYNE, 31
GWIN, 178
GWINN, 22 27
GWYN, 165 184
GWYNN, 22 46
GYER, 7 9 48
GYRE, 42
HACKENS, 98
HACKER, 72 202
HACKNEY, 107 113 116
  125-126 137 143 150
  153 172
HACKSON, 97
HADDON, 142 146
HADDOX, 151 155
HAFFLEY, 151
HAFLEY, 141 152
HAGAN, 22 50
HAGER, 180
HAGGARD, 157
HAGLER, 97
HAGUEWOOD, 92
HAIL, 4 12-13 22-23 25
  30-31 42 80 87 106 109
HAILE, 23 44
HAILEY, 92
HAINES, 1 23
HAINEY, 204
HAINS, 23 75 82 86
HAIR, 23 46 111 124 130
  133 140
HAIRE, 23 136
HAKINS, 71 109
HALCOM, 150
HALE, 2-3 6 12 15 23 26-
  30 32 36 40 47 51 93
  115 123 143 151 157
  200
HALEAM, 197
HALEY, 76 81 84 87-90
HALFACRE, 1
HALFORD, 90
HALL, 6 23 43 72 74-77 80
  82 88-91 99 103 117
  121 125 135 142 153
  172-173 198 205
HALLAHER, 94
HALLIBURTON, 85
HALLUM, 183
HALOWAY, 23
HALPAIN, 140-141
HALTER, 155
HAMACK, 91

HAMBELTON, 95
HAMBLETON, 71 192 202
HAMBRIGHT, 97
HAMBY, 96 154
HAMELTON, 108 111 148
HAMENTREE, 131
HAMER, 23 136
HAMIL, 134 139 151
HAMILL, 129 145
HAMILTON, 2 6 23 34 76
  102 104-105 130 132
  139 146 157 173 194
  203
HAMIT, 1 23
HAMLIN, 1
HAMMER, 7 14 23 43 47
  54
HAMMETT, 12
HAMMIL, 106 131
HAMMILL, 132
HAMMIN, 23
HAMMINTREE, 144
HAMMITT, 23
HAMMON, 23 126
HAMMONDS, 7 9
HAMMONES, 97
HAMMONS, 104
HAMMONTREE, 108 118
  124 128-129 132-133
  137-138 141-142 145
  150 153
HAMONTREE, 143
HAMPTEN, 72
HAMPTON, 15 17 23-24
  34 43 50 155 178
HANCOCK, 169-170 174-
  175 179-180 186-188
  192-193 196
HANDCOCK, 86
HANDLEY, 99
HANDLY, 99
HANDSBROUGH, 172
HANES, 75 139
HANKINS, 155 184 191
HANKS, 55
HANLEY, 15 138 152
HANNA, 105-107 128
HANNAH, 11 24 41 50 71-
  72 82 84 97 103 105-
  106 108 128 144 147
  150 174 202
HANNUN, 203
HANSLEY, 1
HANSON, 138 204
HAONES, 121
HARBER, 85

HARBOR, 74
HARBOUR, 73 75 78
HARCEY, 92
HARDAN, 106
HARDCASTLE, 101
HARDEN, 55 146
HARDESTER, 81
HARDIN, 49 72 115 157 202
HARDING, 1 160
HARDISTER, 78 81
HARDWICK, 97 121 200
HARDY, 200
HARE, 5
HAREWOOD, 97
HARGESS, 99
HARGIS, 114 116
HARGISS, 100-101
HARIS, 24 95
HARISON, 99
HARISS, 100 170
HARKINS, 168
HARLAND, 198
HARLE, 108
HARLEAN, 85
HARLEN, 170
HARLEY, 72 86
HARLIN, 97 192
HARMON, 8 11 24 36 47 118 122 146
HARNEY, 193
HARP, 106
HARPALL, 185
HARPER, 24 72 75 80-81 89-90 121 123 126 134 140 155 157
HARPOLE, 72 170 172
HARPOLL, 87 92
HARREL, 186
HARRELL, 104
HARRELSON, 152
HARRES, 121
HARRINGTON, 72 173 185
HARRIS, 5 12 24 27 36 44 77 95 99 101-103 112 114 116 118 121-122 124 126 128-131 136- 137 140 143 146 148 152 156-157 165 167 169 171-174 176-178 187 194 197
HARRISON, 1 14 24 27 34 36 42 55 72 91 100-101 103 132 155 157 176 180 188-189 193 196-

HARRISON (cont) 198 200 204
HARRISSON, 74 76 78 86
HARRON, 92
HARSHBARGER, 24
HART, 7 24 86 105 107 111 113 118 123-124 126 138 148-150 156 170 196 204
HARTMAN, 5 20 24 27 46
HARTS, 88
HARTSELL, 11 21 24 31 39-40 122 139 141 146
HARTSFIELD, 181 195
HARTSIL, 54
HARVELL, 177
HARVESON, 97
HARVEY, 3 9 24 31 39 49 96 98 127-128 134 137 144 155 189 193
HARVY, 90 189
HARWARD, 94
HARWOOD, 72
HASKELT, 117
HASKET, 118
HASKEW, 139
HASS, 173
HASSELL, 204
HATCHER, 24 119 123 157
HATCHETT, 92 99
HATFIELD, 1
HATHAWAY, 188
HATHEHAWAY, 179
HATHWAY, 24 125 186
HATLER, 6
HATTER, 7
HAULKNER, 152
HAUN, 24 157
HAUNWORTH, 25
HAUTER, 136
HAVEN, 102
HAVENS, 98 129 161
HAVERN, 99
HAW, 202
HAWERD, 98
HAWK, 99
HAWKINS, 32 78 88 93 96 153 196
HAWS, 10 23-24 29
HAYDEN, 141 151
HAYDON, 132
HAYGOOD, 24
HAYNES, 91 96 137 154
HAYNS, 92
HAYS, 7 25 31 45 81 87 90

HAYS (cont) 95 102 123 151 156 165 167 170 173 189-190 195
HAYSE, 130 140-141
HAYTER, 94
HAYWOOD, 191
HAZE, 155
HAZLETT, 10
HEAD, 90
HEADERICK, 52
HEADRICK, 25 44 50 137 147
HEARN, 166 178 180 189 192 194-195 197-198
HEARTSELL, 28 154
HEATH, 83 121
HEATHCOCK, 85
HEATHRICK, 164
HECTOR, 78
HEDERICK, 157
HEDGEPATH, 191
HEDLER, 25
HEDRICK, 23 128 133 136 140 153
HEFLIG, 197
HEFLIN, 166 183 194
HEFTON, 190
HEGARTY, 176
HEISKELL, 25
HELEMES, 97
HELLIN, 14
HELLMAN, 94
HELTON, 123 200
HELVIN, 25
HEMP, 37
HENDERSON, 1 12 99 103 107 111 116-118 120- 122 124-125 127 131- 132 136-137 140 147- 148 152-154 157 169- 170 175 196
HENDRICHSON, 147
HENDRICK, 78-79 85 101 165
HENDRICKS, 72 90 105 200
HENDRICKSON, 128 134 144 149
HENDRIXON, 32 198
HENDRIXSON, 144 148
HENDRY, 34 54
HENIGER, 127
HENLEY, 16 25 139 148 153
HENLY, 25 51 101 103

HENLY (cont) 157
HENNEY, 112
HENNY, 157
HENRY, 25 28 76 86 97-98 102 106 113 116 121 124-125 128 132 134 136-138 140 144-146 148-151 153-155 157 169 180 184
HENSLEY, 9 12 24 102 124
HENSON, 104
HERALD, 25
HERALDSON, 188
HERN, 29 188
HERNDON, 100 104 187
HEROD, 88
HERRIFORD, 102
HERRING, 204
HERROD, 104 165
HERROLD, 25 30
HERROLE, 143
HERT, 25
HERTSELL, 31
HESLIP, 99
HESS, 77 82 84 91 121 157
HESSE, 96
HESSON, 195
HETHERLY, 22 25
HIATT, 152
HICE, 25
HICH, 142
HICHOLS, 157
HICKEY, 72 74 114 125-126 134 155 200
HICKLAND, 113-114
HICKMAN, 6 25 87 142 157 176-177 182-184 188
HICKS, 25 72 76 79 81 93 95 112 114 120 126 157 168 186 193
HICKY, 43 94
HIDEN, 95
HIDER, 25
HIESKELL, 138
HIGDON, 186
HIGENS, 97
HIGGINS, 6 25 75 80 83 157 169 177
HIGGS, 162-163
HIGHTOWER, 182
HIGNIGHT, 86
HILBERT, 25
HILES, 113

HILL, 1 23 25 55 81 93 95 100-101 103 124 135 157 173-174 181 184 190 193 195
HILLERD, 2
HILLHOUSE, 101
HILTON, 25
HIMBROUGH, 92
HIMES, 25
HINCH, 18
HINES, 25 86 93 103 187
HINET, 157
HINKLE, 19 25-26
HINLY, 157
HINSHAW, 99 150
HINSON, 147
HINTON, 139
HINTSON, 165
HIPS, 96
HIRFLEY, 105
HISKS, 113
HISTEN, 157
HITCH, 125 130-131 143-144 147 150-151 155
HITCHCOCK, 110
HITE, 89 189
HITES, 94
HITS, 104
HITTLE, 120
HIX, 112 114 122 126 134 140 146 149-151 153-154
HIXSON, 2
HOAK, 183
HOATSELL, 144
HOBB, 183
HOBBS, 84 92 149-150
HOBSON, 180 186
HOCKINS, 98
HODGE, 16 19 26 55 90 124 181
HODGES, 3 23 26 28 38 76 95-96 104 134 157 169 171 188 192
HODGSON, 1
HOFF, 106
HOFMAN, 26
HOGAN, 71-72 202
HOGDWOOD, 175
HOGE, 2 104
HOGG, 73-74 84 106 108 187
HOLAWAY, 89
HOLBERT, 190
HOLCOMB, 85 93 148
HOLDEFIELD, 196

HOLDER, 80 99 102-103
HOLEMAN, 91
HOLLAN, 90
HOLLAND, 2-3 38 40 89-92 157 165 185 189
HOLLANDWORTH, 168
HOLLARD, 168
HOLLEBY, 26
HOLLERS, 134 136
HOLLINGSWORTH, 126 134 139 145 190 194
HOLLINSWORTH, 174 184
HOLLIT, 164
HOLLMAN, 189
HOLLOMAN, 56
HOLLOMON, 178
HOLLOWAY, 99 107 114 144 190 200
HOLLY, 49 99
HOLMAN, 196
HOLMES, 26 75 80 84-85
HOLMS, 157
HOLOWAY, 108
HOLSINGER, 38
HOLT, 26-27 31 81 83 89 116
HOLTS, 38
HOMBARGER, 47
HOMES, 102
HONEY, 56
HONEYCUT, 26
HOOBS, 95
HOOD, 97 113 123 134-135 139 142 155
HOOFS, 157
HOOFT, 157
HOOK, 105 140 150
HOOKER, 30 101 157 172 197
HOOKS, 105 121 128 135 151
HOOLAND, 55
HOOPER, 95 133-134 141 157
HOOSE, 2
HOOVER, 89 146
HOOZER, 170
HOPE, 26 114
HOPKINS, 18 26 39 73 75 87 167 187
HOPPERS, 26
HOPSON, 165
HORN, 90-91 177 179-180 184 196
HORNSBERRY, 178

HORSE, 190
HORSKINS, 89
HORTON, 3 5 25-26 34 45 50 167
HOSIER, 38
HOSKINS, 181
HOSS, 16 26 29 33 46 48 54
HOTCHKISS, 94
HOUDESHELL, 72
HOUGHS, 91
HOUK, 113 116 134 157-158
HOUSE, 26 73 204
HOUSEHOLDER, 137
HOUSTON, 4 10 26 44 105 107 112-114 116 119 121-122 124 126 129-132 137 139-140 148-149 151 194
HOWARD, 1 7 26 56 77 84 89-90 93 95 98 104 106 135 147 158 174 178 183
HOWE, 183
HOWEL, 26 35 95-96 146 169 175
HOWELL, 74 89 91-92 97 150 169
HOWERD, 98
HOWILL, 185
HOWLET, 96
HOWSER, 26
HOYLE, 26 33
HOYT, 133
HUBBARD, 82 87 92 130 167-168 188
HUBER, 158
HUCHISON, 108 130
HUCKABEE, 83
HUCKABY, 125 155
HUCKBY, 92
HUCKLAND, 110
HUDDLESTON, 171 176 178 196
HUDERSON, 96
HUDGEONS, 131 135
HUDSON, 95 139 145 158 161-162 174 180-181 183 192 204
HUDSPETH, 99
HUFAKER, 98
HUFF, 158
HUFFAKER, 158
HUFFHINES, 45 51
HUFFMAN, 3 26 118 120

HUFFMAN (cont) 131 134 136
HUFFS, 158
HUFHINES, 16 26-27
HUFMAN, 27 31
HUGELS, 176
HUGGARD, 158
HUGGINS, 181
HUGHES, 30 55 72 109 135 138
HUGHS, 1 97 103 196
HUGLE, 185
HULENE, 56
HULING, 114
HULL, 177 186
HULMER, 27
HULSE, 18 27 49
HUMAN, 80
HUMBERT, 95
HUMBLE, 56
HUMEL, 27
HUMMOND, 38
HUMPHRES, 21 52
HUMPHREY, 164
HUMPHREYS, 18 22 27 39 42 47 49-50 52 54-55 136
HUMPHRIES, 31 52 95 133 169
HUMPHRIS, 87
HUN, 99
HUNBERT, 97
HUNT, 3 12-13 15 17-18 23 27 31 33 37-38 40 46 48 82 85 90 93-94 100-103 112-113 135 137 143 148-149 151 155 166 169 171 174 183-187 194
HUNTER, 2 6 13 20 22 27 31 36 44 76 86 116 118 158 170 175-176 185 194-195
HURIAN, 27
HURLEY, 72 101
HURLY, 103-104
HURST, 96 158
HURT, 174
HURVEY, 27
HUSKY, 158
HUSSEY, 108-110
HUSSONG, 122
HUSTON, 11 27
HUTCHENS, 93
HUTCHENSON, 103
HUTCHERSON, 90 98 182

HUTCHERSON (cont) 189
HUTCHESON, 139 189
HUTCHINS, 27 80
HUTCHISON, 21 106 141 202
HUTSELL, 154
HUTSKINS, 13
HUTSON, 2 40 76 103 108 186
HUTTEN, 139
HUTTON, 103 105 128 130 137 149 155
HYDER, 27
HYLES, 101
HYMES, 5
HYTE, 19
IDLETT, 165
IDWELL, 199
IGOR, 98
IMPSON, 167
INESTER(?), 158
ING, 92
INGERSOL, 27
INGLE, 8 27-28 37
INGLIS, 1
INGRAM, 78 98 112 130-131 138 152 196
INGRUM. 118
INMAN, 126 132
INNIS, 1
INSER, 13
INSOR, 28
IRBY, 170 191
IRELAND, 99 158
IRIAR, 112
IRICK, 144
IRLAND, 118
IRVIN, 14 28 47 111 158
IRVINE, 49
IRWIN, 14 22 28 32 39 45-46 52 90 107 116 151 154 168-169 171 179
ISACKS, 103
ISBELL, 82
ISENBARG, 28
ISENBARGER, 19
ISENBERG, 28
ISENBERGH, 26
ISENBURG, 46
ISER, 4
ISH, 129
ISLER, 28
ISOM, 109
IVEY, 100 142
IVINS, 151

IVY, 93 158 164
JACK, 74 88 115 120
JACKS, 28
JACKSON, 2-3 5 12 14 16
  18-20 24 28 30 32 44
  76-78 80 82-83 86-87
  89 91 94 100-102 105-
  106 109 114 116 125
  133 135 143 167-168
  174 176 180-181 183
  185 191-192 196 198
  200 205
JACOB, 182
JACOBS, 18 82 91 123 142
  167 175 181
JADWIN, 165
JAMES, 28 75 80 87 91 96
  104 110-113 116 118
  121-122 135 142 158
  165
JANES, 124 126
JAQUES, 28
JARIMAN, 183
JARMAN, 196
JARRET, 96
JARRETT, 49
JASPER, 100
JAY, 102
JEANS, 101
JEDWIN, 171
JEFFERS, 85
JEFFREY, 103
JEFFREYS, 85
JEFFRIES, 124 134
JENKINS, 15 27-28 40 44
  89 96 102 116 128 146
  154 158
JENNINGS, 28 103-104
  166 168-169 171-172
  175-176 178 190 196
JENTRY, 112
JEST, 102
JESTER, 12
JEWELL, 170
JILES, 23
JIMESON, 95 119
JINKENS, 140
JINKINS, 188
JINNINGS, 195
JOB, 14 23 32 52
JOBB, 16 25 28 52
JOBE, 7 17-18 21 28
JOHN, 56
JOHNS, 189
JOHNSON, 28-29 56 80-81
  88 94 99 101-102 111

JOHNSON (cont)
  123 127 135 143 154
  158 163 165-166 168-
  170 172-173 177-181
  183-184 187-189 192-
  195 197
JOHNSTON, 20 29 42 54
  75 80-81 91 93-94 96
  98 104-105 108-110
  113-115 118 122 125-
  126 128 130-131 139
  146-147
JOINER, 101 173 187 190
JOLLY, 187-188
JONES, 1 6 12 16 20 28-29
  33 40 44 50 53 71-73
  75 77-79 81 85-88 91
  93 95 97-104 106 108
  110 112-113 116 118
  120 126 128 130-131
  133-134 137 139-140
  142 144 148 150-153
  155 158 167 172-173
  175-176 178-180 182-
  183 187-189 194-195
  197
JONSLAN, 196
JONSTON, 1 95
JOPLIN, 178 188 197
JORDAN, 41 82 92-93
JORDEN, 99-101
JORDIAN, 79 93
JORDON, 50 111 121
JOSLIN, 79-80 91
JOURDEN, 84
JOURNEY, 109
JOUSTER, 111
JOYNEL, 194
JOYNER, 179 188
JULIAN, 126 134 140
JULIEN, 2
JUSTICE, 29 107
JUSTIN, 190
KAGLE, 29 40 122 150
  158
KANARD, 140
KANNON, 29
KARNES, 158
KAVANAUGH, 102
KAYHILL, 29
KAYTON, 123
KEAMY, 134
KEAN, 29
KEANE, 8
KEATH, 29 90 193
KEATHLEY, 92 94

KEATHLY, 91
KEBLER, 3 29
KEE, 138 140
KEEBLE, 126 128 137 140
  149 153
KEEBLER, 29
KEEL, 29
KEELE, 29
KEELER, 158
KEELING, 151 166
KEEN, 29 41
KEENAN, 55
KEENE, 19 29 46
KEENER, 5 29 158
KEER, 17
KEES, 29
KEESEE, 104
KEESLER, 29
KEETON, 104 182 191 193
KEIN, 17
KEITH, 1 89 102-103 145
KEIZER, 29
KELBY, 29
KELING, 95
KELL, 75
KELLER, 119 122-123 128
  134 137 142
KELLEY, 26 29 36 43 50
  81 96
KELLOR, 24
KELLOW, 29
KELLY, 12 30 32 36 38 79
  100-101 103 107 110
  116 158 166 181 187
  195
KELM, 158
KELSELY, 30
KELSEY, 30
KELSO, 117 200
KELSOE, 109
KELSON, 158
KELSY, 40
KELTNER, 129 138
KEMP, 171 179 200
KENADAY, 89
KENADY, 30 82
KENATHIN, 158
KENDRICK, 109 111
KENEDAY, 102
KENEDY, 102 128 186
KENESTER, 158
KENLEY, 101
KENLY, 104
KENNADY, 135
KENNAMAN, 138
KENNEDAY, 85

KENNEDY, 2 23 30 34 39 50 52 73-74 115 117 123 125-126 142 196
KENNELLY, 55
KENNER, 30 96
KENNERLY, 102
KENNEY, 30 125 135 137
KENNICK, 30
KENNIMAN, 121
KENSALL, 2
KENT, 170
KEPLINGER, 24 30 47
KEPPLE, 48
KERBEY, 98 111
KERL, 30
KERO, 158
KERR, 96 103 122 132 140 142-146 149-150 152-153 158 164
KERRICK, 141
KERSELAS, 25
KERSEWN, 20
KETCHENS, 107
KEVIT, 86
KEY, 113-114 127 130 132 139-141 151
KEYFAUVER, 15
KEYKENDALL, 100 102
KEYS, 28 30 52 141
KEYWOOD, 111
KHUN, 42
KIBLER, 24 30 48
KIDD, 128 141 146 148 151
KIFER, 158
KIKER, 2 10 15 30 47
KILBOURN, 126
KILBOURNE, 117
KILBURN, 128 153
KILE, 117
KILGORE, 72 102
KILLINGSWORTH, 96
KILPATRICK, 97 126
KIMBERL, 114
KIMBRO, 88 170
KIMBROUGH, 101
KIMMERY, 30 37
KINCADE, 188
KINCAID, 99
KINCANNON, 95 98
KINCANON, 98
KINCHALOE, 22
KINCHELOE, 9 15 23 27 30 54
KINCHELS, 22 30
KINDEL, 30 34

KINDRED, 191
KINDRICK, 112
KINESTER, 97
KING, 11 17-18 25 30 74-75 77-78 80-81 85 87 95 100-101 103-104 106 108 111 119 128 130 133 137 141 144-145 154 158 161-162 166 173 178 186 196
KINGING, 95
KINLEY, 78
KINNAMAN, 130 146
KINNEDY, 36
KINNEMAN, 148 152
KIPLINGER, 51
KIRBY, 56 111 126 128-129
KIRK, 30 33
KIRKENDOLL, 200
KIRKPATERICK, 133
KIRKPATRIC, 95
KIRKPATRICK, 123 139 142 146 151 173 179 185-186 188 194
KIRKSEY, 79-80 87
KIRSEY, 77
KIRTIS, 150
KISER, 140
KITCHEN, 135 200
KITE, 164
KITHCART, 118
KITSMILLER, 30
KITZMILLER, 16 26
KIZER, 150 155
KLOUSE, 30 50
KNIGHT, 30 84 126 154 158 167 171 181 185 188 191
KNOBLETE, 121
KNOTTS, 176
KNOX, 80 93 97 127
KONKEN, 30
KOON, 29
KOONCE, 184
KOONTZ, 31 35
KORTZ, 31
KOUNSE, 146
KOZIAH, 45
KRANE, 27
KROUS, 31
KROUSE, 26
KRUTZER, 28
KUMRAY, 12
KUNS, 148
KURTS, 47

KUYKENDALL, 71-72 202
KYKER, 31 51
KYLE, 110
KYSER, 31
LACETER, 168
LACEY, 81
LACKENS, 22
LACKEY, 31 106 108 111
LACKING, 193
LACKY, 19 22 33 104 189
LACT, 165
LACY, 31 38 50 87 164
LAGAN, 108
LAIN, 31 41 95 98 128 139
LAINE, 168
LAKE, 108 200
LAMAR, 71
LAMB, 2
LAMBERT, 96 107 113 120 129 145 147 151 169 177-178 180 185
LAMBERTH, 170
LAMBURT, 170
LAMBURTH, 101
LAMBUT, 181
LAMBUTH, 170
LAMMON, 24
LAMMONS, 74
LAMON, 29 31
LAMONS, 76
LAMPKIN, 94
LAND, 171 190
LANDERS, 92
LANDIN, 89-90
LANDON, 25 31
LANDRAN, 78
LANE, 1 31 54 86 95 97 101 113 120-121 123 126 132 134 144 150 175 182 189 192 196 203-204
LANEY, 132
LANG, 1
LANGFORD, 130 136
LANGHAM, 103
LANGLEY, 56 74
LANGLY, 100
LANGSTON, 98 155 158 175
LANGSTONE, 176
LANING, 158
LANKFORD, 74 165 184 200
LANNS, 192
LANSDEN, 94 174

LANSDON, 94
LANSDOWN, 4
LANTIN, 172
LARGE, 158
LARKINS, 99
LARRESON, 96
LARTZ, 44
LASATER, 104 171 173 196
LASHBROOKS, 31
LASITER, 181
LASLY, 28
LASSITER, 87 183-184 187 189
LATHAIN, 92
LATHAM, 137 141
LATHER, 31
LATIMER, 203-204
LATIMORE, 2 138 202
LATTA, 86
LATTIE, 74 84
LATTY, 93
LAUDERDALE, 203-204
LAUDERMILK, 13 31 35
LAUGHTER, 86
LAURENCE, 2
LAUTERMILT, 47
LAVEDY, 158
LAW, 31 100 112 120 123 146 148 151 171 195
LAWNESS, 188
LAWPASER, 130
LAWRENCE, 2 31 113 118 168 172-174 184
LAWSON, 31 95 97 120 158
LAY, 96 98
LAYMAN, 13 31 158
LAYMON, 86
LAYNE, 128
LEA, 98 103 126 144 151-152 158
LEAB, 38
LEACH, 3 31 100 102
LEADBETTER, 116
LEAGUE, 155
LEAKES, 43
LEAMAN, 52
LEAMONS, 78
LEATHERDALE, 107
LEAVY, 2
LEBOW, 131 139
LEDBETTER, 56 94 101
LEE, 1 31 56 94 104 117 125-126 128 140 186 196

LEECH, 167
LEEKE, 191
LEEMAN, 182
LEEPER, 138 149
LEETH, 187
LEETON, 80
LEGAT, 87
LEGATE, 80
LEGERWOOD, 158
LEGG, 95 105 142
LEGGATTE, 88
LEINBACK, 134
LEITH, 180
LEKINS, 18
LEMANA, 72
LEMANS, 25 94
LEMASTER, 55
LEMINGHAM, 126
LEMMON, 31
LEMMONS, 79
LEMON, 47
LEMONS, 114
LENNEAR, 200
LENTZ, 55
LEONARD, 13 20 31 78 166
LEORD, 99
LERMON, 198
LESLIE, 16 31
LESSENBERG, 31
LESSENBERY, 14
LESTER, 185 196
LETSINGER, 15
LETT, 99
LEVEL, 95
LEVENTER, 141
LEVERTER, 141
LEVERWILL, 158
LEVY, 84-85
LEWELLING, 158
LEWILLING, 158
LEWIS, 1 31 55 74 76 78 95 104 128 134 158 169 171 173 178 191
LIGGON, 176-177 189
LIGHT, 31
LIGON, 168 186
LIKENS, 107
LIKING, 45
LILARD, 97
LILBURN, 16 31 37
LILE, 77
LILIARD, 97
LILLY, 156
LINCH, 1 187 190
LINCOLN, 164

LINDER, 31 97
LINDLY, 158
LINDSEY, 71 166
LINDSY, 158
LINEBARGER, 32
LINEBAUGH, 32
LINEBERGER, 7 18
LINES, 162
LINGER, 32
LINGUMPHELTER, 119
LINK, 180
LINLEY, 102
LINN, 32
LINVILLE, 11
LINZEY, 55
LIPSAY, 200
LISENBERG, 32
LISENBY, 32 39 51
LITE, 90
LITLE, 7
LITTLE, 7 30 32 46 52 75 82-83 86 103 123 171 Phebe 8
LITTLEFIELD, 75 85 89
LITTLEPAGE, 100
LIVINGLAY, 185
LIVINGSTON, 1
LLOYD, 185
LOASH, 195
LOCKARD, 56
LOCKE, 170
LOCKMILLER, 165
LOFTIS, 123
LOFTISS, 114
LOGAN, 39 103 108 114 122 125 127 136 138-139 142 146-148 151 154 170 172
LOGUE, 167
LOHEA, 55
LOMAX, 167
LONDON, 166
LONEY, 101
LONG, 27 32-33 44 91 96 98 100-101 110 115 133 144 150 153-154 158 192
LONGBOTTOM, 132
LONGLEY, 96
LONGMIRE, 10 24 32
LOONEY, 1 32 41 71-72 94 202
LOONY, 2
LOPWASSER, 32
LORENCE, 144
LOSON, 95

LOTT, 4
LOURENCE, 88
LOVE, 32 73 80 82 92 103 115 118 126 143 158 161
LOVEDY, 158
LOVEGROVE, 32
LOVEL, 106
LOVELACE, 32 106
LOVELADY, 158
LOVEWELL, 72
LOW, 120 122 124 141 148-150 153 158
LOWARY, 89
LOWDY, 32
LOWE, 104 119 198
LOWERY, 74 106 119 124 130 185
LOWRANCE, 44
LOWREY, 32
LOWRY, 43 82-83 92 98 123
LOYD, 32 100 132 186
LUCAS, 32
LUCH, 168
LUCKET, 130 147
LUCKETT, 119
LUDERDEAL, 98
LUDON, 32
LUMPKIN, 186-187
LUMPKINS, 192 194
LUNCE, 195
LUNSFORD, 32
LUNTSFORD, 32
LUSK, 1 34 55 97-98 102 158
LUSSER, 19
LUSTER, 32 80 145
LUTE, 144
LYLE, 32
LYNCH, 17 84 172
LYNN, 72
LYON, 32 55 77 79 142 193 195 203
LYONS, 10 18 32 108
LYRE, 135
LYSENBY, 32
LYTAKER, 73 83
LYTLE, 55
LYTTLETON, 101
M'CLUSKY, 55
M'DONNALD, 94
M'KY, 94
M'LEAN, 55
M'MILLAN, 94
MABIES, 178

MACAFEE, 138
MACANELLY, 28 32
MACKEN, 3
MACKEY, 123 130 141
MACKLEROY, 83
MACKLIN, 151
MACLESTER, 97
MACLIN, 122 141
MACNATT, 165
MACY, 200
MADDEN, 112 122
MADDOCKS, 188
MADDOX, 168 173
MADLOCK, 13 172
MAGEE, 47
MAGNESS, 169
MAHALAND, 171
MAHAN, 1
MAHOLLAND, 166 182
MAHON, 76
MAHONEY, 32
MAHONN, 98
MAIDEN, 11 29
MAINARD, 88
MAINOR, 84-85
MAINS, 8 15 33
MAIZE, 144
MAJOR, 111 189 197
MAJORS, 104-105 107-108 110 116
MALCAM, 130
MALCOM, 116 151
MALCOMB, 158
MALCUM, 141
MALLAN, 195
MALLONE, 21 33
MALLONEE, 8 33
MALON, 33
MALONE, 74 85
MANCOOSKY, 142
MANDINSSALL, 97
MANES, 158
MANESS, 98
MANESSE, 98
MANEY, 203
MANGRUM, 158
MANING, 158 197
MANIS, 158
MANN, 33 101 158 168 170 194
MANNING, 166 195
MANSCO, 202
MANSFIELD, 33 183 190
MANSKER, 71 202
MANSON, 113 117
MANUEL, 109

MANY, 158
MAPLES, 158
MARCH, 33
MARCHBANKS, 78
MARE, 17
MARES, 33
MARICLE, 195
MARK, 26
MARKS, 47
MARKWOOD, 33
MARLER, 170
MARLOW, 165 170 172 177 182
MARON, 98
MARONE, 126
MAROON, 119 128
MARR, 11 33
MARSH, 33
MARSHAL, 99-100
MARSHALL, 33 158 172 174 179
MARSHILL, 40
MARSHL, 10
MARTAIN, 33
MARTAN, 33
MARTEN, 51 96
MARTIN, 1-2 5 10-13 16 21 26-27 30 32-34 51 53 55 72 75 85 90 94 103 105 112 115-116 118-120 127 136-137 141-142 147 149-150 153 158 171 178-179 184 188 190-191 193
MARTON, 169
MASANNIS, 31
MASENGALE, 26
MASH, 43 113
MASHBURN, 44
MASINGILL, 33
MASON, 33 38 74 79 113 158 186 192
MASSEE, 88 93
MASSENGAIL, 20 33
MASSENGALE, 30 39 55
MASSEY, 79 91 180 182 184-185 195
MASSINGALE, 33
MASSY, 33 133
MASTERS, 100
MASTIN, 202
MASTISA, 81
MATHAY, 181
MATHES, 6 26 33 41 108 149
MATHEWS, 34 46 72 74

MATHEWS (cont)
92-93 116 136 153 193
MATHIS, 77 83 85 87 101
MATHUS, 107
MATKOCKS, 106
MATLOCK, 33 51
MATSON, 150
MATTHES, 33
MATTHEW, 156 158
MATTHEWS, 33-34 41 84 90 139 150 158
MATTOCKS, 158
MAUK, 6 33-34
MAUKE, 10
MAUPIN, 145 148
MAUS, 97
MAXEY, 72 172
MAXLEY, 85
MAXWELL, 3 34 54 72-74 106 110 112 114 122-123 128 136 140 143 145 148 154 178 193-195
MAY, 30 34 37 41 81 96 101 103-104 109 117 128 133 137 175
MAYBERRY, 99 101
MAYFIELD, 34 39 80 85 90 92 97-98 102 204
MAYHO, 107
MAYO, 72 117 119 125 187
MAYS, 77 84 131 168-169 181 191 195
MAZE, 135-136 139 149-150
MCADAM, 18
MCADAMS, 18 21 23 34 54
MCADOW, 166 170
MCAFEE, 27 148
MCAFFRY, 117 174
MCALELLY, 81
MCALISTER, 24 34 39 103-104
MCALLAN, 112
MCALLELLY, 81
MCALLEN, 166 182
MCALPIN, 166 182
MCALROY, 116-117
MCANAHAN, 158
MCANALLY, 99
MCAVERY, 85
MCBEE, 101-102
MCBRIAN, 158
MCBRIANT, 130 150

MCBRIDE, 1 27 76-77 95 100-101
MCBRIENT, 148
MCBROOM, 24 34 101
MCBRYAN, 158
MCBRYANT, 129
MCCABE, 112
MCCADELL, 48
MCCAIN, 106
MCCALE, 128
MCCALESTER, 97
MCCALL, 7 26 34 45 138
MCCALLIE, 115 120 123-124 140 143 146 148
MCCALLON, 118 127
MCCALLY, 118 158
MCCALVY, 90
MCCAMERON, 107
MCCAMISH, 34 95
MCCAMMON, 106 132
MCCAMPBELL, 118-119 129
MCCAMY, 103 112
MCCANDLAS, 109
MCCARDELL, 34
MCCARDLE, 34 45
MCCARIEN, 105
MCCARRELL, 103
MCCARROLL, 34 129
MCCARTER, 105
MCCARTNEY, 113 117-118 167
MCCARTY, 34 95-96 158
MCCASELIN, 96
MCCASLAND, 126
MCCASLIN, 84-85 116
MCCAUGHAN, 110
MCCAULY, 144
MCCAY, 112
MCCERG, 141
MCCHANDLER, 158
MCCHESNEY, 109 117 129
MCCLAIN, 29 117 120 124 133 143 147 181
MCCLANAHAN, 109
MCCLANE, 96
MCCLANEHAN, 143
MCCLANNAHAN, 105 118
MCCLARY, 74 76 85 91 158
MCCLAY, 72
MCCLEARY, 30
MCCLEHERRIN, 104
MCCLELLAN, 34

MCCLELLAND, 56
MCCLELLEN, 103
MCCLENDON, 101
MCCLEUR, 88
MCCLORG, 136
MCCLOUD, 11 28 83 99
MCCLOUR, 81
MCCLUNG, 115 120 123-124 133 135-136 138 200
MCCLURE, 13 34 37 76 88 106 113 117 120 124 129-131 143-144 147 150
MCCLURG, 122 136 141
MCCLURKIN, 122
MCCLUSKEY, 103
MCCLUSKY, 103-104
MCCOLAM, 23
MCCOLESTER, 97
MCCOLIP, 29
MCCOLISER, 97
MCCOLLAM, 48
MCCOLLIN, 181
MCCOLLOCH, 105 108 111
MCCOLLOM, 109 115 135 145
MCCOLLUM, 32
MCCOLM, 13
MCCOMB, 109
MCCONALD, 107
MCCONEL, 142
MCCONNAL, 105
MCCONNEL, 33-34 113 151
MCCONNELL, 108 122 128 130 137-138 140 145 152 155
MCCOOL, 116 126 129 145
MCCORD, 27 34 43 99 103 109 112
MCCORDLE, 34 48
MCCORKEL, 34
MCCORKLE, 51 77 176 191
MCCORMACK, 78 101
MCCORMICK, 102
MCCORTNEY, 81
MCCOWEN, 167 191
MCCOWN, 104 158
MCCOY, 34 41 43 52 95 141 165 167
MCCRACKEN, 3 30 34-35 54

MCCRACKIN, 46 95
MCCRARY, 190-191
MCCRASKEY, 35
MCCRAY, 6 9-10 16 27 35 48 50
MCCREA, 35
MCCREY, 50
MCCRORY, 2
MCCROSKEY, 115 121 145
MCCROSKY, 35 158
MCCROY, 125 134 147
MCCULLEY, 98
MCCULLOCH, 112 127-129 145 147
MCCULLOCK, 77 100 108 116
MCCULLOUGH, 135
MCCULLUCK, 100
MCCULLY, 35 114 126 129-130 134 153
MCCUNY, 161-162
MCCURDY, 118 121 123
MCCURREY, 35
MCDANIEL, 24 40 77 99 104 123 149 155 158 169-170 173 184 186 197
MCDEAMON, 194
MCDERMENT, 170 173
MCDERMET, 86
MCDERMITT, 80
MCDONALD, 1 35 47 161-163 174 185 197
MCDONNELL, 179
MCDONNOLD, 94
MCDONOLD, 116
MCDORNART, 194
MCDOUGALD, 83-84
MCDOUGLE, 75
MCDOUGOLD, 93
MCDOWELL, 87 106-107
MCDUMMET, 86
MCEFEE, 4 15
MCELDRY, 123
MCELROY, 100 180
MCELWRATH, 202
MCELYEA, 165 171-172
MCEWEN, 35 75 86
MCFADDIN, 121
MCFALL, 35 91 96
MCFARLAND, 41 83 91 115 155 167 169 175 183
MCFEARSON, 95
MCFEE, 135-136 141 150

MCGARETT, 86
MCGARRITY, 85
MCGAUGHEY, 106
MCGAUGHO, 98
MCGAUGHY, 105 158
MCGAUHY, 114 117
MCGEE, 35 45 55 74 104 119 179
MCGEEHAN, 13
MCGEHEE, 85 177
MCGEMPSY, 53
MCGHEE, 11 16 35 51 53 98 118 123 126 128 130 132 143 149 154
MCGHILL, 151
MCGILL, 120 123 141 143 146
MCGINLEY, 121 123 136-137 151
MCGINNIS, 34-35
MCGINTY, 35 49
MCGLOTHLIN, 204
MCGLOUGHLIN, 35
MCGOWAN, 100
MCGOWN, 100
MCGREER, 19
MCGREW, 135
MCGRIF, 180
MCGUFFY, 101
MCGUIRE, 28 105 120 200
MCGUISE, 15
MCHAFFY, 153
MCHANEY, 170
MCHENRY, 115 196
MCHERN, 102
MCHESS, 158
MCHEW, 158
MCILHERON, 142
MCINTIRE, 26 35
MCINTOSH, 35 73
MCINTURFF, 35
MCIVER, 74
MCJIMSEY, 35
MCJUNKIN, 98
MCJUNKLIN, 98
MCKAIN, 102 203
MCKAMY, 119 122 126 128 134 146
MCKASKEL, 140
MCKASKELE, 142
MCKASKLE, 137
MCKAY, 35
MCKEE, 89 108 194
MCKEEHAN, 35
MCKEEHIN, 35

MCKEEL, 95
MCKEEN, 71-72 202
MCKEIGG, 112
MCKELWRATH, 72
MCKENDRICK, 74
MCKENRY, 116
MCKENSIE, 2
MCKENZEY, 106
MCKEOWN, 81
MCKEZICK, 87
MCKIHEN, 54
MCKINAN, 158
MCKINLEY, 150
MCKINLY, 150 158
MCKINNEY, 83 106 186
MCKINSEY, 158
MCKINZIE, 122
MCKIRBY, 77
MCKISICK, 158
MCKNEELY, 86-87
MCKNIGHT, 79 82 87 90 173 180-181 185 192
MCKRAKEN, 35
MCLAIN, 149
MCLANAHAN, 118
MCLARITON, 102
MCLARY, 82 84
MCLAUGHLIN, 102
MCLEARY, 73
MCLELLAN, 1
MCLEMORE, 73
MCLEOD, 93
MCLEROY, 192
MCLIEN, 49
MCLIN, 12 33 35 143
MCMACKEN, 22 35
MCMACKIN, 35-36
MCMAHAN, 81 144 147-148 158-159
MCMAHON, 74 88 90
MCMELLOON, 143
MCMENAS, 139
MCMENNAWAY, 169
MCMENUS, 141
MCMILAN, 163
MCMILLIN, 76 117 170
MCMILLION, 96
MCMILLON, 94
MCMINN, 83 95-96 101-102 183
MCMISTION, 100
MCMULLEN, 73
MCMULLIN, 80
MCMURRAY, 121 131 155 191
MCMURRY, 107 115-116

MCMURRY (cont) 128 130 133 159 193 204
MCNAB, 109
MCNABB, 5 36 48 97-98 118 131 151
MCNALLY, 120
MCNEAL, 15 34 36
MCNEALE, 34
MCNEAR, 97
MCNEELEY, 72 113 166
MCNEELY, 145 168 171 173
MCNEES, 36
MCNEILY, 112
MCNIGHT, 171
MCNUT, 36
MCNUTT, 20 98 105 109 115 129 145 152
MCNUTTY, 92
MCPEAK, 169
MCPHERSON, 36 101
MCQUAGE, 129
MCQUAGUS, 132
MCQUEEN, 105
MCRANALDS, 113 142
MCRANDALS, 120
MCRANDLS, 107
MCREYNOLDS, 123 139 145-146 149 152-153
MCROBERTS, 36 141
MCROY, 154
MCRUNNALS, 95
MCSPADDEN, 168 176
MCSPADEN, 96 173
MCSPADON, 96
MCSTUART, 36
MCTEER, 105-106 110 116 120 123 138 145 147 150-151
MCWHERTER, 87 181
MCWHINNEY, 112 114
MCWHIRTER, 168 172-173 177 180 187-188
MCWHORTER, 36 45 77-78 85 102-103 169
MCWILLIAMS, 144 146
MEAGLE, 179
MEAK, 196
MEAKS, 186
MEALLEY, 195
MEANS, 94 137 155
MEARS, 12
MEDEORIS, 82
MEDLIN, 172 177 185
MEDLING, 181 197

MEDLOCK, 5 21 24 36 43 51 119 150-151 169
MEDNIS, 116
MEE, 96
MEEK, 155
MEEKS, 100 110
MEGINNIS, 36
MEHUR, 159
MELELELAN, 159
MELONE, 122
MELONEY, 100
MELSON, 155
MELTER, 97
MELTON, 89 130 141 167 175 193
MELVIN, 7 11 17 23 36 42 45 49
MENIFOLD, 139
MENIS, 130
MERCER, 13 36
MERIDITH, 167
MERONE, 141
MERRETT, 97 132
MERRIET, 134
MERRIMAN, 200
MERRIT, 159
MERRITT, 93 174 185 194
MESLVANY, 159
MESSEMORE, 54
MESSER, 22 36 39 51
METCALF, 38 101-102
MEURHEAD, 84
MIARS, 46
MICHAELS, 197
MICKLE, 110 166
MIDGET, 177
MIDLETON, 162
MILBURN, 4 12 17 19 36 72
MILES, 111 174 185
MILHORN, 36
MILLAR, 17 36
MILLEGAN, 192
MILLER, 1 8-13 16 24-27 36-40 43 45-49 54 73-74 77 80 84 91 94 96 99 104-105 108-109 113 122 125 134 137 144 152 155-156 159 164 174 176 180 184-185 190 193 197 204
MILLIGAN, 121
MILLION, 9 34 37 54
MILLS, 96 105 143 159 179
MILLSAPS, 56

MILSAP, 56
MILSAPPS, 129
MILSAPS, 132 143-144
MILTON, 121 194
MINIS, 115 133 136
MINNIS, 112 152
MIRACK, 82
MIRES, 152
MISER, 37 126-127 144 153
MISKELLY, 55
MISSINGER, 37
MITCHEL, 5 37 73 109 170 180
MITCHELL, 3-4 8-10 20-22 35-37 39-40 44 48 53 75 77 79 81 84-85 98-99 119-120 134 145 159 169 173-174 177 180 185-187 192 195 197 200
MITCHENER, 185
MITTS, 76-77
MIXON, 74 85
MIZER, 150 153
MNING, 158
MOBEY, 191
MOBLEY, 73
MOBLY, 73
MOCK, 37 159
MODGLIN, 173-174
MOFFET, 7
MOFFETT, 107
MOFFITT, 118
MOHON, 95
MOLER, 28 43
MONAN, 77
MONDINE, 192
MONTEETH, 37
MONTGAUE, 159
MONTGOMERY, 2 14 71 76 87 90-91 102-104 106-111 115-116 120 122 124-126 129 131-132 134 141 143 147 159
MOODY, 74 97
MOON, 2 37 159 195
MOOR, 51 98 103 106
MOORE, 1-2 4-5 15 24 35 37-38 45-46 72 75 78-79 81 84 86-87 89 94 99-100 103-105 110 114 122 126 128-129 132-133 135 137 141 143 151-152 159 164

MOORE (cont)
169-170 172 174-175
177 179 184-185 194
196-198
MOOREFIELD, 116
MOORELOCK, 143
MOPIN, 159
MORE, 35 107 110 153
MORELOCK, 149
MORGAN, 1 11 13 30 36-
38 51 72 74 76 83 85
100 103 138 159 181
188 200 202
MORIS, 24
MORISON, 53
MORPHUS, 93
MORPING, 159
MORRES, 143
MORRICE, 128
MORRIS, 2 17 38 56 76-77
89 91 100-102 104 125
127 138 159 166 182
193 196
MORRISON, 34 38 44 72
100 104 107 120 165
167 200 203
MORRISS, 174 184
MORROW, 102
MORRSON, 102
MORSE, 125
MORTEN, 96
MORTON, 84 92 103 122
130 137 147 179
MOSELEY, 189 191
MOSELY, 85 186 188
MOSER, 127 174 192
MOSES, 118
MOSHER, 127
MOSIER, 127 195
MOSLEY, 177 195
MOSS, 38 72-73 75 88-89
101-102 169 175 185-
186 190 192
MOSSES, 116
MOTHERAL, 182
MOTHERALL, 204
MOTISE, 97
MOUNT, 96 185 188
MOUNTCASTEL, 96
MOWDY, 38 52
MOWL, 19
MOXLEY, 192
MUIRHEAD, 78
MUIRHEID, 78
MULISON, 180
MULKEY, 38 42

MULKY, 4
MULL, 200
MULLEN, 14
MULLENDOVE, 159
MULLIN, 102
MULLINAUX, 53
MULLINDORE, 159
MULLINOX, 38
MULLINS, 38
MULVANIS, 150
MURAY, 97
MURCHEAN, 83
MUREY, 50
MURPHEY, 76
MURPHREY, 88
MURPHY, 75 77 84 91 107
115 128-129 132 140-
141 145 159
MURR, 32 38
MURRAY, 12 28 38-39 47
50 115 129 139 164
MURREL, 96
MURREN, 124 139
MURREY, 97
MURRILL, 39
MURRIN, 154
MURRY, 5 8-9 17 19 25 34
39 43 53 132 150 180-
181 195-196
MUSE, 104
MUYRHEAD, 92
MYDYETT, 81
MYERS, 35 39 41 51 134
154 187
MYGIAR, 25
MYRES, 191
MYRICK, 83 166
NABOURS, 102
NAFF, 39
NANCE, 120
NARRAMORE, 2
NASBIT, 39
NASH, 39 137-138
NATIONS, 159
NAVE, 39 109 164
NAZWORTHY, 100
NEAL, 39 104 120 143 146
179 197
NEDING, 76
NEDRY, 87
NEEDHAM, 53 76 78
NEEDY, 13
NEEL, 125 132 170-171
NEELEY, 72 202
NEIL, 114 172 174 187
NEILSON, 55 83 86

NEILY, 108
NEIMAN, 151
NEIMON, 134
NELLUMS, 104
NELMS, 101 104
NELSON, 2 4 8 10 12 15-
16 25 28-30 33 35-36
38-40 42 46 48-49 52
54 75 97 102-103 148
154 168 196
NEMON, 120
NETHERLY, 20
NETHERTON, 106
NETTLES, 83 180 189
NEVILL, 100 162
NEVILS, 86
NEW, 174 198
NEWBERRY, 41 139 154
NEWBY, 165 190
NEWELL, 89
NEWHOUSE, 84
NEWLAND, 40
NEWMAN, 40-41 50 112
154 159
NEWPORT, 1
NEYMAN, 136 139 142
NIAMAN, 110
NICHALSON, 150
NICHOLAS, 40
NICHOLASSON, 87
NICHOLS, 27 40 95 102
137-138 140 159 183
NICHOLSON, 55 104 117
143 171 183-184
NICKELS, 105
NICKINGS, 183 192
NICKS, 166 168
NIGHT, 128 190 195
NINE, 40
NIPPER, 135
NIXON, 165
NOAH, 101
NOBLE, 132 139
NOBLES, 78-80 84 87
NOBLET, 128 136 142
NOBLETT, 100
NOBLS, 85
NOEL, 140
NOLAND, 42
NOLE, 36
NOLEN, 141
NORMAN, 96 100 178 201
NORRINGTON, 13
NORRIS, 10 40 50 53 71-
72 187 202
NORSE, 145

NORTH, 29
NORTHCOTT. 74
NORTHCUT, 76 100
NORTHCUTT, 82 90
NORTHERN, 90
NORTHINGTON, 13 38 40
NORTON, 6 104 127 137-138 159
NORWOOD, 103 117 125 136
NOWALAND, 46
NOWLAN, 40
NOWLIN, 55
NUCHOLS, 154
NUCKLES, 92
NYE, 203
O'CONNEL, 159
O'KELLY, 95
O'NEAL, 7 93
OAKES, 80
OBRIANT, 150
OCONNER, 121
OCONNOR, 121
ODDLE, 40
ODEAR, 151
ODELL, 17 40 78
ODEN, 29 40
ODLE, 19 28-29 40 90
ODNEAL, 40
ODOM, 187
ODONNELL, 19
ODUM, 40 172
ODWIN, 21 40
OER, 112
OFFICER, 98
OGEL, 96
OGLE, 96 150 152 159
OGLESBY, 76 78 80
OLDFIELD, 104
OLDHAM, 55 104
OLER, 40
OLIVER, 31 35 40 49-50 101 123 154 190 201
OLSABROOKS, 91
ONEAL, 91 150 169 174 182 201
ONEIL, 186
ONELE, 97
ONLEY, 96
ORGAN, 171 187 190 195
ORINDULPH, 40
ORMAN, 134 136
ORMAND, 122-123
ORMES, 75
ORMOND, 125 142
ORR, 40 96-97 124 131-

ORR (cont) 132
ORSBURN, 97
ORTON, 55
ORZBURN, 104
OSBROOKS, 192
OSMAS, 40
OSMENT, 172 183
OSTEEN, 56
OVERHOLER, 40
OVERHOLSER, 17 40 43 45 48 52
OVERHOLSTER, 52
OVERHOLT, 40 53
OVERHOLTS, 25
OVERHOTS, 35
OVERTON, 155 201
OWEN, 1 39-40 50 173-174 177 186-188
OWENS, 5 40 73 99 111 152 159 177 179
OWINS, 102
OWNSLY, 159
OZMENT, 174-175
PACELY, 139
PACK, 180
PADGETT, 127
PAGE, 12 14 37 45 74 88-89 92 99 118
PAIN, 5 40 52 143 203
PAINTER, 20 30 40-41 99
PAISLEY, 192
PALMER, 106 108 149-150 175 178-179 191 193
PALMORE, 55
PANBEAN, 159
PANKEY, 165
PANTER, 193
PANTHER, 110 120
PANTOR, 25
PARDUE, 32
PARISH, 77 104 168
PARKENS, 96
PARKER, 9 14 16 20-21 24 28 30 39 41 72-73 75 79 81 96 132-133 143 159 171-172 175 192 194
PARKES, 96 145
PARKESON, 50
PARKHILL, 107
PARKINS, 144
PARKMAN, 186
PARKS, 2 16 18 41 79 96 101 104 115 118 122

PARKS (cont) 137-138 143
PARMER, 159 202
PARSONS, 125 154 159 173
PARTEE, 90
PARTEN, 166
PARTIN, 132
PASTE, 22
PATE, 41 87 91 98 115 120 152 159 179
PATERSON, 159
PATISON, 91
PATRICK, 41 93 125 132 139 148 197
PATTEN, 33 41
PATTERICK, 144
PATTERSON, 8 41 49 75 78 80-81 87 89 92-93 97 99 111 113 141 155 159 165 177 179 182 184 189-191 193 196-197 203
PATTON, 7 13 17 21 27 35 41 54 72-73 77 99 102 113 166 175 190 197
PATTY, 112 117 155
PAUL, 77 112 115 124 131 144
PAYNE, 1 16-17 41 49 55 104 122 129 151 162-163 178-180
PAYTON, 71 202
PEA, 102
PEACE, 190
PEACOCK, 189
PEAK, 170
PEAKE, 97
PEAL, 72
PEARCE, 41 73 111 155
PEARCEFIELD, 7
PEARCY, 189
PEARSON, 128 159
PEARY, 88
PECK, 103
PECKS, 80
PEELE, 202
PEEPLES, 5
PEMBERTON, 170 175 179
PENDERGRAFT, 154
PENEEL, 165
PENHUM, 41
PENIEL, 186
PENN, 93
PENNEL, 118

PENNEY, 87
PENNY, 41 188
PENTECOST, 155 181
PEOPLES, 5 41 44 96
PERDUE, 100
PERIMAN, 182 191
PERKINS, 41 55 103 128-130 137 139 155 194
PERKONS, 41
PERRY, 2 73-74 98 103 145 167 175 202
PERRYMAN, 159
PERRYWOOD, 170
PERTIN, 159
PESTERFIELD, 130-132 148
PETERS, 1
PETERSON, 32 41 52 121
PETICOCK, 103
PETIS, 82
PETTET, 97
PETTUS, 84
PETTY, 100 159 174 186
PEW, 137
PEWIT, 41
PEYTON, 2 201
PHALING, 87
PHAREZ, 26
PHARIS, 159
PHARRIS, 97 159
PHELP, 173
PHELPS, 179
PHILIP, 14 122
PHILIPS, 41 85 92 125 186 195
PHILLIPS, 4-5 17 34 41 45 50-51 74 115 118 120 122 125 133 137 147 151 155 165 170 172 174-175 180 183 185-186 192
PHIPPS, 183 204
PHIPS, 99
PICKENS, 41 114 116 125 159
PICKERING, 150
PICKET, 102
PIERCE, 124 159
PIERCY, 18
PIGG, 133
PIKE, 102 184
PILLOW, 55
PIMBERTON, 182
PINEXO, 108
PINION, 91
PIPKINS, 74

PITCHFORD, 75
PITCOCK, 6 21 28 31 41-42 51
PITCOCKE, 42
PITMAN, 42 119 131
PITNER, 159 165 192 197
PITTS, 159
PIVELEY, 49
PLEMING, 145
PLUMBLEE, 125
PLUMER, 125
PLUMLEE, 138
PLUMMER, 122 134 136 159
POE, 104
POFFORD, 42
POGUE, 201
POINDEXTER, 153
POINTER, 42
POLAND, 42 118 144
POLLAND, 123
POLLARD, 73-75 80
POLLEN, 111
POORE, 27
POPE, 27 83 88 93-94 114
POPLAND, 134
POPLIN, 136
PORE, 42
PORTER, 20 42 54-55 80 89 92 105 108 111 122 126 129 152-153 159 165 175
PORTERFIELD, 167
PORTMAN, 1
POSEY, 95 115
POSSEY, 110
POTER, 95
POTTER, 148
POTTS, 97-98 180
POULSTON, 42
POUND, 88
POVIANCE, 166
POWEL, 32 179
POWELL, 100 118 196-198
POWERS, 165 170 180
PPOOL, 168
PRATER, 145 149
PRATHER, 42
PRATT, 39 42
PRECHET, 95
PRESCOTT, 56
PRESNELL, 42
PRESSER, 45
PRESTON, 175 201
PREVITT, 123

PREWITT, 85
PRICE, 21 26 40 42 50 53-54 91 93 96 98 100 104 118 123 145 152 159
PRICHARD, 35 190
PRICHERD, 104
PRIDE, 108 116
PRIDEY, 96
PRIDY, 79
PRIESTLY, 176 197
PRIM, 179-180
PRIMMER, 42
PRING, 19 42 45
PRINGE, 97
PRISTON, 159
PRISWOOD, 159
PRITCHARD, 3 143
PRITCHETT, 91
PRIVET, 148
PRIVIT, 136
PRIVITT, 131
PROCTOR, 99 173 178
PROFET, 42
PROFFIT, 22 42
PROPHET, 159
PROWEL, 96
PRUITT, 75-76
PUCKET, 181
PUCKETT, 80 176 178 188-189 192 195
PUE, 118 188
PUGH, 42 129 131 137 168 172 194 196
PULLEN, 72
PULLIN, 166
PURCELL, 42
PURCES, 4 14
PURDEN, 42
PURSELL, 24
PURSLEY, 178 187
PUTNAM, 77
QUALES, 94
QUALLS, 176
QUARLES, 176 193
QUARLS, 187
QUICK, 89
QUILLEN, 42
QUILLIN, 40
QUIMBY, 42
QUINLEY, 172 174
QUINN, 171
QUISENBURY, 99
RACKLEY, 80 93
RACKLY, 80
RADER, 159
RAGAN, 86 91 95 117 148

RAGAN (cont)
  150 154
RAGASDALE, 75
RAGEN, 38 97
RAGSDALE, 103 169 193
RAINES, 125
RAINEY, 173
RAINS, 42 55 76-79 81 96
  134 140 159 201
RAINWATER, 159
RAINWATERS, 159
RALSTON, 41-42 48
RAMBO, 153
RAMSEY, 53 72 82 98 125
  129 159 180 193
RAMSOWER, 123
RANDALES, 159
RANDALLS, 159
RANDLES, 159
RANDOLPH, 40 42 97 196
RANGE, 11 16 29 32 42-43
  54
RANKEN, 43
RANKIN, 43 77 80 109-
  110 113-114 120-121
  127-128 140 146 150
  152 204
RANKINS, 43 100
RANSBARGER, 119
RAPER, 117
RARIDEN, 201
RASBERRY, 86
RASSER, 114
RATHER, 167-168
RATLEY, 100
RATTERCE, 186
RAWLINGS, 2 104
RAY, 43 91 93 97 109-110
  120 129 165 173 175
  179 184 190
RAYNES, 129
REA, 145 194
REACE, 111
READ, 103 118 191
READER, 181
READING, 168
REAGAN, 105 115-116
  118 122 125 133 137
  143 147-148 159
REAL, 95
REALY, 170
REANNER, 49
REASON, 92
REASONER, 43
REAVE, 40
REAVES, 43 102-103

RECARD, 11
RECEMPECKER, 127
RECTOR, 26 43 51 54 94
REDDING, 182 188
REDFORD, 201
REDIGO, 191
REDINGS, 159
REDMAN, 43
REDMON, 120
REECE, 43 98 159
REED, 19 35 43 49 75 77
  79 88 90 92 97 100 106
  141 145-146 150 161
  163 178 181 187 194
  198 203
REEDER, 43 46 112 201
REEL, 98
REESE, 120 171 174 177
  185 188 191 197
REESER, 43
REEVES, 31 43 89 173 186
REGAN, 106 123
REGANS, 148
REGISTER, 21 24
REID, 100-101 112 125
REIFF, 165
REMERTON, 113
REMINGTON, 114
REMON, 189
RENCE, 159
RENFRO, 134 159
RENNELS, 129
RENNO, 24
RENNOR, 43
RENSBARGER, 155
RENSHAW, 185
RENTFRO, 89
RESER, 43
RESSER, 22
REW, 174
REYNOLD, 171
REYNOLDS, 1 81 117-118
  127 185 189 194
RHEA, 43 108 115-116
  119-120 127 130 133-
  134 137-138 140-141
  197 201
RHO, 72
RHODES, 30 55 110
RHOEDS, 102
RHULE, 201
RHYMES, 102
RHYNE, 122
RIAGAN, 159
RIAS, 187
RICARD, 21 43

RICE, 2 43 99 101-102 125
  127 131 136 141 159
  167 173 181 183-184
  191 193-194
RICH, 99 179
RICHARD, 4
RICHARDS, 43 103 127
  139 159 166 201
RICHARDSON, 43 73 77
  79 82-83 87 92-93 97
  106 118 159 177 181
  184 186 191
RICHERSON, 161-162
RICHEY, 43 99 108 143
  147
RICHMAN, 120
RICHMON, 78
RICHMOND, 179-180 185
RICKARD, 43
RICKER, 42
RICKET, 147
RICKETS, 175
RICKETTS, 171 179
RIDDEL, 98
RIDDLE, 8 12 32 38 43
  101 104 163 191
RIDER, 108 122
RIDG, 133 145
RIDGE, 105
RIDGEWAY, 77
RIDGWAY, 82 92
RIDINGS, 159
RIDLEY, 72 202
RIEFF, 167
RIFE, 185
RIGESLY, 43
RIGGIN, 159
RIGGINS, 102
RIGGS, 43
RIGSBY, 43 45 50 89
RIGSLY, 93
RIKERT, 43
RILEY, 43 103
RILY, 103
RINEARI, 159
RINEHART, 24
RINEHEART, 43
RINGAN, 159
RINGGOLD, 87
RINIER, 159
RIPLEY, 47
RIRD, 159
RITCHEY, 11 43
RITCHIE, 44
RIVES, 98
ROACH, 73-74 79 81 85-

ROACH (cont)
  86 88 95 113 119-120
  133-134 143 148-151
  155 171 173-175 189
  196
ROAD, 177
ROADS, 110
ROAN, 141 197
ROANE, 106 187 192 198
ROAREX, 143
ROARK, 101-102
ROBB, 80 92 171
ROBBINETT, 105
ROBBINS, 74 80 84 94
  152
ROBENETT, 120
ROBENETTE, 105 116
ROBENITT, 121 139
ROBERSON, 1-2 46 56
ROBERT, 99
ROBERTS, 1 25 44 47 52
  55 74 93 99-101 105-
  106 109 126-127 136
  159 202
ROBERTSON, 2 17 44 51
  75 83-85 89 92 96 99
  101 103 112 118 120
  124 127 129 131 159
  165 167 169-170 172-
  173 176 181 185 189
  191 195-197
ROBINS, 79 100
ROBINSON, 2 19 25 44
  103 111 118 134 181
  197
ROBISON, 7 44 142 201
RODDEY, 44
RODDY, 79 111-112 123
  130-133 136-137 153
  155
RODEY, 80
RODGERS, 7 14 44 90
RODINGS, 159
RODY, 79
ROGAN, 17 44 72
ROGERS, 2 6 19 32 43-44
  80 90 95-97 105-108
  110 113 115 119 122-
  123 131 133-134 138
  140-141 145 151 154
  159 165 171-173 175-
  176 181 183 185 187-
  188 194 196 201 203
ROLAND, 44 104
ROLLER, 44
ROLLINS, 31

ROLLS, 82 192
ROLSTON, 44
ROMINE, 169
ROMINES, 159
ROMINS, 159
ROMLAND, 159
ROMLING, 171
RONALDS, 92
RONNELS, 14
RONY, 90
ROOKER, 84 111-112 118
  201
ROONEL, 101
ROOP, 147
ROORK, 115 118
ROPER, 96 120
ROSE, 26 30 44 46 127
  137-138 141 147 154-
  155 159
ROSS, 1 44 51 74 76 83-85
  97 102-103 114 116
  130 138-140 145 150
  155 167 170 179 190
ROSSEN, 104
ROSSIN, 154
ROSSOM, 109
ROTRAMBLE, 188
ROUHOOFT, 159
ROULSTON, 115 140
ROUNDTREE, 82
ROUNTREE, 90
ROUSE, 114
ROUTEN, 191
ROUTH, 115 159
ROUTON, 188
ROWAN, 106 113 138 142
ROWARK, 101
ROWLAND, 169
ROWLIN, 99
ROWLING, 179
ROYLSTON, 44
ROYSTON, 35 52
RU, 97
RUBLE, 7 30 34-35 44 48
RUCKER, 92 111 193
RUDD, 151 153-154 159
RUDDER, 138
RUFF, 176
RULE, 71 134 145
RULL, 1
RULMON, 168
RUNALDO, 76 84
RUNNILS, 109
RUNOLDS, 73 89
RUNYAN, 159
RUPLE, 44

RUSELL, 175
RUSH, 44 116 120-121 130
  132
RUSS, 78
RUSSEL, 96
RUSSELL, 3 16 23 43-45
  55 77 97 99 102-103
  105 107 109-110 116-
  117 120 122-123 127
  129 137 141 143 145
  148 152 155 177 201
RUSSLE, 135
RUST, 77 81 84
RUSTIN, 45 159
RUSTON, 155
RUSY, 103
RUTCHLEDGE, 182
RUTH, 96
RUTHERFORD, 104
RUTLAND, 176 195
RUTLEDGE, 27 72 170
RUTLET, 26
RYAN, 201
RYEN, 115
RYESTER, 33
RYKER, 8
RYLAND, 33 45 143
RYLEY, 45
RYMAL, 45
RYMIL, 21
RYMILL, 13
RYON, 45
S--DLY, 95
SACKETT, 45
SACKRAN, 97
SAFFELL, 130 134 138
SAFFORD, 97
SAGE, 159
SAILOR, 21 40 45
SAIN, 92
SAINTCLAIR, 125
SALLENS, 159
SALLY, 96
SALMON, 99
SALT, 10
SALTS, 9 16 25 34 37 40
  45-46
SAMMONS, 75 80
SAMMS, 45
SAMPELS, 98
SAMPLES, 113 116 118
  124 128 132 134 139
  149
SAMPSON, 159
SANDERS, 45 49 99 104
  148 172 184-185 190

SANDERS (cont)
  194 202
SANDERSON, 79
SANDFORD, 83 175
SANDS, 4 9 22 45 50 168
  173 177 185-186
SANFORD, 79 97
SAPPINGTON, 121
SARGANT, 19 103
SARGENT, 44 103
SARTAIN, 99
SARTEN, 46
SATERFIELD, 188
SATTERFIELD, 45 97 181
SAULS, 182
SAUNDERS, 86 116 159
SAWESBEER, 45
SAWTELL, 134 147
SAWYERS, 55 91 120 167
SAY, 138
SAYLOR, 7 45
SAYLORS, 102
SCALF, 38 45
SCALLARN, 75
SCALLION, 86-87
SCALLORN, 77
SCALP, 12
SCALPH, 37
SCARET, 167
SCARULOCK, 2
SCHANNON, 190
SCHRIMSHEER, 118
SCOBEY, 165 171 175
SCOBY, 2 174 192
SCOGGINS, 99 152
SCOSSY, 2
SCOT, 178
SCOTT, 45 49 74 76 79 84
  92-93 96 103 111-113
  118 126 129-131 134
  139 145 150 154 159
  165 168 178 182 190
  196
SCRIPSHIR, 114
SCROGGS, 45 120 130
  134
SCRUGGS, 139 159-160
SCURLOCK, 190 193
SEABALL, 45
SEAHORN, 45 97
SEALE, 162
SEALS, 153 177
SEARCY, 155 172 197
SEARS, 1
SEAT, 74 77 82 191 193
SEATON, 124 160

SEATT, 188
SEAWELL, 174
SEAY, 88 180 193
SEBASTIAN, 204
SECREST, 127
SEDWICK, 73
SEE, 79
SEEBASTAIN, 127
SEEBOLT, 45 49 95
SEEHORN, 36 45
SEFLETT, 96
SEHORN, 53
SELF, 81
SELL, 45
SELLARS, 46 76 78 80 84
  176
SELLERS, 46 73-74 89 93
  180
SELMON, 101
SELPH, 80
SERATT, 74
SERBER, 46
SERRATT, 88 92
SERTAIN, 100
SESSAM, 101
SETSELLER, 10
SETTER, 175
SETTLE, 177
SEVIER, 9 29 39 42 49 164
SEWEL, 98
SEWELL, 77 124
SEXTON, 92-94 113 122
  127 144
SHACKLEFORD, 46
SHADDEN, 124 141 146
SHADDIN, 121
SHAHAN, 122 160
SHAKLE, 101
SHAM, 77
SHAMBLIN, 120 160
SHANE, 79 81 96 180
SHANKLE, 101
SHANKLIN, 25 27 105
SHANKS, 44 46 125 168
  179 181
SHANLEY, 1
SHANNON, 46 55 172 181
  190
SHANON, 5
SHAOUR, 72
SHARFEY, 46
SHARP, 1 94-95 104 108
  112 114 123 141 145
  154 160 172 202
SHARPE, 167 197
SHARROD, 75

SHAVER, 135 143 146
SHAW, 46 55 84 87 89 110
  127 155 171 175 179-
  181 190 194 202
SHAWLEY, 52
SHEALS, 101
SHEARER, 51 88
SHECKEL, 100
SHEDDEN, 124
SHEEN, 204
SHEETS, 46
SHEFFIELD, 46
SHEID, 102
SHELBY, 72 178
SHELL, 127 144 201
SHELLEY, 202
SHELTON, 46 96-97 118
  127
SHEMBRIDGE, 196
SHEPHARD, 186
SHEPHERD, 46 104
SHEPPARD, 25 72 173
SHERELL, 100
SHERFEY, 11 20 22 46-47
SHERFFEY, 46
SHERFY, 6 16 36
SHERMAN, 13 93
SHERN, 91
SHERON, 77
SHERRALL, 106
SHERRELL, 191
SHERRILL, 43 46 100 152
  182 187 190 194
SHERROD, 75
SHERRON, 84 92
SHERROOL, 169
SHETTERLY, 127
SHEWBIRD, 160
SHEWBREAD, 160
SHICKORD, 188
SHIELD, 160
SHIELDS, 4 7 11 22 33-34
  39 45-46 108 134 142
  144 147 151 154 160
SHILS, 109
SHIP, 194
SHIPLEY, 6 13 18 22-23
  46 96 201
SHIPMAN, 102
SHIRRELL, 150
SHOAT, 1
SHOEMAKER, 17
SHOOK, 97 116 120 125
  134 142 144
SHORAS, 175
SHORT, 46 93 104

SHORTER, 168 192
SHOT, 124
SHOULDS, 160
SHOUN, 10
SHOUTTS, 160
SHRADER, 160
SHROPSHIRE, 104
SHUGART, 117
SIDDLE, 165
SILAS, 101
SILCOCK, 46
SILCUERK, 98
SILLAMAN, 195
SILLOMAN, 196
SILMAN, 100
SILMON, 100
SIMERLEY, 154
SIMERLY, 46 136 155
SIMMONS, 8 33 47 85 89 96 99 101 104 113
SIMMS, 115 134 139
SIMON, 99
SIMONS, 78 99 112 115 123 127 133 140
SIMPSON, 20 32 40 46-47 56 72 81 104 110 145 181 186 192
SIMS, 1 103-104 133 183 186 192 196
SINGLETON, 80 82 111 115 128-129 133 136 138 142 152 154
SINK, 160
SISK, 8 47 176
SIVELS, 96
SKEAN, 193
SKELTON, 47 97
SKILES, 39 47
SKILLERN, 2
SKIPPER, 47
SLAGLE, 12 36 44 47 53
SLANTON, 98
SLATACE, 111
SLATON, 47
SLAUGHTER, 44 47 156
SLEMMONS, 47
SLEMONS, 131
SLIEGER, 47
SLIGER, 6 8-9 27 32 39 46-47 134
SLIMMONS, 40
SLOAN, 82 86 92 106-109 114 117 122 139 149
SLOVER, 96
SLYGER, 19 23 28 31 47 52

SMALLING, 47
SMALLWOOD, 160
SMALLY, 101
SMART, 110 172 175 193
SMAWLEY, 20
SMEDLEY, 98
SMILSER, 54
SMILY, 104
SMITH, 1-4 8 15 19-21 23 26-27 29 31 33 40-41 45 47-48 50 53-56 71-75 77-81 83 85-90 92 94 97-104 109 112-116 122-123 126-127 129 131-132 134-136 141-143 145 148 152 154 160 165-168 170-172 176 178-180 182-184 187-189 192 194 196-198 202
SMITHERS, 201
SMITHPETER, 164
SMITZER, 48
SMOOT, 135 138
SMOTHERS, 204
SNAPP, 5 16 18 21 25 29 35 39 42-43 48 160
SNEED, 154 160 189-190 196
SNIDER, 112 114-115 117 120-122 133 138-139 141 143 152 155
SNODDY, 72 195
SNODGRASS, 48
SNOWDEN, 87
SNYDER, 26
SOAP, 104
SOLOMON, 31
SOLTZ, 49
SOMERS, 169 177
SOMMUNS, 183
SOUL, 18
SOULTS, 155
SOUTHERN, 193
SOUTHFIELD, 55
SOUTHWORTH, 197
SOW, 160
SPADLEN, 180
SPARKES, 161-162
SPARKMAN, 77
SPARKS, 48-49 99 101 155 189
SPARROW, 171 174
SPARRY, 176
SPATE, 74
SPEARS, 14 48 83 165

SPECK, 48
SPEED, 176
SPEERS, 48 152
SPELLINGS, 87 92
SPENCER, 55 72 86-87 99 135 141 160-161
SPERES, 81
SPERRY, 194
SPHERE, 81
SPIGHT, 79 83
SPILMAN, 106 147-148
SPINKS, 195
SPORE, 34
SPRADLEN, 172
SPRADLIN, 47 123 133 136 145 189
SPRADLING, 8 144
SPRAGAN, 115
SPRIGO, 47
SPRIGS, 96
SPRING, 7 28 98 176 178 181 186 191 193
SPRINGS, 44
SPURGEN, 48
SPURRIERS, 48
SPYKER, 103
SQUIBB, 3-4 48
STACKHOUSE, 48
STACUP, 76
STAFFORD, 92 160 177
STAGS, 104
STALCUP, 77
STALLIONS, 2 130 133-134 154 160
STAMPHILL, 100
STAMPS, 104
STAN, 93
STANBERRY, 48
STANBURY, 35 48 150
STANDEFER, 1
STANDEFORD, 168
STANDFORD, 168
STANDIFER, 101
STANDLE, 181
STANDLEY, 183
STANDRIDGE, 101-102
STANFIELD, 48 125 131 134 147
STANFILL, 2
STANFORD, 48
STANLEY, 77 81 83 160 177
STANLY, 184
STANSBURY, 17 160
STANTON, 49 123
STAPLES, 99

STAR, 49
STARKEY, 146 160
STARKY, 137
STARLIENS, 123
STARMER, 9
STARNES, 15 37 42 49 56 176
STARNS, 21 34 40 49
STARR, 17 46 72 122
STATON, 75 80 87
STAUNLOR, 141
STAVER, 160
STEATY, 160
STEEL, 72 149 160 202-203
STEELE, 49 119 124 133 137 146 165 183 186
STEEN, 1
STELLAR, 82
STELLER, 89
STEOVELL, 97
STEPENSON, 190
STEPHENS, 1 16 33 49 53 56 74 96 103-104 106 122-123 141 160 196 198 201
STEPHENSON, 27 34-35 48-49 119 122 137 171 187
STEPHISON, 79
STERLING, 121 141 154
STERRETT, 168
STEUART, 84
STEVENS, 16 49 51 184
STEVENSON, 1 176 182 190
STEWART, 6 43 73 84 88 94-95 108 133 138 147 150 197-198
STIGALL, 110
STILL, 56 165 172-173
STILLER, 83
STINE, 201
STINER, 160
STINETT, 160
STINNET, 1 127 139
STINNETT, 152 154
STINSON, 140
STOCKARD, 164
STOCKTON, 109 160
STODDARD, 77
STOKES, 104 176
STONE, 19 49 56 81-82 86-87 90 111 116 118 127 131 135 138-139 179 185

STORMER, 22 49 54
STOUT, 49 53 201
STOVAL, 204
STOVALL, 99 103 193
STOVER, 49
STRAIN, 11 49 119 145 151
STRAINE, 126
STRANAHAN, 151
STRAUTHER, 86
STREET, 99 103
STRICKLAND, 104 155
STRICKLIN, 104
STRIPLY, 95
STRODER, 202
STROTHER, 2 86
STROUD, 31 37
STUARD, 102 113
STUART, 39 44 47 49 81 86 102-103 113 120 166-167 173 178 184 190 193
STUBLEFIELD, 191
STUCKEY, 102
STUDDURT, 156
STUMP, 55
STURDIVANT, 104
SUGG, 181
SUGGS, 185
SUIT, 133
SULIVAN, 103
SULLENS, 1
SULLINS, 46 49 133
SULLIVAN, 103 172 174 176 181-184 188
SUMMARY, 97
SUMMENS, 97
SUMMER, 49
SUMMERMAN, 49
SUMMERS, 3 19 49 172 185 195
SUMNER, 72
SUPATALLER, 160
SURATT, 79
SURBEY, 49
SUSONG, 23
SUTHERLAND, 125 183
SUTTEL, 95
SUTTEN, 148
SUTTLES, 29 50
SUTTON, 2 50-51 72 104 133 147 171 175-176 198
SUVELY, 160
SWAFFORD, 97
SWAIN, 143

SWAINY, 204
SWAN, 135 138 198
SWANAY, 50
SWANEY, 50 185
SWANGER, 122
SWANN, 193
SWATZELL, 50
SWEARINGEN, 120
SWEAT, 182
SWEATT, 180
SWEET, 10 31
SWEETON, 1 99-100
SWESESHER, 98
SWICEGOOD, 50
SWINDLE, 180-181
SWINEY, 178
SWINGLE, 15 184
SWINGLEY, 172
SWISHER, 98 133 145
SWODDY, 160
SWOLER, 100
SWONGER, 42
SWORDS, 50
SYLVESTER, 50
SYPERT, 175 187 194
TADLOCK, 33 38 50
TAIT, 171 173
TALBERT, 113 135
TALBOT, 160
TALBOTT, 131 135
TALENT, 124 150
TALFORD, 31
TALIAFERRO, 84 88
TALIVER, 160
TALLENT, 118 137-138 145
TALLEY, 167 178 180 194
TALLY, 101 103 139 178-179 181-182
TANCKERSLEY, 97
TANER, 82
TANNER, 160
TAPP, 15 50
TARBET, 148 151
TARPLEY, 180 193 195
TARRANT, 156
TARRANTS, 102
TARRER, 187
TARVER, 178 184-187 196
TARVIN, 81
TARWATER, 99-100
TATE, 8 50 94 119-120 129 136 148 155 164
TATOM, 92
TATUM, 166

TAYLOR, 4-7 23 27 29-30 40 46 48 50 53-55 73 78-79 91-92 94-96 98-100 102-105 111-112 116 127 131 133 139-140 143-145 148 155-156 160 165 167 172 174-175 177-179 185-186 188 190 192-193 196
TAYLOT, 98
TEAFATELLER, 149
TEAGE, 160
TEAGUE, 106-107 186
TEDFORD, 107-108 113 129 131 133 136 146 149 151-152
TEDLOCK, 30 50
TEEFATELLER, 138 147 150
TEEFETELLER, 116
TEFETALLOR, 136
TELFORD, 24 166 182 195
TEMPLE, 42
TEMPLETON, 96
TEMPLIN, 14 26 52
TERRELL, 72 78
TERRILL, 93
TERRY, 1 25 45 76 106 169 172
THACKER, 11 44 50
THARO, 112
THARP, 112 119 147
THEDFORD, 73 75-76 80 86 88-89 92
THETFORD, 81-84
THOMAS, 1 10 50 75-76 82 85 88 90 95 98 115 125 128 135 145 148 154 160 164-165 167-168 170-171 174 183 185 189 191 194 198 203
THOMASON, 154
THOMISON, 195
THOMPSON, 1-2 9-10 34 42 50 54-56 71 79 81 85-86 92 94 98 100 104 106-107 110 112 114 116-117 119-123 125 129 131 133-136 138-147 152-153 160 165-168 173 176 179 189 195-196 198
THORN, 192-193
THORNBURY, 160

THORNHILL, 98
THORNTON, 44 102
THORP, 19
THOURNBURGH, 98
THRASHER, 100
THRATCHER, 102
THREEWIT, 7
THREEWITTS, 42
THRESHER, 50
THROWER, 169 173 185 192
THURMAN, 1 138
TICKER, 121
TILFORD, 179 194 197
TILGHMAN, 94
TILLEY, 35
TILSON, 3 13 15 18 25 50 53
TIMBERMAN, 108-109
TINCLE, 72 89
TINDEL, 117
TINER, 95
TINKER, 3 26 30 50
TINKLE, 74 78
TINSLEY, 1
TIPPET, 106 171
TIPPIT, 166 182
TIPTON, 2 44 50 54 80 105 110-111 113 120 123 126 129-131 133 137-145 147-148 150 152 164 167 172 183 185 192 194
TITTLE, 50
TODD, 85 123 132 183 196-197
TODHUNTER, 100
TOLLER, 80
TOLLY, 142
TOMBS, 85
TOMPKINS, 50-51
TONEY, 53 139
TOOL, 110
TOOLE, 154
TOOLY, 190
TOOMA, 201
TOOMY, 160
TOOPES, 126
TOPPIN, 54
TORBET, 117 127 151
TORBETT, 127
TORBIT, 121
TOSSEN, 31
TOTEN, 87
TOTTEN, 75 77
TOWEL, 71

TOWELL, 203
TOWLS, 160
TOWNESLEY, 128
TOWNS, 97
TOWNSEN, 103
TOWNSEND, 201
TOWNSLEY, 123 153
TRACY, 183 188 194
TRAINER, 82 155
TRAMMEL, 1 72
TRASY, 175
TRAVILIAN, 177
TRAVILLIAN, 168
TRAVIS, 101
TRAYNER, 81
TRAYNOR, 87 91 98
TREADWAY, 51
TREAVILLIAN, 170
TRENT, 99 142
TRENTHORN, 160
TREPLETT, 98
TREUMEN, 88-89
TRIAS, 107
TRIBBLE, 170
TRICE, 126 129 145 177 183
TRIER, 183
TRIGG, 204
TRIMBLE, 105-106 111
TRISTY, 182
TRIVATHAN, 18
TROSPER, 83 90-91
TROTTER, 51 98 124 146 160
TROUSDALE, 203
TROUT, 83
TROVILION, 197
TROXEL, 201
TRUETT, 184 188
TRUHUTTS, 98
TRUNDLE, 152
TRUSSELL, 100
TRUSTY, 77 173 176
TUBB, 99-100
TUBBS, 100 107
TUCK, 120 126 131 136 139 141 144 148 154-155
TUCKER, 33 35-39 48 51 54 72 80 83 98 100 111 122 130 136 142-143 146-147 155 165 169 175-176 178 188 192 194-195 198
TULLOCH, 112 125-126 138 149

TULLUCH, 114
TULLY, 100
TUNIS, 160
TURMIN, 97
TURNAGE, 180
TURNER, 2 85 92-93 95
  119 160 168 173 175
  185 188-189 194
TURPIN, 89 188
TWEDY, 7 51
TWORKMAN, 51
TYLER, 3 80 84
TYLOR, 7 26
TYRELL, 183
TYSON, 73 79 88
UMSTEAD, 79-80
UNDERDOWN, 160
UNDERHILL, 197
UNDERWOOD, 51 126-127 133 160 178 196
UNKNOWN, 160
UPSHAW, 122
UPTON, 106 108 124-125
USHER, 73
UTLEY, 83
UTTER, 115 120-121 129 136
UZZELL, 2
VADEN, 51
VAN, 51
VANBIBER, 1
VANCE, 12 44 51 115 154
VANDERPOOL, 150
VANDEVENTER, 51
VANDIVER, 101
VANHOOSER, 165
VANN, 114 118
VANPELT, 103 125 135
VANPSETT, 144
VANTREECE, 192
VANTREESE, 188
VANZANT, 99 103
VARNELI, 160
VARNELL, 160
VARNILL, 160
VARRNELL, 160
VAUGHAN, 175
VAUGHN, 36 51 82 88 90 101 134 169
VAUGHT, 106 110-114 117 122-123 138
VAUGN, 21
VAUN, 105 160
VAUSKOE, 39
VAUT, 105 108 111
VERNATTA, 173

VERNON, 95-96 104
VICARS, 110
VICKERS, 79 88 140 147 149
VICKERY, 56
VINCENT, 113
VINEYARD, 142 146 151-152 154-155
VINYARD, 138
VIVRETT, 188 191
VOLENTINE, 93
VONN, 97
VOWEL, 196
WADDELL, 51
WADDILL, 51
WADDLE, 20 25 48 51 129 133 160
WADDY, 148
WADE, 75 83 114-117 167
WADKINS, 187
WAESNER, 39
WAFFORD, 101
WAGGONER, 10 51-52
WAGNER, 104
WAGONER, 104
WAID, 113
WAKER, 96
WALDEN, 41 51 118
WALDREN, 32
WALDRIP, 86
WALDROPE, 43
WALKER, 1 10 16 27 31 33 40 51 55 72-74 79 82-83 86-89 95 101-102 104 106 108-113 115 119 122 124-125 133-134 142 147 152 154 160-161 165 168 177 179 182 185 192-193 196-197
WALL, 51 124 160 183 185 203
WALLACE, 51 100 102-103 106-107 109-110 112 114-115 119 125 127 129 132 135 138-139 141 143 145 149 152 201
WALLEN, 1 103
WALLER, 8 51 136 139
WALLICE, 85
WALLING, 201
WALLINGFORD, 87
WALLINGSFORD, 82 85 92
WALLS, 125 166

WALPOLE, 56
WALTER, 34
WALTERS, 3 8 37 51 187
WALTON, 2 55 71 78 195
WAMACK, 167
WANN, 97
WARD, 1 79 82 129 141 148 160 166-167 171 178 180 183 186 195 197
WARDLAW, 55
WAREN, 51
WARMACK, 166-167 175
WARRAN, 92
WARREN, 38 52 91 93 104 115-116 125 131 133 135 143 151 160 162 175 182 188 191 193-195 201
WARRIN, 79 92 94
WASHBURN, 108
WASHINGTON, 55
WASSHAM, 107
WATENBARGER, 35 52
WATENBURGER, 52
WATER, 187
WATERS, 110 126 132 136-137 139 152 155 173 177 180 183 190
WATKINS, 52 147 152 177
WATLEBERGER, 52
WATSON, 8 20 40 52 81 83-85 88 100 109 112 127 155 160 164 170 201
WATTENBERGER, 9 52
WATTERS, 160
WATTINBERGER, 52
WATTS, 30 77
WAY, 139
WAYLAND, 160
WEAKLEY, 55
WEALS, 72
WEAR, 53 97 107 109-110 126 128-129 131 133 140-141 144-145 160
WEATHERFORD, 52
WEATHERLEY, 97
WEATHERLY, 196
WEATHERS, 122 124
WEATHERSPOON, 75
WEAVER, 1 104 116 133 139
WEBB, 16 35 41 46 52 55 73 75 77 85-86 89-90 92 96 117 124 129 148

241

WEBB (cont)
  160-161 169 175 182
  185 193
WEBBER, 99 192
WEBSTER, 143 145 148
WEEKS, 104
WEIR, 43 52 102-103 106
  108-110 114 119-120
  126 150 180 184
WELBURN, 120
WELCH, 55 74 79 83 85-
  87 172 176 186
WELDON, 114
WELLS, 122 136 160 169
  201
WELSH, 131
WESLECK, 52
WESLEVENCY, 98
WEST, 12 32 40 52 96 150
  170 172 179
WESTFIELD, 97
WESTMORELAND, 125
WESTON, 52
WETHEFORD, 52
WETHERLY, 185
WETHERS, 122 148
WETHERSPOON, 111
WHEALY, 160
WHEAT, 52
WHEELER, 14 32-33 52
  104 112 115 125 127
  134-137 141-142 147
  150 176 182 192
WHEELOCK, 13 15 22 28
  36 42 44 52-53
WHEELOR, 40 52
WHEYBY, 160
WHICHARD, 85
WHILOCK, 52
WHISLER, 22 52
WHISTER, 6
WHISTLER, 52
WHITABERRY, 96
WHITAKRE, 4
WHITE, 5-6 11 14 16 21 23
  26-27 29-30 35 37 41
  43 46-47 50-53 55 73-
  74 77 85-88 90 93 96
  98-99 108 110-112 117
  119 122-123 127 129
  131 137 144-145 149
  153 155 160 167 177
  184 189 191 203-204
WHITEHEAD, 25 146
WHITENBARGER, 107
  111

WHITENBERGER, 111
WHITLEY, 78 84 171 180
WHITLOCK, 38 52-53 186
  190
WHITLY, 103
WHITSON, 13 17 36 39-40
  53 88 166-167 195
WHITT, 104
WHITTENBARGER, 115
  150
WHITTENBERGER, 105
  117-118 123 137 140
WHITTLE, 160
WHITTON, 192
WHITWORTH, 175
WHURLEY, 20
WIAN, 53
WIATT, 47
WICKER, 95
WIER, 1 109 186 190
WIETT, 98
WIGGIN, 102
WIGGINGTON, 138
WIGGINS, 9 119-120
WIGGINTON, 104
WIGINTON, 137
WILBORN, 78
WILBOURNE, 81
WILBURN, 76-77 147
WILCOX, 160
WILEMAN, 99-101
WILES, 53 128
WILEY, 53 172 196
WILHIGHT, 95
WILHITE, 53
WILKERSON, 180
WILKESON, 11
WILKINS, 83 93
WILKINSON, 53 100 111
  119 141
WILKISON, 32
WILKS, 93
WILL, 155
WILLARD, 53 172
WILLCOX, 53
WILLERD, 191
WILLETT, 53
WILLIAM, 55 103 124 160
WILLIAMS, 3-4 6 11 18-
  19 22-23 29 45 47 49
  52-53 55 71 73-76 79-
  80 82-83 86 88-89 91-
  92 97-98 101-106 108
  110 113 117 120 125
  129 131-133 137-138
  143 145-146 148-150

WILLIAMS (cont)
  160 166 170-171 174-
  176 178-179 181-182
  184-185 189-191 193-
  195 198 201-203
WILLIAMSON, 55 88 143
  146 160 165 167 184
  187 191 196
WILLIFORD, 104 191
WILLIS, 56 80 99 101 107
  111 185 190
WILLIT, 53
WILLS, 53
WILLSON, 53 78
WILMATH, 175
WILSON, 6 9 25 34 43 54
  72 77-78 80 91 95-97
  99 102 104 109-110
  113-115 117-120 124
  129 133 135 139 143
  145 148 150 152 154
  160 163 165-169 171
  177 179 184 186 189
  191 202-203
WIMBERLEE, 121
WIMBERLEY, 100 144
WIMBERLY, 131 136 153
WIMPA, 100
WIMPY, 96
WINBERG, 53
WINCHESTER, 40 72 125
  139 193 202-203
WINDELL, 48
WINDER, 154
WINDERS, 54
WINE, 44
WINES, 118
WINFORD, 104 197
WINGORE, 2
WINKLE, 54
WINKLER, 54
WINN, 2 100
WINSET, 155 194
WINSETT, 196
WINSTON, 164 174 188
  197
WINTER, 126 147
WINTERS, 14 102 143-144
  185
WISEMAN, 117 125 141
  151
WIST, 160
WITCHER, 111 118
WITERNER, 160
WITHERLY, 191
WITHERSPOON, 73 90 93

WITHERSPOON (cont) 168
WITT, 104 155
WITTENBARGER, 54
WODS, 104
WOLARD, 94
WOLF, 49 54
WOLLARD, 184
WOMACK, 1 101-102
WOOD, 2 6 8 34-35 54 56 80 89 100 102-104 109 147 160 169 173 176 179 193 196-197
WOODALL, 100 205
WOODARD, 75 93 119 133
WOODDY, 117
WOODEN, 96 119 125 134 140
WOODET, 96
WOODEY, 96
WOODRUFF, 54
WOODRUM, 168 179 185 196
WOODS, 31 54 73 81 88 90 94 96 98-100 107 111 119 125 137 145 160 183
WOODSON, 85 156
WOODVILL, 187
WOODWARD, 168 171-172 174 180 189 202
WOODY, 112 119 154
WOOLARD, 179
WOOLDRIDGE, 172
WOOLLARD, 177 182
WOOLLEN, 176

WOOLSEY, 54
WOOTEN, 99 170
WORD, 83 85 87-88 91 94 166 170-171 189
WORHAM, 54
WORKMAN, 42 54
WORLEY, 54 72 94
WORMACK, 111 179
WORRELL, 96
WORSHAM, 111
WORTHAM, 174 178 189
WORTHAN, 173
WORTHEM, 103
WORTHINGTON, 8 27
WORTMAN, 54
WRAY, 101 170 175 179 190 192
WRENSHEY, 54
WRIGHT, 5 34 54-55 76 79 85 99 116 127 132 141 145 147 153 155 168 170 173-175 177 179 182-187 194-196 202
WRITE, 87 101
WRYE, 180
WYAT, 104
WYATT, 54
WYER, 203
WYETT, 54
WYINGTON, 6
WYLEY, 121 137
WYLIE, 54
WYLY, 118
WYNN, 172-173 182 195 198
WYNNE, 167 173-174 176 191

YANCEY, 105
YANCY, 91
YANDLE, 197
YARNELL, 131 181 190
YATES, 55 72 82 84 94 104-105 139 152
YEAGER, 22 32 39 52 54 99
YEARBORY, 82
YEARGIN, 155
YEARLY, 54
YEARNELL, 171
YEAROUT, 115 124 134 136-138 144 148-149 152
YOAKHAM, 1
YOAKIM, 97
YOAKIN, 96
YORK, 10 76 83 160 175
YOUBANKS, 184
YOUNG, 5 10-11 15 17 21 27 30 32 34 36 39 42 44 53-54 72-73 84 86 101-102 104 107 115 119 124 126 132 135 139-140 146 155 167 172 176 181-183 187 191 196 198 203-204
YOUNGBLOOD, 101
YOUNT, 120 143
YOUNTT, 123
YOUREE, 165 192
YUNT, 113
ZEIGLER, 72
ZERICOR, 73
ZETTY, 25
ZIMMERMAN, 54-55

Other Heritage Books by Sherida K. Eddlemon:

Missouri Genealogical Records and Abstracts:
Volume 1: 1766-1839
Volume 2: 1752-1839
Volume 3: 1787-1839
Volume 4: 1741-1839
Volume 5: 1755-1839
Volume 6: 1621-1839
Volume 7: 1535-1839

Missouri Genealogical Gleanings 1840 and Beyond, Volumes 1-9

1890 Genealogical Census Reconstruction: Mississippi, Volumes 1 and 2

1890 Genealogical Census Reconstruction: Missouri, Volumes 1-3

1890 Genealogical Census Reconstruction: Ohio, Volume 1
(with Patricia P. Nelson)

1890 Genealogical Census Reconstruction: Tennessee, Volume 1

A Genealogical Collection of Kentucky Birth and Death Records

Callaway County, Missouri, Marriage Records: 1821 to 1871

Cumberland Presbyterian Church, Volume One: 1836 and Beyond

Dickson County, Tennessee Marriage Records, 1817-1879

Genealogical Abstracts from Missouri Church Records and
Other Religious Sources, Volume 1

Genealogical Abstracts from Tennessee Newspapers, 1791-1808

Genealogical Abstracts from Tennessee Newspapers, 1803-1812

Genealogical Abstracts from Tennessee Newspapers, 1821-1828

Tennessee Genealogical Records and Abstracts, Volume 1: 1787-1839

Genealogical Gleanings from New York Fraternal Organizations
Volumes 1 and 2

Index to the Arkansas General Land Office, 1820-1907
Volumes 1-10

Kentucky Genealogical Records and Abstracts, Volume 1: 1781-1839

Kentucky Genealogical Records and Abstracts, Volume 2: 1796-1839

Lewis County, Missouri Index to Circuit Court Records, Volume 1, 1833-1841

Missouri Birth and Death Records, Volumes 1-4

Morgan County, Missouri Marriage Records, 1833-1893

Our Ancestors of Albany County, New York, Volumes 1 and 2

Our Ancestors of Cuyahoga County, Ohio, Volume 1
(with Patricia P. Nelson)

Ralls County, Missouri Settlement Records, 1832-1853

Records of Randolph County, Missouri, 1833-1964

Ten Thousand Missouri Taxpayers

The "Show-Me" Guide to Missouri: Sources for Genealogical and Historical Research

CD: Dickson County, Tennessee Marriage Records, 1817-1879

CD: Index to the Arkansas General Land Office, 1820-1907 Volumes 1-10

CD: Missouri, Volume 3

CD: Tennessee Genealogical Records

CD: Tennessee Genealogical Records, Volumes 1-3

www.ingramcontent.com/pod-product-compliance
Lightning Source LLC
Chambersburg PA
CBHW060817190426
43197CB00038B/1861